Inside the Commodity
Option Markets

Inside the Commodity Option Markets

JOHN LABUSZEWSKI
JEANNE CAIRNS SINQUEFIELD

JOHN WILEY & SONS
New York • Chichester • Brisbane • Toronto • Singapore

Library of Congress Cataloging in Publication Data:

Labuszewski, John.
    Inside the commodity option markets.

    Bibliography: p.
    Includes index.
    1. Commodity exchanges. 2. Put and call transactions.
3. Hedging (Finance) 4. Financial futures.
I. Sinquefield, Jeanne Cairns. II. Title. III. Title:
Commodity option markets.
HG6046.L225   1985   332.64'5   84-25808
ISBN 0-471-89607-1

Printed in the United States of America

10 9 8 7 6 5 4 3 2

Foreword

Economic history is the story of the gradual exten-
sion of the economic community beyond its origi-
nal limits of the single household to embrace the
nation and then the world.

Ludwig Von Mises, The Theory of Money and Credit

The 1970s witnessed the beginning of the largest transformation in the history of futures markets and perhaps world monetary and capital markets with the introduction of financial futures—currency and interest rate futures. These developments had their counterpart in the equity markets with the development of exchange traded equity options. Prior to the 1970s futures trading had been undergoing subtle but important changes with the extension of trading from primary agricultural commodities to semiprocessed and fully processed commodities as well as live animals. These innovations paved the way for the subsequent introduction of trading in the financial arena.

The 1980s began a second wave of innovation in futures markets with the inception of trading in options on futures markets, stock index futures, and the extension of futures trading in the financial arena to time zones throughout the world. Some of these developments also had counterparts in the equity markets with the development of trading in equity options on stock indices. The former new contracts have not only revolutionized futures trading but have concommitantly had a significant impact on the world's financial markets. Financial institutions and corporations have been provided with important new tools which will permit them to more effectively manage their currency, interest rate, and equity risks. An inevitable effect of these changes has been to produce a demand for a new profession of risk managers. In turn, these new risk managers are finding it necessary to rely on academics and practitioners to provide them with a complete analytic understanding of how these markets can be used. This publication presents an excellent introduction to the use of one of these important new tools—options on futures contracts.

On October 1, 1982 the Chicago Board of Trade introduced trading in options on Treasury Bond futures contracts. This was followed by options on gold futures, S&P futures, and most recently deutsche mark futures. It is interesting to note in an area of innovation where most new products fail most options contracts which have been introduced in the past two years have proven to be successful. In some instances the success has been remarkable. The options on Treasury Bond futures have averaged nearly 25,000 contracts a day in the first eight months of 1984. Furthermore the open interest is now the second largest of all futures markets and actually surpassed the Treasury Bond futures contract itself at one point during the year. Gold and DM have enjoyed success and only sugar has languished in what is a truly remarkable record for new products.

These developments have had an enormous impact on the exchanges themselves. New memberships have been created which provide access to markets for individuals who specialize in these more complex products. The success of these new markets has also required the construction of new trading pits. Market makers have been expanded into complicated trading strategists employing new techniques such as conversions, reverse conversions, delta neutral hedges, and a wide variety of other techniques. These individuals have come from equity markets, financial futures markets and directly out of MBA programs at major universities.

The impact on the users of these markets have been even more profound. Research departments in commercial banks, non-bank dealers in primary government securities, and bullion dealers have been expanded to analyze these new markets. Traders have become more facile in using these new tools to effectively manage risks in everything ranging from gold bullion to deutsche marks. Many of those skeptics who condemned these new developments with an incomplete understanding of these markets have recognized that these new products allow them to assume any risk profile which is consistent with their objectives of profit maximization.

It is important to recognize that these tools also provide additional opportunities not afforded by futures markets. They provide not only a way to provide a floor or ceiling for price risk but also provide a means for hedging volatility. Furthermore options may provide a whole new basket of products in the cash markets. Interest rate cap products are one simple example. As these markets develop it seems reasonable to argue that many new products will emerge which will provide opportunities for those people not directly involved in these markets.

This book answers many of the questions that professional risk managers will be asking about options on futures products. It was particularly valuable as an introductory treatise and describes in lay terms some of the more complicated options pricing models. Of particular interest are the concluding chapters dealing with commercial applications. The interested reader should be able to extrapolate more about the use of these models once basic models and applications have been understood.

These new markets are all in their infancy. Furthermore the next few years will witness the introduction of options on other financial futures and metals as well as agricultural futures. Further penetration of existing markets as well as the expansion of options into traditional futures markets will require a greater understanding of options on futures contracts. Individuals that develop an understanding of the uses of these techniques will inevitably become more important to their respective institutions and corporations. As a secondary effect they can provide significant benefits to the world in managing risks ranging from the business cycle to agricultural cycles and catastrophes. It is important to welcome all readers of this book into the new and exciting area of risk management.

RICHARD L. SANDOR, PH.D.
Senior Vice President
Drexel Burnham Lambert Inc.
Chicago, Illinois

Preface

The past few years have been exciting times for the futures industry. Importantly, in late 1982, options on futures contracts were finally approved and began trading. Both of us worked on the development of these new products: Jeanne on the Chicago Board of Trade's option on T-bond futures contract and John on the Midwest Commodity Exchange's options on gold futures contract. While we physically wrote these contracts, many individuals provided input and molded the final products. They include various members and staff of the futures exchanges, industry experts, and staff at the CFTC. Especially important was Richard Sandor, one of the fathers of financial futures.

One slightly unnerving aspect of the work was the limited amount of literature available on commodity options. We decided to try and fill this void by writing this book. We felt that there was a heterogeneous audience for such a book—from farmers to CEOs, account executives to floor brokers. Thus the book was designed with two purposes. First, this book provides a solid introduction to commodity options, including an in-depth discussion of option pricing. Second, the book can be used as a basic resource by providing details on individual option contracts, and separate analyses and examples of the major types of trading strategies.

A variety of people have helped with the ideas in this book. This includes Ramakrishnan Chandrasekar, Michael Kamradt, James Meisner, Henry Otto, and Randall Sheldon, all current or former staff members of the Chicago Board of Trade. We'd also like to thank our spouses Heidi and Rex for their support.

JOHN LABUSZEWSKI
JEANNE CAIRNS SINQUEFIELD, PH.D

Chicago
March 1985

Contents

7   Risk Management with Options   271

List of Tables

List of Figures

Inside the Commodity
Option Markets

1

Introduction

Interest in commodities in general has grown tremendously during the past decade. U.S. commodity futures exchanges have experienced an almost exponential volume growth. The concept of a commodity has also been expanded. Commodity exchanges now offer futures in trading in products as diverse as petroleum and government securities, in addition to the traditional commodities such as grains and livestock.

Both the commodity futures and security exchanges have recently begun trading options on commodities (futures and physicals). Commodity options, of course, are nothing new. They have been offered in many forms through the years for products as diverse as gold, wheat, and tulip bulbs. However, exchange-trade commodity options in the United States were prohibited since 1936. This ban was lifted in 1982 when both the Commodity Futures Trading Commission (CFTC) and the Security Exchange Commission (SEC) approved exchange-traded commodity options. This change is partially due to the success of exchange-traded stock options, and growing public interest in commodity options.

Commodity options promise to become an important trading vehicle for the investing public as well as an important hedging tool for commercial enterprises. Traders who are armed with an in-depth expertise of these rapidly evolving markets are likely to be better prepared to take advantage of opportunities as they present themselves than are ill-prepared traders. This book does not purport to present a sure-fire get-rich-quick-scheme; however, we do intend to provide the investing public, commercial enterprises, account executives, and other interested observers with a perspective on the evolution of the industry, a firm grounding in the fundamentals of commodity option trading, a working knowledge of the available markets, and also a flavor for some of the subtleties associated with the markets.

The introduction of commodity options markets by organized exchanges may be considered an event analogous to the establishment of the Chicago Board Options Exchange (CBOE). CBOE was organized in 1973 to trade corporate stock options. This was in contrast to the loosely organized "over-the-counter" (OTC) put and call dealers market, which traded stock options prior to the inception of the CBOE. CBOE, along with a handful of other security exchanges that trade stock options, are now the dominant forces in the stock option market. The diminished significance of the OTC stock option market may be attributed to the efficiencies and integrity associated with the organized exchange method of trading. We expect the exchange-traded commodity options market to overshadow the current dealer commodity option market.

The focus of this book is on exchange-traded commodity options. Two types of commodity options are being offered—options on futures and options on the actual commodity. Two different government agencies regulate these options. The Security Exchange Commission regulates all options on actual securities. This includes options on stocks, and other securities including Treasuries, GNMAs, and domestic CDs. The Commodity Futures Trading Commission regulates all options on futures contracts and all options on actual commodities excluding securities. The reader should be aware that there are important differences in regulatory requirements between these two agencies.

This book is divided into seven chapters. Chapter 1 reviews the fundamental concepts and terminology associated with options and futures. Chapter 2 reviews the history of exchange-traded options in the United States. Chapter 3 compares options on futures, options on actuals, and dealer options. Chapter 4 describes the various types of commodity options that will or are being offered by exchanges and dealers. Chapter 5 presents option pricing models for various types of commodity options (options on futures, physical commodities, cash indices, and interest-bearing securities). Chapter 6 discusses option trading strategies. This includes applications and examples. Chapter 7 discusses commercial applications for commodity options. The appendices provide additional information on margins, followed by a glossary.

FUNDAMENTAL CONCEPTS

Any analysis of options trading—commodity or stock options—must begin with a review of the fundamental concepts and terminology associated with the option trade. Fortunately, commodity options share much of the same fundamentals with stock options. The reader who is familiar with stock options, therefore, might wish to skip ahead to the next section.

Put and Call Options

An option is a contractual agreement contingently to purchase or sell a particular asset or financial right, such as a commodity or a commodity futures contract, for a specific price within a specific time period.

There are two basic types of options, a "call" option and a "put" option. A *call* option gives the holder (or option buyer) the right, but not the obligation, to *purchase* the underlying commodity. The call writer (or option seller) is obligated to sell the particular commodity upon the holder's demand and in accordance with the previously agreed-upon conditions. Similarly, a *put* option gives the holder the right, but not the obligation, to *sell* the underlying commodity. The put writer is obligated to buy the particular commodity upon the holder's demand and in accordance with the previously agreed-upon commodities.

The easiest way to recall the distinction between a call and a put option is by associating the implications of the terms "call" and "put" with the contractual rights of the option holder. The call option holder buys the right to purchase the commodity underlying the call option. The right to purchase is implied by the term "call." On the other hand, the put option buyer buys the right to sell the commodity underlying the put option. Again, the right to sell is implied by the term "put." Oftimes, one will hear of a call option holder "calling" the underlying commodity from the writer, or conversely, of the put option holder "putting" the underlying commodity to the writer. This process is also referred to as exercising the option.

Option Expiration

The option holder's right to exercise the option contract expires on the expiration date. There is an important distinction between the option expiration date and the exercise date. The exercise date is the date upon which the option is actually exercised while the expiration date is the last day upon which the option may be exercised. These terms are needed to differentiate between a "European" and an "American" option. A European option can only be exercised on the expiration date. Its expiration date is the same as the exercise date (if indeed the option is exercised by the holder). An American option, on the other hand, can be exercised at any time prior to the expiration date at the holder's discretion. Thus the exercise date can be different from the expiration date. We will concentrate our attentions on American options common to the domestic option markets.

Strike Price

When a holder of an option exercises the option, he buys, in the case of a call option; or sells, in the case of a put option. This trade is transacted at a particular price agreed upon by both the buyer and seller at the time the option is "written." (A writer or option seller is considered to have "written" or "granted" an option when the option is sold.) This price is known as the "strike" or "exercise" price. If two individuals were to enter an option contract, they would negotiate the strike price as well as other contract terms. Where there are a large number of option buyers and sellers, however, it is inconvenient or even chaotic to negotiate the strike price of individual option contracts. Exchange-traded options, therefore, are characterized by a standardized strike price and other contract terms. Exchanges permit only traders to negotiate the option price or "premium."

Typically, more than one strike price is established for each commodity option with a particular expiration date. The strike price is set so that there are strike prices in the immediate pricing vicinity above and below the price of the underlying instrument. Normally, these strike prices are set at regular intervals.

Option Premium

The option "premium" is the price one pays to buy the option, or the price one receives for selling the option. The premium is negotiated between the buyer and seller at the time the option is written. Generally, a call option premium rises as the price of the underlying instrument rises and drops as the underlying price drops. The holder of a call option, then, is hoping that the underlying price will rise. A put option premium generally declines as the price of the underlying instrument rises and rises as the underlying price declines. In this case, the holder is hoping that the underlying price will go down while the writer is hoping that the underlying price will go up.

This type of price behavior may be explained with an example. Assume that the price of gold were $500 and the strike price on a gold physical call option were $400. The holder would make $100 by exercising the option. When he exercises the call option, the holder pays the writer $400 and receives the gold. The gold may subsequently be sold for $500 in the open market and the holder will thereby realize a $100 profit. (This profit is decreased to the extent of the premium originally paid to acquire the option.) Clearly, a call option is more valuable when the underlying price is $500 than when the underlying price equals $400 or even $300. This example is reversed for put options. If the price of gold were $300 and the put option strike price equaled $400, the holder would make $100 by exercising the put. If the underlying price were $400 and $500, the put option would be considerably less valuable.

Option Identification

An option contract for a particular commodity may be fully identified by reference to whether it is a put or a call, the expiration date, and the strike price. These contract terms are called the option "type," "class," and "series." All put options are regarded as options of the same type as are all call options. Options of the same type that share a common expiration date are said to be of the same class. Finally, all options of the same type and class that have the same strike price comprise an option series.

Exchange-traded options are standardized with respect to the option contract terms. The exchange sets particular strike prices and particular expiration dates. Only the premium varies once the option is listed as available for trading. This standardization or "fungibility" generally differentiates exchange-traded options from dealer options, which are not always so standard-ized. Exchange-traded options also permit traders to liquidate or offset long or short positions before expiration and without exercising the option. Thus, if one were to enter an "opening sale" or an "opening purchase" of a particular option series, the trader could subsequently cancel that short or long position by engaging in a "closing purchase" or a "closing sale," respectively.

RISK/REWARD STRUCTURE

The central and perhaps most confusing feature of an option contract is that the holder and writer assume very different risk/return postures. The holder's risk is limited to the price of the option or premium paid on purchase, whereas the writer's risk is practically unlimited. The holder's potential return is practically unlimited while the writer's potential return is limited to the pre-mium received on purchase. Why, given this arrangement, would a trader want to sell an option? Let's examine the risk/reward structure of an option contract more closely.

Ways to Profit from an Option

There are two ways in which a holder can profit from buying an option contract. A holder can take his profit by exercising the option or by selling the option contract before it expires. Let's assume that the holder bought a sugar physical call option contract for 2 cents a pound when sugar was selling for 15 cents a pound. The strike price is 16 cents a pound.

If the price of sugar stayed at the 15-cent level, the holder would not be in-clined to exercise the option. If he did so, he would be buying sugar at 16 cents when it is only worth 15 cents in the market. But let's say that the price of sugar went up to 20 cents. At 20 cents, the holder could exercise the option at 16 cents and sell the sugar in the cash market for 20 cents, or a 4-cent profit. As we learned in the prior section, the premium would have gone up if the price of the underlying commodity—in this case sugar—had gone up. Assume that the premium had risen to 7 cents; in this case, the holder can sell the option at the increased premium and realize a profit of 5 cents. The holder's profit equals the difference between the closing sale price of 7 cents and the opening purchase price of 2 cents.

Similarly, there are only two ways in which an option holder can profit from writing an option. An option writer can take his profit by "buying back" the option contract before it expires or by waiting for the option to expire. If our sugar call option buyer in the previous example had not exercised the op-tion because sugar prices remained static or declined, the writer would receive the full premium paid to him when he sold the option contract to the holder. Let's say that the price of sugar went down to 10 cents a pound. In this case, the call option premium would have declined; the writer could buy the same call

TABLE 1.1   IDENTIFYING AN OPTION

	Type	Class	Series
Put or call	A gold put		
Expiration		A December gold put	
Strike price			A $400 December gold put

TABLE 1.2   OPTION PREMIUM MOVEMENT

	Underlying Price Goes Up	Underlying Price Goes Down
Call option premium	Goes up	Goes down
Put option premium	Goes down	Goes up

TABLE 1.3   RESULTS OF AN OPTION TRANSACTION

	Holder	Writer
Exercising the option	Profits by exercise by the in-the-money amount (less the premium)	Loses by exercise by the in-the-money amount (cushioned by the premium)
Option expiration	Loses the entire premium	Profits by the entire premium
Closing or offsetting transaction	Profits if premium increases; loses if premium decreases	Profits if premium decreases; loses if premium increases

option with the same expiration and strike price at the lower premium. In this way, the writer cancels or offsets the original option sale with an option purchase. The profit is implied in the difference between the premium at the time of the opening sale and the time of the closing purchase.

In-the-Money, Out-of-the-Money

An option holder would exercise an option only when he could turn a profit on it. Naturally, it would be foolish to exercise an option when one incurred a loss by so doing. An option writer is also interested in whether the holder can be expected to exercise the option; because if there is no exercise, the writer keeps the premium, which could then be regarded as pure profit.

In order to identify options that represent likely candidates for exercise, one must examine the relationship between the strike price and the underlying commodity price. In the case of a call option, the holder could profitably exercise an option when the underlying commodity price is greater than the strike price. The holder would be buying at the low strike price and would be able to sell at the higher prevailing price. (The price that was originally paid for the option or premium is irrelevant in the consideration of whether or not to exercise the option because it is a "sunk" or irretrievable cost.) If the prevailing price were lower than the strike price, there would be no incentive to exercise a call option because to do so would result in a loss to the holder.

Because the question of whether an option might be exercised or not is asked so frequently, the option trade has developed expressions to distinguish options that are likely to be exercised from those that are not likely to be exercised. An "in-the-money" option is one that is likely to culminate in an exercise, whereas an "out-of-the-money" option is one that is not likely to be exercised. Specifically, an in-the-money call is one where the underlying commodity price exceeds the strike price while an out-of-the-money call is one where the underlying commodity price is less than the strike price. The terms are simply reversed for put options—an in-the-money put is one where the underlying commodity price is less than the strike price while an out-of-the-money put is one where the underlying commodity price is greater than the strike price. If the underlying market price equals the strike price, then the option is referred to as an "at-the-money" option and it is indeterminate whether the holder would want to exercise it or not.

Options Diagram

Figure 1.1 illustrates the potential profit or loss that may accrue to the holder or writer of a call option contract. Let's assume that the call may be exercised for a gold futures contract and that the holder will wait until the ex-

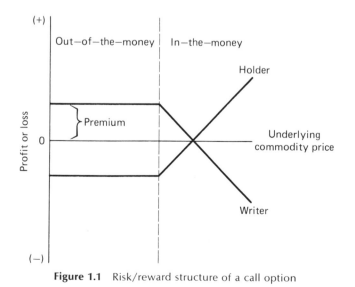

Figure 1.1   Risk/reward structure of a call option

piration date to decide whether to exercise the option or let it expire. The option premium is $40 per ounce and the striking price is $400 per ounce. The holder loses while the writer receives the entire premium if the option is permitted to expire (regardless of whether the option is in- or out-of-the-money).

The holder can be expected, however, to exercise the option if it is in-the-money. The holder profits when exercising the option by the in-the-money amount less the price originally paid as premium. If, for example, the holder exercises the option when the underlying gold contract is worth $450, the holder makes $50 upon exercise less the $40 premium for a net profit of $10 per ounce. If the holder exercises the option when the underlying gold contract is worth only $430, then the holder makes $30 upon exercise less the $40 premium for a net loss of $10 per ounce. If the price of gold upon exercise equals $440 per ounce (at-the-money), then the holder breaks even—neither profiting nor losing as a result of the transaction.

The writer's profit and loss scenario is represented as a mirror image of the buyer's profit–loss scenario. When the price of gold equals $450 upon exercise, the writer loses $50 upon exercise but his loss is cushioned by the $40 premium and the writer's net loss is $10. When the price of gold equals $430 upon exercise the writer loses $30 through the exercise but retains the $40 premium for a $10 net profit.

It is interesting to note that it may be in the best interest for the holder to exercise an in-the-money option even when a net loss results. A holder always turns a profit by exercising an in-the-money option, which at the least, helps to cushion the original outlay to buy the option. If, of course, the option is out-of-the-money, the holder will almost invariably prefer to let the option expire and lose the premium to the writer.

The profit–loss associated with a put option is illustrated in Figure 1.2. The call option holder profits from an increase in the underlying gold price while a put option holder profits from a decline in the underlying price. The call option

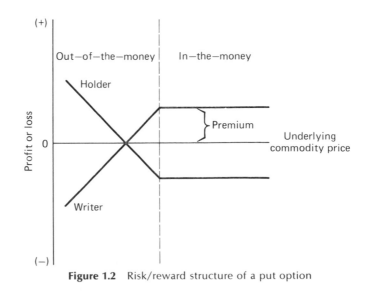

Figure 1.2   Risk/reward structure of a put option

writer profits when the underlying price remains constant or declines and the put option writer profits when the underlying price remains constant or increases.

Covered Call Writing

A basic strategy in stock option trading is covered call writing. This is also an important strategy in commodity options. Covered call writing is a strategy where one writes or sells a call option while simultaneously owning a similar amount of the underlying commodity. By writing an option against a commodity, the risk of owning the underlying commodity is always decreased. The basic purpose of such a strategy is to increase the income on the underlying commodity. The premium provides an increase in income, and provides partial protection against a decline in the price of the underlying commodity. Such a strategy will outperform outright ownership of the commodity if the commodity price falls, remains the same, or rises slightly. The strategy limits the profit if the price of the underlying commodity increases substantially. The profit–loss associated with writing a covered call option is illustrated in Figure 1.3.

Let's assume that an investor owns a 100 troy ounces of gold, which is currently selling at $380 per ounce. If this investor then sells a March $400 call option for gold, he establishes a covered write. Assume the premium is $40 per ounce. If the price of gold is less than $400 at expiration, the writer receives $40. This $40 will cover some or all of any price decline. For example, if gold falls to $340, the premium will provide protection for all of this downside loss. If gold falls below $440, he will incur a loss on the overall position. The potential profit of this is limited to $40. This is because the writer is obligated to sell the gold at the strike price of $400.

In general, the maximum profit for a covered write carried to expiration occurs when the strike price equals the commodity price at expiration. This assumes that an option premium is always at least equal to its intrinsic value. An investor's breakeven point at expiration occurs when the loss on the underlying

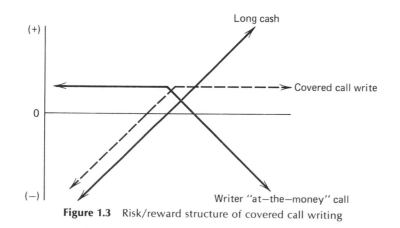

Figure 1.3   Risk/reward structure of covered call writing

commodity equals the premium. However, the investor must consider the costs of holding a commodity in evaluating such a strategy. This includes any financing, storage and transportation costs, plus any coupon or interest received.

Futures Contracts

To trade options on futures, an investor also needs a basic understanding of futures contracts. This section provides a basic review of fundamental concepts and terminology associated with futures contracts. The reader who is familiar with futures contracts, might want to skip ahead to Chapter 2.

Long and Short Futures Contracts

A futures contract is a standardized agreement to buy or sell a fixed quantity of a commodity for future delivery at a price negotiated through auction. Both parties of a future contract are obligated to perform as long as the contract remains open. There are two types of futures positions, a short and a long futures position. A short futures contract entails the obligation to deliver the underlying commodity if not offset prior to delivery. A long futures contract entails the obligation to buy the commodity if not offset prior to delivery.

Risk/Return Structure for Futures

Unlike options, the risk/return structure for a long and a short futures position is symmetric. The holder of a long futures position gains if the futures price increases and loses if it decreases. The holder of a short futures position gains if the futures position decreases and loses if it increases. Gains and losses on both sides are realized on a daily basis. This is accomplished by futures contracts being marked-to-market on a daily basis. Figure 1.4 illustrates the potential profit or loss from long and short futures positions.

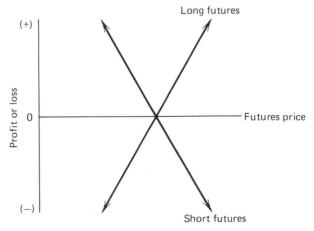

Figure 1.4   Potential loss/gains of long and short futures positions

Futures Prices

Futures prices are determined by auction in open outcry markets. The primary determinant of a futures price is the cash price of the underlying commodity. Other variables that affect futures prices include the cost of financing, insurance, transportation, and any coupon payments received from holding the underlying commodity. Agricultural commodities are also affected by the old crop/new crop variable. Arbitrage normally keeps futures prices within certain boundaries around the cash price of the underlying commodity. For example, a T-bond futures price should not be higher than the cash price plus the cost of carrying the commodity to delivery. Otherwise, there is a risk-free arbitrage whereby a trader buys the commodity and goes short the futures, and then carries it to delivery. Therefore the cash price of a commodity is highly correlated with its futures price. Since most commodities are not exchange traded, futures prices are often used to obtain basic information on pricing.

Hedging or Transferring Price Risk with Futures and Options

A hedger can use futures to "lock in a price." Figure 1.5 illustrates the use of a short futures position to hedge a long cash position. Any gains or losses in the cash position would be offset by losses or gains in the futures position. The effectiveness of such a hedge depends upon several factors. First, it depends on the relationship between the cash and futures prices. This is referred to as *basis risk*. Basis risk occurs when the cash price and the futures price move differently. For example using a T-bond futures contract to hedge a corporate bond would incur more basis risk than to hedge a T-bond. Second, a futures hedge requires that a trader know exactly the quantity he wants to hedge. For example, a T-bond dealer makes a bid for a $100 million of T-bonds in the Treasury auction. However, he may only receive part of his bid. If he were

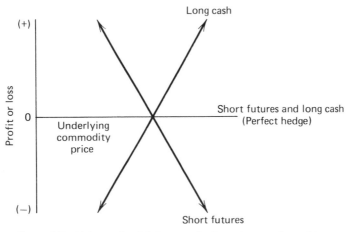

Figure 1.5 Using a short futures to hedge a long cash position

using futures to hedge his expected position, he would be overhedged, and be subject to price risk on his futures positions.

An investor can also use long options to hedge price risk. Long options can be used to lock in a floor price (long put/long cash) or a ceiling price (long call/short cash). Figures 1.6 and 1.7 illustrate the use of long options to hedge long or short cash positions. The most that an option buyer can lose is his option premium, whereas he can take advantage of price movements in his favor. The decision to use either futures or options to transfer price risk should consider the cost of the two markets (premiums versus basis risk and margin calls) versus potential return of options. Options are a better vehicle when quantity risk is important. Options should not be considered as substitutes for futures, but rather as an alternative hedging/trading vehicle. Many investors use both markets to hedge price risk.

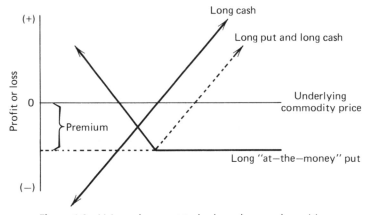

Figure 1.6   Using a long put to hedge a long cash position

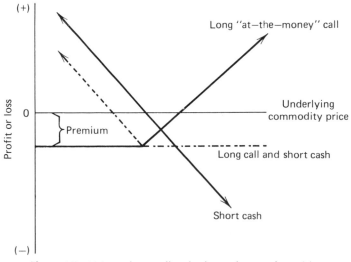

Figure 1.7   Using a long call to hedge a short cash position

2

History of Options Trading in the United States

The history of options trading in the United States is replete with instances of intervention by the federal government. This discussion, therefore, deals more with episodes of regulatory intercession than with trading experience.

THE PRE-COMMODITY EXCHANGE ACT ERA

Commodity options have been known by many names including privileges, indemnities, bids, offers, advance guarantees, and decline guaranties. Commodity options first surfaced domestically somewhat over a hundred years ago when privileges, a form of commodity options, appeared on the floors of the nation's grain exchanges. There were two types of privileges—bids and offers, which correspond roughly to puts and calls. The buyer of a bid had the privilege of selling grain futures to the privilege seller while the buyer of an offer had the privilege of buying grain futures from the privilege seller. Rather than negotiate premiums, a fixed commission was charged for a bid and an offer, the strike price of which was adjusted below and above current market prices. Privileges could be obtained that expired by the end of the day, within a week, or within a month; thus they were referred to as "dailies," "weeklies," and "monthlies."

Privileges proved to be very popular during the volatile up and down markets of the 1860s. They were met with considerable opposition, however, from farm groups who petitioned their state governments to prohibit option and futures trading. These farmers felt that malevolent speculators were responsible for volatile grain prices and were guilty of price manipulation. Accordingly, privileges were officially frowned upon by grain exchanges such as the Chicago Board of Trade, which adopted a rule in 1865 that denied privilege traders the protection of the exchange:

> *Privileges bought or sold to deliver or call for grain or other property by members of the Association shall not be recognized as a business transaction by the Directors or the Committee of Arbitration.*

This did not effectively discourage trading of privileges, and the rule was subsequently eliminated in 1869.

The Illinois legislature became involved in the option trading controversy in the 1870s. Lobbyists for farm groups and for traders and businessmen pushed hard to protect their respective interests and eventually some compromised reforms were passed. These reforms proved ineffective in curbing the trade of privileges despite an 1885 ruling by the Illinois Supreme Court that found privileges to be illegal. The difficulty with enforcing a ban stemmed from the difficulty of making a fair distinction between options and futures and from the fact that exchange members almost universally ignored the regulations.

The U.S. Congress became involved with the issue in the early 1890s when grain prices declined and farmers blamed the drop on the evils of speculation. Congress came very close to adopting a general ban on options, but nevertheless failed to act. In the 1920s, the issue reemerged, and in 1921, Congress passed the Futures Trading Act. This act imposed a prohibitive tax on earnings from privilege trading. In 1922, Congress passed the Grain Futures Act, which required exchanges and their members to maintain and file reports concerning privilege trading and also authorized the Secretary of Agriculture to conduct investigations of exchange operations. Failure to comply with the act could result in revocation of an exchange's status as a futures market. The effect of the 1921 and 1922 acts was effectively to end all commodity option trading on exchanges. A subsequent 1926 decision by the Supreme Court in *Trusler v. Crooks,* however, found the tax imposed by the 1921 act unconstitutional.[1] Option trading immediately reemerged on the grain markets.

The dates of July 19 and 20, 1933, are significant in the grain trade. On those dates, wheat prices collapsed dramatically and privilege trading was labeled the culprit. As a result of political pressure from the farm lobby, Congress passed the Commodity Exchange Act of 1936, which banned all commodity option trading in certain enumerated domestic commodities including wheat, cotton, rice, corn, oats, barley, rye, flaxseed, grain sorghums, mill feeds, butter, eggs, and Irish potatoes. In 1938 the list was expanded to include wool tops, in 1940, fats, oils, cottonseed meal, cottonseed, peanuts, soybeans, and soybean meal, and 1968, livestock, livestock products, and frozen orange juice. The result was that commodity options completely disappeared from the domestic commodity exchange.

LONDON MARKETS

Meanwhile, options trading continued actively in London until the outbreak of World War II. Volumes remained minimal until the late 1960s when

---

[1] *Trusler v. Crooks,* 269 U.S. 475 (1926).

Americans, who were prohibited from trading options in the United States, "discovered" the London markets. Many domestic brokerage firms began to offer their services as intermediaries between American customers and members of the London exchanges. The American customer was at something of a disadvantage in this respect because the clearinghouse guaranties of the London exchanges extend only to the local exchange members and not to the American customer.

Options were available in London in a number of diverse commodities including cocoa, coffee, copper, silver, sugar, lead, tin, and zinc. In contrast to so-called American options, London options could only be exercised on the expiration date. London options were and are available for expiration in three, six, and nine months' time. These London options are exercisable for a futures contract in the particular commodity.

The popularity of London options grew tremendously in the early 1970s. Unfortunately, the domestic option market during this period was characterized by some widely publicized scandals involving option-based get-rich-quick schemes. Some domestic retailers sold options to the public at excessive premiums and without "covering" their short option positions through ownership of the underlying commodity. The most notable case during this period was *SEC v. Goldstein, Samuelson, Inc.*[2] Goldstein had become the proprietor of a "Ponzi" arrangement, that is, he sold options uncovered under the assumption that if some of the options were exercised, they could be paid out of premiums received from new customers. Unfortunately, the bubble burst and the resulting scandal had far-reaching implications—reports were that investors who had become involved in this pyramid scheme lost $70 million.

OPTIONS BANNED

None of the retail sales abuses that allegedly occurred during this period were actually connected with exchange-traded options. Nevertheless, Congress decided to review federal regulation of commodity futures and option trading in order to prevent further scandals of this nature. The Commodity Futures Trading Commission Act of 1974 was the result of this review. The new law created the Commodity Futures Trading Commission (CFTC) as an independent agency charged with the administration of the Commodity Exchange Act.

The new law continued the prohibition of exchange-traded options for the commodities enumerated prior to 1974. In addition, the CFTC was empowered to extend the prohibition to any other commodities covered under the new act or to permit options on previously nonenumerated commodities to trade under whatever conditions it deemed appropriate.

Congress initially required the CFTC to develop regulations that would permit options to begin trading within a year. The CFTC responded by adopt-

---

[2] "Note, Federal Legislation for Commodity Option Trading: A Proposal," 47 *D. Cal. Law Rev.* 1418, 1426 (1974).

ing regulations that would permit options to be traded off-exchange by closely supervised firms already engaged in the offer and sale of the physical commodity underlying the option. The regulations were made effective in 1977 when the CFTC licensed 60 firms to transact business in London options and "dealer" options. The latter type of option is sold by the dealer in the physical commodity and is "covered" by the dealer's inventory of goods.

Sales abuses continued to occur, however, and in June 1978, the CFTC decided temporarily to suspend all sales of commodity options in the United States. The only exceptions to the ban included options traded between commercials and dealer options offered to the public, provided that the grantor firm was able to demonstrate financial capability. The exception to the ban was made in response to intense congressional pressure and near certainty that Congress itself would act to permit existing dealer option grantors to remain in business if the CFTC did not.

In 1978, Congress passed the Futures Trading Act of 1978. This law had the effect of reinforcing the commission's ban on options and required the CFTC to develop a plan that would adequately regulate options before the ban was lifted. It also recognized and sanctioned dealer options under specific circumstances.

OPTIONS PILOT PROGRAM OF 1981

For some time, the CFTC had discussed the possibility of permitting domestic commodity exchanges to trade options exercisable in futures contracts, much like London options. The purported purpose of the pilot program was to gather evidence to determine the economic benefits of options, to examine the effectiveness of customer protection rules, and to examine the effect that options trading would have on futures.

In September 1981, the CFTC published final rules that would govern exchange-traded options on the commodities that were enumerated prior to 1974. In December 1981, eight domestic commodity futures exchanges submitted applications to trade options exercisable in futures contracts ranging from precious metals to imported agricultural commodities to financial instruments. Trading in options on T-bond, sugar, and gold futures began in late 1982. Trading in options on S&P 500 and NYSE futures began in January 1983. Options on German mark, live cattle, soybeans, wheat, cotton, and silver futures began in 1984. Other option futures contracts currently proposed include those on hogs, corn, GNMA-II, and heating oil.

SECURITY EXCHANGES

While Congress and the CFTC had often taken measures that prohibited options trading on commodities, there was no similar ban on options exercisable for security instruments such as corporate stock.

Consequently, options exercisable in stock were traded actively in the over-the-counter markets under the auspices of the Put and Call Dealers Association. In 1973, the Chicago Board Options Exchange, an offshoot of the Chicago Board of Trade, began trading stock options under strictly supervised conditions. In 1973, only 18 stocks were listed for trading, but this number grew to over 200 to date. In addition, other security exchanges such as the American Stock Exchange, the Pacific Stock Exchange, the Philadelphia Stock Exchange, and the Midwest Stock Exchange began to list stock options.

In the 1980s, these security exchanges became interested in expanding the scope of their option markets to include trading of debt instruments, such as Treasury securities and GNMAs, domestic CDs, and foreign currencies. In December 1981, the chairmen of the Securities and Exchange Commission (SEC), which regulates the security exchanges and the CFTC, agreed that the SEC would have jurisdiction over options on actual security instruments such as T-bills and bonds, while the CFTC was to retain jurisdiction over options on futures contracts for security instruments as well as other physical commodities that are not security instruments. This agreement was formally approved by Congress in late 1982. Trading in options on actual T-bills, T-notes, T-bonds, and currencies began in late 1982. Options on five stock indices (all cash settled) (S&P 100, S&P 500, AMEX Major Market Index, AMEX Market Value, NYSE Composite) began in 1983. Other proposals include options on GNMAs, domestic CDs, and gold bullion.

3

Commodity Option Markets Today

Option contracts may be written for almost any kind of asset or financial right. Of course, the regulatory framework permits only certain kinds of option contracts to be traded. Nevertheless, commodity option markets are or will soon be available for a wide range of different commodities.

The commodities that are the subject of option contracts, or "underlying" commodities, may be categorized on the basis of whether they may be exercised for a "physical" or "actual" commodity, or a futures contract. For example, there are dealer options for physical gold bullion, whereas options for gold futures contracts are being traded by commodity futures exchanges. There are also options for futures contracts based upon Treasury securities as well as options for actual Treasury securities offered by security exchanges.

Actual commodities may be further classified by whether or not they generate interest income. For example, an actual Treasury bond generates interest income for the holder of the security, whereas any income generated from a commodity such as gold or silver must be in the form of price appreciation. An option for an interest-bearing commodity closely resembles a stock option that generates periodic dividend income with the qualification that interest income is guaranteed while dividend income is contingent upon the corporation's success and dividend policy. A futures contract, whether it is based upon an interest-bearing commodity or not, never generates interest income. Therefore options on futures are very much like options on non–interest-bearing commodities.

Option contracts written for futures contracts or actual commodities serve the same basic economic functions. Options provide insurance against adverse price movements for commercial market participants and provide speculators with a vehicle that may be used to profit from commodity price movement while limiting the risk associated with adverse fluctuations. There are, however, some important differences that arise from the use of different underlying commodities.

OPTIONS ON FUTURES CONTRACTS

Futures contract options are offered by the nation's commodity futures exchanges and are regulated by the Commodity Futures Trading Commission's option pilot program of 1981, and the agricultural option pilot program of 1984. The first pilot program limited each commodity exchange to a single option market on those commodities for which option trading was not prohibited prior to 1974. This meant that options could only be traded for futures contracts on precious metals such as gold, silver, and platinum; financial instruments such as Treasury bills, T-bonds, GNMAs, bank certificates of deposit, and Eurodollars; some agricultural commodities such as sugar, cocoa, and coffee; and energy products such as heating oil and gasoline. For details about what is actually offered or proposed, see Chapter 4.

Options on futures contracts will prove to be a highly leveraged, versatile means to invest or to insure the value of an asset against adverse price movements. Options on financial futures will allow market participants to combine the substantial leverage and profit potential of futures with the limited risk of options. The following description explains the mechanics of futures options, their economic function, and advantages over options on actuals.

HOW FUTURES OPTIONS WORK

A futures option gives an option buyer the right, for a price (the option premium), too sell (put option) or to buy (call option) a specified futures contract at a specified price (the striking or exercise price) at any time prior to the expiration of the option. The option buyer's obligations are completely satisfied when he pays the premium for an option, with one exception. If the buyer elects to exercise his option, he is required to post an initial margin for the futures position he establishes. This margin may be taken from the gains he makes on the difference between the prevailing futures price and the option striking price upon exercise of the option.

In return for the option premium, an option seller incurs the risk of being assigned a notice of exercise, in which case he will automatically become the seller (call option) or buyer (put option) of a futures contract at the option striking price. The option seller is required to post a daily margin to cover his liabilities until the option expires, is offset, or is exercised. The liabilities of the option seller are backed by his margin account balance. Settlement of an exercised option requires a set of debits and credits that transfer the option exerciser's gains from the option seller's margin account to the option buyer's margin account.

The basic difference, therefore, between options on futures and options on actuals (either stocks or commodities) is the nature of what is delivered when the option is exercised. When an option on a future is exercised, both the buyer and seller of an option receive futures positions. When an option on an actual is exercised, the buyer of a call (or the writer of a put) receives the actual stock or commodity, while the seller of the call (or the buyer of the put) receives payment. There are also options (on stock indices) that are settled for cash.

ECONOMIC FUNCTION OF OPTIONS ON FUTURES

The foregoing involves important differences, while maintaining certain similarities. Let's first clarify the relationships and similarities, namely, their related economic functions. Options on actuals provide a means to insure the value of an asset against adverse price movements; options on futures also provide this insurance because there is a direct relationship between the price of a commodity and the price of a futures contract on the same commodity. The futures price is essentially a marketwide assessment of what the price of the underlying commodity will be sometime in the future. Since futures prices track cash prices, a futures option can be used to insure against the same price movements as an option on the actual commodity.

Second, options allow investors to benefit from changes in the price movement of a commodity without actually owning it. This is true whether one trades an option on a future or an option on an actual, since (as noted) futures prices track cash prices.

It has also been suggested that futures prices (if available) can be used in determining programs for options contracts. Joseph M. Burns said in 1979:

> *The implicit premium of an option contract should not be estimated on the basis of the current spot price that is expected to exist in the contract expiration month. The forward or futures price . . . could be used as a proxy for the expected future spot.*[1]

This argument is supported by market practices in the dealer option market. Dealer options on gold, copper, and silver are designed to match the futures contract standards; this is so the futures prices can be used in setting premiums. Thus it appears that anyone using options on actuals would have to be looking at futures prices.

DIFFERENCES BETWEEN OPTIONS ON FUTURES AND OPTIONS ON ACTUALS

The most important differences between options on futures and options on actuals are related to the pricing of the underlying commodity, deliverable supply, cost and risk of exercising, and flexibility.

First, the pricing of an option is affected by the availability and quality of

---

[1] J. M. Burns, "A Treatise on markets, Spots, Futures and Options," American Enterprise Institute, Studies in Economic Policy, 1979.

the pricing of the underlying commodity (i.e., future, stock, or commodity). For example, the Government National Mortgage Association—collaterized depository receipt (GNMA-CDR) futures market is very liquid and actively traded, with continuous prices available on a centralized exchange.

The cash market for GNMA certificates is neither consistently liquid nor traded on a centralized exchange. GNMA cash prices are often based on dealer indications rather than actual trades. In this case, the price of GNMA-CDR futures would be more efficient than GNMA certificates. With the price of options being tied to the price of the underlying commodity, prices for options on GNMA-CDR futures should be more efficient than for options on actual GNMAs. Any comparison of options on futures and options on actuals, therefore, needs to compare the pricing information available for the future and the commodity.

Second, the potential for manipulation of an option is affected by the deliverable supply of the underlying commodity. For options on futures, the deliverable supply of futures contracts is infinite. The deliverable supply of a commodity or stock, however, is finite. Therefore, the absolute size of deliverable supply for a commodity option could affect the potential for manipulation or squeezes.

Third, the cost of exercising an option depends upon the underlying commodity. When an option on an actual is exercised, the buyer of a call (writer of a put) is required to pay in full for the actual delivered by the writer of the call (buyer of a put); therefore, both a buyer and/or writer move from a leveraged to an unleveraged position. When an option on a future is exercised, a buyer of a put or a call is only required to put up additional margin money if the current futures price is less than the strike price plus the premium, while no additional money is required from the writers. A buyer or writer of an exercised option on a future therefore moves from one leveraged position to another. Since it is less costly to finance a leveraged position, it will be less costly to exercise an option on a future than an option on an actual.

The riskiness of exercising an option also depends upon the underlying commodity. Assume an investor uses an option to protect himself against adverse price movements of the underlying commodity. For example, an investor either is long T-bonds and buys a put option, or is short T-bonds and writes a put option. What happens when an option on an actual is exercised? The buyer of the put, in the former case, will have to realize any capital gains or losses on the T-bonds delivered. The writer of the put, in the latter case, could receive T-bonds that could not be used to satisfy his short position. Therefore, when an option on an actual is exercised the cash and option transactions are intermixed.

When an option on a futures is exercised, the investor continues to receive protection against price movements by the futures contract. The buyer of the put in the former case receives a short futures position to hedge his cash T-bond position. The writer of the put, in the latter case, will have a long futures position to hedge his short T-bond position. The investor can offset his futures position and buy or sell specific T-bonds at the exact time he desires to realize his capital gains or losses. The investor can separate his cash and option transactions.

Fourth, the portfolio management opportunities of an option depend upon its underlying commodity. For example, when an option on a GNMA actual is exercised, the buyer of a call (and the writer of a put) receives the actual GNMA certificate. Since GNMAs are not traded on a centralized exchange it may be difficult for an investor to trade this instrument. When an option on a GNMA-CDR futures is exercised, both buyers and writers establish futures positions. Since GNMA-CDR futures are traded on a centralized exchange, it would be easy for an investor to trade this instrument. Therefore, an option on GNMA-CDR futures would provide an investor with greater flexibility in the management of his portfolio than an option on an actual.

Options on financial futures thus have important advantages over options on actuals, including more efficient pricing, lower cost and lower risk of exercising, and greater flexibility for portfolio management.

OPTIONS ON ACTUAL COMMODITIES

Options on interest-bearing commodities such as actual Treasury bills, T-notes, GNMAs, and T-bonds are to be offered by the nation's security exchanges that are regulated by the SEC. Options trading on securities exchanges first surfaced in 1973 with the formation of the Chicago Board Options Exchange. The success of financial futures such as T-bill, T-bond, and GNMA futures in the late 1970s and continuing into the 1980s prompted these exchanges to explore ways to trade options on actual debt securities and currencies in addition to corporate stock.

An option on a physical commodity may be attractive to commercials who are interested in using the option market to take or make delivery of the actual commodity. Upon exercise of an option on a physical, the actual commodity is delivered. When an option on a futures is exercised, a specific futures contract is received (e.g., December 1983 T-bonds). The holder of the futures contract must then wait until the delivery month for delivery to occur.

Another difference is that options on futures, except those with cash settlement, expire in the month prior to delivery month. Normally futures prices converge to cash prices during the delivery month. Differences between futures prices and cash prices occur before the delivery month. This could affect the effectiveness of an option being used for price protection against an underlying cash position.

Obviously there are some potentially important differences between options on physicals and options on futures. However, both provide the basic function that any option provides: price protection and speculative opportunity. If options on both a physical and a future are available, the critical decision factor on which to trade is liquidity. Interestingly, options on T-bond futures are the more liquid contract, rather than the options on actual T-bonds. In April 1984, the former were trading ±40,000 a day while the latter were trading only ±1,000. However, options on stock indices that settle for cash are more liquid than options on stock index futures.

4

Available or Proposed Options Markets

A number of exchange-traded commodity options have begun trading in the United States. As of 1984 26 have been approved by either the CFTC (12) or the SEC (14), 24 were trading, and 8 are awaiting approval. This includes options on various stock indices, currencies, financials, metals, bulk commodities, and agricultural products.

Table 4.1 lists the proposed and approved options by regulatory agency and exchange. Tables 4.2 and 4.3 provide the salient features of these option contracts offered by the futures and option exchanges. Table 4.4 provides salient features of some non–exchange-traded commodity options offered by CFTC-approved dealers.

Commodity options that should be approved in the near future include those submitted under the CFTC's physical option pilot program (AMEX gold bullion) and its agricultural option pilot program (grain and livestock futures).

All of these commodity options have important similarities. First, they all provide what any option provides, insurance against price increases or declines. *An option is an option is an option.* Second, all these commodity options will be exchange traded. Exchange-traded options have important advantages over available dealer or forward market options. In exchange-traded options all transactions are ultimately between the clearing members and the clearinghouse. In this manner the clearinghouse becomes a party to every trade; in effect, it becomes the buyer to every seller and the seller to every buyer. This is unlike forward or dealer markets where parties to a transaction deal only with each other. This enhances market performance in several ways. One, it eliminates concern over the credit rating of the party on the other side of the transaction. Two, it frees the original trading partners from delivery or offset from each other. Three, it provides the maximum flexibility in deciding when and how to close out a position. Four, because of the guarantee of the clearinghouse, fails are no longer a problem as they can be in the forward market.

TABLE 4.1 PROPOSED[a] AND APPROVED COMMODITY OPTIONS IN THE UNITED STATES, 1984

SEC Regulated Type	Exchange	CFTC Regulated Type	Exchange
A. Stock Index Options[b]		A. Stock Index Options[b]	
S&P 100 Index	CBOE	NYSE Composite Index futures	NYFE
S&P 500 Index	CBOE	S&P 500 Index futures	CME
Major Market Index	AMEX		
AMEX Market Value Index	AMEX	B. Currencies, Financials	
NYSE Composite Index	NYSE	German mark futures	CME
		T-Bond futures	CBT
B. Currencies, Financials		GNMA-II futures	CBT[a]
British pound	PSE		
Canadian dollars	PSE	C. Bulk Commodities	
Common marks	PSE	Gold futures	COMEX,MCE[c]
Swiss franc	PSE	Silver futures	COMEX
Japanese yen	PSE	Heating oil futures	NYMEX[a]
13 Week T-Bill	AMEX,NYSE[c]		
U.S. T-note	AMEX,NYSE[c]	D. Agriculture Commodities	
U.S. T-bond	CBOE,NYSE[c]	Corn futures	CBT[a],MCE[a]
GNMA	CBOE[c]	Cotton Futures	ANYCE[a]
Domestic CDs	AMEX	Hog futures	CME[a]
		Live cattle futures	CME[c]
C. Bulk Commodities[c]		Soybean futures	CBT[c],MCE[a]
Gold bullion	AMEX[a]	Sugar futures	CSCE
		Wheat futures	KCT,MPLS, MCE[a]

SEC Regulated
AMEX   American Stock Exchange
CBOE   Chicago Board Option Exchange
NYSE   New York Stock Exchange

CFTC Regulated
CBT   Chicago Board of Trade
CME   Chicago Mercantile Exchange
COMEX Commodity Exchange, New York

PSE   Philadelphia Stock Exchange

CSCE	Coffee Sugar & Cocoa Exchange
KCT	Kansas City Board of Trade
MCE	Mid America Commodity Exchange
MPLS	Minneapolis Grain Exchange
NYCE	New York Cotton Exchange
NYFE	New York Futures Exchange
NYMEX	New York Mercantile Exchange

[a] Proposed but not approved by appropriate regulatory agency.

[b] These contracts are all settled for cash. Others require either delivery of physical commodities or futures contracts. The exception is for options on stock futures. They are also settled for cash on last day of trading.

[c] Approved, but not yet trading.

This is, however, a lot of new contracts to try and understand. In this chapter, we describe these various commodity markets while evaluating the risks and potential of specific commodity option contracts. Commodity markets are different from stock markets. First, except for futures, most commodities are not exchange traded. For example, domestic CDs, currencies, GNMAs, Treasuries, heating oil, stock indices, and sugar are not exchange traded except as futures contracts. Gold and silver, however, are exchange traded. Second, commodities are not homogeneous. This results in pricing differentials within the same commodity. For example, GNMAs can have different coupons, issue date, and so on. Third, for bulk commodities like heating oil and agricultural commodities like grains and livestock, location and storage are important. This is not important for financial instruments or stocks. Finally, each commodity has its own trade practices. For example, domestic CDs trade in basis points, Treasury bonds in ⅛ths, and soybeans in ¼¢ per bushel.

This chapter has eight sections. Options based on the same underlying commodities are discussed together. This includes options on GNMAs, domestic CDs, U.S. Treasuries, stock indices, heating oil, metals (gold, silver), currencies, agricultural products (sugar, grains, livestock).

For each commodity we discuss the underlying commodity including (1) pricing, uses, and supply; (2) existing forward and futures markets; and (3) the option contract(s) including its attractive features, potential risks, and types of investors.

OPTIONS ON GNMAs (GOVERNMENT NATIONAL MORTGAGE ASSOCIATION) CERTIFICATES

Options on GNMA certificates have been approved for trading on the Chicago Board Options Exchange. Options on GNMA-II futures are being proposed by Chicago Board of Trade.

To trade these options, a trader must understand both the underlying cash and forward/futures markets. A GNMA certificate is a standardized, mortgage-backed financial instrument with principal and interest payments guaranteed by the U.S. government. The introduction of GNMA certificates in the early 1970s enabled institutional and individual investors to lend money to the home mortgage industry. This resulted in savings and loan associations and banks expanding their mortgage investment activities.

Each GNMA represents a pro-rata share of single-family residential mortgages pooled together to back the certificate. All mortgages in the package must have the same stated rates of interest and maturity dates. GNMAs have an original maturity of around 30 years and are issued in minimum denominations of $25,000 with increments of $5,000. A typical GNMA is issued in $1 to $3 million dollars.

These certificates are called pass-through securities because interest and principal payment on mortgages are passed through to the certificate holder after dealer fees are deducted. Certificate holders are guaranteed timely payment of principal and interest by the U.S. government, even if the individual homeowner or GNMA issuer defaults.

Pricing

GNMA certificates are traded in a centralized dealer market. Transactions are negotiated over the phone between dealers or between dealers and investors. These dealers include the largest brokerage firms, banks, and financial institutions. Cash prices are available in the *Wall Street Journal,* wire services, and from dealers. GNMAs are priced in the cash market on a yield basis, with a minimum bid ask being $\frac{8}{32}$nds; that is, $2,500 per million. A round lot is $1 million. However, the bid/ask for odd lots or coupons other than the current production rate can be substantially larger; that is, $\frac{16}{32}$–$\frac{32}{32}$. GNMA futures are also traded at the Chicago Board of Trade, providing continuous exchange-traded futures prices.

Uses

GNMAs are packaged by mortgage bankers, savings and loans, and other approved GNMA originators and then sold to investors as fixed-income investment. GNMAs are attractive to fixed-income investors such as pension, profit-sharing, and trust funds because of their more frequent payment stream (i.e., monthly rather than semiannual). The cash flow characteristics of GNMAs do differ from other types of fixed-income securities. Payment of principal and interest is made to investors as received. Since mortgages can be paid off early, this results in uneven payment streams. GNMAs are also attractive to investors interested in diversifying their portfolio.

Supply

GNMAs were first issued in 1970. By December 1982, the total amount outstanding was over $166 billion, with varying amounts available for different coupons. New GNMAs are issued at or below the current production rate set by FHA/VA. The current production rate is normally the most liquid issue. This rate has ranged from 7.5% to 17% during the last five years. Variables that affect the housing market in terms of numbers sold are also related to the number of new GNMAs issued.

Forward Market

A forward market, for both mandatory and standby commitments, exists for GNMAs. In such nonregulated markets, participants agree to trade GNMA certificates—usually primary issues—for delivery at some future price. Prices are fixed and negotiated for each transaction. A trader may not close out his position without his trading partner's consent. The credit standing of the other side of the transaction is important. Defaults occur in this market, since there is no uniform or formal mechanism for requiring cash as a security deposit to ensure performance. Mandatory commitments perform a similar function to futures contracts, while standby commitments are like put options. The advantage of forward market transactions is that they can be tailor-made to meet the exact needs of the participants.

Futures Markets

Futures markets in GNMAs were first introduced by the Chicago Board of Trade in 1975. Futures represent a firm commitment to buy or sell a specified commodity during a specified month, at a price established through open outcry in a central, regulated marketplace. The only liquid GNMA contracts are those offered by the Chicago Board of Trade, that is, GNMA-CDR futures contract and GNMA-II futures contracts.

GNMA–CDR Futures

A buyer who takes delivery on a GNMA-CDR contract receives a CDR (collateralized depositary receipt) backed by GNMA certificates. The holder of the CDR may

Surrender the CDR for GNMAs
Hold it and receive $635 per month per receipt
Redeliver it into the futures market
Sell it in the cash market

If a CDR is surrendered, either $100,000 principal balance of 8% GNMAs or an equivalent principal balance of *any* other GNMA coupon to yield 7.96% at par can be delivered. For example, an equivalent principal balance of GNMA 16s is $62,208.40. The CDR can be more valuable than the value of GNMAs received at surrender. This is because the CDR is a perpetuity, paying a fixed $635 per month.

The GNMA-CDR contract was designed to facilitate futures trading, and to avoid in the delivery month the cumbersome process of buying and selling GNMAs in a cash market. This is due to the nature of GNMAs cash markets. GNMAs are bearer instruments. They must be registered at Chemical Bank in New York in order to forward payment of principal and interest, or to break down GNMAs into smaller pieces. A typical GNMA sale entails five or more days, with the principal and interest payments often lagging a month or more. Normally some interest must be retrieved from earlier owners. This makes physical delivery of GNMAs cumbersome.

GNMA-II Futures

In early 1984 the CBT began trading a new GNMA-II futures contract. This contract results in delivery of actual GNMA certificates. The invoice price is adjusted depending upon the coupon delivered (if other than 8%). Delivery can occur over a number of days in the delivery month. However, the actual GNMAs that can be delivered (in terms of coupons) can change depending upon recent changes in FHA/VA current production rates. The proposed option contract is based on this relatively new futures contract. Of interest is how this contract will trade during periods of volatile interest rates, since such changes can affect what is deliverable grade.

Options Market

Two types of options on GNMAs have been proposed—options on actual GNMA certificates and options on GNMA-II futures.

Options on GNMA Actuals

CBOE (see Table 4.2) has received approval to trade an option on a $100,-000 GNMA single family pass-through certificate. Investors should carefuully read the actual contract terms before trading. The contract is designed to match cash market practices. First, when an option is exercised, there are certain restrictions on which GNMAs may be delivered depending upon the current production rate, that is, the official FHA/VA mortgage rate. Second, there is a time difference between when an option can be exercised and when delivery occurs.

These characteristics can have some adverse consequences for the unwary trader. For example, suppose a trader writes a covered option, that is, short calls against cash 16% GNMAs. If the current production changes, these GNMAs may no longer be deliverable into the contract. Another problem is exercise has to occur at least 12 business days prior to the single delivery day allowed per month. The difference between exercise time and delivery could affect the profitability of a trade. An option could be exercised that was in-the-money at exercise time. However, the value of the underlying GNMAs could change substantially during the 12 days required to obtain delivery. The trader may need to hedge this risk through the futures or forward market. Third, a trader in a spread (long and short a call) could find one side of his trade exercised, yet have to wait another month to be able to exercise the other side. Obviously understanding contract details will be important in successfully trading this contract.

Options on GNMA-II Futures

The CBT has submitted for approval options on GNMA-II futures. If such an option is exercised, both the buyer and the writer will receive offsetting por-

TABLE 4.2 SUMMARY OF SECURITY EXCHANGE OPTIONS

Exchange	AMEX	AMEX	AMEX[a]	CBOE	CBOE	PSE	NYSE[a]
Underlying commodity	T-bills: four contracts, $1,000,000 with 13 weeks to maturity, $200,000 13-week, $500,000 26-week, and $100,000 26-week	T-notes: 5- to 7-year term, two contracts—$100,000 and $200,000	90-day domestic CDs $1,000,000	30-year T-bonds, two contracts—$100,000 and $20,000	$100,000 GNMA pass-through certificates	Foreign currencies 12,500 British pounds, 62,500 German marks, 62,500 Swiss francs, 6,250,000 Japanese yen, and 50,000 Canadian dollars	T-bills; four contracts $1,000,000 with 13 weeks to maturity, $200,000 13 week, $500,000 26 week, and $100,000 26 week
Trading months	Mar., June, Sept., and Dec.	Mar., June, Sept., and Dec.	Mar., June, Sept., and Dec.	Mar., June, Sept., and Dec.	Mar., June, Sept., and Dec.	Mar., June, Sept., and Dec.	Mar., June, Sept., and Dec.
Last trading day	Third Friday of expiration month	Third Friday of expiration month	Third Friday of expiration month	Third Friday of expiration month	Third Friday of expiration month	Second Friday of expiration month	Third Friday of expiration month
Expiration	Saturday following last trading day	Saturday following last trading day	Saturday following last trading day	Saturday following last trading day	Saturday following last trading day	Saturday following last trading day	Saturday following last trading day
Strike price intervals	100 basis points	2 points	100 basis points	2 points	2 points	$0.05 in pounds, $0.02 in marks, $0.02 in francs, $0.02 in dollars, $0.0002 in yen	100 basis points
Premium quotation	1 basis point ($25 and $5)	1/32 points ($31.25 and $6.25)	1 basis point ($25)	1/32 points ($31.25 and $6.25)	1/32 points ($31.25)	Quoted in terms of American dollars	1 basis point ($25 and $5)

[a] Proposed, but not trading.

32

TABLE 4.2 SUMMARY OF SECURITY EXCHANGE OPTIONS (Cont'd.)

Exchange	NYSE	AMEX	AMEX	AMEX	CBOE	CBOE
Underlying commodity	NYSE Composite Index × $100 cash settled	Gold bullion[a] (100 troy oz.) settled in cash based on second London gold fixing price on following business day	Major Market Index (20 stocks) × $100 cash settled	Market Value Index (800 stocks) × $100 cash settled	S&P 500 Index × $100 cash settled	S&P 100 Index × $100 cash settled
Trading months	Monthly	Monthly	Monthly	Monthly	Monthly	Monthly
Last trading day	Third Friday of the month	Third Friday of the month	Third Friday of the month	Third Friday of the month	Friday preceding the third Saturday	Friday preceding the third Saturday
Expiration	Saturday following last day of trading	Saturday following last day of trading	Saturday following last day of trading	Saturday following last day of trading	Saturday following last day of trading	Saturday following last day of trading
Strike price intervals	5 points where 1 point is $100	Same as COMEX	5 points where 1 point is $100	5 points where 1 point is $100	5 points where 1 point is $100	5 points where 1 point is $100
Premium quotations	1/16 of a point ($6.25)	10¢ per oz. ($10.00)	2/16 ($6.25)	1/16 ($6.25)	1/16 of a point ($6.25)	1/16 of a point ($6.25)

[a] Proposed, but not trading.

TABLE 4.2 SUMMARY OF SECURITY EXCHANGE OPTIONS (Cont'd.)

Exchange	NYSE[a]	NYSE[a]
Underlying commodity	Spcific T-note issues, $100,000 and $20,000	Specific T-bond issues, $100,000 and $20,000
Trading months	Feb., May, Aug., and Nov.	Feb, May, Aug., and Nov.
Last trading day	Day prior to expiration	Day prior to expiration
Expiration	Third business day prior to fifteenth calendar day	Third business day prior to fifteenth calendar day
Strike price intervals	2 points	2 points
Premium quotation	1/32 point ($31.25 and $6.25)	1/32 point ($31.25 and $6.25)

[a] Proposed, but not trading.

tions in a GNMA-II futures contract. This avoids some of the problems inherent in the option on GNMA actuals discussed above. However, the GNMA-II futures contract is sensitive to changes in current production rate (see section on GNMA-II futures).

Attractive Features

GNMA options should be an attractive substitute for existing standby commitments (puts) available in the forward markets. Exchange-traded GNMA options will remove the risk of default, while providing active secondary markets for offsetting option positions. In fact, it should be similar to the introduction of exchange-traded stock options, which resulted in their being used rather than dealer put and call options. For example, GNMA originators currently buy standby commitments (puts) and obtain price insurance during the period between when mortgages are issued and a GNMA certificate can be issued (normally 45 to 180 days). These originators will be able to trade both puts and calls.

Potential Risks

GNMA options can have special risks when (if) an option is exercised. GNMA certificates were designed to provide some homogeneity to the selling off of mortgages. However, individual GNMA pools can vary widely from each other. First, unlike Treasury instruments, GNMAs can be prepaid at any time. For example, if a homeowner decides to move, he can sell his house and pay off his mortgage. This means there is uncertainty about the income stream over time. The prepayment pattern is affected by such factors as coupon, geographical concentration, date issued, and so forth. Prepayment risk also causes GNMAs trading above par to price differently from those below par. For example, assume you bought a GNMA 16% for 104. If the GNMA immediately prepaid, you would receive only $100. Rapid prepayment of premium GNMAs can and does occur.

Second, the current production rate restricts what can be delivered on both the CBOE's GNMA option contract and the GNMA-II futures contracts. In the past few years the current rate has ranged from 8% to 17%. This change in current production rate is also related to changes in yields on GNMAs.

Third, since GNMAs are not exchange traded it may be difficult for individuals to obtain good prices when buying or selling odd lot GNMAs. The $100,000 contract size of both options is considered an odd lot in the cash market. This can put an individual at a disadvantage when buying and selling GNMAs to make or take delivery of the option on the actual or the GNMA-II futures relative to the GNMA dealers and larger traders.

Finally, the risk of GNMA options depends upon factors that affect levels of interest rates. Interest rates can be highly volatile. Increased interest rates can also reduce the number of new GNMAs issued as new housing starts decline.

Types of Investors

Options on GNMAs should be attractive to those mortgage banks and savings and loan associations already active in the existing forward and stand by commitment markets. In addition, investors in GNMAs such as pension funds, GNMA dealers, and brokerage firms can use this market to hedge or increase the yields on their investments.

OPTIONS ON 90-DAY DOMESTIC CERTIFICATES OF DEPOSIT

Options on domestic CDs are approved for trading on the American Stock Exchange in New York. Table 4.2 provides the salient features of this contract. Certificates of deposit (CDs) are receipts for funds deposited in a bank for a specified period of time and at an agreed-upon rate of interest. Deliverable grade CDs are those from a restricted list of domestic banks in $1 million dollar negotiable pieces with a fixed rate of interest and an original maturity of no more than six months. CDs differ from time deposits in that they are negotiable. CDs were first introduced in 1961 by the Citibank in New York, and are now a major source of bank funds.

Pricing

Fixed-rate CDs are normally priced on a yield basis rather than on a discount basis. For example, the price of a new $1,000,000 face value CD would be $1,000,000. At maturity, the investor would receive $1 million plus interest. The following formula is used to calculate the price of fixed-rate CDs in the secondary market:

$$\text{Price} = \text{Face Amount} \times \frac{360 + (\text{Original Life}) \times (\text{Coupon Rate}}{360 + (\text{Remaining Life (Settlement Yield)}}$$

A CD issued directly by a bank to an investor is called a primary CD. A CD sold by a dealer or investor to another dealer or investor is called a secondary CD. Normally the yields on primary CDs for a specific bank and maturity are lower than for secondary CDs. Banks provide quotes for primary rate CDs with various maturities. These rates can vary between banks, and are negotiable for investors on a purchase of $5 million or more. The secondary market consists of approximately 35 bank and nonbank dealers. Dealers quote bid and offer rates by the month in which the CD matures. This differs from banks, which provide quotes for specific maturities. The bid/ask spread is normally 10 basis points for the top tier banks. However, changes in creditworthiness of particular banks and other market factors can affect this spread, and yields for specific bank CDs.

The price of CDs is affected by the following variables: creditworthiness of the banks, outstanding supply, interest rates on other short-term instruments, negotiability, and other market factors that affect short-term interest rates. Prices of specific CDs by bank, coupon, and maturity can be obtained by direct contact with banks or dealers. Telerate, Quotron, and other wire services also provide quotes for primary and secondary top tier CDs. A 90-day domestic CD futures contract at the Chicago Mercantile Exchange offers continuous exchange-traded futures prices.

Uses

Large fixed-rate CDs are purchased by a variety of investors. These include corporations, financial institutions, state and local governments, foreign banks and governments, pension funds, nonprofit organizations, and individuals. CDs provide both safety of principal and attractive current yields. CD yields are higher than Treasury bills, but often lower than bankers' acceptances, commercial paper, and Eurodollar deposits. There is also an active secondary market for the top tier banks' CDs.

Supply

In 1961, outstanding negotiable CDs totaled $2.8 billion. By the end of 1982 this increased to $132 billion. However, the deliverable supply of CDs that can be delivered on the AMEX option contract is restricted. Total supply of CDs that meet contract standard has been nearer to $5 billion. A portion of this supply, due to informal agreement between banks and investors, is held to maturity. Another sizable proportion can be held by dealers. Yet banks can always increase the supply by issuing more CDs. Therefore, supply should be sensitive to price.

Futures Markets

Futures in 90-day domestic CDs began trading in 1981. The only currently liquid contract is available at the International Monetary Exchange in Chicago. This contract calls for delivery of late month fixed-rate CDs that mature in the third month after delivery month. Only top tier banks determined by a survey of major dealers are deliverable. Each CD must be a $1-million-dollar face amount, with an original maturity of less than six months. Current contract months are March, June, September, and December. The invoice price uses the same formula as the above cash price for CDs, except yield is replaced by the futures settlement yield. Delivery occurs only in the last half of the delivery month. Given the continuous pricing information available from this market, it should be an important tool in successfully trading options on domestic CDs.

Option Markets

Options on domestic CDs are currently approved for trading on the AMEX. Table 4.2 provides the salient features.

Attractive Features

Options on domestic CDs expand portfolio strategies available to investors in domestic CDs and other short-term financial instruments. Like most options, it allows investors to protect the principal value, or issuers to establish ceiling prices. This market may be particularly attractive for dealers in domestic CDs for both risk management and market arbitrage, and for banks who issue CDs.

Potential Risks

An investor trading in options on domestic CDs is subject to several risks. First, short-term interest rates can be volatile. Second, banks can influence yields and deliverable supply through their issuance patterns. Third, the liquidity and yields of specific bank CDs can vary. For example, the writer of a call should expect to receive the "cheapest" CD with the largest bid/ask spread if his option is exercised. Fourth, the list of deliverable banks can be changed. This affects the risk of writing covered calls (short call, long CDs) and buying puts to protect CD positions. Finally, writers of options should be able to arrange for financing in the case an option is exercised. The normal invoice price or cost is over $1,000,000 per contract.

Types of Investors

Options on domestic CDs should be attractive to those firms and individuals already active in buying and selling CDs and CD futures. This includes dealers, banks, financial institutions, corporations, pension funds, and wealthy individuals. Speculative interest should be obtained from individuals already active in stock options, and professional option traders.

OPTIONS ON U.S. TREASURY SECURITIES AND BOND FUTURES

There are two types of options on U.S. Treasuries being offered in the United States. First, the SEC-regulated option exchanges are offering options on specific Treasury bonds, notes, and bill issues. Table 4.2 provides the salient features of these contracts and their trading locations. Second, the Chicago Board of Trade, a CFTC-regulated futures exchange is trading an option on its U.S. Treasury bond futures contract. Table 4.3 provides the salient features of

TABLE 4.3 SUMMARY OF FUTURES CONTRACT OPTIONS

Exchange	MCE[a]	CBT	COMEX	CME	CME	NYFE	CSCE	NYMEX[a]
Underlying commodity	33.2 oz. gold futures	$100,000 T-bonds futures	100 oz. gold futures	Standard & Poor's 500 × $500 futures	W. German marks $125,000 futures	NYSE Composite Index × $500 futures	112,000 lb. raw sugar #11 futures	1,000 barrel #2 heating oil futures
Trading months	Mar., Apr., June, Aug., Sept., and Dec.	Mar., June, Sept., and Dec.	Apr., Aug., and Dec.	Mar., June, Sept., and Dec.	Mar., June, Sept., and Dec.	Mar., June, Sept., and Dec.	Mar., July, and Oct.	Mar., July, Sept., and Dec.
Last trading day	Second Friday of month prior to option month	First Friday at least 5 business days before first notice day of futures	Second Friday of month prior to option month	Third Thursday of contract month (same as futures)	Second Friday immediately preceding third Wednesday of contract month	Business day preceding last business day of month (same as futures)	Second Friday of month prior to option month	Second Friday of month prior to option month
Expiration	Saturday following last trading day	Saturday following last trading day	Last trading day	Last trading day	Last trading day	Last trading day	Saturday following last trading day	Last trading day
Strike price intervals	Depends on current gold price: $10 under $300, $20 between $300 and $500, $30 between $500 and $800, $40 over $800	2 points where 1 point is $1,000	Depends on current gold price: $10 under $300, $20 between $300 and $500, $30 between $500 and $800, $40 over $800	5 index points where index point equals $500	1 index point where 1 index point equals $1,250	2 index points where index point equals $500	Depends on current sugar price: ½¢ in 2 nearby months, 1c in deferred if under 15¢; 2¢ if over 15¢ and under 40¢; and 4¢ over 40¢	Depends on current oil price: 1¢ under 50¢, 2¢ between 50¢, 3¢ between $1.10 and $2, and 4¢ over $2
Premium quotation	2.5¢ per oz. (83¢)	1/64 point (15.63)	10¢ per oz. ($10)	0.05 index point ($25)	0.01 index point ($12.50)	0.05 index point ($25)	0.01¢ per pound ($11.20)	0.01¢ per gallon ($4.00)

[a] Contract details are subject to change. Please contact exchange for current contract specifications.

TABLE 4.3 SUMMARY OF FUTURES CONTRACT OPTIONS (Cont'd)

Exchange	CME	CME	CE	KCBT	MCE	MPLS
Underlying commodity	Hog futures (30,000 lbs.)	Live cattle futures (40,000 lbs.)	Cotton futures (50,000 lbs.)	Wheat futures (5,000 bushels)	5 Wheat futures (5 × 1,000 bushels)	Wheat futures (5,000 bushels)
Trading months	Feb., Apr., June, July, Aug., Oct., and Dec.	Feb., Apr., June, Aug., Oct., and Dec.	Mar., July, and Dec.	Mar., May, July, and Dec.	Mar., May, June, Sept., and Dec.	Mar., May, June, Sept., and Dec.
Last trading day	Fourth business day prior to first business day of delivery month of futures contract	Fourth business day prior to first business day of delivery month of futures contract	First Friday of month preceding delivery month futures contract	First Friday that precedes first notice day by at least 10 business days	Friday that precedes notice day by at least 10 business days	Friday that precedes first notice day by at least 10 business days
Expiration	Same as last trading date	Same as last trading date	Saturday following last day of trading	Saturday following last day of trading	Saturday following last day of trading	Saturday following last day of trading
Strike price intervals	2¢ per lb.	2¢ per lb.	Deferred contracts 2¢ per lb. nearby contract; If cotton is less than 74.5¢ per lb., 1¢ per lb., if greater than 74.5¢ per lb. 2¢ per lb.	10¢ per bushel	10¢ if less than or equal to $4.50; 20¢ if greater than $4.50	10¢ per bushel if less than or equal to $4.50 per bushel; 20¢ per bushel if greater than $4.50 per bushel
Premium quotations	0.00025¢ per lb. ($7.50)	0.000025¢ per lb. ($10.00)	1/100¢ per lb. ($5.00)	1/8¢ per bushel ($6.25)	1/8¢ ($6.25)	1/8¢ per bushel ($6.25)

TABLE 4.3 SUMMARY OF FUTURES CONTRACT OPTIONS (Cont'd)

Exchange	CBT	COMEX	CBT	CBT	MCE
Underlying commodity	GNMA-II futures	Silver futures (5,000 oz.)	Corn futures 5,000 bushels	Soybean futures 5,000 bushels	5 soybean futures (5 × 1,000 bushels)
Trading months	Mar., June, Sept., and Dec.	Same as futures	Nov., Jan., Mar., May, July, Aug., and Sept.	Nov., Jan., Mar., May, July, Aug., and Sept.	Jan, Mar, May, July, Aug, Sept., and Nov.
Last trading day	First Friday at least 5 business days before first notice day of futures	Second Friday of the month prior to underlying futures contract months	First Friday that precedes by at least 10 business days first notice day	First Friday that precedes by at least 10 business days first notice day	Friday that precedes first notice day by at least 10 business days
Expiration	Saturday following last trading day	Saturday following last trading day	Saturday following last trading day	Saturday following last trading day	Saturday following last trading day
Strike price intervals	2 points where 1 point equals $1,000	Depends on current price: 25¢ per oz. less than $5.00, 50¢ per oz. if equals $5.00 to $15.00, $1.00 per oz. if more than $15.00	25¢ per bushel	10¢ per bushel	10¢ per bushel
Premium quotations	1/64 point ($15.63)	1/10¢ per oz. ($5.00)	1/8¢ per bushel ($6.25)	1/8¢ per bushel ($6.25)	1/8¢ per bushel ($6.25)

this contract. There are important differences as discussed in Chapter 3 between these two types of options. However, factors that affect the pricing of the actual securities are important in both options.

Pricing

U.S. Treasury securities are issued directly by the U.S. government, through public auction, and backed by its full faith and credit. These securities can vary in liquidity, depending on amount outstanding, time since issuance, ownership patterns, and so on. Price information is available from several sources. First, the major newspapers provide daily prices. Second, Telerate, Quotron, and other services provide on-line dealer quotations. However, each service provides information from only a limited number of dealers, and lists bid/ask prices rather than actual transactions. Finally, liquid futures markets in 90-day Treasury bills, 10-year Treasury notes, and long-term Treasury bonds provide continuous pricing information. Futures markets are open for trading in T-bills, T-notes, and T-bonds from 8:00 A.M. to 2:00 P.M. CST. Treasuries can be bought and sold before and after these times in the cash market.

A recent event shows the importance of futures markets in these markets. In December 1982, the United States announced an auction for a new Treasury bond. This was scheduled for when the CBT bond futures market was closed. The bond dealers persuaded the U.S. Treasury to move the auction date to a day when the futures market would be open. The dealers needed the futures market to hedge their positions and for pricing information.

Uses

Purchase of Treasury securities provides a relatively safe, interest-bearing investment. They are purchased by individuals, corporations, banks, and pension funds, among others. Government securities can also be purchased to mature on or about a date to meet the anticipated future expenditures. The *Treasury Bulletin* and the *Federal Reserve Bulletins* are important sources of information on ownership patterns, amount outstanding by issue, and historical bid/ask prices. Ownership patterns and outstanding supply can affect the sensitivity of available supply to demand. For example, pension funds hold sizable amounts of Treasury debt. However, they have trading restrictions that make them less sensitive to price. Major bond dealers can also hold a sizable proportion of a particular issue.

Supply

The U.S. government determines the total outstanding supply. They issue three types of Treasury securities: bills (T-bills), notes (T-notes), and bonds (T-bonds).

T-Bills. Treasury bills are short-term securities. T-bills are issued either weekly maturing in either three or six months, or monthly maturing in one year. T-bills are in book entry form only, with sales being made through the Federal Wire. They are marketed on a discount basis, with the face amount being paid to the investor on a maturity date.

T-Notes. T-notes are intermediate-term securities with an issuance to maturity of from 2 to 10 years. Notes are not discount instruments, but are sold at par, with biannual coupon payments. Interest or coupon rates are determined by the auction in which the securities are sold. Only the two-year T-notes are currently issued on a regular basis; that is, monthly. Information on other scheduled auctions can be obtained from financial sections of major newspapers or by calling any Federal Reserve Bank.

T-Bonds. T-bonds are the same as T-notes except that their minimum maturity at issuance is 10 years. T-bonds are available in a wide range of maturities and coupons. T-bonds are more sensitive to price than T-bills due to the longer term to maturity. Also, T-bonds, unlike T-notes, may have call provisions. This means the government may call the issue on any interest payment day any time less than five years to the maturity date.

The total amount of marketable Treasury securities is very large. In December 1982, the total outstanding was $283 billion of T-bills, $438 billion of T-notes, and $103 billion of T-bonds. However, the supply of specific issues varies. For example, the 11¾% T-bond of 2005-10 has an outstanding supply of $2.6 billion, while new 2-year auctions have been from $6 to $7 billion. Available supply of specific issues can also be affected by who owns them. Certain investors, for example, pension funds and banks, have buy and hold strategies. They are often reluctant to sell these securities regardless of price.

Futures Markets

There are currently three liquid futures markets on U.S. Treasury securities. Futures on long-term T-bonds and 6½%-10-year T-notes are traded at the Chicago Board of Trade, and futures on 90-day T-bills at the Chicago Mercantile Exchange. The T-bill contract calls for delivery of a specific T-bill issue that matures in 90 days. Delivery on T-notes and T-bonds can occur on any day during the delivery month. A variety of T-notes or T-bonds are deliverable. In this case, the invoice price is adjusted depending upon the maturity and coupon of the T-note or T-bond delivered, based on an 8% standard. The T-note and T-bond contracts are less sensitive to problems of deliverable supply than the T-bill contract. Traders should be aware that on the T-note and T-bond futures contracts the last day of trading occurs seven business days prior to the last delivery day of the month. Since the futures settlement price is set on the last day of trading for the remaining delivery days, there can be considerable risk in making or taking delivery at the end of the month. Normally, only professional traders stand for delivery. Importantly, these futures markets are very liquid. Some researchers believe that these markets, besides providing important hedging and pricing benefits, have improved the efficiency of the underlying cash markets.

Options Markets

Options markets on both Treasury securities and Treasury futures have been available since October 1982. The former markets require delivery of specific Treasury issues, purchased in the cash market. The latter requires delivery of futures contracts by book entry through the clearing corporation. Interestingly, only the futures option has developed into a truly liquid market. In early 1984, open interest in Treasury bond futures options had passed 190,-000 contracts, while volume was as high as 40,000 contracts a day. The options markets on actual Treasuries are trading less than 1,000 contracts a day. One explanation may be that the bond futures are exchange traded, while actual Treasury securities are not. Thus, continuous pricing is available for the futures along with a more liquid underlying market. The CBT $100,000 T-bond futures trade from 50,000 to 125,000 contracts a day, or $5 to $12 billion. Secondary transactions of a specific T-bond may only be $1 to $2 billion a day. The bid/ask spreads are also wider in the cash market than the futures market.

Attractive Features

Treasury options expand portfolio strategies available to investors in U.S. Treasuries. Like most options, they allow investors to both protect inventory value and establish ceiling prices. However, a key difference from other types of commodity options is that Treasury securities are income bearing. Options can therefore be used to adjust the risk and return of various Treasury portfolios. They can also be used by speculators who want to fine tune their predictions about future interest rates, while limiting the risks that occur in outright futures positions.

Potential Risks

Interest rates can be highly volatile. Yield curves, which outline the relationship between shorter- and longer-term Treasuries, can also range from positive to flat to negative. The U.S. government can also affect yields of specific issues through its issuance pattern. Besides these basic factors, there are different risks for futures options than for options on actual securities.

Options on Treasury Securities

Exercise is more risky for options on securities than options on futures. Options on securities can be exercised at any time prior to maturity. Contract terms require delivery of specific Treasury instruments. Specific issues can be in short supply immediately prior to the expiration of an option. The price of a Treasury issue can also change after delivery occurs. Many of the contracts also call for delivery of odd lot sizes. All of these factors can affect the profit of particular option strategies, if exercise occurs. The bid/ask prices on specific issues can also affect the bid/ask prices available in the options market. Therefore, individual investors should be careful when writing uncovered call options on actual Treasuries.

Options on T-Bond Futures

Options on T-bond futures have the same type of risks that options on any futures contract has. The futures price tracks the "cheapest to deliver," and trading in futures and options on a given day is limited to prices plus or minus the trading limit over the prior day's settlement price. However, neither of these factors appear important. In fact, options on T-bond futures are the most liquid of the new commodity options (adjusted for the dollar size of the underlying commodity).

Types of Investors

Options on Treasuries should be attractive to those firms and individuals already active in buying and selling U.S. Treasuries and Treasury futures. This includes dealers, banks, brokerage firms, corporation pension funds, insurance companies, and individual investors. Sophisticated money managers also use these options to expand available portfolio strategies.

OPTIONS ON STOCK INDICES AND STOCK INDEX FUTURES

There are two types of options on stock indices currently trading. First, the option exchanges are offering options on actual stock indices. These options, when exercised, are settled based on the cash value of the spot index. These include options on (a) S&P 100 Stock Index (CBOE), (b) S&P 500 Stock Index (CBOE), (c) Major Market Index (AMEX), (d) AMEX Market Value Index, and (e) NYSE Composite Index (NYSE).

Second, the futures exchanges are offering options on stock index futures. On final expiration day, these options are automatically exercised and settled in cash based on the closing price of the underlying index. Prior to expiration, exercise results in assignment of a futures position. The three futures options are (a) S&P 500 Index futures contract (CME), (b) S&P 100 Index futures contract (CME), and (c) the NYSE Index futures contract (NYFE). Tables 4.2 and 4.3 provide the salient features of these options contracts.

Pricing

Prices of the underlying stock indices are based on the cash prices of the stocks in the indices. However, each index (S&P 100, NYSE Composite, S&P 500, AMEX Index, and AMEX Market Value) differs in how it is constructed and/or the number of stocks in the index. The indices are constructed as follows:

CBOE 100 Index. This is a capitalized, weighted index based on 100 stocks that are option listed at the CBOE. This index is also adjusted for mergers, delistings, and rights offerings. On April 6, 1984, this index equaled 152.49. The index is published by CBOE and available in newspapers and through wire services. CBOE has constructed the daily value of the index back to January 2, 1976. All the stocks in this index are both traded on a major U.S. stock exchange and option listed at the CBOE. Interestingly, the top 10 stocks account for a substantial proportion of the total market value. The S&P 100 index futures (CME) are also available through newspapers and wire services.

NYSE Index. This is also a capitalized, weighted index based on all stocks traded on the New York Stock Exchange (± 1500 stocks). This stock index is also adjusted for new listings and delistings, mergers, and rights offerings. On April 6, 1984, this index equaled 89.48. The index was first published by the NYSE on May 28, 1964. However, the weekly data is available back to January 7, 1939, based on the discontinued index of the Security and Exchange Commission converted to the NYSE base. The NYSE Index futures contract (NYFE) began trading in mid-1982. NYSE Index futures prices are also widely disseminated through newspapers and wire services.

S&P 500 Index. This is also a capitalized, weighted index based on the 500 large companies in terms of capitalization. This index is also adjusted for mergers, delistings and new listings, and rights offerings. On April 6, 1984, this index equaled 155.48. The index is published by Standard and Poor, Inc., and is widely available through newspapers and wire services. The index, based on 500 stocks, was first published in March 1957. Prior to that, it consisted of the 90 large stocks. The S&P 500, like the NYSE Index, is a widely used proxy for a market index. S&P 500 futures began trading in mid-1982. S&P 500 futures prices are also widely disseminated through newspapers and wire services.

AMEX Major Market Index. This index is a price weighted index based on 20 stocks:

$$\sum_{i=1}^{20} \frac{\text{Price } i}{\text{Divisor}}$$

The divisor is adjusted for stock splits, mergers, delistings and new listings, and rights offerings. The index is published by the American Stock Exchange and is available through newspapers and wire services. The index is perceived as a substitute for the Dow Jones Industrial Average of 30 stocks. Major Market Index futures contracts are being proposed by the Chicago Board of Trade. On May 31, 1984, the index equaled 107.73.

AMEX Market Value Index. This index is a capitalized, weighted index based on all stocks traded on the American Stock Exchange (±800 stocks). This stock index is adjusted for new listings, and delistings, mergers, and rights offerings. The index is published by the American Stock Exchange and is widely available through newspapers and wire services. Because of the weight of oil companies, this index is not as good a proxy for the total market as other market indices. Futures contracts on this index are traded on the Chicago Board of Trade. On May 31, 1984, this index equaled 197.00.

Uses

Stock indices are widely used as proxies for market movements. Because of their varying constructions, these different indices reflect various market movements. The NYSE and S&P 500 are the most widely known indices.

Supply

There is no physical delivery of stock on these options contracts. However, all indices are tied to the prices of their underlying stocks. These indices should be difficult to manipulate, given the large number of stocks and total capitalization involved. However, the SEC is investigating charges that stocks underlying the CBOE 100 option were manipulated immediately prior to expiration of the May 1984 contract.

Options Markets

Options markets already exist for options on *individual* stocks. These markets began in 1973 at the CBOE. These are widely used for both speculative and hedging activity. However, it is more costly to use these individual stock options to hedge the entire market than options on a stock index. This is due to correlation of stock prices. The volatility of an entire index is less than the volatility of the sum of individual stock options.

Trading in options on stock index futures (NYSE, S&P 500, S&P 100) and options on S&P 100 Index, AMEX major Market Index, and ASE Market Value Index began in early 1983. The volume and open interest has been growing rapidly. In 1984 they were often the most liquid options traded on a particular stock exchange.

Futures Markets

Futures on stock indices (NYSE Index, S&P 500, and Value Line) began trading in early 1982. All futures contracts on stock indices are settled by cash on the last day of trading. The futures contracts have been considerably more volatile than the underlying indices. This is probably for two reasons. First, it is easier and faster to use futures markets in anticipation of major market moves than to buy or sell entire portfolios of stocks. Second, it is difficult to arbitrage the futures contracts, since it requires buying or selling a diversified portfolio of stocks. Importantly, these futures contracts, especially the NYSE Index and S&P 500, offer very liquid markets. For example, the S&P futures contract trades from 50,000 to 60,000 contracts a day, with a contract size around $75,-000. Interestingly, the open interest is less than the daily volume. Normally, the reverse is true in futures contracts.

Attractive Features

Options on both stock indices and stock index futures expand the portfolio strategies available to financial institutions and money managers. Chapter 7 provides an expanded discussion of such strategies and concepts. Stock index options allow stock investors to protect the principal value of their stock portfolios. Investors shorting portfolios of stocks can buy puts to establish ceiling prices. These new markets should be attractive to investors in the stock markets and the stock options market. In addition, a composite of stocks tends to be less volatile than its components. Since volatility plays a key role in the pricing of options, it is likely to be cheaper to hedge portfolios using stock index options than by using a portfolio of options on individual stocks. The cash settlement features also allow investors to avoid the costs of making or taking delivery if exercised.

Potential Risks of Stock Index Options

The stock market can be very volatile. Numerous economic and political factors can influence the prices of individual stocks and the stock market as a whole. Therefore, there is substantial opportunity for both profit and loss in these new markets. Liquidity is important in each of these options. When comparing volume, the readers should remember that a S&P 500 future option contract is approximately five times as large as a S&P 100 Index option.

There are also some subtle differences between options on stock indices and stock index futures. First, there are differences when exercise occurs. Options on stock indices are always settled for cash. Options on stock index futures, if exercised prior to expiration, result in futures positions. On the last day, they too are settled for cash. Obviously a futures position is more risky than being cashed out.

Second, early exercise is more likely for index future options than options on individual stocks. This is because of the different margin requirements for futures and stocks. When buying stocks, an investor must put up at least 50%. The margin requirement for futures is approximately 10%. A "deep-in-the-money" option with a delta close to 1 (i.e., the stock future moves 1, the option moves 1), therefore has the same risk position as the underlying stock or future. When the "in-the-money" amount is greater than the margin requirement for the stock or future, the same position can be obtained by exercising or offsetting the option and using the proceeds to obtain a future or stock position. Obviously, this situation occurs earlier for the future option than for the stock option. The increased likelihood of early exercise should also increase premiums for options on index futures.

Third, options on futures have one important advantage over options on indices without futures contracts. They allow the use of the underlying futures contract to change one's risk position. For example, a writer of a call can buy a future to construct a synthetic short put. Investors in options or individual stocks can buy or short sale individual stocks to do the same. It is more difficult to change one's position in options on stock indices. Buying or shorting an index or stocks takes time, and the currently available index futures are not perfectly correlated with one of the AMEX stock indices.

Fourth, options on stock indices and index futures can respond faster to market conditions than the underlying stocks. It takes time even in a very efficient market for actual trades in stocks to occur, that is, to reflect changes in the market. This suggests that these options can be more volatile or move at different times from the underlying markets.

Types of Investors

Options on stock indices and stock index futures should be attractive to the same firms and individuals already active in buying and selling stocks and stock options. This includes stockbrokers, brokerage firms, banks, financial institutions, corporations, pension funds, and individual investors. Professional money managers should also use the market to expand portfolio strategies.

OPTIONS ON HEATING OIL FUTURES

Heating oil is just one of over 2,000 refined petroleum products. However, refinery operations of crude oil are directed toward production of two or three major products, such as gasoline, kerosene, and fuel or heating oils. No. 2 is one of five different grades of fuel oil. The main home heating oil is No. 2. Importantly, the heating oil market has undergone substantial change due to unstable sources of crude, the emergence of OPEC, competition from other energy sources and revisions of federal regulation.

The NYMEX is proposing to trade options on heating oil No. 2 in futures. A trader in this market should understand: (a) what affects pricing in the underlying cash markets and (b) the New York Mercantile Exchange's heating oil futures contract.

Pricing

There are three major sources of heating oil prices:

1. *Platt's Oilgram,* which reports the day-to-day prices of a range of petroleum products
2. Posted prices of major refiners
3. Heating oil futures traded at the NYME and CBT

It is important to note that the cash prices in *Platt's Oilgram* lag the market by at least one day. Also, prices of actual transactions can differ considerably from posted prices. As in many commodity markets, futures provide an important source of price information.

Uses

The predominate use of No. 2 heating oil is for residential and commercial heating. Other uses include melting and heating processing in the glass and ceramics industries, as feedstock in the petrochemical industry, as fuel for furnace heating in the metallurgical and electronic fields, to fuel diesel and similar engines, for electrical and other power generation, and as fuel for trucks, maritime vessels, and railroads.

There are many factors that influence residential demand for heating oil. These include conservation habits, existing type and size of housing units, climate differences by region, and supply and price of substitute fuels. In the short run, residential demand for fuel oil is relatively inelastic. A consumer with an oil-burning furnace must buy fuel oil. In the long run, consumers can replace such heating systems for more cost-effective systems. Changes in weather conditions can also have a large impact on demand.

Supply

Heating oil is a refined petroleum product obtained from crude oil. Thus, both supply of crude oil and refinery operation can affect the supply of heating oil. Refineries are generally designed to process specific types of crude oil. Refinery production is geared to produce more of the profitable products. In the United States, the design of refineries limits heating oil to 20% to 24% of the yield of a barrel of crude oil. Because the flexibility in refinery operations is limited and storage expensive, supply of U.S. heating oil cannot be expanded quickly. In times of unanticipated increases in demand, more expensive imports must be used.

Supply of heating oil is also affected by location. Refineries are found in 42 states. Bulk terminals and bulk stations maintain stocks in principal markets. They then sell to large industrial firms, jobbers, and independent oil dealers. Because of transportation costs, refiners in the West cannot compete with refiners in the Gulf Coast for northeastern markets. The major means of transportation are pipelines and water. Trucks and railroads are less important.

Forward Markets

A large proportion of the market transactions in heating oil takes the form of contractual arrangements, that is, approximately 85% to 90%. The key contract terms are the mode of delivery and the price. The contracts cover forward delivery of 6 to 12 months with price based at delivery. Major participants in these forward markets include domestic and international refiners, bulk terminal operators, importers, and large industrial concerns. As in most forward markets, occasionally there are defaults.

Futures Markets

Futures markets in heating oil began trading at the New York Mercantile Exchange in 1980. This contract calls for physical delivery in New York of 5,000 barrels of No. 2 heating oil. On May 30, 1984, this contract traded 7,800 contracts, with an open interest of 19,000 contracts. The Chicago Board of Trade recently began trading a futures contract on heating oil that calls for a receipt delivery contract based on Gulf delivery. While deliverable supply is not a problem in the NYME contract, physical constraints can limit the actual deliveries that can be made in New York during a particular 24-hour period. In 1982, delivery problems occurred due to this constraint. The use of physical delivery rather than receipt delivery also affects who can realistically take delivery.

Options Markets

The NYME has submitted to the CFTC an option contract on its heating oil futures contract. Table 4.3 provides the salient features. Approval should be received sometime in 1985, with trading beginning shortly thereafter. Delivery of a futures contract will be done by book entry through the clearing corporation. Expiration of the option will occur in the month prior to the expiration of the underlying futures contract. Position limits for speculators will be 2,000 contracts.

Attractive Features

Heating oil options will have important uses by commercial firms. Refiners and bulk terminals and stations can use options to protect inventory value. Refiners, jobbers, and independent oil dealers can combine risk management of their heating oil dealings with market arbitrage. Commercial users of heating oil can buy call options to establish ceiling prices, while retaining the potential for lower prices.

Potential Risks

Prices of heating oil can be highly volatile. Production costs are sensitive to the price of crude oil as well as the demand for other competing refined products. Supply and price of crude can be affected by cartels such as OPEC, and by federal regulations. Demand for heating oil is also heavily influenced by weather conditions.

Basis risk (difference between cash and futures prices) may also be important. The NYME futures contract prices off of New York delivery. This can differ from cash prices of heating oil in the West or Gulf Coast due to locational differences and supply.

Types of Investors

Options on heating oil futures should be attractive to firms already active in buying and selling of heating oil. This includes refiners, bulk terminals and stations, wholesalers, large industrial firms, jobbers, and independent oil dealers.

METALS (GOLD, SILVER)

Cash Markets

To trade either options on gold or options on silver, traders should understand what affects their underlying cash markets. Both gold and silver concentrate a great deal of value in small volume and weight. Both gold and silver are used as industrial materials, in manufacturing jewelry, held in bullion for investment, and have active futures markets. Prices of gold and silver tend to rise when stocks and bonds are shaky or during inflationary periods. Increasingly, portfolio managers are recommending their purchase to diversify portfolios. They are also a barometer of world anxiety.

Pricing: Gold

Traders normally make use of three mechanisms to establish gold prices. This includes the Zurich interbank price, the London fixing, and the spot or nearby delivery contract price on the New York and Chicago futures exchanges. In addition, trading is conducted in Hong Kong.

Uses: Gold

Industrial demand at 78% is the largest use of gold. The major use is for gold jewelry, followed by applications in electronic components, space and aviation, dentistry and medicine, and commemorative medallions and coins. Investment in gold bullion is also used as a protection against inflation and eroding currency values.

Supply: Gold

The major producers of gold are South Africa, the Soviet Union, Canada, and the United States, with non-Communist countries accounting for 80% of the total world supplies of gold. Large supplies are held by most central banks, and the IMF as reserves. Sales of gold from these sources can affect available supplies for investors. The two major centers for gold trading are Zurich and London.

Gold Futures

Futures markets in gold ingots are conducted on the Chicago Board of Trade, the MidAmerica Commodity Exchange, the International Monetary Market of the Chicago Mercantile Exchange, the New York Mercantile Exchange, and the Commodity Exchange, Inc., in New York. The most liquid market is on the COMEX, which accounted for 91% of the volume traded in the United States in 1982. The basic difference is the trading unit, that is, either 100 troy ounces, 33.2 troy ounces, or 1 kilo. All futures contracts call for delivery of either a warehouse or depository receipt, with the actual gold being held at approved vaults in either New York or Chicago.

Options Markets

The COMEX began trading options on gold futures (100 troy ounces) in October 1982. Prior to that, only dealer options on gold actuals were available. The MidAmerica Commodity Exchange has also received approval from the CFTC to trade options on its 33.2-troy-ounce gold futures contract. The American Stock Exchange has also submitted an option on gold bullion contract to the SEC. This contract is cash settled based on the second London gold fixing price on the following day after an option is exercised. This avoids problems of physical delivery of either gold or a futures contract. This gold fixing price is based on transactions and would be very difficult to manipulate. The salient features of the option on gold bullion are presented in Table 4.2, gold futures contracts in Table 4.3, and the Mocatta dealer option on 100-troy-ounce gold is in Table 4.4.

Options on gold futures expire in the month prior to the futures delivery

TABLE 4.4 SUMMARY OF DEALER OPTIONS

Firm	Mocatta[a] Metals Corp.	Mocatta[a] Metals Corp.	Mocatta[a] Metals Corp.	Mocatta[a] Metals Corp.	Mocatta[a] Metals Corp.	Mocatta[a] Metals Corp.	Mocatta[a] Quality Corp.	Mocatta[a] Quality Corp.
Underlying commodity	100 oz. Gold	50 South African Kruggerands	10 Canadian maple leafs	1,000 oz. silver	$1,000 face value silver half-dollars	$1,000 face value silver dollars	25,000 lb. copper	50 oz. platinum
Trading months	Jan., Mar., Apr., June, July, Sept., Oct., and Dec.	Jan., Feb., Apr., May, July, Aug., Oct., and Dec.	Feb., Mar., May, June, Aug., Sept., Nov., and Dec.	Feb., Mar., May, June, Aug., Sept., Nov., and Dec.	Jan., Mar., Apr., June, July, Sept., Nov., and Dec.	Jan., Feb., Apr., May, July, Aug., Oct., and Nov.	Feb., Mar., May, June, Aug., Sept., Nov., and Dec.	Jan., Feb., Apr., May, July, Aug., Oct., and Nov.
Expiration	First business day of month	First business day of month	First business day of month	First business day of month	First business day of month	First business day of month	First business day of month	First business day of month
Strike price intervals	$25 per oz.	$25 per oz.	$25 per oz.	$1 per oz.	$200	$1,000	4¢ per lb.	Depends on current platinum price: $25 under $700, $50 over $700

[a] Although several firms other than Mocatta offer similar options, Mocatta appears to be the most popular dealer.

month. This is to allow time to offset assigned futures contracts obtained through exercise. This means that a trader in options on futures can avoid buying or selling the actual gold, even though his options position is exercised. The trading of the options on gold futures at the COMEX occurs adjacent to the gold futures trading. This facilitates arbitrage between the two markets.

Attractive Features

Gold options have important uses by commercial firms. Bullion dealers can use options to protect their inventory value, and to protect forward sales and expected future spot sales. Metal dealers can also combine risk management for their gold dealings with market arbitrage. Mining firms can buy put gold options to establish price floors, while retaining the potential for higher prices for their products. Jewelry manufacturers can buy gold call options to establish ceiling prices while still being able to profit if the gold price declines. Options on gold are also attractive, since they separate option and cash transactions.

Potential Risks

Prices of gold can be highly volatile, and are especially sensitive to world events. Major owners and suppliers of gold can affect world gold prices through buying and selling. In addition, there are special risks for options on futures. First, there is basis risk between gold and gold futures prices, which can affect the profitability of particular options. Second, futures options can be exercised after the close of trading. This is especially important on the last day of trading, which is normally a Friday. The next trading day of the futures position that one receives through exercise is not until the following Monday. Finally, futures markets have trading limits based on the prior day's settlement prices. In volatile times, this could restrict futures trading. However, no such trading limits exist for the option, or for cash gold prices.

Types of Investors

Options on gold futures should be attractive to firms already active in buying and selling gold. This includes gold refiners, miners, dealers, manufacturers, and other carriers of gold inventories. In addition, investors in gold bullion and coins can use this market to either hedge their gold or increase their returns.

Pricing: Silver

London and New York are the principal world silver cash and futures markets. The silver cash markets in London are the London Metals Exchange (LME) and the London Silver Market, with the latter being the most important. Cash markets are also available in Chicago, Zurich, Singapore, and Hong

Kong. Futures markets in New York and Chicago also provide important pricing information.

Uses: Silver

There is industrial and nonindustrial demand for silver. Silver is used extensively as an input in the production of batteries, photographic material, solder, tableware, electrical and electronic industries, and in the dental and medical professions. Industrial uses account for 99% of U.S. silver consumption. Silver is also held by many investors in the form of jewelry or coins.

Supply: Silver

There are three major sources of supply of silver bullion. The largest source is as a by-product in the mining and refining of base metal ores—copper, lead, and zinc. Therefore, the demand and price factors for these metals directly influence the level of silver production and its pricing. Silver production also comes from primary silver mining operations. Other important sources are secondary production of recycled silver, and silver stocks held by individuals, firms, and governments. The major producers in order of importance are Mexico, Canada, Peru, United States, Australia, and the Soviet Union. Substitutes are available for silver in the electronic and electrical fields. Therefore, use of alternative materials could become a significant factor in silver demand.

Silver Futures

Futures markets for silver ingot bars are conducted on the Chicago Board of Trade, the Commodity Exchange, Inc., and the MidAmerica Commodity Exchange. Silver forward contracts are also traded on the London Metals Exchange. The most liquid market is the COMEX, which accounted for more than 85% of the volume traded in the United States in 1982. The basic difference is the trading unit, that is, either 5,000 or 1,000 troy ounces. Delivery occurs through warehouse or vault receipts. The actual silver bars are held at approved vaults in either Chicago or New York.

Option Markets: Silver

Options on silver physicals, both puts and calls, are currently offered by CFTC approved dealers. Table 4.4 provides salient features on dealer options offered by Moccata Metals on 1,000 silver, silver half-dollars, and silver dollars. COMEX is trading an option on its 5,000-ounce silver futures contract (see Table 4.3). This contract has the same features as the options on gold futures.

Attractive Features

Options on silver futures should have the same advantages of any exchange-traded options. Silver options have important uses by commercial firms, similar to that for gold.

Potential Risks

Prices of silver can be highly volatile, and can be affected by the supply and demand for other base metals. Development of alternative materials could also affect the demand for silver. The actual risks of trading options on silver also depend on actual contract terms. For example, when and how exercise can occur, relationship to futures contracts and deliverable supply of silver could be important.

Types of Investors

Options on silver should be attractive to firms already active in buying and selling silver. This includes silver refiners, miners, dealers, manufacturers of jewelry, photographic materials, solder, batteries, and tableware. In addition, investors in silver can write puts to hedge prices or increase their returns.

OPTIONS ON FOREIGN CURRENCIES

Options on foreign currencies (British pound, Canadian dollar, German mark, Swiss franc, and Japanese yen) are trading on the Philadelphia Stock Exchange. Recently, options on the German mark futures contract began trading at Chicago Mercantile Exchange. Most countries in the world issue their own currency. Different currencies can be bought and sold through the foreign exchange market. Such transactions consist of an exchange of one country's currency for another's at a particular rate. The foreign exchange market is very efficient.

Pricing

Currencies are traded through banks and brokers. The central actor of the foreign exchange market is the commercial bank, through which most foreign exchange transactions occur. This activity among banks is referred to as the "interbank market" and is the core of the foreign exchange market. It is in this forum that exchange rates are determined. Trading is concentrated in the major financial centers of the world: New York, Chicago, London, Frankfurt, Zurich, Hong Kong, Singapore, and Tokyo. The foreign exchange market operates 24 hours a day. Foreign exchange rates are available in the *Wall Street*

Journal, wire services, and from commercial banks. Most transactions are spot (64%) as versus forward or swap transactions. Exchange rates are normally quoted in terms of foreign currency units per U.S. dollar. One exception is British pounds where the quote is U.S. dollars per foreign currency quote. Currency futures markets on the Chicago Mercantile Exchange are another important source of price information.

Uses

The primary reason for foreign exchange transactions is to complete a transaction for some particular good or service produced in another country. Individuals and companies involved in this market rarely buy and sell currencies for the purpose of holding different currencies.

Supply

Exchange rates are determined by the supply and demand for foreign currencies. Like any other commodity, currencies are demanded by a variety of actors in the marketplace. The interaction of these forces results in an equilibrium rate of exchange between two currencies. Governments also intervene in the market to alter an unacceptable equilibrium by either buying or selling their own currency. Governments can also increase or decrease the money supply, thereby affecting exchange rates.

Forward Market

In 1980 forward transactions accounted for 6% of all foreign exchange transactions. This involves buying and selling currencies with the intent of taking delivery or receiving payment more than two days after the agreement is reached. The maturity of the forward contract or date of delivery may be set days, weeks, months, or in a few cases, years in advance. The rate at which the exchange will take place is fixed at the time of the agreement. Forward exchange contracts with banks have two potential drawbacks. First, many banks require certain customers to maintain compensating balances until the forward contract comes to maturity. The opportunity costs of keeping funds in a bank may be significant if more profitable investment opportunities exist outside the banking environment. Second, depending upon the financial wherewithal of the potential hedger, banks may not be willing to agree to a forward contract. This effectively may present many individuals from hedging in the foreign exchange forward market.

Forward transactions usually take place between banks and their customers. Commercial banks often find that "swap" transactions are more efficient than forward contracts in the interbank market. Over 30% of all foreign currency transactions between banks are in the form of "swaps." A swap is the simultaneous purchase or sale of a currency for one value date and a sale or purchase of the same currency for another value date. A swap transaction is a convenient way for banks to utilize otherwise idle currency balances or to cover themselves when they hold an unbalanced portfolio of foreign currencies

Futures Markets

Futures markets in foreign currencies were first introduced by the International Monetary Market (now a division of the Chicago Mercantile Exchange) in 1972. This includes futures on the British pound, German mark, Swiss franc, Canadian dollar, Mexican peso, Japanese yen, Dutch guilder, French franc, and Italian lira. The futures market provides a vehicle for bridging the gap between speculative and hedging interest in the foreign exchange markets. Although the forward market can be used by large corporations to hedge their foreign exchange risks, it is quite difficult for the individual or the smaller corporation to hedge through this mechanism. Banks dealing in forward foreign exchange contracts tend to cater to large, multinational corporations. Banks do not exclude the smaller hedger outright. However, they tend to give a customer an unfavorable quote if the bank does not wish to service the customer's needs. Likewise, speculators are virtually excluded from the forward exchange market on the forward side. Although there are no laws prohibiting private citizens from speculating, banks are generally disinclined to facilitate such activity, in preference to large-volume customers. Whereas banks have provided forward markets to large hedgers, the futures markets have served smaller hedgers, and more importantly provided a means of applying the risk capital of speculators to large and small hedgers alike.

Foreign currency futures are currently traded in the following sizes at the IMM:

25,000 British pounds
100,000 Canadian dollars
125,000 West German marks
35,000,0000 Japanese yen
125,000 Swiss francs

These futures contracts are quoted in terms of U.S. dollars, rather than in European terms. Futures contracts also have daily price fluctuation limits. Futures markets usually terminate on the "second business day immediately preceding the third Wednesday of the contract month," except if Wednesday is a holiday. There is also a two-day lag between termination of trade and delivery day on the contract. Contract months are March, June, September, and December. Delivery of foreign currencies is made in the country of origin by the seller. These contracts are becoming an increasingly important source of pricing information on foreign exchange rates.

Options Markets

Options on foreign currencies are currently trading on the Philadelphia Stock Exchange and Chicago Mercantile Exchange. Tables 4.2 and 4.3 provide their salient features. Exercise results in delivery of the actual currency, in its country of origin for the former, and a futures contract for the latter.

Attractive Features

Foreign currency options should provide an alternative strategy to using only forward or futures contracts to hedge foreign exchange risk. For example, when the exact amount of foreign currency to be hedged is not known, options could be an attractive tool. This market may be particularly attractive for corporations dealing in foreign markets, whose profitability is tied to the exchange rate, and for banks for both risk management and market arbitrage.

Potential Risks

An investor trading in options on foreign currencies is subject to several risks. First, foreign exchange rates can change dramatically within a very short period. Second, action by a government can influence its own foreign exchange rate, and restrict the ability to take funds outside a foreign country. Third, these options are currently not very liquid. This can make it difficult to trade out or into positions. Finally, writers of options (PSE) should be able to arrange for both financing and delivery at a foreign bank in the case an option is exercised. The availability of futures options will make it easier for the smaller player to exercise options and to arbitrage off the futures.

Types of Investors

Options on foreign currencies should be attractive to individuals and firms already active in the foreign exchange market. This includes banks, brokers, financial institutions, corporations, and individuals. Speculative interest should be options from individuals and institutions already active in currency futures.

OPTIONS ON AGRICULTURAL FUTURES

The CFTC is beginning a pilot program for options on agricultural futures. U.S. futures exchanges have submitted proposals to trade options on grains (soybeans, wheat, corn, and cotton) and livestock (live cattle, and hogs). Trading began in soybeans, live cattle and wheat in late 1984. Such options contracts are limited to exchanges where the underlying futures contract is traded.

Agricultural futures (wheat) began trading in the United States in 1848, followed by other major commodities such as corn, soybeans, soybean meal, cotton, potatoes, live hogs, frozen concentrated orange juice, oil, sugar, coffee, cocoa, cattle, and pork bellies.

Grains are divided into classes and subclasses according to shape, texture, color of the kernel, and in some cases by areas of production. Livestock has similar types of grading. Exchange regulations governing deliveries against futures contracts spell out very specifically the grades or quality of the commodity to be delivered. Some grades are deliverable at the futures contract price. Others are deliverable at discounts or premiums to the futures price. Invoice prices on futures are also adjusted for location and storage facility of the commodity delivered. Such differentials obviously can affect which grade at which location is cheapest to deliver, and result in transportation of a commodity from one location to another. Therefore, pricing of agricultural products is substantially more complicated than pricing of a homogeneous commodity where location is unimportant, for example, T-bills and silver.

Pricing

For most of these commodities, futures markets are the major source of price information. Both cash and forward transactions are priced relative to futures prices. Futures prices are affected by the same variables as cash prices. This includes available supplies and the demand for specific commodities. Therefore, information such as domestic production, imports, exports, stockholdings, and domestic use is important in determining price. The U.S. Department of Agriculture provides estimates of these numbers, which are further analyzed by various commodity firms. Continuous futures prices are available through wire services and are widely published in newspapers such as the *Wall Street Journal.* Local radio stations also provide up-to-date information on futures prices for agricultural products.

Uses

Futures markets are widely used by individuals and firms involved in agriculture. This includes those involved in growing, marketing, processing, industrial users, exporters, and the like. Commercial firms use futures:

1. To reduce the risk of commodity price fluctuation
2. To provide a substitute for intended cash price transactions
3. For arbitrage

Speculators in futures markets include floor traders, spreaders, and position traders. Speculators have no commercial interest, but use these markets to try and make profits.

Supply

The supply of agricultural commodities can be substantially affected by the success or failure of a new crop or changes in the cost of raising livestock. Grain reserve programs, export embargoes, and international commodity agreements can also affect domestic supplies and therefore prices. There is also distinctive seasonality in supply of different commodities. For example, supply is greater after, rather than before, harvest. Also, there is a difference in storable (grain) versus nonstorable commodities (livestock). Weather coonditions can also affect supply in various locations. Importantly, expectations about potential supplies and demands, both domestically and internationally, can change quickly. This can result in rapid, large price changes. Futures prices for agricultural commodities can therefore be very volatile compared to other investments.

Futures Markets

Futures markets are a primary source of pricing for agricultural products. However, only a few futures markets (wheat, corn, soybeans, hogs, and live cattle) are liquid markets. Liquidity is very important in agricultural futures markets. It affects the ease of trading in and out of these markets. Measures of liquidity include daily volume and open interest. This information is published daily in major newspapers, and is available directly from the exchanges. A crude rule of thumb is one outside piece of paper will result in three additional transactions. Therefore, daily volume and open interest should be examined before transacting large orders. Otherwise, large orders can push prices up *or* down.

Options Markets

Options on agricultural commodities expand the risk management strategies available to firms involved in agriculture. Like most options, they allow investors to protect principal value and establish ceiling prices.

Attractive Features

This market may be particularly attractive to producers of commodities. Currently, producers (i.e., farmers) either use futures to lock in prices, or forward markets to sell their crops in advance of harvest. Given the uncertainty surrounding the quality to be produced, futures hedges can result in their being over- or underhedged. Options can be used by farmers and processors in combination with futures to hedge both quality risk and price risk. Warehousemen and exporters can use options to increase the returns on their actual or anticipated inventory.

Potential Risk

Agricultural futures prices can be highly volatile. Government actions, weather, pests, and international events can quickly affect the expected supply and demand for agricultural products. For example, unexpected crop failures can dramatically affect the price. Open interest near delivery month can also be important, since there is a finite deliverable supply of each agricultural commodity. Prices have been known to be substantially higher prior to a harvest, and during severe winters that restrict transportation. Deliverable standards on futures contracts can affect what is cheapest to deliver and futures prices. Therefore, an investor in options on agricultural futures should be knowledgeable both about the underlying commodity and the contract terms and conditions for the futures contracts.

Types of Investors

Options on agricultural futures should be attractive to firms and individuals already active in buying and selling agricultural commodities. This includes farmers, ranchers, merchants, processors, storers, grain elevators, and exporters/importers. Speculators should include those already trading agricultural futures and other options markets.

OPTIONS ON SUGAR FUTURES

Options on domestic agricultural products were prohibited under the Commodity Exchange Act. However, as mentioned earlier, steps were made to change this provision. Strangely, there are a few agricultural products that were not explicitly enumerated under this Act. This includes sugar. Therefore, the Coffee, Cocoa, and Sugar Exchange was able to obtain approval and began trading in 1983 an option on their sugar futures contract.

Pricing

Cash prices for refined and raw cane and beet sugar are published daily in the *Wall Street Journal* and weekly in *Milling and Baking News*. Monthly prices are published quarterly in the U.S.D.A. publication "Sugar and Sweetener Outlook and Situation." The CCSE #11 raw sugar and the MidAmerica Commodity Exchange refined sugar futures contracts are a major source of price information in the United States. Both cash and forward transactions are priced relative to current futures prices. Futures prices are affected by the same variables as cash/forward prices. Therefore, information such as domestic production, imports, stockholdings, domestic use, storage costs, and transportation costs are important in determining price. The U.S.D.A. provides estimates of these numbers, which are further analyzed by various commodity firms. Continuous futures prices are available through wire services and are widely published in newspapers. Local radio stations also provide up-to-date information on futures prices.

Uses

Sugar is one of the most universally used food ingredients. Beverage companies, bakeries, and candy and processed food producers are all major uses of sugar in the United States. Intermediaries in cash sugar transactions are an important component in the distribution pattern of cash sugar in the United States. They act as a bridge between the raw sugar producer, the refiner, and the end user. These intermediaries include operators, cash brokers, distributors, liquifiers, and baggers.

Supply

In 1980, over 85 million metric tons of centrifugal sugar were produced throughout the world. The United States was the world's fifth largest sugar producer. Brazil was the largest followed by the Soviet Union, India, and Cuba. The United States is also a major importer of sugar.

Major sources of sugar are sugar beets and sugar cane. Other caloric sweeteners include corn sweeteners and honey and maple syrup. Sugar beets are grown in the United States by approximately 14,000 farmers in 16 different temperate climate states. Sugar cane is grown in the warmer climate states of Hawaii, Louisiana, Texas, and Florida. The entire year's sugar beet crop reaches the sugar refinery during September and October. Sugar cane refining is less seasonal than beet refining, since refiners can obtain their raw products from the world as well as the domestic market. There are 25 major sugar refiners in the United States.

Sugar beets and sugar cane prices can, at the discretion of the Secretary of Agriculture, make available sugar price supports. There are also import duties on raw sugar, while the International Sugar Agreement also calls for the build-up of reserve stock as prices on the world market decline.

There is a distinctive seasonality in supply of raw sugar. Weather conditions can also affect supply in various locations. Prices of substitutes for sugar beets and sugar cane, such as corn sweeteners, can also affect demand and prices.

Futures Markets

The CSCE #11 sugar futures contract is a primary source of pricing for sugar in the United States. This is a very liquid contract, widely used by both U.S. and foreign producers and refiners of sugar. However, only professionals should stand for delivery in this market, since delivery often occurs outside the

United States. A one lot is also an odd lot. It takes approximately 100 #11 futures contracts to equal the size of one delivery vessel.

Forward Markets

Almost all of the sugar that moves from the sugar grower to the refiner is forward contracted. Currently, there is no price determination in advance, and there exists a myriad of methods to establish a price in the future all dependent on the refiner's ability to market the sugar. Refiners may sell directly to users on a fixed forward price basis, or within a corridor of prices that are adjusted based on the eventual published list or market price of sugar when shipment is made. Purchasers of raw sugar from producers outside the United States often forward contract basing the price off the N.Y. futures market. However, since refined and raw markets do not always move in tandem, buyers and sellers of refined sugar do not base the price off the N.Y. market.

Options Market

The CSCE (see Table 4.3) is currently trading options on sugar futures. Such options are similar to other options on futures contracts. Expiration occurs in the month prior to delivery month of the futures contract. Exercise results in offsetting futures positions.

Attractive Features

Sugar futures options expand the risk management strategies available to growers, intermediaries, and refiners of sugar. Like most options, they allow investors to protect principal value and establish ceiling prices. Currently, farmers of sugar beets or sugar cane either use futures to lock in price, or forward markets to sell their crops in advance of the harvest. Options can be used to hedge prices when uncertainty surrounds the quantity to be produced. Farmers and refiners can use options in combination with futures to hedge both price risk and quantity risk. Intermediaries such as operators, cash brokers, distributors, liquifiers, and baggers can either use options to reduce price risk or to increase the returns of their actual or anticipated inventories.

Potential Risk

Sugar prices can be highly volatile. Government actions, weather, and pests can quickly affect the expected supply and demand for sugar. Seasonality of prices should also be considered, in addition to events that affect transportation and storage. Standards of futures contracts can also affect what is cheapest to deliver, causing a divergence between futures and cash prices. Therefore, an investor in options on sugar futures should be knowledgeable about the sugar market and the #11 sugar futures contract.

Types of Investors

Options on sugar futures should be attractive to firms and individuals already active in buying and selling sugar and sugar futures contracts. This includes sugar beet and sugar cane farmers, refiners of sugar beets and sugar cane, intermediaries such as operators, cash brokers, distributors, liquifiers, baggers, and major purchasers of sugar such as beverage companies, bakeries, and candy and processed food producers.

CONCLUSIONS

The above only provides an introduction to these various commodity options. Additional information can be obtained from the Security and Futures Exchanges on the (a) underlying commodity, (b) detailed option contracts, (c) futures contract, and (d) historical price and volume data. Of interest is which contracts will be successful. The preliminary information suggests that options on futures are better than options on actuals where physical delivery of the commodity is required (T-bonds, GNMAs, and currencies). However, both types of contracts can exist when options on actuals are settled for cash (e.g., stock index options and gold bullion). The agricultural options should provide a new dimension to our commodity markets.

5

Option Pricing

As is true in other investment forums, profitable option trading is contingent upon the trader's ability to recognize and capitalize on profit opportunities as they arise. As discussed above, there are two basic ways in which option buyers and sellers profit from an option transaction. An option buyer profits by exercising in-the-money options or by selling options prior to expiration, assuming that the premium appreciates over the original purchase price. An option seller profits when an option is left to expire (as is expected when the option is out-of-the-money) or when the option is bought back, assuming the premium depreciates in value. Options are, of course, derivative from the underlying commodity and their price is affected by movements in the underlying market price. If the underlying price moves in-the-money, then it is possible to exercise an option and turn a profit. As a result, the price of the option rises to reflect the enhanced profit opportunity. If the underlying price moves out-of-the-money, then it becomes more likely that the option will be permitted to expire and the seller will retain the premium. When this happens, the value of holding the option as reflected in the premium falls.

An obvious strategy, then, is to forecast price movements in the underlying commodity market. When the forecast is bullish, the recommended strategy is to buy calls or sell puts; when the forecast is bearish, the recommended strategy is to sell calls or buy puts. Although the strategy is obvious, it is not always obvious when the underlying market may be expected to move in a bullish or bearish direction. Many techniques may be called upon to help determine the probable direction that the market price will move. In some cases, however, it may prove impossible to apply these techniques to good effect. Additionally, many other traders may be using substantially similar techniques and so other methods may be indicated to avoid losing the competitive edge.

The option premium is a direct reflection of the potential returns associated with the option. By studying the level of the option premium and how it relates to general market conditions, a trader may be able to assess whether an option is over- or underpriced. The process of evaluating the premium in relation to its "fair market value" or simply fair value may be quite complicated and employ confusing mathematical formulas. This does not negate the importance of understanding the concept of fair value. Although not every option trader may be expected to base his strategies solely on fair value calculations, every trader should, at a minimum, be familiar with the concept and be able to reference fair value calculations to avoid buying overpriced or selling underpriced options.

FAIR VALUE OF AN OPTION

The fair value of an option must be assessed in relation to alternative investment opportunities that may exist. Keep in mind that expected returns generally must compensate for risks incurred. Thus a higher risk investment must be associated with higher expected returns in order to attract investment capital. This is intuitive insofar as rational investors prefer investments with the highest expected returns for a given risk level or the lowest risk level for a given expected return.

Options are extremely flexible risk management tools and may be used for many different purposes. A writer of options, for example, takes on a practically unlimited downside risk in return for the potential to earn a limited profit. That limited profit, as reflected in the premium, must be sufficient to compensate for the possibility that large losses may result. Similarly, an option buyer gives up a limited sum in return for the possibility that large profits may result. The premium must reflect the nonsymmetrical nature of the bargain struck between the option buyer and seller. This, in essence, is "fair value."

The fair value of an option has been defined by Gastineau (1979) as:

> *The price at which both the buyer and the writer of the option should expect to break even, neglecting the effect of commissions, after an adjustment for risk. Fair value is an estimate of where an option* should *sell in an efficient market, not where it [necessarily] will sell.*[1]

But how can an option trader tell when the market is efficient and is fairly pricing an option? The balance of this chapter wrestles with this problem at some length.

Importance of the Fair Value Concept

Before we go on to explore the theory and calculation of fair market value, the importance of the concept should be established. Obviously, nobody wants to pay more than the fair price to buy or receive less than the fair price to sell a commodity. By paying too much or receiving too little, it is obvious that an option trader is diminishing his profits below a fair level. But he is also increasing

[1] Gary Gastineau, *The Stock Option Manual* (New York: McGraw-Hill, 1979).

the risks associated with his trades because he has too little protection in the form of profits to cover the risks inherent in the position.

Consider the case of a grocer who consistently buys tomatoes at 55 cents per pound when the going wholesale price is 53 cents. Even if our grocer sold the produce at the going retail price of 57 cents, his profit margin of 2 cents is lower than it otherwise could be. In effect, the grocer is increasing the probability of bankruptcy, since overhead costs including labor, rent, and electricity are beyond his control and may be subject to sudden increase. Thus his returns may be insufficient to compensate for the associated risk of doing business. If our grocer were to buy tomatoes at the going wholesale price of 53 cents but sell them at 55 cents, 2 cents lower than the prevailing retail price, his returns would once again be too low to compensate for the risk of doing business. Additionally, the grocer may be able to use the shelf space allocated for tomatoes to sell a more profitable variety of produce. He is therefore losing the opportunity to realize greater profits.

Just like the grocer, the option trader must avoid purchasing overpriced or selling underpriced options in order to maintain risk/return parity. If an option trader is able to buy underpriced and sell overpriced options, he will gain a competitive edge in the marketplace. If our trader could always pay less than fair market value or sell higher than fair market value, then over the long run, the trader will perforce achieve greater than average returns. Unlike tomatoes, however, it may not be obvious when an option is under-, over-, or fairly priced.

Some traders may prefer to use the option markets to take on risk in the hopes of achieving higher returns on investments. The holder of a call option, for example, hopes that the market may appreciate significantly so that a large profit may be realized while risking a limited amount of money. All other things being equal, our trader would prefer to pay less for the option holding returns at a particular level. To illustrate, assume that a gold call option is available with a $400 per ounce strike price and the underlying gold market is trading at-the-money. The most optimistic price forecasts predict that gold may appreciate to $460 before expiration. The option is priced at $20. In this case, the call buyer risks the $20 premium for a possible maximum return of $40 ($60 upon exercise less $20 premium). The ratio of maximum profit to maximum loss in this case is two to one. What would happen if the option were trading at 50% less, or $10. In that case, the call holder risks the $10 premium for a possible profit of $50 ($60 upon exercise less $10 premium). The ratio of maximum profit to maximum loss is now five to one. By varying the premium by 50% downwards, the reward/risk ratio goes up 250%!

Let's compare the risks and returns associated with buying the gold option at $20 versus buying the option at $10 where the price of gold at option expiration varies over a wide range.

As is apparent, the returns associated with purchasing the call at $10 dominate over the returns associated with purchasing the call at $20, by a consistent $10. The breakeven point is equal to $410 where the option is purchased at $10, while the breakeven point is equal to $420 when the option is purchased at $20.

(1) Gold Price at Expiration	(2) Returns Where Premium = $10	(3) Returns Where Premium = $20	(4) (2) Less (3)
$380	($10)	($20)	$10
400	(10)	(20)	10
410	0	(10)	10
420	10	0	10
460	50	40	10
Reward/risk	5 to 1	2 to 1	

The reward/risk ratio is extremely sensitive to changes in the option premium.

Other traders may prefer to use option markets to reduce the risks associated with their normal commercial activities. A gold dealer may hold considerable inventories from which to sell upon demand and may be apprehensive about the possibility of significant price declines and resultant losses. This risk may be managed by writing covered call options, a strategy that is discussed in depth in Chapter 7.

Assume that our gold dealer writes calls while holding an equal quantity of gold. Assume that the calls are struck at-the-money at the prevailing gold price of $400 and the most pessimistic forecasts predict that gold will decline to $340. Our gold dealer would prefer to receive the highest premium possible to insulate himself against the potential $60 loss on his inventories. Assume that the call is priced at $20. In this case, the worst possible result would be that the dealer will lose $40 ($60 loss on exercise plus the $20 premium). Note, however, that he is better off having sold the call by $20 than he would have been had he not sold the call. If gold stays at $400, the dealer can sell his inventories at $400 in the open market or through exercise, retaining the $20 premium as a bonus of sorts. If the price of gold appreciates $20, the call will be exercised and the dealer will receive $400 for the sale of his physical inventories and retain the $20 premium for a total of $420, a sum that equals the current market price of gold. If the prevailing price of gold appreciates over $420, then the gold dealer would have been better off by not writing calls because his returns are limited to $20, but this may be regarded as a missed opportunity and not an out-of-pocket expense. Thus the call writer risks losing $40 for a maximum potential profit of $20, but this result may be preferable to risking a $60 loss despite the limited potential return. In this case the reward/risk ratio is one to two. But what would happen if the calls were sold for only $10? In that case the covered call writer would risk losing $50 ($60 loss on exercise plus the $10 premium), while the potential return would be limited to $10. The reward/risk ratio is now one to five and again this illustrates the sensitivity of the reward/risk ratio to a changing option premium.

Let's compare the results of this covered writing strategy where the option is sold at $20 and when the option is sold at $10.

The returns associated with a covered writing strategy where the option premium equals $20 are always $10 greater than the returns where the premium equals $10. The breakeven point is at $380 where the options are sold at

(1) Gold Price at Expiration	(2) Returns Where Premium = $20	(3) Returns Where Premium = $10	(4) (2) Less (3)
$340	($40)	($50)	$10
380	0	(10)	10
390	10	0	10
400	20	10	10
420	20	10	10
Reward/risk	1 to 5	1 to 2	

$420 or $10 more than the $390 breakeven point when the options are sold at $10. Whether buying or selling options the reward/risk ratio is extremely sensitive to changes in the option premium.

No matter if the option trader's motive is to take on greater risk in the hopes of realizing large profits or if the motive is to reduce the risks of large losses, the importance of identifying the fair value of an option cannot be underestimated.

Option Pricing Parameters

Although we have explained why an option trader should be interested in determining the fair value of an option, we are still no closer to finding out how to make such an assessment. But before a complete model can be specified, let's define some of the factors that restrict the option premium within certain parameters and discuss the rationale underlying these restrictions.

Implicit in the term "fair value" is the fact that options are indeed valuable in a monetary sense, or at least may be valuable under some circumstances. Options may be regarded as contingent claims on the underlying commodity, be it a physical commodity, a security, or a futures contract. The holder of an option, by virtue of his power of discretion to exercise the option or not, coupled with the possibility of profit associated with the underlying instrument, owns a valuable item. Because the option holder can be expected to exercise the option only under such conditions where a profit may ultimately be expected, and because the maximum loss associated with the long option position is foregone initially and irretrievably upon purchase, there are no circumstances under which the option will have negative value.

This is not to suggest that an option holder can never lose as a result of an option transaction. Nor can it be said that conditions conducive to a profitable exercise of an option will invariably be realized. Indeed, many options are purchased and ultimately have no value whatsoever. This, however, is the worst case scenario (at least from the perspective of the option buyer). In other words, option premiums will always be greater than or equal to zero.

The *terminal value* of an option, or the premium on the expiration date, is always equal to the greater of the in-the-money valuation or zero. When expiration is imminent, an option holder has only two alternatives. He can exercise the option or he can abandon the option by permitting it to expire unexercised. Since expiration is imminent, an option holder cannot continue to hold the option in the hopes that the premium will rise and the option can be sold at a profit. A rational option holder will exercise the option if it is in-the-money and let it lapse when it is out-of-the-money. The return associated with exercising an in-the-money option is the in-the-money amount while the return associated with letting an option lapse is zero (without considering the original premium, which is an irretrievable "sunk" cost and shouldn't enter into a decision to exercise an option or not).

If an option was in-the-money upon expiration date and someone was willing to buy the option for more than the in-the-money amount, then option traders would sell the option knowing that the premium they receive exceeds their loss of the in-the-money amount when the option is exercised. Similarly, if someone was willing to sell the option for less than the in-the-money amount, then traders would buy the option knowing that the premium paid is less than the profit of the in-the-money amount on exercise. If an option were out-of-the-money and someone was willing to buy the option at all, then traders would sell knowing that the option could not be exercised at a profit.

Letting C denote the premium associated with a call option, U the underlying commodity price, and E the exercise or strike price, we may represent the terminal price of a call option as follows and as shown in Figure 5:1:

$$(5.1) \qquad C_{\text{terminal}} = \begin{cases} U - E & \text{where } U > E \\ 0 & \text{where } U \leq E \end{cases}$$

The definitions of in-the-money and out-of-the-money are simply reversed in the context of a put option. Consequently, the terminal value of a put option P may be represented as follows and as shown in Figure 5.2:

$$P_{\text{terminal}} = \begin{cases} U - E & \text{where } U < E \\ 0 & \text{where } U \geq E \end{cases}$$

The terminal option value reflects the maximum amount that the premium may assume. We have already discussed why an option premium can never be less than zero or negative. If an option were available at a price less than the in-the-money amount, arbitrageurs would immediately buy the option and exercise it, realizing the difference between the in-the-money amount and the premium as profit. Arbitrageurs would continue buying until the profit opportunity ceased to exist, bidding up the option premium in the process to at least equal the in-the-money amount.

The minimum value of an option may be referred to as the option's *intrinsic value*. The intrinsic value is always equal to the greater of zero or the in-the-money valuation. Of course, an option premium will not always equal the intrinsic value; often the premium will be considerably more. For example, an option buyer may anticipate that the price of the underlying commodity will appreciate significantly between the current and the expiration date. Under

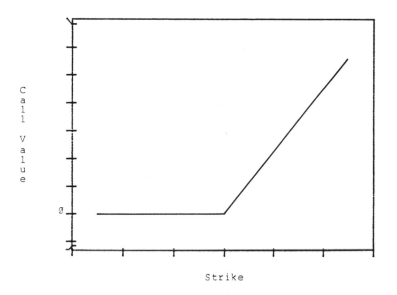

Strike

Underlying Market Price

Figure 5.1 Terminal value of a call option

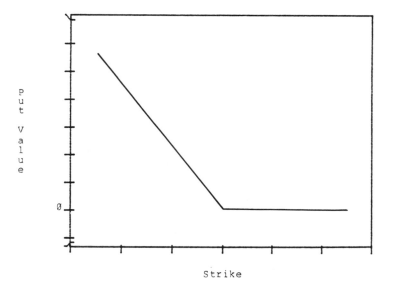

Strike

Underlying Market Price

Figure 5.2 Terminal value of a put option

those circumstances, he may be willing to pay far more than the intrinsic amount for the privilege of holding a call option. Conversely, where it is anticipated that the underlying commodity price will fall, traders may pay far more than the intrinsic value to purchase a put option.

A valid rule of thumb is that where there is more time between the current and expiration date, the underlying commodity price may wander within a wider range. Thus the longer the term to expiration, the greater the probability that the option will be profitable to exercise. Therefore, an option premium will generally be higher as the term to option expiration is extended. The value of an option in excess of its intrinsic value is often referred to as its *extrinsic* or *time value*. The option premium may be represented as the summation of its intrinsic and extrinsic value:

$$\text{Premium} = \text{Intrinsic Value} + \text{Extrinsic Value}$$

Figures 5.3 and 5.4 show the intrinsic, extrinsic, and total (premiun) value for a call and a put.

Just as an option's intrinsic value may be equal to zero, an option may similarly have negligible or zero extrinsic value. An option will have no extrinsic value when expiration is imminent. Additionally, it may have no extrinsic value where it is so far out-of-the-money that the possibility that it will someday be in-the-money before it expires and thus permit a profitable exercise is extremely remote. In no case, however, can an option have negative extrinsic value, just as an option can never have negative intrinsic value.

On the upward end, an option premium is constrained by the total price of the underlying instrument. An option is a derivative instrument and derives its value from the possibility that profits may be possible by taking a position in the underlying commodity market. If, for example, a call option premium approaches or exceeds the total purchase price of the underlying commodity, then there would be no economic incentive to buy the option. If the premium approaches or exceeds the underlying commodity price, then the prospective call option buyer would do just as well to buy the underlying commodity outright. The risk associated with the underlying commodity is its total price, which in this case is comparable to the total risk on the option represented by the premium. The returns associated with an option are comparable to those on the underlying commodity. But to profit from a long position, the option must be exercised. Thus the holder pays the premium plus the exercise price, a sum that presumably exceeds the total price of the underlying commodity.

Similarly, a prospective put option buyer would not pay a premium that approaches the total sale price of the commodity. The put option buyer hopes that the commodity price will decline. Clearly, it would be absurd to pay a premium for the right to sell a commodity that was comparable to the total sale price of the option.

Taking this discussion to an extreme, assume that a call option has a zero strike price. The option contract is then the functional equivalent of a contract

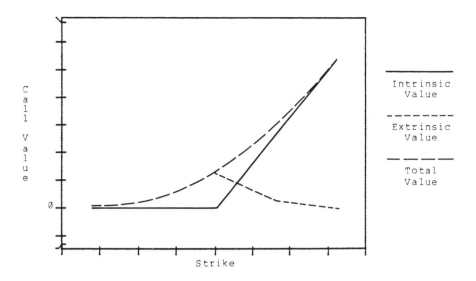

Underlying Market Price

Figure 5.3 Intrinsic and extrinsic value of a call

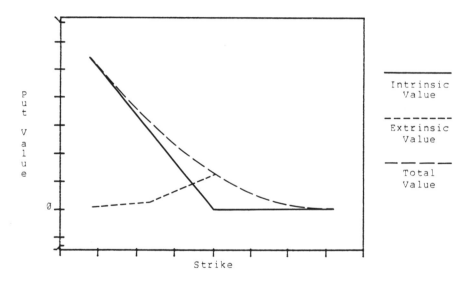

Underlying Market Price

Figure 5.4 Intrinsic and extrinsic value of a put

on the underlying commodity outright. The risks and potential returns associated with the option and the outright position would be equal. The option would always be in-the-money and would always be exercised. The returns on such an exercise where the strike price is zero would be the price of the underlying commodity, less the premium. Neglecting the effects of transaction costs, there would be no difference between buying the call option and buying the underlying commodity. The premium, therefore, would always equal the price of the underlying commodity and could never be more than the underlying commodity price.

The restrictions on an option premium as discussed above may be represented for a call as follows and as shown in Figures 5.5 and 5.6:

$$U \geq C \geq \begin{cases} U - E & \text{where } U > E \\ 0 & \text{where } U \leq E \end{cases}$$

And for a put:

$$U \geq C \geq \begin{cases} E - U & \text{where } U < E \\ 0 & \text{where } U \geq E \end{cases}$$

Breakeven Option Pricing

Our definition of fair market value references a premium at which the buyer and seller "should expect to break even." Of course, option traders do not enter the market in the hopes of merely breaking even; they enter the market in the hopes of making a profit. Nevertheless, some traders realize large losses or earn large profits and some do so consistently (although a trader could not, obviously, sustain large losses indefinitely). So what does this expectation of breaking even mean?

The term "expectation" implies an assessment of probability. Although traders may not be able to forecast precisely what their returns might be on each transaction, they may be able to assign a probability to a variety of possible outcomes. For example, over a large number of trials, one would expect that a coin tossed in the air would land heads up 50% of the time and tails up 50% of the time. Thus, over 20 trials the coin should land heads up 10 times and tails up 10 times. Over 10 trials, the coin should land heads up 5 times and tails up 5 times. Over 2 trials, the coin should land heads up once and tails up once. But if there is only one trial, does this mean that the coin will land on its edge?

Just as a coin may land either on its head or tail on any one trial, an option transaction may result in a profit or a loss on any one occasion. The expectation that a trader will break even is effective only over a large number of trials or transactions. Over a large number of occasions, if the transaction is entered into at the option's fair market value, the trader should expect to break even. This holds true in a statistical sense over a large number of transactions even if

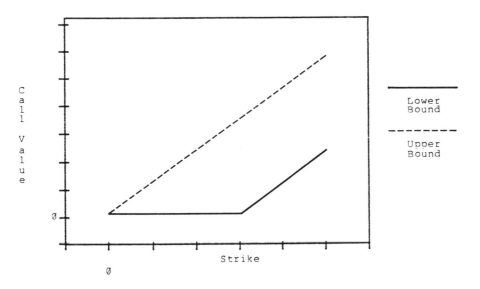

Underlying Market Price
Figure 5.5 Restrictions on a call option premium

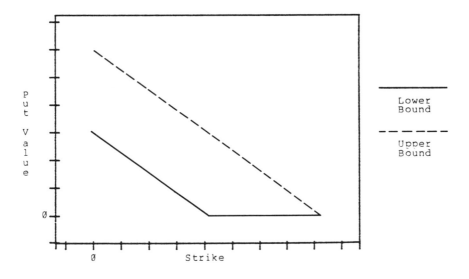

Underlying Market Price
Figure 5.6 Restrictions on a put option premium

trades are entered into on a random basis. Of course, some traders lose and some profit over a large number of transactions. Referring back to the example of the coin toss, one might observe that if a coin is shaved in a peculiar way, this may influence the probability that it will land heads or tails up. Similarly, if an option trader is wise and consistently recognizes circumstances wherein the option is under- or overpriced relative to its fair market value, he may consistently turn a profit.

Let's develop a simplistic option pricing model to demonstrate this point. Recall that an option's terminal value equals zero or the in-the-money valuation, whichever is greatest. Terminal value in equation 5.1 may also be expressed as Max $(0, U - E)$. Assume that the terminal value of the underlying commodity, that is, the price of the underlying commodity at the option expiration date, can assume only two different values, U_1 and U_2. The two possible terminal values of a call option, C_1 and C_2, will thus be equal to either Max $(0, U_1 - E)$ or Max $(0, U_2 - E)$, respectively. The returns that accrue to the option holder will equal the terminal value of the option less the original call premium C. But only one of the two outcomes can occur, and therefore our trader must assess the probability that one or the other outcome will be realized. The probability that the terminal commodity price will equal U_1 may be represented by $P(U_1)$ while the probability that the terminal commodity value equals U_2 may be represented by $P(U_1)$. Since there are only two possible outcomes, $P(U_1) + P(U_2) = 1$. It follows that the probability that U_2 will become the terminal commodity price equals $(1 - P(U_1))$. The call holder's expected return Exp(R) may be represented as:

$$\text{Exp}(R) = P(U_1)\text{Max } (0, U_1 - E) + (1 - P(U_1))\text{Max } (0, U_2 - E) - C$$

But we know that an option trader is expected to break even from the option transaction. Accordingly, Exp(R) must be set equal to zero before we may solve the equation to find the fair market value of the original call option premium C. Solving for C we have:

(5.2) $C = P(U_1)\text{Max } (0, U_1 - E) + (1 - P(U_1))\text{Max } (0, U_2 - E)$

Let's use equation 5.2 to solve a simple problem. Assume that the price of gold equals $400 per ounce and that a gold option is available that is struck at-the-money. Gold is expected to either rise to $450 or decline to $350 by the time the option expires. There is a 50% probability attached to either outcome. Figure 5.7 details this example with returns. How much would a trader be willing to pay for a call option with these specifications?

$$C = (.5)\text{Max } (0, 350 - 400) + (1 - .5)\text{Max } (0, 450 - 400)$$
$$= (.5) (0) + (.5) (\$50)$$
$$= \$25$$

In this case, the option is valued at $25 per ounce. We can see that over a large number of transactions, the option buyer would expect to break even on

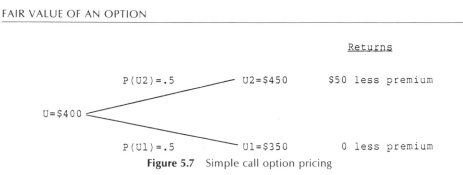
Figure 5.7   Simple call option pricing

the purchase. In 50% of the cases, the option holder would make $50 upon exercise reduced by the $25 premium for a return of $25 per ounce. In the other 50% of the transactions, the option would expire worthless and the holder would be out the original $25 premium. He makes $25 half the time and loses $25 half the time and thus breaks even. The same would hold true for the option writer. Where the option is exercised, the seller loses $50 cushioned by the $25 premium for a net loss of $25; where the option expires unexercised, the seller retains the full $25 premium. Thus the buyer's and seller's expected return is zero.

In addition, note that we have assumed that the expected return on the underlying commodity likewise is zero. A trader who goes long at $400 would expect to earn $50 half the time and lose $50 half the time. Likewise, a trader who goes short the underlying commodity would expect to earn $50 half the time and lose $50 half the time. Thus traders would be indifferent to buying or selling the underlying commodity. But if the commodity could be bought at $390, then traders would be inclined to buy because their expected return would be $10. They would make $60 half the time and lose $40 half the time. By buying the commodity in order to take advantage of this situation, traders would bid up the price to its fair market value of $400.

Similarly, when the option is priced at $25, traders are indifferent to buying or selling because the returns under either strategy would be equal over a large number of transactions. But what would happen if the option could be purchased for $20? In this case the buyer's expected return would be $5. He could expect to earn $50 less $20 premium or $30 net half the time and lose the $20 premium half the time. This implies an expected return of $5 to the buyer and an expected return of negative $5 to the seller. And, of course, by buying the option at $20, traders would bid the price up to its fair value of $25.

Neutral Hedge Ratio

Some option traders may be unsatisfied with the prospect of losing $20 half the time even if the expected return is $5. A trader may be able to take advantage of mispriced options without incurring the risk of loss by hedging the option position with an offsetting position in the underlying commodity market. For example, a long call or a short put position may be offset by a short position in the underlying commodity. A short call or a long put may be offset by a long position in the underlying commodity. By taking on an offsetting position to hedge the acquisition of a position in a mispriced option, a trader may be able to lock in profits; this is an effective form of *arbitrage*. Arbitrage may be thought of as transactions aimed at taking advantage of mispriced options by taking on a hedge or offsetting position. The ability to engage in this type of arbitrage forms the basis of this model of fair option pricing.

The arbitrageur's most critical problem is to execute a perfect hedge transaction. To do this, he must determine the ratio of units of the underlying commodity to units of option contracts that will minimize the risk in the net position. The idea is to precisely match price fluctuations in one market with offsetting price fluctuations in the other market. Let's assume that the call option in our preceding example was fairly priced at $25. Assume that our option trader buys one call option and sells an equivalent amount of the underlying commodity. What would his returns be?

(1) Probability	(2) Terminal Commodity Price	(3) Return on Long Call	(4) Return on Short Commodity	(5) Net Return (3) + (4)
50%	$350	($25)	$50	$25
50	450	25	(50)	(25)
Expected return		0	0	0

In this case, our trader is no better off having executed the hedge than when he was outright long the call position. His possible returns are simply reversed; when the market is down a profit ensues and when the market is up a loss ensues. What our trader neglected to consider is that the movements in the option premium and the commodity price do not match. The expected fluctuation in an option premium relative to a given fluctuation in the underlying commodity price is often referred to as the option's *delta* and may be used to determine the option's *neutral hedge ratio,* which we shall denote as b^*. The asterisk associated with this symbol is intended to show that the neutral hedge option/commodity ratio is *optimal* in the sense that the implementation of a hedge in that ratio reduces risk to a minimum. The term b may be used to symbolize a option/commodity ratio that is not optimal in the sense that it doesn't minimize risk.

The delta or neutral hedge ratio may be determined by examining the ratio of possible fluctuations in the option premium (ΔC) to corresponding fluctuations in the price of the underlying commodity (ΔU). The term "Δ" or the greek letter "delta" refers to changes in price.

(5.3) $$\Delta = \Delta C / \Delta U$$

The delta in this case may be calculated as:

$$\Delta = (C_2 - C_1)/(U_2 - U_1)$$
$$= (50 - 0)/(450 - 350)$$
$$= .5$$

Taking the reciprocal of delta gives us b* $=1/\Delta = 2$. This indicates that a ratio of two option units to one commodity unit leads to a risk-neutral hedge. In other words, for every two call options sold, one unit of the underlying commodity should be purchased to reduce risk to a minimum. To illustrate, consider the following results of a two-for-one options to commodity hedge:

(1) Probability	(2) Terminal Commodity Price	(3) Return on Two Long Calls	(4) Return on Short Commodity	(5) Net Return (3) + (4)
50%	$350	($50)	$50	0
50	450	50	(50)	0
Expected return		0	0	0

Using a hedging strategy, an arbitrageur can take advantage of situations where an option is mispriced without incurring the risk of loss. Assume that the call option was trading at a $30 premium. The option is overpriced by $5 and so the appropriate strategy is to sell two call options and buy one unit of the underlying commodity.

(1) Probability	(2) Terminal Commodity Price	(3) Return on Two Short Calls	(4) Return on Long Commodity	(5) Net Return (3) + (4)
50%	$350	$60	($50)	$10
50	450	(40)	50	10
Expected return		10	0	10

In this case, our arbitrageur locked in a $5 net profit per option contract or a $10 aggregate return for the two options because he was perfectly hedged in the underlying commodity market. Market participants could be expected to continue selling calls and buying the underlying commodity as a hedge until the price of the calls declined or the price of the underlying commodity appreciates to the point where further arbitrage profits would be impossible. Because this transaction is essentially riskless, arbitrageurs would execute the trade even if only a small profit margin would be realized. The ability to reap such riskless profits should cause the option to be consistently priced at its fair market value.

Although the delta factor for calls can be expressed with a positive number, for example, .3 or .7, the delta factor for puts is often expressed as a negative number, for example, $-.3$ or $-.7$. The reason for this is simple: a call is an option to buy while a put is an option to sell. This means that call premiums can be expected to increase in response to an advance in the price of the underlying commodity and decline in response to a drop in the price of the underlying commodity. A put premium, however, can be expected to *decrease* in response to an advance in the underlying commodity price and *increase* in response to a decline in the underlying commodity price.

Obviously, however, it is nonsensical to think of a hedge using a negative number of option contracts. So when one takes the reciprocal of the delta to arrive at a neutral hedge ratio of options to underlying commodity, that reciprocal is generally expressed as a positive number. As a result, one sometimes sees deltas for put options expressed as a positive number. Although this convention is not *technically* correct, it is often more convenient to apply this simplification. Be aware, however, that call deltas are positive and put deltas are negative.

Return on Investment

Thus far, our examples have illustrated the concept of fair value making the assumption that both buyer and seller should expect to break even and that their respective returns are zero. This begs the question of why an investor should bother with an option at all if the expected return is zero? If an option buyer must pay the seller the premium upon purchase, he has an investment in the option. Shouldn't the option buyer expect some positive return for his investment? The answer to this question is a resounding yes!

Assume that an investor could borrow or lend without limitation at a particular interest rate r per time period t. Where an option buyer is required to pay the premium in full upon purchase and in cash, the buyer has an investment in the contract. This cash could readily, under our assumptions, be invested at the interest rate r. One dollar (\$1) applied at interest rate r over one time period t would yield $\$1(1 + r)$ at the end of the time period. And, assuming that the interest is compounded, one dollar should earn $\$1(1 + r)^t$ over t time periods. An investment in a call option should yield $C(1 + r)^t$ less C over t time periods. Thus equation 5.2 may be modified as follows:

$$C(1 + r)^t = P(U_1)\text{Max}(0, U_1 - E) + (1 - P(U_1))\text{Max}(0, U_2 - E)$$

or

(5.4) $C = 1/(1 + r)^t[P(U_1)\text{Max}(0, U_1 - E) + (1 - P(U_1))\text{Max}(0, U_2 - E)]$

Going back to our example where the price of gold is expected to either increase to \$450 or decline to \$350 from the current price of \$400 by expiration with a 50/50 probability, let's apply our modified formula. Assume that the interest rate $r = .10$ or 10% per time period $t = 1$. Recall that the fair price of this call option was determined to be \$25. Applying equation 5.4 we have:

$$C = 1/(1 + .1)^1 \ [\$25]$$
$$= .909 \ [\$25]$$
$$= \$22.73$$

The unadjusted return on this option is expected to be \$25. (Since the return without consideration of the premium paid up front will be \$50 or zero with a 50/50 chance.) A rational investor, however, would not pay \$25 one period in advance for this option. Because there is a *time value* associated with cash implied by the opportunity to invest the cash at interest, a rational investor would pay less than $25 for the privilege of holding the option. If the option were purchased at $22.73, our investor would in effect earn 10% interest or $2.27 on the investment of $22.73 because:

$$\text{Exp}(R) = (1 + r)^t \text{ (Investment)}$$
$$\$25 = (1.10) \ (\$22.73)$$

The option writer enjoys the use of the $22.73 premium during the life of the option. Since he can invest this money at 10% interest, his expected loss at expiration of $25 is compensated by the $22.73 premium plus the $2.27 earned in interest over the life of the option. Since both buyer and seller may hedge their respective positions by taking on an offsetting position in the underlying market, their option positions are essentially riskless. The option buyer is assured of a riskless return of 10% on the investment. This interest rate r may be referred to as the *riskless rate of return* and represents the percentage returns associated with a guaranteed investment. An investor will always prefer ventures that have the lowest risk for a given return or the highest return for a given risk. This rate will therefore be low relative to investments that are even marginally risky.

Just as an option trader anticipates some return on cash invested in an option contract, he will similarly anticipate a positive return on cash invested in a commodity. If gold is expected to either appreciate or decline $50 with an equal probability, then the expected return on the commodity is zero. Why would any investor want to invest in gold if the expected return is zero?

Recall that the returns associated with an investment are expected to increase as a function of invested capital. If no cash is invested, can one expect a return? Consider the types of commodities that may be the subject of an option contract. In particular, consider a futures contract. The investment in a futures contract is equal to the original or initial margin paid to secure the contract. Recall that this original margin is often paid not in cash but with instruments that do not imply an opportunity cost. An original margin may be put up in securities such as Treasury bills or even in letters of credit in some cases. The holder of a futures contract, therefore, does not forfeit any opportunities by buying or selling a futures contract. Still, there *is* risk associated with a long or short futures position, which may lead to profit or loss. Some market observers believe that futures prices reflect the market's weighted average opinion regarding the ultimate price of the commodity at the time the futures contract comes due for delivery. For the moment, let's apply this assumption. Let's make a further assumption: the futures market *unbiasedly* reflects these future values. If we assume that the futures market only inadvertently misjudges the ultimate price of the commodity at futures contract maturity, then we may surmise that the *expected* return on a futures contract, over a large number of trials, is zero. More will be said about this point later.

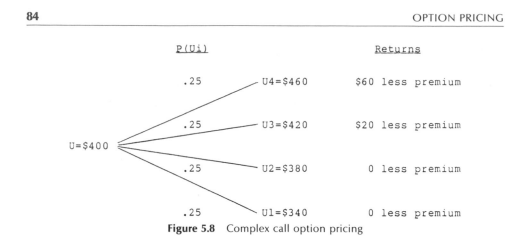

Figure 5.8   Complex call option pricing

Thus far, it has been assumed that the terminal price of the underlying commodity can assume only two different values. This clearly is unrealistic so let's extend the analysis to accommodate the possibility that the terminal commodity price may assume a number of discrete price levels. These discrete price levels may be denoted by U_i where $i = 1, 2, 3, \ldots . n$. The probability that U_i will represent the terminal commodity price may be represented by $P(U_i)$ where the summation of $P(U_i)$ equals 1. In this case, the fair value of a call option may be represented by the summation of the probability of a particular terminal commodity price multiplied by the associated terminal option price, discounted to reflect the investment in the option contract:

$$(5.5) \qquad C = 1/(1 + r)^t \; \sum_{i\,=\,1}^{n} P(U_i)\mathrm{Max}(0,\, U_i - E)$$

where
$$\sum_{i\,=\,1}^{n} P(U_i) = 1$$

Let's develop an example by assuming that the current price of gold is \$400 and there is a call option available that is struck at-the-money. Gold is expected to vary in the range of \$340 to \$460 between the current and expiration dates at discrete \$40 intervals. Thus the set of possible terminal underlying commodity price $U_i = (\$340, \$380, \$420, \$460)$ for $i = 1, 2, 3, 4$ (see Figure 5.8). For simplicity, assume that there is a uniform probability that the terminal commodity price will be any of the possible values U_i. Accordingly, $P(U_i) = 1/n$ or there is a 25% probability that any of the possible terminal commodity prices will be realized. The riskless rate of return is 10% and there is one period remaining until expiration. Applying equation 5.5, we have:

$$C = 1/(1 + .1)^1 \; [(.25)\mathrm{Max}(0,\, 340 - 400) + (.25)\mathrm{Max}(0,\, 380 - 400) + (.25)\mathrm{Max}(0,\, 420 - 400) + (.25)\mathrm{Max}(0,\, 460 - 400)]$$
$$= .909 \; [\$20]$$
$$= \$18.18$$

Over a large number of transactions, a trader could expect to break even by either buying or selling the call at $18.18. A trader who goes long a call at $18.18 can expect to lose the premium half the time and earn $20 and $60 upon exercise a quarter of the time, respectively. Because there is an investment in the option, a trader expects to be compensated for his lost opportunities at the riskless rate of return. One may note that the term $Max(0, U_i - E)$ equals zero and thus drops out of consideration where U_i is less than or equal to E or where a call option is out-of-the-money. Presumably, we may find some value of U_i where $U_i > E > U_{i-1}$. Denoting this value of U_i as U_k, we may refine equation 5.5 somewhat further as:

$$(5.6) \qquad C = 1/(1 + r)^t \sum_{i=k}^{n} P(U_i)\ (U_i - E)$$

Diffusion Price Movement

In the foregoing example, we assumed that it was equally likely that gold would fluctuate $60 as it was to fluctuate $20 between the current and expiration dates. But is this assumption representative of normal commodity price behavior? One might suspect that gold is more likely to move $20 than $60 within a particular time period. Additionally, we have implied that the price of gold may leap from $400 directly to $460 without assuming any of the intervening values. This too is misleading, so let's construct a *diffusion* model of commodity price behavior, where the underlying commodity price diffuses outward from the current value in a steplike function over time.

Assume that gold is currently priced at $400 and there are three time periods before option expiration. Gold prices will either move up or down from the current level in discrete $20 increments. The likelihood of moving in either direction is 50%. When there are two periods before expiration, gold will have moved up $20 to $420 or down $20 to $380. These two values for the underlying commodity price may be represented by the notation $U_{i,t}$ where $t = 2$ periods to expiration. The set of possible values of U_i, t where $t = 2$ is ($380, $420) for $i = 1, 2$. The probability of $U_{i,t}$ may be represented by $P(U_{i,t})$, and it is clear that $P(U_{i,2}) = .50$ or 50% for $i = 1$ or $i = 2$. Following the lower path on our probability tree, assume that gold declines to $380. By the time there is only one period to expiration $t = 1$, gold will have moved up $20 to $400 or down $20 to $360. Following the upper path, assume that the price moves to $420 by $t = 2$. By $t = 1$, gold will have moved to $440 or $400. Thus the set of possible values of $U_{i,t}$ where $t = 1$ is ($360, $400, $440) for $i = 1, 2, 3$.

What is the probability that gold prices will equal $360 by $t = 1$? If the price of gold at $t = 2$ is $380, then we know there is a 50% chance that gold will decline $20 to $360 by $t = 1$. The *conditional* or contingent probability of realizing a particular price given that a known price is realized in the preceding period may be represented as:

$$P(U_{i,t} \mid U_{i,t+1})$$

The overall probability of realizing a particular price level in a particular period $P(U_{i,t})$ may be determined by:

(5.7) $$P(U_{i,t}) = P(U_{i,t} \mid U_{i,t+1}) \, P(U_{i,t+1})$$

The conditional probability of realizing a price of \$360 given that \$380 was realized in the preceding period or $P(\$360_{t=1}, \$380_{t=2})$ equals .50 or 50% and we know that the probability of realizing a price of \$380 by $t = 2$ or $P(\$380_{t=2})$ is likewise .50 or 50%. Thus

$$\begin{aligned}
P(\$360_{t=1}) &= P(\$360_{t=1} \mid \$380_{t=2}) \, P(\$380_{t=2}) \\
&= (.50)(.50) \\
&= .50 \text{ or } 50\%
\end{aligned}$$

When we reach option expiration, gold may assume a price between \$340 and \$460 at \$40 intervals, or $U_{i,t}$ for $t = 0$ is (\$340, \$380, \$420, \$460) for $i = 1, 2, 3, 4$. The probabilities associated with these terminal values may be determined using the same method as above. For example, gold may achieve a price of \$340 only by moving down the path from \$400 to \$380 to \$360 and on to \$340.

$$\begin{aligned}
P(\$340_{t=0}) &= P(\$340_{t=0} \mid \$360_{t=1}) \, P(\$360_{t=1}) \\
&= (.50)(.25) \\
&= .125 \text{ or } 12.5\%
\end{aligned}$$

Gold may achieve a price of \$380 by expiration either through \$360 or \$400. Thus

$$\begin{aligned}
P(\$380_{t=0}) &= P(\$380_{t=0} \mid \$360_{t=1}) \, P(\$360_{t=1}) + \\
&\quad\ \ P(\$380_{t=0} \mid \$400_{t=1}) \, P(\$400_{t=1}) \\
&= (.50)(.25) + (.50)(.50) \\
&= .375 \text{ or } 37.5\%
\end{aligned}$$

The probabilities associated with the set of possible terminal commodity prices \$340, \$380, \$420, and \$460 are 12.5%, 37.5%, 37.5%, and 12.5%, respectively (see Figure 5.9). Using equation 5.5, but ignoring the discount factor, we may calculate the call option premium as:

$$\begin{aligned}
C &= (.125)\text{Max}(0,\, 340 - 400) + (.375)\text{Max}(0,\, 380 - 400) + \\
&\quad\ (.375)\text{Max}(0,\, 420 - 400) + (.125)\text{Max}(0,\, 460 - 400) \\
&= 0 + 0 + (.375)(20) + (.125)(60) \\
&= \$15
\end{aligned}$$

Applying the Delta or Neutral Hedge Ratio

Over a large number of transactions, the option trader would be indifferent to buying or selling the call at \$15. If the option were priced over \$15, traders would rush in to sell, driving the price down to its fair market value; and if the

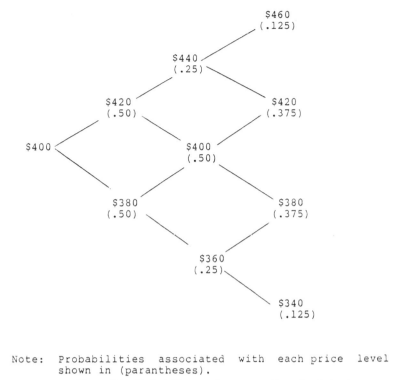

Figure 5.9   Probability tree for commodity price behavior

option were priced less then $15, traders would buy and drive the price up to its
fair market value. And, of course, traders could be expected to attempt to lock
in possible arbitrage profits by taking on an offsetting position in the underlying commodity market. But what would be the appropriate neutral hedge
ratio?

If the price of gold moves from $400 to $460, the call premium moves from
its original value of $15 to a terminal value of $60. This implies a delta factor of
$(60 - 15) / (460 - 400) = .75$, or four option units to every three commodity
units. But what if the underlying commodity price moves from $400 to $340
and the premium declines from $15 to 0? In this case, the delta factor is
$(0 - 15) / (340 - 400) = .25$, or four option units to every one commodity units.
Which of the two neutral hedge ratios should a prudent trader apply?

The answer is neither: delta is valid only for relatively small movements in
the underlying commodity price and must be adjusted frequently in order to
precisely offset risks. If we consult our probability tree, we find that the underlying commodity price will move from the original $400 to either $420 or $380 as
a next step. In order to calculate the appropriate neutral hedge ratio, we must
determine what the call premium would be where the underlying commodity
price assumes the values of $380 or $420 at time $t = 2$ periods to expiration. But
before we can do this, we must know what the fair call premiums are where
there are $t = 1$ periods to expiration.

If there is but one period to expiration and the price of the underlying commodity equals \$440 (denoted by $U_{i=3,t\,=\,1}$), there are only two relevant branches on the probability tree. The terminal price of the commodity may assume the values of either \$420 or \$460 with 50% probability. The terminal call premium must equal either $\text{Max}(0, 420 - 400)$ or $\text{Max}(0, 460 - 400)$ or \$20 and \$60, respectively. Equation 5.2 may be applied (ignoring the time value of money for the moment) to determine the call premium $C_{i\,=\,3,\,t\,=\,1}$:

$$C_{3,1} = (.50)\text{Max}(0, 420 - 400) + (.50)\text{Max}(0, 460 - 400)$$
$$= (.50)(20) + (.50)(60)$$
$$= \$40$$

Working backwards using this equation, we may fill in the call premiums at all forks of the probability tree (see Figure 5.10). Thus we find that where there are $t = 2$ periods to expiration, the call premiums associated with a \$380 and \$420 gold price are \$5 and \$25, respectively. The delta factor may be calculated as:

$$\Delta = (C_{2,\,2} - C_{1,\,2})/(U_{2,\,2} - U_{1,\,2})$$
$$= (25 - 5)/(420 - 380)$$
$$= .50$$

Taking the reciprocal of the delta factor, the appropriate hedge ratio is two option units to every single commodity unit. If the initial call premium were overpriced at \$18, an arbitrageur would sell two calls and buy one unit of gold.

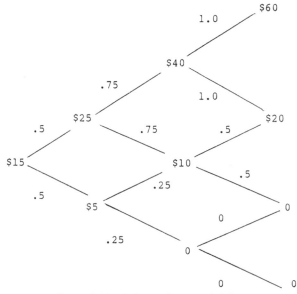

Figure 5.10   Call premiums and deltas

Assume that by $t = 2$ periods to expiration, the equilibrium premium was restored. If gold moved to $380, our arbitrageur could buy back the two calls at $5 a piece for a $26 gross profit and sell the gold at $380 for a loss of $20, locking in a net $3 profit per option. Similarly, if gold moved up to $420, the two calls could be bought back at $25 a piece for a $14 loss while the gold could be sold for a $20 profit, again locking in a net $3 profit per option.

Assume that the price of gold moves up to $420. At this point, the neutral hedge ratio must be adjusted to reflect the possibility that gold will move to $400 or $440. The neutral hedge ratio may be calculated as .75, or four option units to three units of the underlying commodity:

$$\Delta = (C_{3,\,1} - C_{2,\,1})/(U_{3,\,1} - U_{2,\,1})$$
$$= (40 - 10)/(440 - 400)$$
$$= .75$$

Note that as the option moves further into-the-money, the neutral hedge ratio increases and as the option moves out-of-the-money, the ratio decreases. The ratio actually equuals 1.0 when the option is exceedingly in-the-money and 0 when it so far out-of-the-money as to negate the possibility of a profitable exercise. When the option is at-the-money, the delta factor equals .5.

Let's consider the effect of opportunity costs, specifically, assume that the riskless rate of return equals 10%. When there are $t = 3$ periods to expiration, the $15 premium must be discounted to reflect the investment in the option contract. Thus the call premium where $t = 3$ equals:

$$C_{t\,=\,3} = 1/(1 + .10)^3 \,[\$15]$$
$$= .75 \,[\$15]$$
$$= \$11.27$$

When there are $t = 2$ periods to expiration, the call premiums of $5 and $25 may be discounted to $4.13 and $20.66, respectively (see Figure 5.11). What would be the neutral hedge ratio in this case?

$$\Delta = (C_{2,\,2} - C_{1,\,2})/(U_{2,\,2} - U_{1,\,2})$$
$$= (20.66 - 4.13)/(420 - 380)$$
$$= .41$$

This implies that (1/.41) or 2.42 option units should be acquired for every single commodity option unit in order to effect a riskless hedge from $t = 3$ to $t = 2$ periods to expiration. Because the reciprocal of the neutral hedge ratio doesn't equal a round number, that is, 1, 2, 3. . . , it may be impossible in practice to implement a perfectly offsetting hedge. But let's assume that the option and commodity units were infinitely divisible and an option trader decided to sell 2.42 option units and buy one commodity unit, reversing these transactions when there are $t = 2$ periods to expiration.

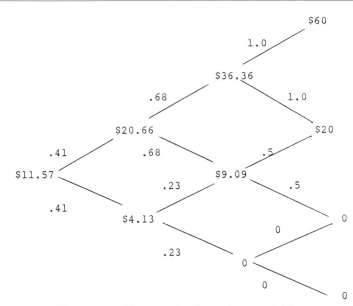

Figure 5.11 Discounted call premiums and deltas

If gold moves from $400 to $420:

Buy gold at $400, sell gold at $420	$20.00
Sell 2.42 options at $11.27, buy 2.42 options at $20.66	(22.73)
Invest premiums of $27.27 (2.42 × $11.27) at 10% for one period	2.73
Total	$ 0

If gold moves from $400 to $380:

Buy gold at $400, sell gold at $380	($20.00)
Sell 2.42 options at $11.27, buy 2.42 options at $4.13	17.27
Invest premiums of $27.27 (2.42 × $11.27) at 10% for one period	2.73
Total	$ 0

The net effect of these transactions is that the option writer broke even. The writer temporarily takes money out of the option market, funds that may be invested at the short-term interest rate. On the other hand, the option buyer invests the premium in the contract. If these transactions were reversed, we would see that the option buyer locks in the riskless rate of 10% on the investment. But let's assume that the option was originally underpriced by $1.27 at $10.00 and that it returns to equilibrium by the time there are $t = 2$ periods to expiration. Let's illustrate how the buyer can lock in a profit over and above the riskless rate of return.

If gold moves from $400 to $420:

Sell gold at $400, buy gold at $420	($20.00)
Buy 2.42 options at $10.00, sell 2.42 options at $20.66	25.80
Borrow premium of $24.20 (2.42 × $10.00) at 10% for one period	(2.42)
Total	$ 3.38

If gold moves from $400 to $380:

Sell gold at $400, buy gold at $380	$20.00
Buy 2.42 options at $10.00, sell 2.42 options at $4.13	(14.20)
Borrow premium of $24.20 (2.42 × $10.00) at 10% for one period	(2.42)
Total	$ 3.38

The $3.38 profit represents a return of $1.40 on each option ($3.38/2.42). Our option buyer locks in a profit actually in excess of the $1.27 because the amount invested in the contract is less than the fair market value. Of course, whenever an option is over- or underpriced, arbitrageurs can be expected to sell and buy, respectively, always driving the price towards the fair market.

WHY DOES AN OPTION HAVE VALUE?

We have gone on at some length developing a simple model of fair value option pricing and in the process have suggested some variables that impact upon fair value. But we have not addressed the fundamental characteristics of what make an option valuable, thus encouraging investors to part with the option premium in order to buy an option. Let's consider these characteristics and how they might differ when the commodity underlying the option contract differs.

An option contract derives its value from the value attached to the underlying commodity for which the option may be exercised. Clearly, if the underlying commodity had no value, then no one would want, for example, to obtain a call option that grants the right to buy the commodity. But the commodities that are the subject of option contracts all have some value or potential value, whether the "commodity" is a futures contract, a physical commodity, or a security. It is the potential to earn a return on the underlying commodity that imparts value to the option contract. Because the means of earning a return on different types of commodities vary, the value of different types of options also vary.

Although an option derives its value from the value of the underlying commodity, it has certain characteristics not associated with the underlying commodity that give it its own special value. The two most prominent of these characteristics may be identified as insurance and leverage value. These two factors are discussed next.

Insurance Value

When an investor buys a commodity—a quantity of silver bullion for example—this implies that he believes that the price of silver will appreciate so that he might dispose of the silver at some subsequent date for a profit. Clearly, a rational investor would prefer not to buy silver when he anticipates that the price will decline. But this is a risk that he nevertheless undertakes. A question that is obviously of interest to our silver buyer centers about the magnitude of this risk, that is, just how much can I expect to lose if the price of silver declines?

This isn't a question that can be answered simply. If our silver buyer constantly monitored the market and could sell the silver at a moment's notice at the prevailing price, then he could minimize possible losses if the market begins to drop. But what if our silver investor can't execute his transactions promptly? Or what if the silver market drops so unexpectedly and precipitously that our investor can't limit his losses to manageable levels? And finally, what if our investor can't take the time frequently to review the status of his investment? All of these risks are associated with buying the physical commodity and are, to one degree or another, unavoidable.

The option premium has often been compared to an insurance premium. This comparison is justified because the analogy between options and an insurance policy is strong. When a homeowner buys a fire insurance policy, he pays a relatively small premium, reserving the right to make a relatively large claim in the event adversity strikes and the house burns down. When a trader buys an option, he foregoes a relatively small premium in return for a potentially large profit. Of course, the analogy breaks down somewhat when we consider that the homeowner normally prefers to forego the fire insurance premium and never make a claim while option traders are hoping to stake their claim for large profits. On the opposite side of the transaction, the insurance company collects a relatively small premium from a number of policyholders and is obligated to pay large sums if a claim is made. An option writer collects the premium and risks large losses if the price of the underlying commodity moves against him.

Because an option holder may exercise the call or put by buying or selling the underlying commodity, respectively, he is afforded the opportunity to profit from price movements of that commodity. Because of the nonsymmetrical nature of the option contract, the holder is "insured" against losing any more than the option premium. This may be considered by many as the best of two worlds—limited risk coupled with unlimited profit potential. But recall that the premium adjusts to compensate for the imbalance between potential returns and potential profits. This is analogous to the fire insurance premium. The policyholder knows that there is a small probability of ever making a claim on the policy and a large probability that the premiums will simply represent a loss. But the policyholder is willing to accept this imbalance because the premiums foregone are small relative to the loss that would be borne if the house burnt down and was uninsured.

If a commodity price is not administered by a governmental program or influenced by monopolistic forces, it may be expected to fluctuate freely in order to adjust to the dynamic availability of supplies and demands placed upon those supplies. If a commodity price exhibits little or not variability, then there will be little or no point in trading an option for that commodity. There will be little motivation to use the option to profit from price movements in the underlying commodity market and no reason to use the option to limit risk. Because every commodity that underlies an option contract will vary in price, possibly in an adverse direction, *every option contract has some insurance value.* The magnitude of this insurance value depends upon the potential magnitude of adverse price movements. Where the price of a commodity may potentially move significantly against a trader, then an option contract takes on enhanced attractiveness because the option buyer may limit his risk to the premium. Of course, the increased appeal of the option is reflected in an increased premium.

Leverage Value

Assume that a commodity could be purchased for $100 and that it was expected to increase in value by $12 a year. Assume further that our investor is faced with the alternative of buying the commodity for $100 or buying a call option with an exercise price at-the-money ($100) for a $2 premium. Which investment would be the most attractive? A $12 receipt from a $100 investment comes out to a 12% return. Alternatively, the call holder earns $10 ($12 upon exercise less the $2 premium) for a $2 investment, or a return of 500%. Clearly, the option trader is able to apply his investment at a much greater return than an outright buyer of the commodity. The advantage enjoyed by the option trader is called *leverage.*

One enjoys leverage when one can increase the potential return without increasing the amount of money invested in a particular venture, or when one can decrease the amount of money invested in the venture without diminishing the potential returns. Returns must, of course, be measured relative to the investment. Because the returns on an option contract are tied to the returns associated with the underlying commodity, it is useful to understand the characteristics of commodity price behavior.

Every commodity that underlies an option exhibits price variability to one extent or another. Hence, profits are possible by investing in a commodity. Although the character of that price movement may vary to a large extent from one type of commodity to the next, there are some common features associated with commodity price behavior that may be identified. For the most part, commodity prices may be described as following the diffusion process described above. That is, today's price is a function of yesterday's price plus some random fluctuation. We may depict the price of a commodity underlying an option at any particular time as:

$$U_t = U_{t-1} + \epsilon_t$$

Where ϵ refers to the random price fluctuation. Obviously, the change in the commodity price from one time period to the next or U_t less U_{i-1} equals the random fluctuation ϵ_t. If the price of a commodity equals $100 at one point and the random fluctuation equals +$10, then the price of the commodity one period later will equal $110 ($100 plus $10). Sometimes, the random fluctuation may be −$10 and the price will decrease from $100 to $90. If the price increases half the time by $10 and decreases half the time by $10, then the average price fluctuation actually is zero. If this fluctuation is truly random, then the change in price yesterday will not provide any reliable indication in which direction the price will fluctuate today. In other words, these price fluctuations are "independent" over time.

This model provides a good description of how a futures price fluctuates over time. The best indication of tomorrow's price is today's price because the unexpected change in price is zero. Although it is likely that there will be some random fluctuation in one direction or the other, it is difficult to predict which direction the market will move in. This is characteristic of an *efficient market*. An efficient market adjusts rapidly in price to fully reflect all information available that bears upon the balance of supply and demand. Because the price adjustment is rapid and because new information about market fundamentals becomes available from time to time on an unpredictable basis, it may be difficult to identify opportunities in the futures market.

From a practical standpoint, it is often quite difficult to identify profit opportunities in a timely manner in the futures market. In addition, if the market efficiently predicts future price levels, this suggests that the expected return in the futures market may be zero. In other words, both buyer and seller of a futures contract can expect to break even, ignoring transaction costs, over a large number of trials. Why would anyone want to enter into an investment where he expects on average to break even?

At this point, let's digress a bit to discuss this statement that no returns can be expected on a futures contract. Futures may be used for many purposes, the most easily identifiable purposes include hedging, that is, using futures to offset risks associated with the underlying cash commodity, and speculation, that is, trading with the intention of capitalizing on anticipated movements in the futures markets. A hedger ostensibly wishes to avoid risk while a speculator takes on risks in the hopes of realizing profits. From a theoretical standpoint, a trader who assumes increased risks must be compensated by some returns. Conversely, a trader who offsets risk must be willing to give up some return in order to limit risk. As we have stated before, increased risk must be accompanied by increased expected returns. The theoretical literature often refers to this "risk premium" that compensates the speculator for taking on risk otherwise borne by the hedger. From this standpoint, at least some participants in the futures markets expect a positive return. But it is unclear that the academic literature has established that this return is reflected in the form of some consistently identifiable pricing trend. Where there are relatively balanced numbers of hedgers who offset risk by shorting futures and by going long futures, it is easy to understand why this risk premium cannot be explained by some price trend.

It is probably fruitless to consider further whether a risk premium is implicit in futures prices, whether a consistent trend may be observed in futures prices, or whether futures traders can expect a positive or negative return over time. As we shall see later, however, it may be more productive to identify relationships between futures and the instruments that may be delivered against a futures contract. To the extent that the option pricing model we are working to develop is based upon the assumption that one can offset option market risk with risk in the underlying market, it is more important to study these *relationships between market prices, rather than absolute price movements*.

Let's return to the concept of leverage and return on investment. Recall that a futures contract generally may be secured or margined with Treasury securities or other instruments such as letters of credit. Because the futures trader may continue to collect interest associated with, for example, Treasury bills posted as original margin on a futures contract, no opportunity cost is implicit in trading futures. A holder of a futures contract has no investment per se in the contract—he enjoys complete leverage because he still participates in returns (or losses) on the commodity.

Options must generally be secured by payment of the full cash premium. The holder of an option enjoys leverage by virtue of the fact that he participates in returns on the commodity without posting the full purchase price of that commodity. But leverage is a relative concept. When an investor purchases an option for a futures contract, the relevant comparison is the leverage on the futures contract relative to the leverage on the option market. Clearly, the holder of an option cannot reduce his investment in the contract below zero. In fact, he is required to pay the premium in cash—he therefore has an investment in the option. But the holder of a futures contract has *no* investment in the contract and enjoys complete leverage. So as long as the option premium is greater than zero, the holder of an option on a futures contract enjoys *negative leverage!*

When an investor buys a physical commodity or a security, he generally must pay cash to secure the commodity. For example, if one were to buy silver when it was selling for $10.00 per ounce, then one would have a $10.00 investment in each ounce purchased. Similarly, if one were to buy $100,000 face value of U.S. Treasury bonds when they were selling at 100% of par, one would have a $100,000 investment in bonds. Investors who buy stock can, of course, margin the stock at 50% but this is not the same as a futures margin. A stock investor who margins a stock purchase at 50% makes a down payment equal to half the value of the stock and borrows the remaining 50% at interest. If we assume that investors may borrow and lend without limitation at the same interest rate r, then an investor who margins stock would be indifferent to paying 100% of the stock price upon purchase or margining the stock at 50%. The investment in a stock, for all practical purposes, equals the full purchase price.

Since there is an investment in a debt security or a physical commodity equal to the purchase price, some return on that investment is expected. But this is incompatible with the presumption that the expected change in the value of a commodity over time is zero. Our model must be adjusted to include a trend component m that is indicative of returns on the commodity investment:

$$(5.8) \qquad\qquad U_t = U_{t-1} + m + \epsilon_t$$

To illustrate, assume that a 10% annual return was expected on an investment in a commodity presently valued at $100. If this return is realized in the form of price appreciation, then the commodity price at the end of one year should equal $110. Since there are 365 days in a year, the price appreciation on any one day equals approximately $0.03 ($10/365), or 3 cents per day. Again, the random fluctuation has a mean of zero but may be considerably higher or lower than zero on any single day. Assume that the random fluctuation on the first day is +$4.20. The price of the commodity will appreciate to $104.23 (the original price of $100 plus the trend component of $0.03 plus the random fluctuation of $4.20). On the second day, the price of the commodity may fluctuate randomly up or down by $4.20, greater than $4.20 or less than $4.20.

When one purchases a physical commodity, one expects a return on the investment. If someone buys silver, for example, he generally does so in the hopes that the price will appreciate so that the metal may be sold for a profit at some later date. But how much should that appreciation be?

To begin, it may be observed that the investor foregoes the returns that otherwise might accrue on the funds invested in silver. Presumably, our investor could apply those funds at the risk-free rate r. Additionally, an investor who buys silver and holds it for subsequent resale will incur certain holding costs h. For physical commodities at large, these holding costs may include storage fees, handling fees, insurance, demurrage, and spoilage. The price of a physical commodity P may be compared to the expected price of a futures contract $\text{Exp}(F)$ on that commodity as:

$$(5.9) \qquad\qquad \text{Exp}(F) = P[1 + (r + h)^t]$$

Where t represents the time remaining until the delivery month on the futures contract. (This is a commonly referenced "cost of carry" model used to determine the fair market price of a futures contract on a particular commodity. It may be observed parenthetically, however, that futures prices are affected by expectations of the future balance of supply and demand in an efficient market. Moreover, information that may impact upon such forecasts becomes available unpredictably, and therefore, over the long run, the expected futures price at any given point might well be depicted strictly in terms of this cost of carry model.) If the risk-free rate r equals 10% per annum and annual holding charges are equal to 5% of the commodity's value, the expected price of a futures contract that may be delivered in one year for a commodity presently valued at $100 equals $117:

$$\text{Exp}(F) = \$100[1 + (.10 + .05)^1]$$
$$= \$100(1.15)$$
$$= \$115$$

When someone buys a call option, he is afforded the opportunity to profit from the price appreciation on the underlying physical commodity. But the premium that is invested in an option generally is far less than the purchase price of the physical commodity itself. Hence, the holder of an option on a physical commodity always enjoys a great deal of leverage. *Options on physicals are said, therefore, to have positive leverage value.*

Let's consider the leverage value of options on debt securities. In particular, consider the purchase of a U.S. Treasury bond. When someone buys a T-bond, funds equal to the purchase price are foregone in return for the periodic receipt of an interest payment. If someone buys $100,000 face value of U.S. Treasury bonds with an 8% coupon at their face value, then one is entitled to be reimbursed for the $100,000 face value when the bonds mature and receive 8% or $8,000 annually in the interim. If interest rates in general are greater than 8%, then a wise investor would pay less than the par value of $100,000 to secure the T-bonds. In that case, he would count the difference between the purchase price and the $100,000 face value as part of the return. To illustrate, a $100,000 face value, 20-year bond with an 8% coupon would be sold at approximately 60% of par or $60,000 to yield 14%. The holder's profits are realized in the form of periodic interest payments plus price appreciation represented by the $40,-000 difference between the $100,000 face value returned upon maturity and the $60,000 original purchase price. And if interest rates in general were less than the 8% coupon, then an investor would pay more than the par value to secure the T-bonds.

The relevant question is how does the yield y on the debt security compare to the risk-free rate r, which often is represented by the return on short-term government securities such as U.S. Treasury bills. Generally, the yield on long-term instruments will exceed the return on short-term instruments. Hence, the yield y on T-bonds can normally be expected to exceed the risk-free rate r represented by the T-bill rate. Consider an investor who buys an option for a Treasury bond. The purchase of an option frees up capital equal to the difference between the purchase price of the T-bond and the option premium for alternate investment use. But if the investor applies this freed-up capital at the riskless rate r, then his returns are actually diminished relative to the returns y associated with the purchase of the T-bond. Thus, *where the return on the debt security that is the subject of the option is greater than the risk-free rate, then the option is said to have negative leverage value.*

If $y > r \Rightarrow$ negative leverage value
If $y < r \Rightarrow$ positive leverage value

Normally, long-term instruments will yield more than their short-term counterparts. But sometimes the yield curve may become inverted and long-term investments may yield less than short-term investments. The term "yield curve" comes from a graphic representation of the relationship of long-term and short-term returns (see Figure 5.12). Usually, long-term investments yield more than short term investments. This is intuitive insofar as more adverse financial events may occur in, for example, 20 years than in 3 months. Hence, investors demand higher returns for long-term ventures. But when unusual financial circumstances prevail, the yield y on a Treasury bond that is the subject of an option contract may dip below the risk-free rate r. When this happens, an option buyer can apply the funds represented by the difference between the purchase price of the debt security and the option premium at the

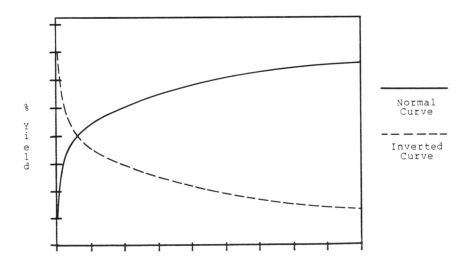

Term Until Maturity
Figure 5.12 The yield curve

risk-free rate r and achieve positive leverage. *When the return on the debt security that is the subject of the option is less than the risk-free rate, then the option is said to have positive leverage value.*

Of course, when the returns on the debt instrument that is the subject of the option contract equals the risk-free rate (when, for example, the subject of the option is a U.S. Treasury bill), then the option has neither positive nor negative leverage value. The price of a debt security S may be compared to the expected price of a futures contract $\text{Exp}(F)$ on that commodity as follows:

$$(5.10) \qquad \text{Exp}(F) = S[1 + (r - y)^t]$$

If the risk-free rate equals 10% per annum and the debt security is yielding 12%, then the expected price of a futures contract that is deliverable in one year for a debt instrument currently valued at $100 equals $98:

$$\text{Exp}(F) = \$100[1+(.10-.12)^1]$$
$$= \$100(.98)$$
$$= \$98$$

FACTORS THAT IMPACT UPON THE OPTION PRICE

When we developed a simplistic model of option pricing, a number of factors were mentioned that affect the fair market price of the option. Perhaps the most critical, but most easily overlooked, factor is the relationship of the strike price to the current price of the underlying commodity. Other factors include interest rates, the term until option expiration, and possible movements in the underlying commodity market, or market volatility. All of these factors were discussed and included implicitly or explicitly within our simplistic option pricing model. Other factors that can have an impact are any payouts that are associated with holding the underlying commodity, carrying costs, and taxes.

Additionally, we have seen how the different types of commodities that may underlie an option can affect the insurance and leverage value associated with the option. The factors that impact upon the price of an option affect insurance and leverage value as well and may have different effects where different types of underlying commodities are considered. Let's explore some of these factors and how they determine the ultimate price of a commodity option.

Underlying Market and Strike Price

The relationship between the price of the underlying commodity and the strike price impacts tremendously on the price of an option. Equation 5.1 depicts this most clearly as the terminal value of an option is defined as the difference between the underlying commodity and the strike price. Where the option is in-the-money, the absolute difference between the market and strike price actually defines the minimum or intrinsic value associated with the option. Therefore, the relationship between the market and strike price generally is the first factor that an option trader will examine when making a pricing assessment.

Fortunately, the relationship between the underlying commodity market and strike prices is directly observable. If a Treasury bond call option has a strike price of 66% of par and the underlying Treasury bond is trading at 68% of par, then the call is 2% of par in-the-money and must be worth at least that amount. If the bond is trading at 64% of par, then the call is out-of-the-money and its intrinsic value equals zero. Of course, if the option in question were a put struck at 66% of par, it would be 2% of par in-the-money when the bond was trading at 64 and 2% of par out-of-the-money when the bond was trading at 68. And, of course, the put option would have an intrinsic value of 2% of par in the former case and zero in the latter case.

Although this was alluded to earlier, the relationship between the market and strike price impacts upon the insurance and leverage value of an option. Consider a put option for gold, struck at $400 when gold was selling for $400, that is, the option is struck at-the-money. This option has a great deal of insurance value because an option holder who is holding gold inventories could be assured that if the price of gold declines significantly, he could always dispose of the metal at $400 or the prevailing price when the option was purchased. But if the option was significantly out-of-the-money such that the strike price was well below the current prevailing price, the put option would have little insurance value. Consider a put option struck at $300 when the prevailing price of gold was $400. In this case, our put holder might take little comfort in the knowledge that he could always sell his gold at $300. On the other hand, the option may be extremely in-the-money. Consider a put option struck at $500 when the market was trading at $400. The put holder who owns this option is in a strong position because he can sell gold at will for $100 per ounce over prevailing prices. But while the insurance value of an option that is extremely in-the-money may be high, this is negated by other considerations as we will see below.

The insurance value of an option grows higher when the option is farther in-the-money. Counteracting that effect is the fact that as the option is farther in-the-money, its leverage value diminishes. Consider the put option struck at $500 when the underlying gold market is trading at $400. The option is $100 in-the-money and the option holder would be required to buy the option for at least $100. But when an option is purchased, the premium generally is passed from buyer to seller in cash. This implies some opportunity cost associated with buying the option. Moreover, this diminishes the leverage value of the option because the investment in the option becomes larger. Since the option holder must pay at least the intrinsic value to secure the option, it makes little sense to buy an option that is extremely in-the-money despite its high insurance value. An analogy can be drawn between two different fire insurance policies, one that offers a great deal of protection for a correspondingly handsome premium and another that offers a relatively modest degree of protection but for a much lower price.

The relationship between the underlying market and strike price affects options on any type of commodity—futures contracts, physical commodities, or interest-bearing securities. But the effect is slightly different on each. Consider an option on a gold futures contract. There is no opportunity cost per se when entering into a futures contract because the margin generally can be put in instruments such as Treasury bills or other interest-bearing securities where no opportunity cost is implicit. But an option for a futures contract must still be purchased for cash. This means that the option has negative leverage value from the start; should the option move farther in-the-money, the more negative that leverage will become. Where an option on a physical commodity is considered, an option on physical gold bullion, for example, the option always has positive leverage value because an option premium will never exceed the full purchase price of the underlying commodity, which must be purchased in cash. Should the option move farther into-the-money, the positive leverage diminishes but it can never become negative. Finally consider an option on an interest-bearing security such as a Treasury bond. A Treasury bond must be purchased in cash but the bond itself generates interest. The leverage value of the bond must be considered by examining the relationship of the short-term interest rate at which an option may be financed to the returns generated by holding the underlying bond. If the bond returns exceed the short-term interest rate, then the option has negative leverage value, and if the bond returns are less than the short-term rate, then the option has positive leverage. In any case, the farther the option is in-the-money, the less leverage associated with the option. If the option begins with negative leverage, its leverage value becomes more negative should the option move farther into-the-money. If the option begins with positive leverage value, its leverage value diminishes as it is farther in-the-money, but it cannot become negative as the option premium cannot exceed the purchase price of the underlying commodity.

The relationship between the market and the strike price defines the intrinsic value of an option. But we know that an option premium may be a good deal greater than the intrinsic value; this excess over and above intrinsic value represents, of course, the extrinsic or time value associated with the option. The option's intrinsic value plus extrinsic value equals the total value of the option premium. Table 5.1 examines the relationship between intrinsic and extrinsic value for options on futures contracts, on physical commodities, and actual debt securities:

Table 5.1 provides a convenient way to compare the two components of an option premium. Note that while the option's intrinsic value grows continually as a function of the in-the-money amount, the option's extrinsic value is greatest when the option is at-the-money and diminishes as the option moves farther into- or out-of-the-money. Table 5.2 compares these prices to the prices of an option on a physical commodity.

Tables 5.1 and 5.2 can be used conveniently to compare the pricing charac-

TABLE 5.1 INTRINSIC AND EXTRINSIC VALUE OF A CALL ON A FUTURES CON-
TRACT[a]

Underlying Market Price	Intrinsic Value	+	Extrinsic Value	=	Total Value
$120	$20		$0.00		$20.00
115	15		0.54		15.54
110	10		1.18		11.18
105	5		2.93		7.93
100	0		4.64		4.64
95	0		2.86		2.86
90	0		1.16		1.16
85	0		0.43		0.43
80	0		0.13		0.13

[a] Where the exercise price equals $100; market volatility is 25%; there are 90 days to expiration; and short-term interest rates equal 12%.

TABLE 5.2 INTRINSIC AND EXTRINSIC VALUE OF A CALL ON A PHYSICAL COM-
MODITY[a]

Underlying Market Price	Intrinsic Value	+	Extrinsic Value	=	Total Value
$120	$20		$3.79		$23.79
115	15		4.05		19.05
110	10		4.58		14.58
105	5		5.18		10.18
100	0		6.62		6.62
95	0		4.23		4.23
90	0		1.93		1.93
85	0		0.79		0.79
80	0		0.25		0.25

teristics of the two options. Because the exercise price is set at $100 for the hypothetical commodity, one can easily compare premiums on the basis of the percentage in- or out-of-the-money. For example, where a call option on a futures contract is 10% in-the-money (where the underlying market price is $110), the premium equals $11.18 or 11.18% of the exercise price. By contrast, the premium for a comparable option on a physial commodity equals $14.58 or 14.58% of the exercise price.

Note that at all levels, the extrinsic value associated with the option on a physical commodity is greater than the extrinsic value associated with an option on a futures contract. This is due simply to the fact that a physical commodity must generally be purchased for cash while a futures contract may be secured for noncash items. Thus an option on a physical security has more leverage value than an option on a futures contract. Moreover, the expected returns on a physical commodity are positive because there is a cash investment

TABLE 5.3 INTRINSIC AND EXTRINSIC VALUE OF A CALL ON AN ACTUAL SECU-RITY[a]

Underlying Market Price	Intrinsic Value	+	Extrinsic Value	=	Total Value
$120	$20		$0.00		$20.00
115	15		0.05		15.05
110	10		0.76		10.76
105	5		2.61		7.61
100	0		4.40		4.40
95	0		2.36		2.36
90	0		1.06		1.06
85	0		0.39		0.39
80	0		0.11		0.11

[a] Where the exercise price equals $100; market volatility is 25%; there are 90 days to expiration; short-term interest rates equal 12%; and the yield on the underlying security is 14%.

in the commodity. Therefore, the price of the commodity is expected to increase over time to cover the opportunity cost represented by a short-term interest rate plus the holding costs associated with the investment. In other words, the price of the physical commodity is expected to trend upward over the life of the option, driving it farther towards or into-the-money.

Table 5.3 compares these premiums to the premiums associated with an option on an actual security. We see that in the case of the option on an actual security, the extrinsic values are actually less than for comparable options on futures contracts or options on physical commodities. This may be attributed to the fact that the security is yielding, in the example in Table 5.3, a rate in excess of the relevant short-term interest rate. Thus negative leverage is associated with the option because the option investor gives up, in effect, the opportunity to realize a yield in excess of the short-term rate by purchasing the security.

The option's extrinsic or time value is affected by these and other factors discussed in the pages ahead, including market volatility, term until expiration, short-term interest rates, holding costs, payout rates, and taxes.

Market Volatility

Market volatility is a term that refers to the degree of variability in the price of the commodity that underlies an option. Volatility may be measured by the changes in the commodity price from month to month, from week to week, or more commonly, from day to day. Market volatility is an important determinant in the price of an option. If gold prices were expected to increase 10% over the next six months, then a call option might be considered an attractive investment. But the option market may have already adjusted for the anticipated increase and the increase is reflected in the option premium. Assume, however, that the latest reports suggest that gold is now expected to rise 50%

over the next six months. This report is likely to cause option traders to buy calls, bidding up call premiums; and sell puts, driving put premiums lower.

Unfortunately, it is not always easy to predict the direction in which a commodity price will fluctuate over the next few months, let alone the next few days. If we believe that commodity markets in general are "efficient," that is, they adjust completely and almost immediately to any new market information, then it is impossible to forecast the direction the market will move in. Therefore, market volatility is often thought of as market movement in either direction, up or down. Following this school of thought, the relevant consideration is the *absolute* change in price, not the direction in which the price may move.

When we developed our simplistic model of commodity option pricing, we assumed that a commodity price could move up or down, with some probability, in discrete steps or increments. In our examples, we had assumed that commodity price movement occurred in increments of $20. Thus, the price of gold could move from $400 per ounce directly to $420 or $380. But clearly this is absurd because if the price of gold were to fluctuate from $400 to $380, for example, it would likely assume quite a few intervening values on the way such as $399, $392, $388, $385, and so on. In fact, the increments can be much finer than that, for gold may be priced to the nearest penny or even in fractional cents. As a practical matter, then, we might assume that the price of gold can fall, not at some discrete intervals, but at any point along a continuum, or a continuous scale.

If prices moved in discrete increments, they would resemble a step process when graphed as in Figure 5.13. In contrast to a step process, when prices move along a continuous scale, their movement looks smooth and uninterrupted. But

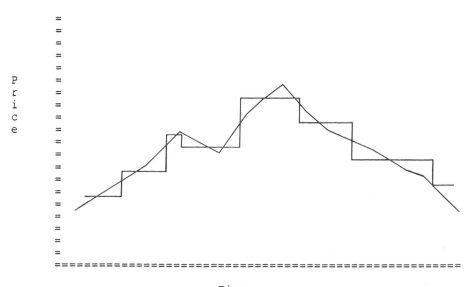

Figure 5.13 Discrete vs. continuous price movements

the jump from a discrete to a continuous movement model is not as dramatic as it appears at first glance. In fact, the continuous process is really an extreme case of a discrete movement process. In our original discrete model, we assumed that gold prices could move up or down by $20 per ounce. What if we assumed that prices could move up or down by only $5 per ounce, $1 per ounce, 1 cent per ounce, or even one-tenth of 1 cent per ounce? If we graphed such movement, we would find that as the increment grows smaller, the graph resembles continuous movement to such an extent that there is no practical distinction.

Thus the variable ϵ_t in equation 5.8 may assume any value along a continuous scale. But how do we get a handle on measuring these fluctuations represented by ϵ_t? To begin, let's assume that these fluctuations are distributed normally in accordance with the familiar bell-shaped curve and that the average fluctuation equals zero. This implies that (where there is no price trend) today's price is the best indication of where tomorrow's price may be and that tomorrow's price, or next week's or next month's price, will be distributed normally as well.

Fortunately, there are statistical tools that we can use to get a handle on the concept of price variability. The statistical measure that can be referenced is called the "standard deviation," often denoted by the Greek letter sigma "σ." As a rule of thumb if the standard deviation equals 10%, for example, of the current commodity price, then you can be 67% certain that the price of the commodity will equal plus or minus 10% of its current value at the end of a year. And you can be 98% certain that the price of a commodity will equal plus or minus two standard deviations or 20% of its current value at the end of a year.

Generally, when calculating the standard deviation of a commodity's price volatility, one takes a series of prices and converts them into rates of return as follows:

(5.11) $$R_t = U_t / U_{t-1}$$

Thus if the price of gold on one day equals $400 and equals $410 the next day, then the rate of return on gold from one day to the next may be calculated as:

$$R_t = 410/400$$
$$= 1.025$$

In other words, the price of gold increased by a factor of 1.025 less 1.0 or 2.5%. If the price of gold instead dropped from $400 to $390, the return may be calculated as:

$$R_t = 390/400$$
$$= .975$$

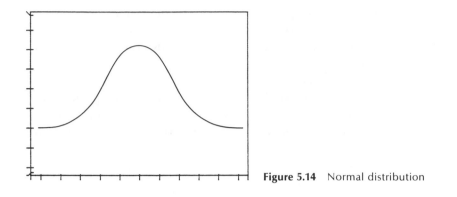

Figure 5.14   Normal distribution

   This indicates that the price is now 97.5% of what it was the previous day or that it dropped by a factor of .975 less 1.0, or 2.5%. Given a series of returns, you can calculate the standard deviation of returns. But before we show that calculation, let's refine the model a bit further. If commodity price movement is normally distributed, this implies that it is equally likely that the price will move up as well as down (see Figure 5.14). But we know that there are natural factors that impede movement in the downward direction. For example, we know that a commodity price can never drop lower than zero—this would imply that sellers have to pay buyers to take a commodity off their hands, clearly an absurd circumstance. Beyond that there are certain natural support levels for a commodity price. If, for example, the price of a commodity declined below the basic cost of production, then producers would cease supplying the commodity and the resulting inadequacy of supplies would drive the price upwards again. Because of these considerations, we must assume that the price of a commodity is "lognormally distributed" (see Figure 5.15). So before we can calculate standard deviation of returns, we must take the natural log of the return, modifying equation 5.11 as follows:

(5.12) $$R_t = \ln(U_t/U_{t-1})$$

   The natural logarithm of 1.025 equals .0247 while the natural logarithim of .975 equals − .0253. This means that a decline in price of $10 is considered more significant than an increase of $10. Given a series of natural log returns, we may calculate the standard deviation of logged returns. Generally, standard deviation is calculated on an annualized basis to assure comparability between two statistics. When calculating standard deviation, you can use daily, weekly, or even monthly returns. As a preliminary step, you must take the average return over the period examined, or:

(5.13) $$\bar{R} = 1/n \sum_{t=1}^{n} R_t$$

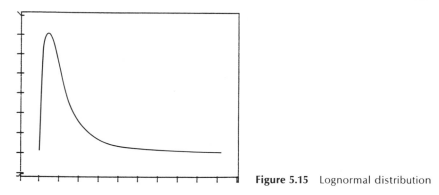

Figure 5.15 Lognormal distribution

Where R refers to the mean return and n equals the number of observations. Let's assume that we're working with daily observations; in that case, the annualized standard deviation of returns may be calculated as:

$$\text{(5.14)} \qquad \sigma = \sqrt{(365/n - 1) \sum_{t=1}^{n} (R_t - \bar{R})^2}$$

If we are working with weekly observations, we would substitute the number 52 for 365; and if monthly observations were used, the number 12 would be substituted for 365. Table 5.4 illustrates how these numbers are calculated using a series of hypothetical commodity prices.

$$\bar{R} = \sum_{t=1}^{n} R_t/n = -.0513/19 = .0027$$

$$\sigma = \sqrt{(365/n - 1) \sum_{t=1}^{n} (R_t - \bar{R})^2}$$

$$= \sqrt{(365/19 - 1)\ .01477}$$

$$= .2995 \text{ or } 29.95\%$$

Market volatility can have an extremely important impact upon the extrinsic value associated with an option. If there is no price volatility at all, of course, an option will have no extrinsic value. Volatility represents the "stochastic" or unknown factor associated with a commodity. It is only where there is some chance that the commodity price will move into-the-money that there will be any interest whatsoever in buying an option. Moreover, there must be some realistic chance of that event occurring; the less realistic the chance, the lower the option premium and the less interest in trading the option.

When volatility is high, an option's insurance and leverage value is high, relative to when volatility is low. The insurance value of an option on a highly variable commodity generally is high because of the risk of adverse price fluc-

TABLE 5.4   CALCULATING STANDARD DEVIATION OF MARKET RETURNS

t	Ut	$\ln(Ut/Ut-1)$	$(Rt - \bar{R})^2$
1	$100	—	—
2	103	.0296	.00104
3	111	.0748	.00601
4	109	−.0181	.00024
5	108	−.0092	.00004
6	112	.0364	.00156
7	110	−.0180	.00023
8	108	−.0183	.00024
9	105	−.0282	.00065
10	107	.0189	.00026
11	105	.0189	.00047
12	105	0	.00026
13	102	−.0289	.00069
14	104	.0194	.00049
15	101	−.2930	.00071
16	98	−.0302	.00075
17	100	.0202	.00052
18	97	−.0305	.00077
19	96	−.0104	.00006
20	95	−.0105	.00006
	Totals	−.0513	.01477

tuation. Where a commodity price is volatile, it can easily move to levels at which commercial interests would be damaged. Under these circumstances, commercial interests may seek out option markets with which to hedge the risk of adverse price fluctuation, or to seek price insurance. By the same token, where price volatility is high, then there is a greater chance that the commodity price will move into-the-money, permitting a profitable exercise. And where greater profits are possible for the same investment, then that investment has greater leverage value.

Table 5.5 examines how the price of a commodity option can be affected under different assumptions about the volatility of the underlying market. It examines the fair value of options on futures contracts, on physical commodities, and on debt securities. Remember that market volatility is expressed as the standard deviation of annualized market returns.

Note that, in all cases, the premium rises if volatility increases. Generally, the premium associated with the physical commodity option is highest and the premium associated with the actual security option is lowest; we will, of course, continue to observe that pattern because of the different price behaviors associated with each underlying commodity.

Term Until Expiration

The extrinsic value of an option is often referred to as its "time value" and for good reason; the term until option expiration represents one of the most important factors that impact upon extrinsic value. A valid rule of thumb is

TABLE 5.5   PREMIUM FOR A CALL OPTION ON A FUTURES CONTRACT, PHYSI-
CAL COMMODITY, AND ACTUAL SECURITY[a]

Underlying Market Volatility	Futures Contract	Physical Commodity	Actual Security
5%	$0.78	$ 3.42	$0.56
10	1.55	4.12	1.70
15	3.11	4.79	2.46
20	3.86	5.88	3.62
25	4.64	6.62	4.39
30	5.42	7.76	5.55
35	6.97	8.92	6.71
40	7.73	9.69	7.09
45	8.50	10.84	8.24
50	9.28	11.63	9.01

[a] Where the exercise price for all options equals $100; the underlying market price is at-the-money or equals $100; there are 90 days to expiration; short-term interest rates are at 12%; the holding costs on the physical commodity are 2% annually; and the yield on the security is 14%.

that, as an option approaches expiration, its extrinsic value declines until expiration when the option's intrinsic value equals its total value (see Figure 5.16). This phenomenon may be attributed to the fact that the insurance value of an option decreases as it approaches expiration. Insurance value is greatest when the option term is longer because there is more possibility that adverse events will occur during a longer time period. By extending the life of the option, one extends the period over which one enjoys its insurance value. This is shown by example in Figure 5.17.

When the life of an option is extended, the probability associated with a

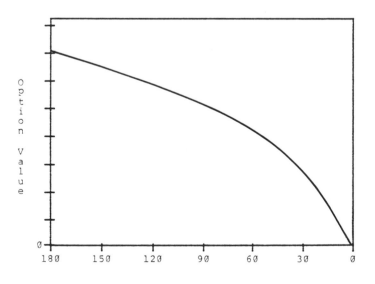

Figure 5.16   Declining time value of an at-the-money option

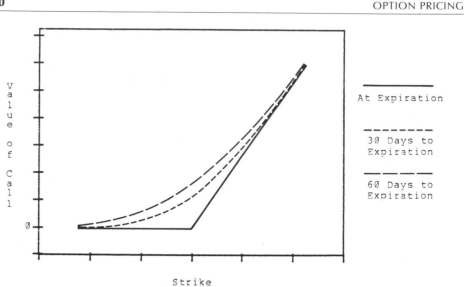

Figure 5.17   Value of call option at different points in time

significant adverse fluctuation is increased. But as discussed above, it is difficult to predict the direction in which a commodity price may fluctuate. So by
the same token, as the life of an option is extended, the probability associated
with a significant favorable price fluctuation is also increased. This means that
whatever leverage value the option has is augmented, the longer the term to
expiration. As we know, the leverage value associated with an option on a physical commodity is always positive; the leverage associated with an option on a
futures contract is always negative; while the leverage associated with an option on an actual security may be positive or negative, depending upon the relationship between the yield on the security and the relevant short-term interest
rate.

Table 5.6 examines how the time value of an option diminishes for the
three different types of commodity options—options on futures, physicals, and
actual securities—as the term until expiration decreases. Because we assume
that the option is struck at-the-money, there is no intrinsic value; rather, the
fair-market premiums derived represent time value exclusively.

Note that, in all cases, the premium falls as the option approaches expiration. Of course, the option on a physical commodity must fall in value faster
because it is worth more to begin with. On the opposite extreme, the option on
the actual security had the least distance to fall because it was valued the least
to start.

Short-Term Interest Rates

Prevailing short-term interest rates can have an effect upon the option premium and its extrinsic value. An option is an investment, and where there is an

TABLE 5.6 PREMIUM FOR A CALL OPTION ON A FUTURES CONTRACT, PHYSI-
CAL COMMODITY, AND ACTUAL SECURITY[a]

Term Until Expiration	Futures Contract	Physical Commodity	Actual Security
360 days	$8.49	$17.48	$7.57
270	8.01	14.36	7.30
180	6.77	10.52	5.91
90	4.64	6.62	4.40
60	3.90	5.21	3.75
30	3.17	3.78	2.68
20	2.38	2.79	2.32
10	1.59	1.79	1.57
0	0	0	0

[a] Where the exercise price for all options equals $100; the underlying market price is at-the-money or equals $100; market volatility is at 25%; short-term interest rates are at 12%; the holding costs on the physical commodity are 2% annually; and the yield on the security is 14%.

investment of capital, some return reasonably is expected. A return is expected because there are alternate investment opportunities available to an investor; so the return expected on an option investment equals the returns foregone on an alternate investment with a similar risk profile. Because an option investment may be rendered riskless by taking on an offsetting position in the underlying commodity market (at least theoretically), the riskless rate of return, commonly represented as the yield on short-term Treasury securities, may be expected on the option investment.

Let's consider how short-term interest rates can affect the option premium. If short-term interest rates rise, then an option investment must yield a larger return to keep pace with alternate investments. This suggests that as short-term rates rise, the option premiums will fall in order to make the option investment attractive to prospective investors. When alternate investments become more attractive to prospective investors, less money is bid for an option premium; consequently, premiums fall and the rate of return on the option investment rises to reflect the increased opportunity costs.

Referring to equation 5.4, we see that the option premium must be discounted by a factor of $1/(1 + r)^t$ in order that the option yield a rate of return r over the term until expiration t. But this analysis may be refined; just as we have assumed that commodity prices move along a continuum, not over discrete intervals, we may assume that interest is compounded continuously. Therefore, instead of the simple discount factor of $1/(1 + r)^t$, we use e^{-rt} where e is the base of the natural logarithm.

Let's consider what the premium associated with options on different types of commodities would look like. First, start with an option for a futures contract. Assume that the option is struck at-the-money at $100; market volatility is 25%; and there are 90 days until expiration. Under these circumstances, the option would have a fair market value of:

Short-Term Interest Rate	Call Option Premium
8%	$4.69
10	4.66
12	4.64
14	4.62
16	4.60

As we can see, as short-term rates go up, the premium associated with an option on a futures contract diminishes. But the decline in the option premium is relatively slight. As mentioned above, there is no investment per se in a futures contract because it may generally be margined with Treasury bills where no opportunity cost is implied. This is not to say that fluctuating short-term rates do not affect commodity prices. Holding futures prices constant, the price of the commodity underlying the futures contract may be expected to decline as short-term rates decrease and increase as short-term rates increase. Holding the price of a commodity underlying a futures contract constant, the futures price will increase as short-term rates decrease and futures will decline as short-term rates increase. Effectively, our model applies the assumption that *futures will remain constant and that underlying prices will fluctuate in response to changing short-term rates.* This assumption is applied throughout the following analysis.

Compare this to a physical commodity. When an investor purchases a physical commodity, he generally must pay in cash; there is an investment in the commodity for which a positive return is expected. At a minimum, an investor generally expects this return to equal the opportunity cost associated with the funds invested, which is represented by two components, short-term interest rates and holding costs. Equation 5.9 reconciled the price of a physical commodity P with the expected price of a futures contract on that physical commodity $\text{Exp}(F)$ considering short-term rates r and holding costs h as:

$$\text{Exp}(F) = P\left[1 + (r + h)^t\right]$$

This equation assumes simple interest; converting into a continuously compounding model we have:

(5.15) $$\text{Exp}(F) = Pe^{(r + h)t}$$

This model suggests that as short-term rates increase, the return on a physical commodity likewise should increase. If the price of a physical commodity is expected to increase over time, then it will trend into-the-money in the case of a call option, and out-of-the-money in the case of a put option. Where a commodity price is expected to move favorably, then the option on that commodity will sell at a higher premium. To illustrate, consider these fair market put and call premiums for an option on a physical commodity. These options are struck at-the-money at $100; market volatility is 25%, there are 90 days to expiration; and holding costs are 2% annually:

Short-Term Interest Rate	Call Option Premium	Put Option Premium
8%	$6.07	$3.63
10	6.35	3.42
12	6.62	3.21
14	6.91	3.02
16	7.21	2.85

Thus, as short-term interest rates increase, premiums for calls on physical commodities can be expected to increase while put option premiums will decrease. This may be explained simply in terms of leverage. Where the underlying commodity is expected to move favorably, greater profits are possible, and where greater profits are possible for a given investment, the option holder enjoys greater leverage. Of course, this leverage is reflected in the option premium.

Holding costs can similarly affect the price of an option on a physical commodity. In our model, holding costs are represented as an annualized percentage of the value of the commodity. Thus holding costs h may be added to the short-term interest rate r in equation 5.14 to produce total carrying costs. Since holding costs and short-term interest rates are treated similarly, then the effects will also be similar. As holding costs increase, the premiums associated with calls on physical commodities increase and the premiums associated with puts decrease.

Finally, consider options for interest-bearing securities. These options may have either positive or negative leverage value, depending upon the relationship between the relevant short-term interest rate and the yield on the secuurity. If the security was yielding a higher rate than the applicable short-term rate, then the option would possess negative leverage; if the security was yielding a lower rate than the applicable short-term rate, then the option would possess positive leverage. Equation 5.10 reconciles the price of a security S to the expected price of a futures contract $Exp(F)$ on that security considering short-term rates r and yield y as:

$$Exp(F) = S[1 + (r - y)^t]$$

This equation also assumes simple interest; converting into a continuously compounding model we have:

(5.16) $$Exp(F) = Se^{(r - y)t}$$

This model suggests that, where short-term rates exceed security yields (negative leverage), the security price may trend down over time relative to a stable futures market. Likewise, if short-term rates are less than security yields (positive leverage), the security price may trend up over time relative to a stable futures market. Where there is more leverage associated with an option investment, call premiums will rise and put premiums decline. Let's illustrate this by deriving fair market premiums for puts and calls on a security. These options are struck at-the-money at $100; market volatility is 25%, and there are 90 days to expiration. For the purposes of this illustration, let's hold yield constant at 14% and look at a range of short-term interest rates.

Short-Term Interest Rate	Call Option Premium	Put Option Premium
8%	$3.97	$5.41
10	4.18	5.14
12	4.40	4.87
14	4.62	4.62
16	4.85	4.37

Note that as short-term rates increase and as leverage becomes increasingly positive, call premiums increase and put premiums decline. Where there is negative leverage, that is, yield is less than the applicable short-term rate, the put premium exceeds the call premium; where there is positive leverage, that is, yield is greater than the applicable short-term rate, the call premium exceeds the put premium. And, where there is no leverage, that is, yield equals the short-term rate, call premiums equal put premiums.

Thus far, we have assumed that the relevant short-term interest rate could be represented by the yield on Treasury bills. But is this assumption valid? There are three factors that call this assumption into question:

1. Option investors cannot perfectly hedge their option positions and may demand returns in excess of the risk-free rate.
2. Investors cannot typically borrow and lend without limit at the same interest rate.
3. The relevant short-term interest rate is likely to change during the life of the option.

It may be difficult perfectly to hedge an option position in the underlying commodity market. For example, it may be difficult for many individuals to sell physical commodities short to cover a long call or short put position. Even if it were possible, it is unlikely that these covering transactions will perfectly hedge risk in the option market. This means that there is always some risk in trading options even if the option position is covered by positions in the underlying commodity. This also means that option traders may demand returns in excess of the risk-free rate on their option positions. (Likewise, the holder of a physical commodity may understandably view such a position as a risky proposition and may view his opportunity costs represented by the risk-free rate in equation 5.9 to be greater than the risk-free rate.) Hence, the relevant short-term interest rate may be higher than the risk-free rate.

The applicable short-term interest rate is the rate at which an investor would otherwise invest funds applied in an option transaction. But an option enthusiast may also borrow funds to trade in options. Unfortunately, most traders cannot borrow and lend at the same rate; typically, investors can borrow at one rate and lend at a somewhat lower rate. But which rate of these two—the lending or the borrowing rate—is the most applicable? The prudent trader will normally derive the fair market premium under both assumptions or split the difference between the two rates.

Finally, we have assumed that the short-term rate is applicable over the life of the option contract. Clearly, however, short-term rates are subject to change. This means that the option premium may reflect the average short-term interest rate anticipated over the life of the option rather than today's rate. In addition, we cannot expect changing short-term rates to exert no influence whatsoever upon the price of a particular commodity underlying the option. The most obvious example of this phenomenon may be identified as financial commodities such as T-bonds or T-bills. Obviously, if short-term rates change, the price of a T-bill that may underlie an option contract is likely to change insofar as short-term rates and T-bill rates are one and the same. Similarly, if short-term rates increase or decrease, then long-term rates such as those represented by the T-bond are likely to increase or decrease accordingly. Beyond that, short-term rates influence the price of other commodities. The price of gold, silver, and even agricultural commodities are influenced to one extent or another by fluctuating short-term rates. Our examples of option premiums and the change in premiums corresponding to changing short-term rates uniformly applied the simple assumption that all other things, including the price of the underlying commodity, would remain static when short-term rates change. Clearly, this is an unrealistic assumption and so care must be taken when examining the results included in this section.

OPTION PRICING MODEL

The option literature is deeply indebted to Professors Black and Scholes whose classic derivation of a stock option pricing model forms the basis of most option pricing models in use today. The formula derived by Black and Scholes takes into account factors such as market volatility, term until expiration, short-term interest rates, and the relationship between market and exercise prices. Unfortunately, it isn't possible to glance at the formula and glean any insight into how it was derived.

Earlier in this chapter, we have developed a simple model of option pricing, under the assumption that commodity futures prices moved in discrete intervals. Referencing equation 5.6 we have:

$$C = 1/(1 + r)^t \sum_{i = k}^{n} P(U_i)\,(U_i - E)$$

TABLE 5.7 EFFECTS OF MARKET CONDITIONS ON A CALL OPTION PREMIUM

Option (on a —)	Increased Short-Term Interest Rates	Increased Price Volatility	Increased Time Until Expiration
Futures contract			
Insurance value	0	+	+
Leverage value	−	+	+
Overall effect	−	+	+
Physical commodity			
Insurance value	0	+	+
Leverage value	+	+	+
Overall effect	+	+	+
Security			
Insurance value	0	+	+
Leverage value	+ or −[a]	+	+ or −[a]
Overall effect	+ or −[a]	+	+

[a] Leverage value may be positive or negative depending upon the relationship between the yield earned on the security and the alternate short-term investment rate.

Now let's convert this formula to its continuous time equivalent:

$$C = e^{-rt} \int_{i=k}^{\infty} N(U_i)\ (U_i - E)dU_i$$

Where N refers to the normal probability distribution, which we assume characterizes commodity price movement. Although we won't illustrate the mathematics involved, this leads us to a form of the Black–Scholes model that is applicable to options on commodity futures:

(5.17)
$$C = e^{-rt}[UN(d_1) - EN(d_2)]$$

where $d_1 = \dfrac{\ln(U/E) + \sigma^2\, t/2}{\sigma\, \sqrt{t}}$

$$d_2 = d_1 - \sigma\, \sqrt{t}$$

Options on Different Commodities

As mentioned above, there are a number of different commodities that could underlie an option contract, including futures contracts, physical commodities, and debt securities. Table 5.7 examines the effects of market conditions on such option contracts. Each of these underlying commodities behave differently so different pricing formulas must be applied for each. Equations 5.15 and 5.16 provide formulas by which to reconcile the price of a physical commodity or a debt security, respectively, with the price of a futures contract thereon. The option pricing model presented in equation 5.17 may be used in the context of options on futures. This means that the price of the underlying commodity U referenced in equation 5.17 equals the price of the subject futures contract F, or $U = F$. Similarly, we may substitute the righthand sides of equations 5.15 and 5.16 into the option pricing formula for U and derive the formula used to determine the fair market value of options on physical commodities and on debt securities.

For options on physical commodities, we have:

(5.18)
$$C = Pe^{ht}N(d_1) - e^{-rt}EN(d_2)$$

$$\text{where } d_1 = \frac{\ln(P/E) + (r + h + \sigma^2/2)t}{\sigma \sqrt{t}}$$

$$d_2 = d_1 - \sigma \sqrt{t}$$

For options on debt securities:

(5.19)
$$C = Se^{-yt}N(d_1) - e^{-rt}EN(d_2)$$

$$\text{where } d_1 = \frac{\ln(S/E) + (r - y + \sigma^2/2)t}{\sigma \sqrt{t}}$$

$$d_2 = d_1 - \sigma \sqrt{t}$$

Using the Formulas

Now that we have arrived at formulas that may be used to calculate the fair market value of commodity option premiums, let's illustrate the use of the formulas. First, let's look at the calculation for the price of an option on a futures contract; specifically, let's consider an option for a Treasury bond futures contract. For the purposes of the calculation, we need to know the values for the term to expiration t, market volatility σ, short-term interest rates r, the underlying futures price U, and the exercise price E. Assume that:

$$U = 58\% \text{ of par}$$
$$E = 60\% \text{ of par}$$
$$\sigma = 20\% \text{ or } .20$$
$$t = 180 \text{ days}; 180/365 = .49 \text{ year}$$
$$r = 12\% \text{ or } .12$$

The call premium on the T-bond futures under these circumstances may be calculated as:

$$C = e^{-(.12)(.49)}[58N(d_1) - 60N(d_2)]$$

$$\text{where } d_1 = \frac{\ln(58/60) + (.2^2/2)(.49)}{.2 \sqrt{.49}}$$

$$= -.1721$$

$$\text{and } d_2 = -.1721 - .2 \sqrt{.49}$$

$$= -.3121$$

$N(-.1721)$ and $N(-.3121)$ may be found by referencing tables for the normal probability distribution provided in the appendix. They are:

$$N(-.1721) \cong .4325$$

$$N(-.3121) \cong .3783$$

When these values are replaced in the formula, we have:

$$C = e^{-(.12)(.49)}[58(.4325) - 60(.3783)]$$

$$= 2.24 \text{ or } \$2,240 \text{ per } \$100,000 \text{ face value contract}$$

Now let's look at the calculation for the price of an option on a physical commodity, specifically, for an option on gold bullion. In addition to the information needed to calculate an option on a futures contract, we also need the holding costs h expressed as an annual percentage of the value of the commodity. Let's assume that:

$$P = \$407 \text{ per ounce}$$
$$E = \$400 \text{ per ounce}$$
$$\sigma = \$40\% \text{ or } .40$$
$$t = 60 \text{ days; } 60/365 = .16 \text{ year}$$
$$r = 12\% \text{ or } .12$$
$$h = 2\% \text{ or } .02$$

Referring to equation 5.18, the fair value of a call option on gold bullion may be calculated as:

$$C = 407e^{(.02)(.16)}N(d_1) - e^{-(.12)(.16)}400N(d_2)$$

$$\text{where } d_1 = \frac{\ln(407/400) + [.12+.02+(.4^2/2)](.16)}{.4 \sqrt{.16}}$$

$$= -.3284$$

$$\text{and } d_2 = -.3284 - .4 \sqrt{.16}$$

$$= -.1684$$

Again, the values of $N(.3284)$ and $N(.1684)$ may be found by referring to the normal probability distribution table in Appendix A.

$$N(-.3284) \cong .6293$$

$$N(-.1684) \cong .5675$$

Substituting these values into the formula:

$$C = 407e^{(.02)(.16)}(.6293) - e^{-(.12)(.16)}400(.5675)$$

$$= \$34.26 \text{ per ounce}$$

Finally, let's calculate the value of an option on an actual security. To make this calculation, we need to know the yield y on the security in addition to the information needed to calculate the value of options on other types of commodities. Assume that the security in question is a Treasury bond and:

$$P = 71\% \text{ of par}$$
$$E = 68\% \text{ of par}$$
$$\sigma = 25\% \text{ or } .25$$
$$t = 45 \text{ days; } 45/365 = .12 \text{ year}$$
$$r = 12\% \text{ or } .12$$
$$y = 14\% \text{ or } .14$$

Referring to equation 5.19, the fair market value of a call option on a Treasury bond under the circumstances described above may be derived as:

$$C = 71e^{-(.14)(.12)}N(d_1) - e^{-(.12)(.12)}68N(d_2)$$

$$\text{where } d_1 = \frac{\ln(71/68) + [.12 - .14 + (.25^2/2)](.12)}{.25 \sqrt{.12}}$$

$$= .5140$$

$$\text{and } d_2 = .5140 - .25 \sqrt{.12}$$

$$= .4273$$

The values of $N(.5140)$ and $N(.4273)$ are found by reference to the normal probability distribution table in Appendix A as:

$$N(.5140) \cong .6950$$

$$N(.4273) \cong .6628$$

Substituting these values into the formula:

$$C = 71e^{-(.14)(.12)}(.6950) - e^{-(.12)(.12)}68(.6628)$$

$$= 4.09 \text{ or } \$4,090 \text{ per } \$100,000 \text{ face value contract}$$

Calculating Delta

An important extra benefit associated with equations 5.17, 5.18, and 5.19 is that the delta factor is derived during the course of calculating the option's fair market value. Recall that the delta factor is a measure of the expected change in the price of the option relative to a change in the price of the underlying commodity. The delta factor may be applied to determine the "neutral" ratio of option to underlying commodity units needed to perfectly offset changes in the value of the option position with changes in the value of the position in the underlying commodity market. The delta factor will enter into the discussion often, in the context of arbitrage strategies and commercial option applications.

Delta will vary from zero to one for a call option, and from zero to negative one for a put option. This implies that option premium fluctuations may be negligible or display a close positive or negative correspondence with the changing value of the underlying commodity. Typically, call options that are at-the-money will be associated with a delta of about .5, indicating that call premium movements will equal about 50% of a fluctuation in the underlying commodity. When an option is extremely out-of-the-money, delta will approach zero. When the option is extremely in-the-money, delta will approach one, in the case of a call, or negative one, in the case of a put, as the option's extrinsic value becomes negligible and the premium becomes a function of the in-the-money amount.

Delta is sensitive to changes in option volatility, term to expiration, and prevailing interest rates but the relationship between market and strike price nevertheless is the most important determinant. Because delta changes when market conditions change, a neutral ratio is valid only over relatively short periods over relatively narrow price ranges. This implies that an option arbitrageur or hedger must constantly monitor market conditions and adjust the ratio of options to underlying commodity frequently.

We had stated that the Black–Scholes model may be used to calculate delta. Specifically, delta may be referenced, in the case of an option on a security or a physical commodity as $N(d_1)$, and as $e^{-rt}N(d_1)$ in the case of an option exercisable for a futures contract. Let's use these formulas to calculate the value of delta over a range of market values. Specifically, Table 5.8 displays deltas for calls on futures, physicals, and securities. For the purposes of these calculations, we assumed that the strike price equals $100, market volatility is 25%, short-term rates are at 12%, holding costs on the physical commodity are 2%, and the yield on the security is 14%.

TABLE 5.8   DELTA FOR CALLS ON FUTURES CONTRACT, PHYSICAL COMMODITY, AND ACTUAL SECURITY

Underlying Market Volatility	Futures Contract	Physical Commodity	Actual Security
$120	.97	.97	1.00
115	.85	.93	.87
110	.78	.87	.79
105	.66	.78	.66
100	.50	.63	.51
95	.35	.47	.35
90	.20	.30	.20
85	.11	.17	.10
80	.04	.07	.04

Over most levels, the delta factors associated with calls on physical commodities exceed the delta factors associated with calls on futures or securities. To understand this phenomenon, we must go back to our discussion of the relative influence of the intrinsic and extrinsic components of the premium over different underlying market price levels. Generally, the extrinsic value associated with calls on physicals exceeds the extrinsic value associated with calls on futures or securities. This is due to the fact that generally more leverage is associated with options on physicals than on futures or securities. We had explained that, generally speaking, delta rises where an option moves farther into-the-money. Conceptually, an increased degree of option leverage is analogous to increasing the in-the-money amount of an option. Thus calls with greater leverage will generally be associated with higher deltas.

Implied Volatility

One of the most difficult problems associated with using these equations to derive the fair market value of an option is to determine the appropriate figures to input into the formulas. It is quite easy, of course, to determine the current value of the underlying commodity, the strike price, and the term to maturity—these figures are readily observable upon inspection. As discussed previously, it is sometimes difficult to determine factors including the relevant short-term interest rate. But at least conceptually, this problem is trivial and may be overcome by carefully determining what the relevant rate is for the individual trader (rather than the marketplace as a whole). Unfortunately, market volatility, as measured by the standard deviation of daily market returns, is not so readily observable.

One may, of course, use an historical series of market returns and calculate a standard deviation in accordance with equation 5.13. But there are some problems associated with that derivation. The first problem involves determining the appropriate historical sample to utilize. One may use an historical series over the last 10, 30, 60, 90, days or more—but which one? Rationally, one must expect the most recent data to be more reflective of current market conditions. This suggests that more recent data be accorded greater weights. But what weights should be employed?

The option trader's intent in determining an historical standard deviation of market returns is to find a value that will be reflective of futures movements. Past movements should be indicative of future movements to some extent; however, their predictive power may be limited in a market where conditions are subject to rapid change. As a result, many traders routinely attempt to derive, not the historical volatility to input into the options pricing model, but what is known as the "implied volatility." The implied volatility is nothing more than the volatility that the marketplace in the aggregate expects will be realized. This figure is "implied" in the current market price.

Our equations used to derive the fair market value of an option consider that fair market value to be a function of the current underlying market price, the exercise price, the term to expiration, short-term interest rates, and other factors (in the case of an option for a physical commodity or for an actual security) in addition to market volatility. In other terms, $C = f(U, E, t, \sigma, r, \ldots)$. If we are able to find a function that provides us with the value for the option premium given certain inputs, surely we must be able to find some function that provides us with a measure of implied volatility given the current value of the premium in addition to these other factors, that is, $\sigma = f(C, U, E, t, r, \ldots)$. Unfortunately, if we attempt to solve our equations for the fair market value of an option for the volatility term, we would find an unsolvable polynomial equation. This suggests that other methods must be employed in order to derive this implied volatility.

Fortunately, other methods are available, but must be put into practice with the aid of a computer. The method that is employed is an "iterative process" and involves taking an initial guess as to what the implied volatility may be and then taking successively finer approximations. In other words, we input all variables into our option pricing model, including a guess as to what the standard deviation of market returns may be. Based upon this set of inputs, we derive a fair market value for the premium and compare this to the prevailing premium in the marketplace. If the derived premium is greater than the market premium, we know that our estimate for volatility is too high; if the derived premium is lower than the market premium, we know that our estimate for volatility is too low. We then adjust our guess and keep on adjusting until the derived premium is within a comfortable tolerance to the market premium. At this point, we have found our implied volatility—or the marketplace's estimate of current volatility.

Several words of caution are in order when deriving this implied volatility. First of all, when making these volatility calculations, you should use it to derive the volatility implied by the most active option series. Generally, the more active a particular market is, the more efficient that market will be. In many respects, there are as many option markets as there are option series and the most active generally will be the most efficient insofar as it should provide the most accurate indicators of "true" market conditions. Beyond that, the ambitious option trader may want to calculate the volatilities implied by all option series and take an average of those implied volatilities, weighted perhaps by the percentage of activity in each. Additionally, it is often advisable to calculate a different implied volatility for each option class. Volatility changes over time and if the marketplace expects a rather stable market in the short term and an uncertain market in the long term, then the market may in effect be using different volatilities for different option classes.

Put/Call Parity

Thus far, our discussion of option pricing has centered about the evaluation of calls while puts have largely been ignored. Put option pricing is conceptually similar to call option pricing subject to one major reversal: a call is an option to buy; a put is an option to sell. The farther an option is in-the-money, the more valuable it will become. Since the definitions of in- and out-of-the-money are simply reversed for put and call options, it's relatively straightforward to determine how the pricing model for puts varies from the pricing model for calls.

The put option premium P on a futures contract may be calculated by modifying equation 5.17 only slightly:

(5.20) $$P = -e^{-rt}[UN(-d_1) - EN(-d_2)]$$

The only differences between equations 5.20 and 5.17 are that we attach a negative sign to d_1, to d_2, and to the equation as a whole where a put is evaluated. (Similar adjustments are required to calculate the premium associated with puts on securities and physical commodities.) In order to illustrate the use of this formula in order to evaluate the fair market value of a put exercisable for a futures contract, consider the same scenario examined in the context of a call on a T-bond futures contract (although we won't provide examples of how to make these calculations for puts on physical commodities or for securities, again, the adjustments to the call pricing formulas are analogous):

$$U = 58\% \text{ of par}$$
$$E = 60\% \text{ of par}$$
$$\sigma = 20\% \text{ or } .20$$
$$t = 180 \text{ days; } 180/365 = .49 \text{ year}$$
$$r = 12\% \text{ or } .12$$

The put premium on the T-bond futures under the foregoing circumstances may be calculated as:

$$P = -e^{-(.12)(.49)}[58N(-d_1) - 60N(-d_2)]$$
$$\text{where } d_1 = \frac{\ln(58/60) + (.2^2/2)(.49)}{.2 \sqrt{.49}}$$
$$= -.1721$$
$$\text{and } d_2 = -.1721 - .2 \sqrt{.49}$$
$$= -.3121$$

The values for $N(-d_1)$ and $N(-d_2)$ may be found by referencing tables for the normal cumulative probability distribution provided in Appendix A. They are:

$$N(-.1721) \cong .5675$$
$$N(-.3121) \cong .6217$$

When these values are inserted into our formula, we have:

$$P = -e^{-(.12)(.49)}[58(.5675) - 60(.6217)]$$
$$= 4.14 \text{ or } \$4,140 \text{ per } \$100,000 \text{ face value contract}$$

Equation 5.20 may also be expressed by the following equation:

(5.21) $$P = C - e^{-rt}(U - E)$$

If one were to calculate the price of a call under these same circumstances, one would find that $C = 2.25$. Substituting this value in equation 5.21, we can confirm that this equation yields the same results as equation 5.20:

$$P = 2.25 - e^{-(.12)(.49)}(58 - 60)$$
$$= 4.14$$

Because the definitions of in- and out-of-the-money are simply reversed for put and call options, there is an inverse relationship between the price of the two instruments. Consider puts and calls on a futures contract where the exercise price equals $100, market volatility is at 25%, there are 90 days to expiration, and short-term interest rates are at 12%.

Underlying Market Price	Put Premium	Call Premium
$120	$ 0.36	$20.00
115	0.98	15.53
110	1.47	11.18
105	3.08	7.94
100	4.64	4.64
95	7.71	2.86
90	10.86	1.16
85	15.00	0.43
80	20.00	0.13

Note that the price of an in-the-money put generally is lower than a comparable in-the-money call. For example, where the put is $10 in-the-money (where the underlying market price equals $90), the premium equals $10.86. Where the call is $10 in-the-money (where the underlying market price equals $110), the premium equals $11.18 or $0.32 higher than the put. This may be explained when we consider that market volatility generally increases with the absolute price level. In this case, we assumed that market volatility (as measured by the standard deviation of market returns) equals 25%. But 25% of $110 exceeds 25% of $90. So while market volatility may remain constant as a percentage of the current price, it decreases absolutely when the commodity price is lower. Thus it's more likely that the call will move an additional $10 in-the-money than the put. For the same reasons, an out-of-the-money put is valued at a higher premium than an out-of-the-money call.

When we consider the relationship between put and call options on underlying instruments such as physical commodities or securities, the leverage associated with the option plays an important role. An option on a physical commodity will always have positive leverage, just as an option on a futures contract will always have negative leverage. This illustration derives the fair market value of puts and calls on a physical commodity, where the exercise price equals $100, market volatility is 25%, there are 90 days to expiration, short-term rates are at 12%, and holding costs are 2%:

Underlying Market Price	Put Premium	Call Premium
$120	$ 0.28	$23.79
115	0.57	19.05
110	1.16	14.58
105	1.75	10.18
100	3.21	6.62
95	5.84	4.23
90	10.00	1.93
85	15.00	0.79
80	20.00	0.75

Because an option on a physical commodity has positive leverage, the values of calls will generally exceed the values of comparable puts. For example, where puts and calls are in-the-money by $10, the call premium of $14.58 exceeds the put premium of $10.00 by $4.58. Likewise, where puts and calls are out-of-the-money by $10, the call premium of $1.93 exceeds the put premium of $1.16 by $0.77. A call holder participates in the price appreciation associated with a physical commodity without incurring the carrying costs associated with owning the commodity. A put holder, by contrast, must stand ready to deliver the commodity upon exercise and by implication bears the carrying costs associated with the physical commodity. Thus call options on physical commodities will generally be priced over comparable put options.

Finally, consider puts and calls on an actual security. Recall that an option on a security may have positive or negative leverage, depending upon the relationship between short-term interest rates and the yield on the security. Where rates exceed the yield, the option has positive leverage, and where the reverse is true, the option has negative leverage. This illustration assumes that the exercise price of the puts and calls on an actual security equals $100, market volatility equals 25%, there are 90 days to expiration, short-term rates are at 12%, and the underlying security yields 14%. Because the yield exceeds the short-term rate, the option has negative leverage.

Underlying Market Price	Put Premium	Call Premium
$120	$ 0.39	$20.00
115	1.04	15.06
110	1.58	10.76
105	3.26	7.61
100	4.88	4.40
95	7.66	2.36
90	11.20	1.07
85	15.35	0.39
80	20.00	0.11

In this example, puts are uniformly priced over comparable calls. Where puts and calls are $10.00 in-the-money, the put premium of $11.20 exceeds the call premium of $10.76 by $0.46, and where the puts and calls are $10.00 out-of-the-money, the put premium of $1.58 exceeds the call premiums of $1.07 by $0.51. A call holder effectively foregoes the positive returns associated with holding the underlying security while a put holder by implication receives those returns. Thus put options on actual securities will generally be priced over comparable call options, but only where the options have negative leverage.

Is the Model Valid?

Almost all option pricing models are based in some respect or another on the basic results found by Black and Scholes. This does not imply, however, that the model may be used precisely to forecast the fair market value of any particular option. One must always bear in mind that the model was derived under some rather strict assumptions and, as such, must be applied cautiously. One of the major restrictions under the model is that the option is held until expiration. Of course, an American option may be exercised when expiration is imminent or at any time subsequent to the initial purchase. Thus the holder of an American option is afforded greater flexibility than the holder of a European option, which may be exercised only upon the expiration date. Where the holder has more flexibility, this implies that the option is worth more.

A further restriction associated with the application of the model is an obvious one—if the values that are input into the calculations are suspect, then the results must likewise be suspect. Some inputs including the current underlying market price, the exercise price, and days until option expiration may readily be observed. Some of the difficulties associated with finding reasonable values for market volatility and short-term interest rates have been discussed in previous sections.

Finally, one must question the ease with which the model may be put into practice. Obviously, most option traders cannot readily calculate these fair market values without the aid of a computer. Fortunately, there are many computer software firms that provide services in this respect. There are several firms that offer access to an interactive computer system that will calculate and display the fair market value of an option premium, often using a modified version of the basic Black–Scholes option model. The popularity of many of these services with the professional commodity option trading community underscores the observation that, although it may be difficult to assess the fair market value of an option, such information is highly valued and, if applied with due caution and reference to the model's historic predictive powers, may become an invaluable option trading aid.

Programming Option Premiums

There are many computer software programs available on the market that enable the user to evaluate the fair market premium of an option. Most of these programs address the evaluation of stock options because stock options have been available for a much longer time than many of the "new" commodity option markets. But as shown above, it is relatively easy to modify the Black–Scholes option pricing formula to evaluate options on futures contracts, physical commodities, as well as securities.

Table 5.9 provides a very straightforward way to evaluate premiums for options on futures, securities, or commodities. This program is written in BASIC—an easily learned computer language that is in use on most microcomputer systems.

This program requires the user to identify the instrument that underlies the option contract, either a futures contract (F), a security (S), or a physical commodity (C). It then goes on to query the user regarding whether the option is a put (P) or a call (C), the option exercise or strike price, the number of days until option expiration, the underlying instrument price, price volatility, and the short-term interest rate. If you are evaluating an option on a security or a physical commodity, the program will query you regarding the annual dividend or coupon, or the annual holding costs, respectively. These figures are to be input in percentage terms.

EXAMPLE.   To illustrate the use of this computer program, assume that you want to evaluate the fair value of a call option exercisable for an actual debt security. The call is struck one point in-the-money at 72% of par—the underlying market price equals 73. There are 30 days until expiration; the coupon rate for the debt instrument equals 11.5%; price volatility equals 9.6%; and the short-term interest rate equals 9.1%. You have retained the program code on a microcomputer and RUN the program. Below is what the program asks you and your responses (underlined):

Underlying type (F/S/C)	? S	RETURN
Option type (P/C)	? C	RETURN
Exercise price	? 72	RETURN
Days to expiration	? 30	RETURN
Security price	? 73	RETURN
Annual dividend or coupon	? 11.5	RETURN
Short-term interest rate	? 9.1	RETURN

Theoretical call premium	=	1.12
Delta	=	.62

Thus the program tells you that the fair value call premium under the specified conditions equals 1.12% of par and that delta equals .62.

By entering this code onto the memory banks of a microcomputer, you have taken a first big step towards building a customized option premium evaluation program. In particular, the subroutines that calculate the theoretical option premium and delta and the normal cumulative probability distribution function from the heart of this program.

TABLE 5.9   OPTION PREMIUM AND DELTA COMPUTER PROGRAM

```
10 PRINT"OPTION EVALUATION PROGRAM"
20 PRINT
30 INPUT"    Underlying type (F/S/C)          ";UT$
40 IF UT$<>"F" AND UT$<>"S" AND UT$<>"C" THEN 30
50 INPUT"    Option type (P/C)                ";OT$
60 IF OT$<>"P" AND OT$<>"C" THEN 50
70 INPUT"    Exercise price                   ";E
80 INPUT"    Days to expiration               ";T
90 T=T/365!
100 IF UT$="F " THEN INPUT"   Futures price              ";U
110 IF UT$="S " THEN INPUT"   Security price             ";U
120 IF UT$="C" THEN INPUT"    Commodity price            ";U
130 IF UT$="S " THEN INPUT"   Annual dividend or coupon  ";H
140 IF UT$="C" THEN INPUT"    Annual holding cost        ";H
150 INPUT"    Price volatility          ";V
160 INPUT"    Short-term interest rate   ";R
170 PRINT
180 GOSUB 1000
190 IF OT$="P" THEN 230
200 PRINT USING"   Theoretical call premium= # # # #.# #";CPRE
210 PRINT USING"   Delta                   = #   #.# #"; CDEL
220 PRINT:PRINT:END
230 PRINT USING"   Theoretical put premium= # # # #.# #"; PPRE
240 PRINT USING"   Delta                  = #  -#.# #"; PDEL
250 PRINT:PRINT:END
1000 'OPTION THEORETICAL PREMIUM & DELTA
1010 IF T<=0! THEN 1500
1020 ENRT=EXP(-R*T/100!)
1030 VRT=V*SQR(T)/100!
1040 IF UT$="F" THEN U1=U
1050 IF UT$="S" THEN U1=U/ENRT-H*T
1060 IF UT$="C" THEN U1=U/ENRT+H*T
1070 D1=LOG(U1/E)/VRT+.5*VRT
1080 D2=D1-VRT
1090 X=D1
1100 GOSUB 2000
1110 ND1=NX
1120 X=D2
1130 GOSUB 2000
1140 ND2=NX
1150 CPRE=ENRT*(U1*ND1-E*ND2)
1160 PPRE=CPRE-ENRT*(U1-E)
1170 CDEL=ND1
```

TABLE 5.9   OPTION PREMIUM AND DELTA COMPUTER PROGRAM (Cont'd.)

```
1180 PDEL=1!−ND1
1190 IF UT$="F" THEN CDEL=CDEL*ENRT
1200 IF UT$="F" THEN PDEL=PDEL*ENRT
1210 IF CPRE<(U−E) THEN CPRE=U−E:CDEL=1!
1220 IF PPRE<(E−U) THEN PPRE=E−U:PDEL=1!
1230 RETURN
1500 IF U> E THEN 1600
1510 IF U< E THEN 1700
1520 CPRE=0!:PPRE=0!
1530 CDEL=0!:PDEL=0!
1540 RETURN
1600 CPRE=U−E:PPRE=0!
1610 CDEL=1!:PDEL=0!
1620 RETURN
1700 CPRE=0!:PPRE=E−U
1710 CDEL=0!:PDEL=1!
1720 RETURN
2000 'NORMAL CDF ROUTINE
2010 Z=.3989423*EXP(−.5*X*X)
2020 Y=1!(1!+.2316419* ABS (X))
2030 NX=((((1.330274*Y−1.821256)*Y+1.781478)*Y−.3565638)*Y+.3193815)*Y*Z
2040 IF X>0! THEN NX=1!−NX
2050 RETURN
```

Source: J. Meisner and J. Labuszewski (1984). "Modifying the Black-Scholes Option Pricing Model for Alternative Underlying Instruments." Unpublished paper.

6
Trading Strategies

An option is one of the most flexible forms of contractual agreements ever developed. Options may be used to take advantage of almost any type of market scenario one can imagine. There are option strategies that can be used to exploit the expectation of increasing, decreasing, or stable prices, or of high or low market volatility. Other strategies may be used to exploit situations where an option may be under- or overpriced relative to other options or the underlying commodity. Options may be available with many different strike prices and terms to expiration on the same underlying commodity. Therefore one generally can tailor a strategy close to the needs of the moment.

Although option strategies may be developed that are very diverse in purpose and nature, they all have one thing in common: they are all motivated by the promise of financial reward. Unfortunately, there is no such thing as a "sure" option strategy; for every reward for which the investor grasps, he takes on a corresponding risk. The risks and rewards associated with option trading generally balance when the option is fairly priced, as discussed in Chapter 5. Astute option traders, however, do not look for situations where risk and potential rewards balance; they look for situations where potential rewards seem to outweigh the associated risk. Many option trading strategies are based upon an assessment of the fair market value of an option in relation to the prevailing market price. However, many other option traders employ fundamental or technical analysis to determine the likely price behavior of the commodity underlying the option. Both of these approaches to commodity option trading are valid; the purpose of this chapter is to describe the strategies that may be employed pursuant to a given expectation of the behavior of the underlying commodity relative to the prevailing price.

For purposes of this chapter, we begin by describing the simplest option strategies first and then proceed to the more complicated. The simplest strategies involve a single option. More complicated strategies involve options in combination with a position in the underlying commodity or with options of a different series. Margin requirements that reflect the risk of such strategies are detailed in Appendix B.

OUTRIGHT OPTION TRADING

An "outright" option trade involves the purchase or sale of a single option series. Examples of outright option trades include the purchase of a call option, the sale of a call option, the purchase of a put option, and the sale of a put option. These strategies are the simplest. It is fairly easy to calculate the potential risk and reward associated with these strategies. They are also motivated by a relatively straightforward market forecast.

Let's consider the market forecasts that would motivate an option trader to enter into an outright option trade. A call represents an option to buy the underlying commodity. The purchase of a commodity implies that the investor is expecting upward or bullish price movement. Conversely, a put represents an option to sell the underlying commodity while the sale of a commodity implies that the investor expects downward or bearish price movement. Option holders own the right to buy in the case of a call and sell in the case of a put. Therefore it is the outright *holder* of an option, not the writer, who subscribes to the bullish or bearish forecast, respectively. (It's often confusing to think of a put holder as bearish because he purchases the option and a purchase generally implies a bullish attitude; therefore, one must think of the put holder's rights to sell by virtue of holding the put.) The risks and rewards assumed by the option writer mirror those assumed by the option holder. This implies that writers subscribe to a price forecast directly opposite to that of the holder. Call writers may be called upon to sell the underlying commodity to the call holder and therefore their price predictions are essentially bearish. Put writers may be called upon to buy the underlying commodity and therefore their price predictions are essentially bullish.

We know from Chapter 5, however, that the option premium must be greater than or at a minimum equal to the option's intrinsic value or the amount by which it is in-the-money. When the option holder initially acquires an option, he forfeits the premium. Therefore, he must hope to retrieve that premium and more in order to turn a profit on the trade. Unfortunately, no profit on the option purchase immediately is possible. If the holder sold the option immediately upon purchase, the returns would simply wash out because he buys and sells at the same premium. If he elects to exercise the option immediately, this implies a profit of zero at best and possibly a large loss. If the option is purchased when it is out-of-the-money, a loss would ensue upon exercise, aggravated by the forfeit of the premium. If the option is purchased when it is in-the-money, a profit upon exercise would be implied; but because the premium must be greater than or equal to the in-the-money amount, the net return must be negative or zero.

These facts suggest that the option writer begins at something of an advantage over the option holder because he receives the premium initially. If the market were to remain stable, the writer would be sure to make a profit. In fact, the time value of the option would decline gradually and prevent the holder from selling his long interest at a wash. The holder of an outright put or call could profit only if his respective bearish or bullish price scenario were realized.

Generally, a significant bear or bull move must be realized before the option could become profitable to exercise, in light of the premium forfeit up front. Therefore an option writer may be motivated to enter into an outright short put or call by a neutral expectation or even one where he expects the market to move slightly in the holder's favor (but not so much so, of course, that it obviates the writer's profits).

The motivations behind outright option strategies can be summarized as follows:

PRICE FORECAST OF OUTRIGHT OPTION TRADERS

	Call	Put
Holder	Bullish	Bearish
Writer	Bearish to neutral	Bullish to neutral

Outright option trades may be the most straightforward of all option strategies. However, they generally may be regarded as the most uncertain insofar as they offer a high degree of both risk and potential return. This suggests that it is very important for an outright option trader to carefully time his purchases or sales in order to be reasonably certain of avoiding a large loss. Of course, the returns that accrue to the option holder, whether positive or negative, are mirrored in the returns that accrue to the option writer. Moreover, the holder's profits are potentially unlimited while losses are limited to the premium; the writer's profits, conversely, are limited to the premium and losses are potentially unlimited. This underscores the importance of timing, especially for the holder of an outright short option position. Nevertheless, it remains important to understand the mechanics associated with taking an outright option position.

Some may observe that if one were to subscribe to a bullish or bearish scenario, it may be easier to buy or sell the underlying commodity directly. In particular, it may be quite easy to buy or sell a futures contract because these contracts are traded on low margins relative to the value of the subject commodity, and in a centralized marketplace where price quotes are easily accessible and one can readily buy or sell with equal ease. But outright options and futures strategies are likely to appeal to distinct sets of traders.

In order to profit from price movement by buying or selling options outright, it is necessary to predict, not only the direction, but also the magnitude of the price fluctuation. When buying calls, for example, it is not enough to know that the price of the underlying instrument is expected to increase. If the price movement does not compensate for the premium paid up front, it may be more lucrative to sell calls instead. The successful outright option speculator is likely to be adept at predicting large or long-term price movements. By contrast, a speculator in futures need only attempt to predict the direction of the movement because he may profit from small fluctuations. The successful futures speculator, therefore, is likely to be adept at predicting relatively small or short-term market movements. Additionally, this implies that speculation in option markets is more likely to be based upon an assessment of the fundamental forces of supply and demand, whereas speculation in futures markets may more likely be based upon charting or technical trading techniques.

The operational character of an option market is conducive to long-term positions, whereas a futures market is more conducive to short-term positions. When a speculator buys an option, he is assured that his maximum loss is limited to the premium. Thus he can afford to take a position and wait for his market expectations to materialize. But when a speculator enters into a futures transaction, he cannot be assured of limiting his losses. A futures trader, subject to "market-to-market," must pay his losses and collect his profits daily in cash. As such, the speculative strategies characteristic of options and futures differ substantially.

The following pages describe in greater detail the mechanics associated with these outright option strategies.

Call Buying

While the purchase of an outright call option is one of the most simple of all option strategies, it has always been the most popular strategy for the trading public. Bullish price forecasts have always been the most alluring of all market scenarios. This is despite the fact that it is possible to profit with equal ease by trading options in a bullish or bearish environment. Where the market is trending upwards, a call buying strategy has two characteristics that recommend it: (1) the call holder's potential losses are strictly limited to the premium forfeit up front, and (2) the call holder enjoys a certain degree of leverage. These points may be appreciated better if one considers the risk/return posture assumed by the investor who buys the underlying commodity outright. If a bull move does in fact occur, the commodity buyer profits to the extent of that move; but if the market unexpectedly declines, our investor may be subject to large losses. Not so for the option holder; while he shares in the profits implied by the bull move (limited to the extent of the premium paid up front), he cannot, bearing error or absurdity, lose more than the forefeit premium. Additionally, the option buyer may enjoy opportunities to participate in these profits. This is despite the fact that his investment in the contract, represented by the premium, generally is much lower than the full purchase price of the commodity. This is a leverage, although as discussed in Chapter 5, a commodity trader may enjoy greater leverage by trading a futures contract instead of an option.

EXAMPLE. An investor is bullish on the price of T-bond futures and is weighing the merits of purchasing the futures contract against the merits of buying a call on the same futures contract. T-bond futures currently are trading at 74% of par and there is available a call struck at 74 selling at $1^{32}\!/_{64}$ths, or a $1,500 premium. If the price of the T-bond futures contract appreciates 5 percentage points to 79, the investor could have made $5,000 had he bought futures or $3,500 had he purchased the call and exercised it when the market was at 79. Note that the return on the call is only $1,500 less than the return on the futures contract—this is, of course, equal to the premium forfeit up front. But if the price of the T-bond futures contract declined 5 points to 69, the investor long the futures contract would lose $5,000 while the call holder's loss would be limited to the $1,500 premium forfeit initially.

Let's examine the risks and rewards associated with the outright purchase of a call option. When we consider the potential profit and loss associated with this, or any other option strategy, we have to be aware of the ways in which one can profit by employing that strategy. One can profit by holding an option when the option is exercised or when it is subsequently sold at a premium in excess of the price at which it originally was purchased. It is customary, however, to examine the implications associated with holding the option(s) until expiration. This, of course, implies that the option holder will be faced with the choice of exercising or abandoning the option when expiration becomes imminent. Although the following text explicitly examines the returns associated with exercise or abandonment, one should keep in mind that resale may be an alternative as well.

The return associated with the exercise or abandonment of a long option may be broken down into two components: the *gross* and the *net* return. The gross return refers to the profit associated with exercising or abandoning the option without consideration of the initial forfeiture of the option premium. Note that the gross return must be greater than or equal to zero. Option holders will not exercise when a negative gross return is expected, but instead, will permit the option to expire unexercised. The net return equals the gross return reduced by the premium forfeit up front. We will see that although the premium should not enter into a decision to exercise or abandon the option, it must be considered as a loss to the holder when calculating the bottom line or net return. When considering a long call option, the gross return may be referenced by the relationship to the underlying market and exercise prices (denoted as U and E, respectively) when expiration is imminent. When the call is in-the-money, that is, when U is greater than E, the holder can be expected to exercise the option. When the call is at- or out-of-the-money, that is, when U is equal to or less than E, the holder would normally refuse to exercise the option. Where the option is exercised, the gross return equals the in-the-money amount or $U - E$; where the option is abandoned, the gross return equals zero. Of course, this gross return must then be reduced by the call premium (denoted as C) to arrive at the net return:

CALCULATING GROSS AND NET RETURNS ON A LONG CALL

When the Call Is Exercised	When the Call Is Abandoned
U	Gross return
(E)	always
Gross return	equals zero
(C)	(C)
Net return	Net return

Presumably, the underlying market price U can rise indefinitely, yielding an "unlimited" potential net profit for the option holder. Practically, of course, one cannot expect the underlying market price to appreciate so dramatically. And in some cases the underlying market may not rise at all. Nonetheless, this theoretically unlimited profit potential represents one of the major features of a call buying strategy that makes it so attractive.

When expiration is imminent, it is always preferable to exercise when a positive gross return is possible. This is true even though a negative net return may occur. Recall that the premium, once forefeit, is an irretrievable sunk cost. Nothing the option holder might do can change this fact; once the premium is paid, the call holder must depend upon bullish underlying market movement in order to realize a net profit. The price that the underlying commodity must achieve in order to provide the option holder with a net profit is called the "breakeven point." In the case of a call option, the breakeven point can be calculated as the option exercise price E plus the premium C forfeit up front, or $E + C$. Only where the underlying commodity price U exceeds $E + C$ will a positive net return become possible.

But what happens if the price of the underlying commodity U rises only a small amount? If the underlying market price rises into-the-money such that U is greater than E when expiration becomes imminent, then exercise is still indicated. This is despite the fact that U may be less than $U + C$. When a call is exercised under these circumstances, the gross profit is positive, although the net profit, in light of the forfeit of the call premium $C,$ is negative.

Another scenario has the underlying market price U less than the exercise price E. When expiration is imminent and these circumstances prevail (the option is out-of-the-money), our option holder will, of course, not exercise the option. If the holder exercises this option, he realizes a negative gross return, exacerbated on a net basis by the forfeit of the premium.

A unique case may occur when the option is at-the-money, that is, $U = E$. Under these circumstances, most option holders will prefer to abandon the option. This is because exercise would entail some transaction costs, as would the subsequent sale of the underlying commodity purchased upon exercise. Of course, some option holders may have an ulterior reason to hold the underlying commodity, for example, if the option calls for the delivery of a physical commodity and the option holder is a commercial entity engaged in the production, resale, or industrial usage of that commodity. Other option holders may elect to exercise when that represents the most convenient or expeditious way of acquiring a long position in the underlying market and they are confident that the market will experience a strong bull move. For example, many of the options on futures contracts permit the holder to exercise the option after the option and underlying futures markets close on a specified Friday afternoon but before they open the next business day. If a bullish economic event occurred between the close and the time that the holder is required to make known his intentions to exercise, then it may be profitable to exercise an at-the-money option, or even a slightly out-of-the-money option.

The foregoing suggests that there are three "zones" defined by the relationship between the underlying market price, the strike price, and the option premium. The first zone falls in the area where the underlying market price U is less than the exercise price E. In that case, a negative gross *and* net return would accrue to the option holder who elected to exercise his option. Practically, of course, the gross return would equal zero because the option would, under normal circumstances, be permitted to expire. A second zone occurs where U is greater than E but where $U + E$ is still less than C. Under these circumstances, the option would be exercised for a positive gross return, but the net return would be negative. Finally, a third zone occurs where the option is in-the-money and the in-the-money valuation exceeds the call premium C. Under these circumstances, a positive gross *and* net return is indicated. A special case exists, of course, where the option is at-the-money, that is, $U = E$. For most purposes, this case may be subsumed under our zone "I" case because, whether the option is exercised or not, the gross return equals zero (without considering transaction costs) and the net return is negative.

GROSS AND NET RETURN "ZONES"

Zone		Gross Return	Net Return
I:	Out-of-the-money	Zero	Negative
II:	In-the-money, U less than $E + C$	Positive	Negative
III:	In-the-money, U greater than $E + C$	Positive	Positive

In order to illustrate the concept of the three return zones, let's consider a simple example of a call option purchase:

EXAMPLE. An option enthusiast has studied the market carefully and has determined that gold prices are likely to appreciate over the next three months. Unfortunately, he is uncertain as to when the bull move will occur but nevertheless is confident that it is imminent. Therefore, he prefers to capitalize on this expectation by buying a call option rather than buying futures. Assume that there is available a call on a gold futures contract that was struck at-the-money at the prevailing market price of $380 per ounce. Further assume that the option premium was equal to $20 per ounce. What would our investor's returns be if the market moves in either direction?

Gold Price at Expiration	Gross Return	Less $20 Premium Equals	Net Return
$340	$ 0		($20)
360	0		(20)
380	0		(20)
390	10		(10)
400	20		0
410	30		10
420	40		20
440	60		40

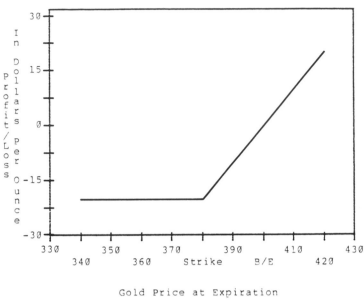

Gold Price at Expiration

Figure 6.1   Return zones for an outright holder

In this example (see Figure 6.1), the out-of-the-money zone I extends from the strike price of $380 on down. As is apparent from the accompanying table, the holder's gross returns equal zero. This is reduced by the $20 premium to net a $20 loss. Zone II (where the option is in-the-money but a profitable exercise is nonetheless impossible) extends from the $380 strike price to the $400 breakeven point. Here the gross return precisely offsets the forfeiture of the $20 premium. To illustrate, where the underlying market is priced at $390 at expiration, the gross profit of $10 (implied by the purchase of a commodity valued at $390 for a mere $380) is negated by the forfeiture of the $20 premium to net a $10 loss. Finally, zone III begins at the breakeven point of $400 and extends upwards. How would these results compare to the purchase of a gold futures contract at the strike price $380, assuming that a futures contract represented the subject of the option contract and, therefore, the futures price equals U?

Gold Price at Expiration	(1) Returns on Long Call	(2) Returns on Long Futures	Difference (1) − (2)
$340	($20)	($40)	$20
350	(20)	(30)	10
360	(20)	(20)	—
370	(20)	(10)	(10)
380	(20)	0	(20)
390	(10)	10	(20)
400	0	20	(20)
410	10	30	(20)

The returns associated with the long outright call dominate the returns associated with the long outright futures contract only at the point of $360 and below, or the strike price E less the call premium C initially forfeit. At points over $360, the returns associated with the futures contract dominate the returns associated with the long call. At the strike price $380 and above, the futures contract dominates the option by a consistent $20. Note, however, that the option holder is insulated from large losses since he can lose no more than the $20 premium—the holder of the long futures contract is subject to practically unlimited loss in the event of a precipitous decline. The call holder, by contrast, can afford to hold his position, confident that he will lose no more than $20 at worst. If the market subsequently rallies, he remains in a favorable position to participate in the profits associated with that rally.

Thus far, we have considered only the purchase of a call struck at-the-money. Although the most active option contracts will be those near to the money, it is not always possible to purchase an option that is exactly at-the-money. Nor is it necessarily a wise strategy, contingent, of course, upon the market forecasts and risk preferences subscribed to by our option enthusiast. Let's consider the purchase of an at-the-money call with in- and out-of-the-money calls.

When contemplating the purchase of a call, there will generally be available options that are both in- and out-of-the-money in addition to options that are, if not precisely at-the-money, at least near-to-the-money, all of which may share a common expiration date. The most significant difference between these three varieties of options is, of course, that each will sell for a different premium (see Figure 6.2). However, options that are in-the-money will invariably

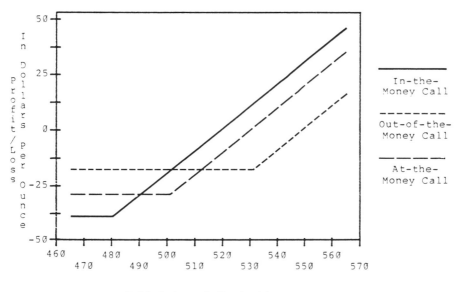

Gold Price at Expiration

Figure 6.2 In-, out-, and at-the-money call purchase

command a higher premium than options of the same class that may be out-of-the-money. In fact, the in-the-money valuation of an option defines its intrinsic value, an important component of the total premium that option will command. Of course, an out-of-the-money option by definition is void of any intrinsic value because it is not in-the-money. Ignoring the time value an option may have premiums for options whose strike prices are low, in the case of calls and high and in the case of puts, will be higher than comparable options of the same class whose strike prices are high and low, respectively.

To illustrate this concept, let's examine the fair market premiums associated with in- and out-of-the-money calls. In this illustration, we use an option exercisable for gold futures where the underlying futures contract is trading at $495 and there are available calls struck at $460, $480, $500, $530, and $560. Market volatility is at 40%, there are 60 days until expiration of this particular class of options, and the relevant short-term interest rate equals 9.5%:

	Strike Price	Premium
Out-of-the-money	$560	$10.41
Out-of-the-money	530	17.83
Near-the-money	500	28.86
In-the-money	480	38.54
In-the-money	460	50.27

In this case, the investor who buys the near-the-money option struck at $500 would forfeit $28.86 per ounce initially even though the option had no intrinsic value whatsoever. Nonetheless, under this set of market conditions, this price is "fair" insofar as the holder of this long call statistically may expect to break even. The breakeven point in that case equals the strike price of $500 plus the $28.86 premium, or $528.86. Currently the underlying market price equals $495. This implies that the market must move upwards in excess of $33.86 before the call may profitably be exercised on a net basis. The purchasers of out-of-the-money calls struck at $530 and $560 would be required to pay a premium of $17.83 and $10.41, respectively. At a glance, these out-of-the-money calls certainly appear to be more attractive than the purchase of the near-the-money call. These buyers are required to pay smaller premiums and, consequently, risk less than the holder of the near-to-the-money option. This is mistaken, however, because the purchasers of the out-of-the-money calls at their fair market value statistically expect to break even just as the holders of the near-to-the-money calls and the in-the-money calls. The holders of these out-of-the-money calls risk less *but* the probability that the option will move into-the-money to permit a profitable exercise is correspondingly less. The breakeven points for the $530 and $560 calls are $547.83 and $570.41, respectively. This means that the market must move from its current prevailing price of $495 up at least $52.83 or $75.41 so holders of the $530 and $560 call can profitably exercise their options. So while the risk assumed by these traders is low, the chances for a profitable exercise are correspondingly diminished. However, holders of the in-the-money options struck at $480 and $460 must pay relatively high premiums of $38.54 and $50.27 in order, respectively, to secure their purchases. These premiums may be high, but the chances that these options will become profitable to exercise on a net basis at some subsequent point is similarly high. (Since these options are in-the-money currently, it is of course profitable on a gross basis to exercise them immediately but it is never profitable on a net basis immediately to exercise an option upon purchase.) The breakeven points for the $480 and $460 options are at $518.54 and $510.27, respectively. This implies that the market must move upwards at least $17.83 and $10.41 to provide holders of these in-the-money options with a net profit upon exercise.

BREAKEVEN POINTS AND MARKET MOVES REQUIRED TO TURN A PROFIT

Strike Price	Premium	Breakeven Point	Market Move to Profit
$560	$10.41	$570.41	$75.41
530	17.83	547.83	52.83
500	28.86	528.86	33.86
480	38.54	518.54	23.54
460	50.27	510.27	15.27

The situation cited above provides another striking example of a theme that has run throughout our discussions; that is, returns and risks must balance. Where nothing is risked, no returns may be expected; and where there is high risk, then returns must be easier to achieve. As a general rule of thumb, then, the farther a call is out-of-the-money, the less cost associated with the call purchase. However, the breakeven point will be higher and the underlying market must move further in order that the holder may turn a profit on either a gross or a net basis. However, the farther the option moves into-the-money, the more risk assumed by a new holder (represented by the premium forfeit upon purchase). Yet the breakeven point will be lower and the movement required to turn a gross or a net profit is smaller. This suggests that prospective option purchasers must assess (1) the likely magnitude of a bull movement, and (2) the degree of confidence they have in this prediction. Investors who subscribe to a bullish scenario and believe that this imminent bull move will be very large may prefer to purchase out-of-the-money calls. Naturally, it is more difficult to predict a major bull move than a slight bull move because the occurrence of major bull moves is less frequent. However, the buyer of an out-of-the-money option pays a smaller premium relative to the buyer of an in-the-money option. Therefore, an out-of-the-money call buyer implies by such a purchase that he expects a large bull move. However, he need not maintain the degree of confidence in such a prediction as does the buyer of an in-the-money option who risks a great deal more. Generally, of course, our in-the-money call buyer looks only towards a relatively slight bull move and the market is always more likely to realize a small than a large move in either direction. The farther the option is in-the-money, the lower the breakeven point will be relative to the current underlying market price but the greater the risk assumed by the option buyer. At some point, in-the-money options will be viewed as unattractive by prospective option purchasers. This is because they risk a great deal and are required to pay this risk capital (represented by the premium) in cash over to the option seller up front. This may be unattractive relative to the prospect of buying futures that may be margined in instruments other than cash, which does not imply an opportunity cost. Additionally, for reasons discussed above, futures are inherently more conducive to short-term speculation than are options. As in all investment forums, risks tend to balance with the opportunity for positive returns.

Once an investor enters into a long call position, he may find that the market will move in accordance with his predictions. Or he may find that his predictions fail to be realized. In the former case, the option generally will be held until the investor is confident that the bull move, the anticipation of which initially motivated the call purchase, has run its course. At this point, the call holder will exercise the option or execute a closing sale; which alternative is chosen depends upon the profit potential associated with each. Generally, however, most options, once purchased, are held for the duration of their life, that is, until they expire. It is easy to hold an option because option holders pay in advance the premium that represents their maximum risk exposure. Moreover, if the market moves sufficiently upward for the option holder to realize a positive net return and there is still some time left before expiration, then the prospect exists that the underlying market may appreciate more. This can make it more profitable to hold the option longer rather than exercise or execute a closing sale immediately. (Commodity traders are often offered the sage advice of "letting profits run and cutting losses short.") But should the market move in an adverse direction (down in the case of a long call) or it becomes apparent in no uncertain terms that a bull move has run its course and the market will now reverse, then the long call holder is best advised to take defensive action.

This defensive action may take many different forms. The simplest of these actions is the execution of a closing sale. This strategy is most attractive where an investor purchases an out-of-the-money call. This is because the loss associated with such a closing sale may be small relative to the loss associated with the liquidation of an option of the same class that was in-the-money. Recall that the delta factor, which defines the expected movement of the option premium relative to a given movement in the underlying commodity market, is smaller for out-of-the-money options than it is for in-the-money options. Therefore the holder of an out-of-the-money call can afford to observe a rather large bear movement in the underlying commodity market than can the holder of an in-the-money option. Remember delta is always equal to or under 1.0. This implies that the change in the option premium will invariably represent only a fraction of the change in the underlying commodity price. This suggests that the losses associated with a closing sale may be only a fraction of the losses implied by the bear movement. Recall, however, that delta is only effective over a relatively short period. Over a longer period, delta will be dynamic and the declining time value of an option may represent a loss in excess of the change in the underlying commodity price. Fortunately for the holder of an in-the-money option, however, when the underlying commodity price moves down and perhaps out-of-the-money, the decline in the premium will slow down. But this is a double-edged sword. The in-the-money call will decline in value faster than the out-of-the-money call when the underlying market declines. But it will also rise in value faster when the underlying market rises. Therefore, should our call buyer prefer to take his profits through a closing sale rather than through exercise, the in-the-money option becomes more attractive. This is mitigated in that delta is effective only for relatively short durations. Where an option begins with a great deal of time value, that time value must decline as the option approaches expiration. In some cases, an option premium may even decline when the option moves into-the-money because of the declining time value of the premium.

EXAMPLE.   Call options are available exercisable for T-bond futures contracts that are both in- and out-of-the-money. Compare the purchase of an in-the-money call with the purchase of an out-of-the-money call. Assume that the underlying market is priced at 76. One investor buys an in-the-money call struck at 74 while another buys an out-of-the-money call struck at 78. Market variability is at 25%; there are 120 days until the expiration of both options; and the relevant short-term interest rate equals 8% per annum. Under these circumstances, the call struck at 74 will have a fair market value of 5.412% of par, or $5,412 per $100,000 face value contract. The call struck at 78 will sell around 3.282% of par, or $3,282 per $100,000 contract. What happens if the market declines 1 percentage point to 75% of par over the next 60 days while all other market conditions remain static? In that case, the in-the-money call struck at 74 drops in price to $3,449 while the out-of-the-money call struck at 78 declines to $1,754. This implies a loss upon a closing sale of $1,963 for the in-the-money call and a loss of only $1,428 for the out-of-the-money call. Consider the results if the underlying market price moved upwards to 77% of par over those same 60 days. In that case, one normally would expect the premiums associated with each option to appreciate and the in-the-money option to appreciate more than the out-of-the-money option. But in this case, the declining time values of the two options overcome the effects of this otherwise bullish move. The in-the-money call struck at 74 declines to $4,678, for a $734 loss, while the out-of-the-money call declines to $2,578, for a $704 loss. Note that the loss associated with the in-the-money option was slightly more than the loss associated with the out-of-the-money call. This is because, although both options were an equal amount in- and out-of-the-money originally, the 74 call had slightly more time value originally and thus the time value had a farther distance to fall over the 60 days.

Generally, it is preferable to liquidate a losing long call position through a closing sale than through exercise. This strategy is usually advisable as the loss implied by the declining value of the premium in response to a bear move (coupled with the premium's natural tendency to decline over time) cannot exceed the loss implied by an exercise. As long as there remains some time value associated with the option, a call holder who desires to liquidate a declining position will always be better off executing a closing sale than exercising the position. Of course, exercise is only feasible where at least a gross profit is possible, that is, where the option is in-the-money. To understand this, consider that the call premium C must be greater than or equal to the underlying market price U less the exercise price E, or $U - E$. The loss implied by the exercise of a declining long call position through exercise is the original call premium less the gross profit of $U - E$ (this is where the option is in our zone "II" described above). But as long as the current call premium has some time value associated with it, that is, it is greater than $U - E$, then the loss through resale will always be less than the loss associated with liquidation through exercise.

Other strategies may, however, be indicated when our call holder holds some residual confidence that a bull move ultimately will be realized. In cases such as these, the call holder's objective is to insulate himself from bear movements while continuing to hold a long call position. These strategies are intended basically to reduce the risk associated with an adverse (bear) movement but are essentially bullish in nature. One strategy that may be pursued would have the long call holder liquidate through a closing sale the declining position but immediately take another long call position at a higher strike price. (This option does not necessarily have to be out-of-the-money; as long as its strike price is higher, the premium will be lower and, therefore, there will be less risk associated therewith.) Another strategy is to take on an offsetting position in another option series. For example, one can sell another call option with the same expiration but with a higher strike price. Then our long call holder creates a bullish vertical spread and reduces the loss associated with a bear move (and reduces the potential profit associated with a bull move). In any event, long call strategies generally hold their allure because the option holder is assured that he cannot lose more than the original option premium. Prudent option traders should always be careful not to overextend themselves and buy options where they cannot afford to lose the premium paid upon purchase. If an option trader cannot afford to lose the premium, he should restrict his option activities to strategies that are inherently less risky to begin than an outright long call.

Call Writing

The sale, or writing or granting, of a call is a strategy that mirrors perfectly, with respect to risks and returns, the strategy of call buying. While outright call buying represents far and away the most common and popular strategy employed by the trading public, call writing on an outright basis represents one of the least popular strategies.

Outright call writing does not represent a popular strategy for the general public for the simple fact that practically unlimited losses may be associated with an outright short call position. An outright short call position may also be referred to as an "uncovered" or "naked" position. The outright call writer does not cover the risks inherent in the short call by any offsetting position. Generally, calls will be written in conjunction with positions in the underlying commodity or other option series. It is, however, important to be thoroughly familiar with the mechanics of the outright short call position in order that discussions of more complicated strategies, which may involve one or more short call positions, may be dissected and understood readily. For those who have completely grasped the risks and returns associated with a long call position, it should be easy to assimilate the concept of a short call position; the risks and returns are simply reversed. The option holder's risks are limited to the premium forfeit up front and profits are, at least theoretically, unlimited. The option writer's options are strictly limited to the premium received initially while the writer's risks may theoretically be unlimited.

EXAMPLE. Assume that an investor is bearish on the price of silver and believes that he may capitalize on this bearish expectation by selling calls. Silver is trading at $12.00 per ounce and there is available an option struck at-the-money at a premium of $0.50 per ounce. Our trader sells this call outright and waits until option expiration to take his profits or recognize his losses. Assume that the price of silver declines to $10.00 per ounce. At this point, the call option holder—the party opposite to our trader—would prefer to abandon the option because clearly it would be foolish to exercise the option by purchasing a commodity at the $12.00 exercise price when it was valued at only $10.00. When the option is abandoned, it expires unexercised and worthless. Consequently, our outright call writer retains the full premium at $0.50 per ounce as option. What would happen if the opposite scenario were realized, that is, the price of silver appreciated $2.00 to $14.00? At this point, the option holder would rationally elect to exercise by buying the commodity valued at $14.00 for the $12.00 exercise price. This implies a gross profit of $2.00 upon exercise for the holder ($U - E$ or $14.00 less $12.00 equals $2.00), reduced by the $0.50 premium. This yields a net profit of $1.50 for the holder. The writer's returns are, of course, a mirror image of those of the holder—the writer realizes a negative return of $1.50. He is required to sell a commodity valued at $14.00 for only $12.00, insulated only by the $0.50 premium, for a $1.50 loss. In this case, then, our option writer risks a loss of $1.50 where the market moves up for a possible profit of only $0.50. Of course, when the option is fairly priced, the statistical probabilities and magnitude of possible profits and losses should balance.

Earlier we had discussed the gross and net returns that may accrue to a call option holder or buyer. But the same concepts may be applied to analyze a call writer's position, with the exception that the returns are reversed in the context of the call sale. Again, the gross return refers to the returns—positive or negative—that accrue directly from the exercise of the option. Because the option will only be exercised when it is profitable for the holder, at least without consideration of the option premium, the writer's gross returns must be negative or at best equal to zero. On a net basis, the writer counts the premium as a positive return, regardless of whether it exceeds or is less than the gross return:

GROSS AND NET RETURNS ON SHORT CALL

When the Call Is Exercised	When the Call Is Abandoned
(U)	Gross return
$\dfrac{E}{\text{Gross return}}$	always
	equals zero
$\dfrac{C}{\text{Net return}}$	$\dfrac{C}{\text{Net return}}$

An in-the-money option should be exercised while an out-of-the-money option should be abandoned. However, the option writer starts at an advantage over the option holder by virtue of the receipt of the premium. This implies that, if the market remains stable, the writer invariably will profit. If an option expires out-of-the-money, the writer's profits equal the full extent of the premium. The maximum profit represented by the premium is diminished by the in-the-money valuation should the option be exercised. But if the market remains stable, or even moves slightly against the option writer's position, the writer still profits on a net basis. Recall that an option can never sell for less than its intrinsic value or the underlying market price U less the exercise price E, or $U - E$. So as long as the underlying market price U remains stable, the writer will retain the call premium C, which must exceed or at a minimum be equal to $U - E$. Another way of analyzing these gross and net profits is by reference to the breakeven point, or $E + C$ in the case of a call. As long as U remains under the breakeven point $E + C$, the writer will realize a net profit. This is, of course, just another way of saying that the writer will invariably profit as long as C exceeds $U - E$. Just as the concept of these gross and net returns may be applied to both call buyer and seller, so can the concept of gross and net return "zones":

GROSS AND NET RETURN "ZONES"

Zone		Gross Return	Net Return
I:	Out-of-the-money	Zero	Positive
II:	In-the-money, C greater than $U - E$	Negative	Positive
III:	In-the-money, C less than $U - E$	Negative	Negative

Let's illustrate the concept of these three return zones in the context of an outright call sale (also see Figure 6.3):

EXAMPLE. A trader has studied the T-bond futures market and believes that it is likely to move downwards slightly or at least remain neutral. As a result, our trader sells a call struck at-the-money at 76-00% of par and receives a 2-00 premium, or $2,000 for a $100,000 futures contract. What would our investor's returns be should the market move in either direction?

T-Bond Price at Expiration	Gross Return	Plus 2-00 Premium Equals	Net Return
72-00	$0		$2,000
74-00	0		2,000
76-00	0		2,000
77-00	(1,000)		1,000
78-00	(2,000)		0
79-00	(3,000)		(1,000)
80-00	(4,000)		(2,000)
82-00	(6,000)		(4,000)
84-00	(8,000)		(6,000)

Zone I in the previous example extends from the strike price of 76-00 and on down. Should the option expire at-the-money or out-of-the-money, the option holder will find no reason to exercise the option: Consequently, the writer will retain the full premium of 2-00, or $2,000. Zone II extends from the at-the-money point of 76-00 up to the breakeven point of 78-00, or the exercise price of 76-00 plus the original premium of 2-00. In this zone, the option sale remains profitable; but, of course, the profit represented by the premium is eroded by the in-the-money valuation. The writer still profits despite the fact that the

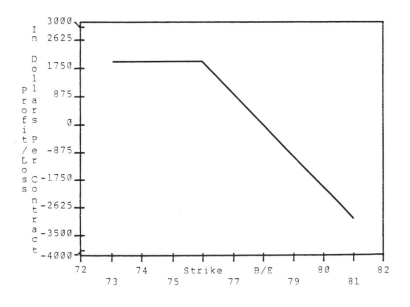

T-Bond Futures at Expiration

Figure 6.3 Return zones for an outright call writer

underlying market actually moved upwards slightly. Of course, in zone III, over the breakeven point, the negative gross returns incurred upon exercise (implied by the requirement imposed upon the writer to sell a commodity at a fixed exercise price when it is actually valued in excess) dominate the premium received.

Earlier we had stated that the same of an outright call option represents a bearish or neutral position. At this point, it is appropriate to somewhat revise these statements. The previous example showed that a trader short a call can still realize a net profit even when the market is slightly bullish. But beyond that, if a trader held a bearish market viewpoint, would he really desire to sell a call? Let's answer that question by means of an example.

EXAMPLE.   There is available a call exercisable for gold futures and struck at-the-money at the prevailing gold futures price of $480, selling for a $20 premium. Our investor is bearish and considering the alternatives of selling the call or selling the underlying gold futures contract. What would our trader's returns be under either of the two alternatives (assuming that both positions would be held until the expiration of the option)?

Gold Price at Expiration	(1) Returns on Short Call	(2) Returns on Short Futures	Difference (1) - (2)
$420	$20	$60	($40)
440	20	40	(20)
460	20	20	0
480	20	0	20
490	10	(10)	20
500	0	(20)	20
510	(10)	(30)	20
520	(20)	(40)	20
540	(40)	(60)	20

These results suggest that, if one held firm bearish sentiments, one may prefer to sell the underlying commodity rather than the call. At all points lower than the exercise price E less the call premium C, the returns associated with the short futures contract dominate the returns associated with the short call (which are fixed at the $20 premium). Our results also indicate that the call writer may profit even where the market moves in a slightly bullish direction. In our zone II, delineated by the exercise price of $480 and the breakeven point of $500, the call writer actually profits, although his profits decline the farther the underlying market price moves upwards. Not so for the holder of the short futures contract; at points in our zone II, the short futures holder realizes a loss. At all points over the breakeven point, both the call writer and short futures holder lose, although the call writer is insulated from the losses implied by the bull movement to the extent of the premium received initially. This suggests that, compared to the short futures position, the short call is actually a rather conservative position. But let's not forget our point here: if one were truly bearish, an outright short call strategy could not be recommended. An outright short commodity position or, as we will see in the subsequent section, a long put strategy is inherently better suited to take advantage of a strong bearish sentiment than a short call.

Thus far we have taken great pains to point out that a theoretically unlimited loss may be associated with a short option position—whether that short position involves a call or a put. At this time, let's digress a bit and discuss why, from a statistical standpoint, this generalization is misleading. Practically, option writers cannot expect "unlimited" losses; an unlimited loss cannot be quantified except in the abstract. Surely there is some way empirically to assess the level of risk. Fortunately, there is such a way, although the routine application of this method will generally require the use of a calculator or a computer.

One may observe that the price of a commodity can never fall below zero. An "unlimited loss" on a short put option occurs when the market falls precipitously (as discussed in greater detail below). Since the market cannot fall below zero, one can easily quantify the maximum risk associated with a short put. Of course, it is unreasonable to expect the market price of a commodity to fall to zero. Certainly we can develop a method to assess risk that renders a finer assessment of risk. Earlier we had discussed the concept of volatility in the underlying commodity market and had quantified this concept through the use of the standard deviation statistic. If we believe that we can assess market volatility and that this assessment provides an accurate indication of future volatility, then we may attach probabilities to possible returns over different time frames. For example, we know that the range bounded by the current market price plus or minus one standard deviation is likely to be realized with an approximate 67% probability. The range bounded by the current market price plus or minus two standard deviations is likely to be achieved 95% of the time; the range bounded by the current market price plus or minus three standard deviations is likely to be realized 99% of the time. Recall that the standard deviation of market returns customarily is expressed on an annualized basis. A second important point to remember is that market fluctuations are assumed to follow, not a strict normal distribution, but a *lognormal* distribution. This implies that one must adjust the raw measure of standard deviation in order to assess the probable range that the underlying commodity price may assume. This adjustment entails taking a logarithmic function: the natural logarithm of the standard deviation (*sd*) expressed on a proportionate basis, for example, 25% equals .25, to the base of the natural logarithm *e:*

$$(6.1) \qquad \text{Bound} = e^{sd}$$

To illustrate how these bounds may be derived, consider the following example.

EXAMPLE.   The current market price of the commodity in question equals
$100—the annualized standard deviation of market returns equals
25%. In order to find the upper and lower bounds of the current
commodity price plus or minus one standard deviation, we must
take $100 times $e^{.25}$ and $100 times $e^{-.25}$. These bounds will equal
$138.63 and $77.88. Our conclusions from these bounds are that we
are approximately 67% confident that the commodity price will fall
between $138.63 and $77.88 within one year. Once again, we see
that a commodity price whose fluctuations follow this lognormal
distribution is more likely to appreciate absolutely than depreciate. What if we were to take the current market price plus or minus
two or three standard deviations? In the case of two standard deviations, we would take $100 times $e^{(2)(.25)}$ and $100 times $e^{(2)(-.25)}$,
or $164.87 and $60.65. Were we to solve for three standard deviations, the range would equal $100 times $e^{(3)(.25)}$ and $e^{(3)(-.25)}$, or
$211.70 and $47.24. This implies that we are 95% confident that the
commodity price will fall within the bounds of $164.87 and $60.65
and 99% confident that it will fall within the bounds of $211.70 and
$47.24.

This measure of standard deviation is convenient to determine the likely
range of commodity prices within the year. However, an option may not have
exactly a year of life in it—its expiration may come prior to the expiration of a
year or sometimes more than a year in advance. This calls for a further refine-
ment of our model. Specifically, we must adjust for the time period we are interested in. If that time period happens to be 120 days, for example, we just
adjust by a factor of 120 days until option expiration divided by 365 days in a
year, or 0.33 = 120/365. Our complete model, then, is as follows:

$$(6.2) \qquad \text{Bound} = e^{(dte/365)(n)(sd)}$$

where *dte* equals the number of days until option expiration and *n* equals the
number of standard deviations in which we may be interested.

EXAMPLE.   The current commodity price equals $100; the standard deviation
of market returns on an annualized basis equals 25% and there are
120 days until option expiration. We maintain a 67% confidence
that the commodity price will fall within one standard deviation
plus or minus from the current market price. These bounds are
defined by $100 times $e^{(120/365)(1)(.25)}$ and $100 times $e^{(120/365)(1)(-.25)}$,
or $108.57 and $92.11. We are 95% confident that the commodity
price will fall within two standard deviations from the current
price or between $117.87 and $84.84. Finally, we are 99% confident
that the commodity price will fall within three standard deviations
from the current price or between $127.96 and $78.15.

Knowing facts such as these, we shall be able to attach probabilities to extreme cases in order to estimate the maximum profit and loss associated with a particular option strategy. We know that the maximum profit associated with a short call strategy equals the premium received initially. What of the maximum possible loss? Although it is theoretically unlimited, we may venture to consider a movement on the order of three standard deviations as representative of a maximum loss. Although we are only 99% confident that market movement will be within plus or minus three standard deviations, this is nonetheless a high level of confidence. Some may be less conservative and prefer to utilize a 95% confidence level, as implied by a movement of plus or minus two standard deviations. We, however, will employ the 99% confidence level for our illustrations.

EXAMPLE.   A call exercisable for a gold futures contract is available struck at-the-money at $500 and goes for a premium of $38.94 per ounce. The annualized standard deviation of market returns equals 40% and there are 100 days until option expiration. With 99% confidence we may state that within the 100-day period until expiration, the market price will remain within the range bounded by $500 times $e^{(100/365)(3)(.40)}$ and $500 times $e^{(100/365)(3)(-.40)}$, or $694.63 and $359.91. Where a call is sold, the worst case scenario would have the market move upwards. Should the market move up to the upper bound of $694.63, the call writer will suffer a gross loss of $194.63 per ounce on exercise, cushioned by the receipt of the $38.94 premium, for a net loss of $155.69. Thus we may state that the maximum reward the call writer may expect equals $38.94, whereas the risk he runs is on the magnitude of $155.69 with 99% confidence.

So far we have only considered examples of the short call strategy where the option in question is struck at-the-money. But, of course, a prospective option writer will generally be faced with the prospect of selling options that are struck both in- and out-of-the-money in addition to at- or near-the-money options. Again, the most obvious difference between options that are struck in- and out-of-the-money is the premiums at which they may be sold. In-the-money options always command a higher premium than out-of-the-money options. How should an option writer evaluate the prospects associated with each of the options available? There are a number of ways: the prospective writer may wish to evaluate his profit if the underlying market price remains stable or if it moves appreciably in either direction. This implies a breakeven analysis in addition to an assessment of the maximum profit and loss.

First, let's consider the scenario where the market remains stable. The fact that in-the-money options are associated with higher premiums suggests superficially that the prospective option writer consider selling in-the-money options in order to maximize his maximum returns. But this supposition ignores the fact that in-the-money options may by definition be exercised by the holder for a gross profit, causing the writer a gross loss and diminishing his net returns. It is far better for the prospective option writer who anticipates a stable market to sell an at-the-money option when the time value is greatest. If the market does indeed remain stable, the time value of the option will slowly diminish, locking in a profit for the option writer equal to the premium. Consider the case where there are call options exercisable for gold futures struck at $460, $480, $500, $530, and $560. The underlying market is trading at $495; market volatility equals 40%; there are 60 days until expiration; and the relevant short-term interest rate equals 9.5%. How would the associated option premiums break down into intrinsic and time value?

	Strike Price	Premium	Intrinsic Value	Time Value
Out-of-the-money	$560	$10.41	$0	$10.41
Out-of-the-money	530	17.83	0	17.83
Near-the-money	500	28.86	0	28.86
In-the-money	480	38.54	15.00	23.54
In-the-money	460	50.27	35.00	15.27

If the call writer expects a stable market, his returns would be limited to the time value of these options. If the option in question moves out-of-the-money, then the writer's profits could equal the full premium. Let's consider the writer's returns where the market moves against him. First of all, one should assess the breakeven point and the bull move required for the writer to realize that breakeven point. Of course, we must remember that the writer starts off in the black, as it were, by virtue of the receipt of the premium. Secondly, we might assess the maximum loss represented by a three standard deviation bull move. This is a movement upwards to $602.94 over the 60-day life of the options in question:

Breakeven Points and Market Moves
to Realize Maximum Profit, Loss, and Breakeven

Strike price	$560	$530	$500	$480	$460
Max return	10.41	17.83	28.86	38.54	50.27
Market move for max return	0	0	0	(15.00)	(35.00)
Breakeven point	570.41	547.83	528.86	518.54	510.27
Market move to break even	75.41	52.83	33.86	23.54	15.27
Max loss	32.53	55.11	74.08	84.40	92.67
Market move for max loss	42.94	72.94	102.94	122.94	140.94

As in all option strategies, if these options are fairly priced, the writer will maintain a statistical expectation of breaking even, at least over a number of trials. Note that maximum losses rise when maximum profits rise. The extreme

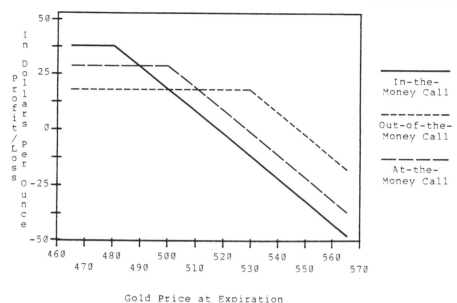

Gold Price at Expiration

Figure 6.4 In-, out-, and at-the money call sale

out-of-the-money option has both the least risk and least profit potential while the extreme in-the-money option has the most profit potential as well as risk (see Figure 6.4). This suggests that conservative option writers will prefer to sell out-of-the-money options and aggressive writers will sell in-the-money options.

Since the maximum loss appreciated with a short call strategy will generally be high relative to the maximum profit, outright call writers will find it advisable to carefully monitor market conditions and take action promptly to limit losses should the market start to move up appreciably. In-the-money call writers should be particularly interested in taking swift action. Their positions may decline in value quicker than the positions of out-of-the-money option writers. Usually, the easiest way to limit loss is simply to engage in a closing purchase. The call writer does not, of course, enjoy the option to exercise and thereby liquidate the position. One should note that the writer has every interest in staying in the market to capitalize on the declining time value of the option. Sometimes the underlying market may experience a significant bull move, and yet, the option writer will profit because the time value of the option has declined in excess of the enhanced value attributable to the bull movement.

EXAMPLE.   An option trader sells a call exercisable for physical silver bullion struck at $12.00 per ounce when the underlying market price equals $11.85. Market volatility is on the order of 35%; there are 120 days until option expiration; the relevant short-term interest rate equals 8%; and holding costs equal 1%. The call is sold for $1.09 per ounce. What should the writer do if the market starts to move against him, that is, a bull movement? The answer depends upon the period over which the bull movement takes place. Assume that the market moved up to $12.60 over the course of the next 10 days. At this point, the fair market value of the option can be expected to appreciate to $1.46 per ounce. It may be wise for the call writer to limit his losses to $0.37 per ounce by engaging in a closing purchase. But what if the market moves up to $12.60 over the next 90 days? By the time there are only 30 days until option expiration, the price can be expected to decline (all other factors remaining stable) to around $0.91 per ounce. Assume that the option writer is fairly confident that this bull move will not continue, or at least that the market will remain under the breakeven point represented by the strike price of $12.00 plus the original premium of $1.09 or $13.09. Our writer may then prefer to stay in the market rather than to execute a closing purchase. This would lock in the $0.18 per ounce profit implied by the difference between the original premium of $1.09 and the current premium of $0.91. The only difference between the two scenarios was the amount of time required for the bull move. Although the market moved upwards in the former case, it did so quickly, resulting in a loss for the writer. In the former case, the declining time value of the option overtook the decline in the premium expected as a result of the option's trend into-the-money.

Put Buying

The outright purchase of a put represents a rather elementary strategy among possible option strategies. Conceptually, it is quite similar to an outright call purchase. The qualification, of course, is that a put purchase is essentially a bearish strategy while a call purchase is essentially bullish. It seems somewhat odd, then, that outright put purchases do not generally represent popular strategies with the trading public, at least not to the extent of an outright call purchase. For the most part, public trading interest historically has been perked by the prospect of a major bull movement. Major bear movements, although equally profitable provided the proper strategy is executed, have been considered rather lackluster in comparison. Of course, it is equally easy to execute a bearish as a bullish strategy (and, unfortunately, equally difficult to pick out appropriate situations in which to apply such strategies). Therefore, the purchase of an outright put should be considered just as viable a strategy as the outright purchase of a call.

Just like the outright purchase of a call, a long put strategy is attractive because the put holder's maximum losses are limited to the initial premium. Additionally, the pursuit of a long put strategy permits the put holder to take a bearish position where it may otherwise be somewhat difficult to apply the same direction in the underlying commodity market. Consider the case of a noncommercial speculator in a particular commodity. In the absence of an option market, it may be difficult to assume a short position in the cash market. Of course, the existence of a futures market where short and long positions may be taken with equal ease may provide an additional outlet for such bearish interest. However, the holder of a short futures contract does not enjoy the benefit of limited risk. In any case, the put holder is afforded the opportunity to participate in returns associated with a bear movement to an extent limited only by the initial premium. This combination of limited risk and theoretically unlimited returns may be quite attractive.

EXAMPLE. An investor is bearish on the price of raw sugar and is considering the alternatives of buying a put exercisable in sugar futures or selling the sugar futures contract outright. Sugar currently is trading at 10 cents a pound in the futures market and a put is available struck at-the-money and trading at a 1-cent per pound premium. If the price of the sugar futures contract declines to, for example, 7 cents per pound, the investor who had sold sugar futures at 10 cents could realize a profit of 3 cents per pound. The investor who had bought a put struck at 10 cents for a 1-cent premium could exercise the put by selling a commodity valued at 7 cents for 10 cents; this implies a 3-cent profit on exercise reduced by the 1-cent premium initially forfeit for a net profit of 2 cents per pound. The return on the put equals only 2 cents—1 cent less than the return on the futures contract. Note, however, that had the futures price appreciated to 13 cents, holding a short futures position would have entailed a loss of 3 cents per pound. At that point, the put holder would have refrained from exercising the option and realized a loss of only 1 cent per pound. So although the put holder participates in the bulk of the bearish movement, his maximum loss in the case of a bull move represents but a fraction of the loss implied by such movement.

Let's examine the profits and losses potentially associated with the long put strategy. This is done by breaking down the returns that may accrue to the put holder on the basis of the terminal price of the underlying commodity, that is, the price the underlying commodity assumes upon option expiration. Our concern with the terminal commodity price implies, of course, that we expect the option trader to hold the put until expiration. At this point he will be faced with the alternatives of exercising the put or abandoning it. We reiterate, however, that the put holder has the choice of liquidating the option prior to expiration by the execution of a closing sale. The profits or losses are implied by the difference between the original put premium and the premium upon sale.

The returns associated with holding a put option may be broken down into a gross and a net return. This is similar to the returns associated with holding a call option. The gross return again refers to the return associated with the exercise or abandonment of the put without consideration of the premium forfeit upon put purchase. The net return refers to this gross return less the original premium paid. The gross return must, of course, be the greater of the in-the-money valuation of the put or zero. This is apparent insofar as a rational put holder will elect to exercise the put only when a profit, at least on a gross basis, is possible. If the option is at- or out-of-the-money, of course, the holder will prefer to abandon the option rather than exercise it for a gross loss. Recall that the definitions of in- and out-of-the-money are reversed in the context of a put option. A put option is in-the-money when the underlying commodity price U is less than the exercise price E. Here a put holder will find it profitable to sell a commodity at some price E in excess of its market value U. Thus the put holder's gross return must equal the greater of the exercise price less the underlying market price $E - U$ or zero. The net return is simply the gross return $E - U$ less the put premium P, or $E - U - P$:

CALCULATING THE GROSS AND NET RETURNS ON A LONG PUT

When the Put Is Exercised	When the Put Is Abandoned
E	Gross return
(U)	always
Gross return	equals zero
(P)	(P)
Net return	Net return

Earlier we discussed the profit potential associated with a long call position. We had implied that the call holder may realize a practically unlimited profit in the event of precipitous price advances. This presumption cannot be applied as readily in the context of a put option. It is obvious that the price of a commodity cannot fall below zero. The put holder profits in the event of bearish price movement. But the amount by which a commodity price may decline is limited to its current value. Zero forms a base below which the commodity price cannot break through. As a practical matter, it is obvious that a commodity price cannot be expected to approach zero under typical circumstances. As discussed in reference to short call positions, we may attach a probability to any particular advance or decline in the underlying commodity market and assess some degree of confidence that the price will remain within certain bounds.

EXAMPLE.   An option trader is bearish on the price of gold futures and decides to take action by buying a put option. The current price of the underlying gold futures contract is $480 and there is available a put option struck at-the-money at $480 and selling at a premium of $37.46. There are 90 days until option expiration; market volatility is at 40%; and short-term rates are at 8%. The central question becomes: what does our put holder risk and what is the magnitude of his potential profits? If we know that the standard deviation of annualized market returns equals 40%, then we may calculate the market decline that corresponds to a bear movement of three standard deviations over the 90-day life of the option. Referring to equation 6.2, that bound may be calculated as the current price $480 times $e^{(90/365)(3)(-.40)}$, or $357.06. Thus we may say with 99% confidence that the market cannot be expected to decline below $357.06. If the market declines to $357.06 by option expiration, then the put holder will be able to exercise the option for a gross return of $122.94, or the exercise price $480 less the terminal commodity price $357.06. This gross return is, of course, reduced by the option premium of $37.46 for a net return of $85.48. This defines the upside potential return associated with the long put. We may similarly state with 99% confidence that the market cannot be expected to move over the current price of $480 times $e^{(90/365)(3)(.40)}$, or $645.27. If the market exhibits this large bull movement, the put holder may be expected to take a loss. However, his loss is limited to the premium of $37.46 despite the large bull move.

The possibility of large bear and bull movements should be examined. However, one should note that these eventualities represent extremes and that a much smaller movement in either direction is more likely. But what would the put holder's returns be if these smaller movements are realized? In order to answer that question, let's construct our familiar return "zones" where the gross and net returns are contingent upon the terminal value of the underlying commodity price. Once more, we may define three zones. Our first zone "I" occurs where the put option is in-the-money so far that both a positive gross return and a positive net return become possible. This zone is delineated on the low end by zero and extends to the point where the underlying commodity price U equals the exercise price E less the original put premium P, or where U equals $E - P$. This point $E - P$ defines the breakeven point for the put option, that is, the terminal value of the underlying commodity where both buyer and seller of the put can expect to break even upon exercise. If a put expires when the underlying market price falls into zone I, the option may be exercised at a gross profit of $E - U$, which exceeds the put premium P. Thus a positive gross and net profit accrue to the put holder under these circumstances. Zone "II" is bounded on the lower end by the breakeven point $E - P$ and on the upper end by the exercise price E. When the terminal value of the underlying commodity falls within zone II, the option may be exercised for a gross profit; but unfortunately for the put holder, the gross profit is exceeded by the original option premium. Thus the put holder experienced a net loss. Finally, zone "III" extends from the exercise price E on upwards. When the terminal value of the underlying commodity falls within zone III, this implies that the option is out-of-the-money and that the holder would prefer to abandon it, limiting his loss to the premium P forfeit up front. In that case, the gross return is zero and the net return corresponding to the put premium P is negative.

GROSS AND NET RETURN "ZONES"

Zone		Gross Return	Net Return
I:	In-the-money, U less than $E - P$	Positive	Positive
II:	In-the-money, U greater than $E - P$	Positive	Negative
III:	Out-of-the-money	Zero	Negative

In order to illustrate the concept of our three return zones in the context of a long put, consider the following example:

EXAMPLE.   An option trader, after carefully considering likely gold market movements, has concluded that a major bear movement is likely over the next few months. While he is uncertain as to the exact timing of this bear movement, he is confident that it is imminent and elects to purchase a put (rather than selling futures in order to capitalize on this price expectation). Assume that there is available a put exercisable for a gold futures contract that is struck at-the-money at the prevailing price of $500 per ounce. This put may be purchased for $20 per ounce. What returns could accrue to our put holder should the market move in either direction?

Gold Price at Expiration	Gross Return	Less $20 Premium Equals	Net Return
$440	$60		$40
460	40		20
480	20		0
490	10		(10)
500	0		(20)
510	0		(20)
520	0		(20)
540	0		(20)

In this example (also see Figure 6.5), zone I, where both a positive gross and net return are possible, extends from the exercise price of $500 less the premium of $20, or $480 on downwards. In this zone, the gross return upon exercise implied by the ability to sell a commodity at an exercise price in excess of the commodity's current value exceeds the premium forfeit up front. Zone II extends from the breakeven point of $480 on upwards to the exercise price of $500. As is apparent from the returns that accrue when the terminal commodity price equals $490, the gross return is positive but is dominated by the forfeiture of the premium upon original option purchase. Finally, zone III extends from the exercise price of $500 on upwards out-of-the-money. In this zone, the put holder would be foolish to exercise by selling a commodity at the exercise price when it is valued in excess of that price. Therefore, the put holder will

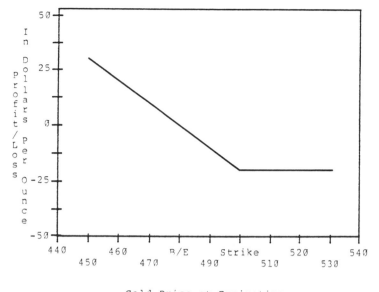

Gold Price at Expiration

Figure 6.5 Return zones for a long put position

abandon the option, realizing a gross return of zero and a net loss equal to the original put premium of $20. Under these circumstances, the benefits associated with a long put as compared to a short underlying commodity position are most apparent. Let's compare the returns that would be associated with each strategy, assuming that a gold futures contract could be sold at $500:

Gold Price at Expiration	(1) Returns on Long Put	(2) Returns on Short Futures	Difference (1) − (2)
$440	$40	$60	($20)
460	20	40	(20)
480	0	20	(20)
490	(10)	10	(20)
500	(20)	0	(20)
510	(20)	(10)	(10)
520	(20)	(20)	0
530	(20)	(30)	10
540	(20)	(40)	20
550	(20)	(50)	30
560	(20)	(60)	40

The foregoing table illustrates that while the put holder foregoes the $20 premium, thereby restricting his participation in the bear movement, he also limits his risk to $20. Thus the trader who had shorted futures at $500 risks a great deal more than the option trader. In our previous example, we had stated that the put holder was bearish but was uncertain as to when the bear move could be expected during the life of the option. If he had elected to sell futures instead of buying a put, he may have limited his staying power in the market. He could have been subject to troublesome margin calls in the event of interim bull movement before the ultimate bear move.

In our discussion of the short call strategy, it was stated that, although a call writer profits by bear movement, the short call strategy is best practiced when a somewhat more neutral scenario is forecast. If one were truly quite bearish, a long put strategy represents a better way to capitalize on that bearish forecast than a short call.

EXAMPLE.   Referencing the situation in the previous example, consider the returns that would accrue to our option trader if he buys a put or if he sells a call in order to capitalize on a bearish forecast. Assume that both puts and calls are available struck at-the-money at $500, exercisable for gold futures, and both trading at $20 per ounce premiums. What returns would be associated with the application of either strategy?

Gold Price at Expiration	(1) Returns on Long Put	(2) Returns on Short Call	Difference (1) − (2)
$420	$60	$20	$40
440	40	20	20
460	20	20	0
480	0	20	(20)
490	(10)	20	(30)
500	(20)	20	(40)
510	(20)	10	(30)
520	(20)	0	(20)
540	(20)	(20)	0
560	(20)	(40)	20
580	(20)	(60)	40

As illustrated, it's far better to buy the put when a large bear movement is expected than to sell a call. Moreover, the long put strategy permits the trader to limit downside risk in the event of a major bull move. Thus, when market volatility is high, one may state that the long put strategy is far more attractive than the short call strategy. If market volatility is low and the underlying commodity price remains fairly stable, then the short call strategy is more attractive than the long put, regardless of whether a slight bear or bull movement is experienced.

Thus far we have only considered long put options struck at-the-money. To complete this analysis, examination of long put strategies using both in- and out-of-the-money puts is warranted. As always, the major distinction between options that are in-the-money from those that are out-of-the-money is the premium they command in the marketplace. Of course, the definitions of in- and out-of-the-money are reversed in the context of puts as opposed to calls. This means that the higher the exercise price, the more the put is worth. To illustrate this concept, consider puts exercisable for physical silver bullion. Assume that silver currently is valued at $10.20 per ounce and there are available puts struck at $9.00, $9.50, $10.00, $10.50, and $11.00 per ounce. The first two options are by definition out-of-the-money because no return is implied by the sale of a commodity at a price less than the prevailing market price. The $10.00 put, although strictly out-of-the-money, is nevertheless near-the-money; and as stated earlier, slightly out-of-the-money options generally are the most popular insofar as these options do not have any intrinsic value to compromise the leverage associated with the option. The final two options, struck at $10.50 and $11.00 per ounce, are in-the-money because a gross profit is implied by the sale of a commodity at a price in excess of the current market price. Assume that market volatility equals 30%, there are 90 days to option expiration, short-term interest rates are at 8%, and holding costs amount to 1% per annum. As a preliminary step, we must determine the premium levels expected to be associated with each option. They are:

	Strike Price	Premium
Out-of-the-money	$9.00	$0.12
Out-of-the-money	9.50	0.24
Near-the-money	10.00	0.41
In-the-money	10.50	0.65
In-the-money	11.00	0.95

As is apparent, the in-the-money puts command successively increasing premiums corresponding to the amount by which they are in-the-money. A low premium generally suggests a relatively low probability of a large return insofar as potential profits and losses must balance when an option is fairly priced. What is of interest at this point is the breakeven point associated with each option as well as the maximum risk and return the put holder may expect (see Figure 6.6).

Breakeven Points and Market Moves to Realize Maximum Profit, Loss, and Breakeven					
Strike price	$9.00	$9.50	$10.00	$10.50	$11.00
Max return	0.71	1.09	1.42	1.68	1.88
Market move for max return	(2.03)	(2.03)	(2.03)	(2.03)	(2.03)
Breakeven point	8.88	9.26	9.59	9.85	10.05
Market move to break even	(1.32)	(0.94)	(0.61)	(0.35)	(0.15)
Max loss	0.12	0.24	0.41	0.65	0.95
Market move for max loss	0	0	0	0.30	0.80

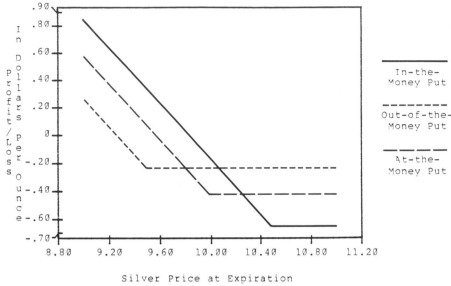

Figure 6.6 In-, out-, and at-the-money put purchase

In the foregoing cases, the maximum return occurs when the market moves sharply downwards. Again, we use the value for a bear movement of three standard deviations downwards; in this case, we are 99% confident that the market will not move down below $8.17. Where the market moves downwards in this magnitude, the put holder who had purchased in-the-money puts may realize the largest returns. Note, however, that the holder of in-the-money options risks a good deal more than the holder of out-of-the-money options, as represented by the original premiums paid to secure the options. When an in-the-money put is purchased, the breakeven point is higher and, therefore, more readily realizable. In addition, the market must actually appreciate before the holder of in-the-money puts is subject to the maximum loss. These results suggest that put holders must (1) assess the magnitude of the bear movement expected, and (2) assess the degree of confidence they maintain in that price forecast. If one expects a large bear movement, then one may be advised to buy out-of-the-money puts, particularly when one has a limited degree of confidence in that forecast. Since major moves occur with less frequency than minor moves, it makes sense that one generally must have less confidence in a dramatic than a relatively weak bearish forecast. On the other hand, if one expects a relatively small bear movement with great confidence, one may become inclined to buy in-the-money puts. Because puts with a variety of strike prices should be available at any given time, option traders should be able to tailor their trading strategy quite closely to the market forecasts to which they may subscribe.

Although a long put strategy may be motivated by the best of market forecasts, sometimes forecasts are not realized in practice. Under those circumstances, put holders may become inclined to limit their losses. This is particularly true for holders of in-the-money options who risk larger sums in pursuit of relatively large rewards. Under these circumstances, the most apparent strategy that may be pursued to limit loss is simply to execute a closing sale of the put. As discussed previously, when an option is in-the-money, the premium will fluctuate more dramatically in response to changing values of the underlying commodity than when the option is out-of-the-money. Because the premium associated with an out-of-the-money option falls slower than premiums associated with in-the-money options, the purchase of an out-of-the-money put may be considered more conservative than the purchase of an in-the-money put. Note, however, that an in-the-money put premium will likewise appreciate less dramatically in response to a favorable movement in the underlying commodity market. Just because delta is always less than, or at a maximum, equal to 1.0 does not suggest that the put holder's losses upon the execution of a closing sale in response to a bullish market will always be less than the losses implied by the bull movement in the underlying commodity. Delta is applicable only over short periods and over relatively small market movements. In addition, over time, the premium will fall as the option's time value declines. In fact, some cases may be constructed where the underlying market moves favorably or downward in the case of a put holder and the premium actually depreciates because of the diminished time value associated with the option.

EXAMPLE.   Put options exercisable for stock index futures contracts are available struck at-the-money at 150 and out-of-the-money at 148; the stock index futures contract is trading at 150. Market volatility equals 20%; there are 120 days until option expiration; and short-term rates equal 8%. Under these circumstances, the fair market values of the at- and out-of-the-money puts equal 6.98 and 5.44 index points, respectively. Both positions were applied in anticipation of a falling market. However, let's assume that the market unexpectedly began to rise to 151 over the next 10 days; at this point, both the 150 and 148 options are out-of-the-money and fall in value to 5.97 and 5.04 index points, respectively. This equates to a loss of 1.01 points (5.97 − 6.98) on the 150 put and 0.40 point (5.04 − 5.44) on the 148 put upon the execution of a closing sale. As we can see, the put that originally was out-of-the-money generates a smaller loss than the put that originally was in-the-money. What losses would be incurred if the market appreciated to the same 151 over a period of 60 days instead of only 10 days? Holding all other factors equal, the 148 put would decline to 3.37 points and the holder would realize a loss of 2.07 index points (3.37 − 5.44) upon the execution of a closing sale. The 150 put would decline in value more sharply to 4.26 index points and the holder would realize a loss of 2.72 index points (4.26 − 6.98) upon the execution of a closing sale. Again, we see that the loss on the at-the-money option exceeds the loss on the out-of-the-money option. What would happen if the market actually declined to 147 over the next 100 days? Presumably, the put holders would profit through the execution of a closing sale subsequent to such favorable price movement. Unfortunately, holding all other things equal, the 148 put declines to 3.45 for a 1.99 index point loss (3.45 − 5.44) while the 150 put declines to 4.13 for an even greater loss of 2.85 index points (4.13 − 6.98). In this case, the time values associated with the two options fell faster than the rise in intrinsic value attributable to a bearish price movement.

The closing sale is the most obvious strategy that can be employed to cut losses short on a declining long put position. Some may suggest the exercise of the put to liquidate the option. However, this is usually inadvisable for the same reasons an exercise of a declining long call position is not recommended: the loss upon exercise must exceed the loss attributable to a closing sale whenever the put has any time value left in it. As a start, it is apparent that a put holder will only exercise an in-the-money put. The gross profit would equal the in-the-money amount or the exercise price E less the underlying market price U while the net return would equal this gross amount less the premium P. If the long put is being closed out to cut short losses, presumably the net return would be negative. Where there is any time value left in the put, the current put premium must be in excess of the original premium P paid to secure the option. Therefore, the loss implied by a closing sale, equal to the current premium less the original premium, must be greater than the net loss implied by an exercise.

Where the put holder has some residual faith that the market ultimately will vindicate his bearish views, the put holder may desire to execute other loss-limiting strategies. These strategies permit the trader to maintain the long put position while holding a countervailing position intended to insulate against a large bull move and the loss of the full premium. For example, the put holder may sell another put of the same class (with the same expiration) but with a lower strike price in order to create a bearish vertical put spread (this strategy is discussed in greater detail in a subsequent section). Another strategy would have the put holder liquidate the original long put through a closing sale and immediately reenter the market with a put whose strike price was somewhat lower. This put would be farther away from the money than the original option, would command a lower premium, and consequently, entail less risk. Of course, long option strategies of the put or call variety are alluring in large part because of the limited risk involved; therefore, the put holder should be prepared to part with the original premium in the event of an adverse event. Those who cannot comfortably buy a put should restrict their activities to less risky option strategies in the first place.

Put Writing

The sale of a put, also known as the writing or granting of a put, mirrors the long put strategy precisely with respect to both risk and returns. Of course, the balance between risks and returns cannot be considered symmetrical insofar as the put writer takes on a theoretically unlimited risk in return for a limited potential return. As mentioned above, call strategies are generally more appealing to the trading public than put strategies. In addition, because of the theoretically unlimited risk associated with the short put, the trading public has made the least use of the short put strategy of the four possible outright option strategies. Conceptually, if one fully grasps the long put strategy, the short put strategy provides no challenge; the returns that accrue to the put writer are the exact opposite of the returns that accrue to the put holder.

EXAMPLE. Our trader is bullish on the price of silver and believes that he could capitalize on this expectation by selling puts. Silver is currently at $14.00 per ounce and an at-the-money option is available trading at a $0.70 premium. The put is sold outright and held until expiration. Let's compare the risks and returns of the put writer to those of the option trader who may have held bearish sentiments and bought the put. Assume that the put holder's pricing forecast is realized and the silver market appreciates $2.00 per ounce to $16.00. At this point, the put holder would be inclined to abandon the option; if the option were exercised, this would imply the sale of a commodity for $14.00 when it is valued $2.00 higher at $16.00. Thus the option would expire unexercised and the put writer would retain the full $0.70 premium and count the same as profit. Likewise, the put holder would be forced to content himself with the forfeiture of the full $0.70 premium. Now consider the case where the put writer's views are contradicted by the marketplace—silver declines $2.00 per ounce to $12.00. At this point, the put holder could be expected to take advantage of the opportunity to sell silver at the $14.00 exercise price when it is valued at only $12.00. The holder would realize a $2.00 profit on exercise less the $0.70 premium forfeit up front for a profit of $1.30 per ounce. The writer would be compelled to buy silver at $14.00 when it is only valued at $12.00—this implies a $2.00 loss cushioned by the initial receipt of the $0.70 premium for a loss of $1.30.

Once again, we may find it useful to break down the returns that accrue to the put writer with varying terminal levels of the underlying commodity. By examining returns associated with terminal values of the underlying commodity, that is, the price of the commodity upon option expiration, it is implied that the put writer is expected to retain the short put position until it expires. A reasonable alternative for the put writer is simply to engage in a closing purchase, thereby offsetting the short put position prior to expiration. When the short put position is retained until expiration, it is the put holder who has the option to exercise or abandon the put, not the writer.

The returns associated with retaining a short put position can be broken down into a gross and a net return, similar to the way in which the returns that accrue to the holder of the long put position can be categorized. Once more, the gross return refers to the return associated with the exercise or abandonment of the put while the net return refers to the gross return, adjusted upwards in the case of a put writer by the initial receipt of the premium. Because the option will only be exercised when it is in-the-money and in the case of a put that means when the exercise price E is in excess of the underlying market price U, the put writer's gross returns can only be negative or in the best case zero where the option is abandoned. Of course, on a net basis, the premium is always counted as profit, although the premium may be more or less than the gross loss:

GROSS AND NET RETURNS FOR SHORT PUT

When the Put Is Exercised	When the Put Is Abandoned
(E)	Gross return
U	always
Gross return	equals zero
P	P
Net return	Net return

If the underlying market price moves downward and the option is in-the-money, then one may expect that it will be exercised. Similarly, an out-of-the-money put will be abandoned. The put writer begins at an advantage over the put holder insofar as he receives the premium initially. Because the premium will at least equal the in-the-money valuation of the option, the market must move downwards to some extent before the holder can realize a profit. Thus if the market remains stable, the writer will invariably realize a profit through the sale of the put; and if the put expires out-of-the-money, then this profit equals the full premium. If the option expires while it is in-the-money, it can be expected to be exercised, of course. But if the market remained stable, this implies that the holder's gross profit on exercise must be less than the premium forfeit. Once again, the writer profits on a net basis. Even if the market moves slightly downwards against the writer, there is still some probability that the writer, not the holder, will realize a profit on a net basis. So long as the underlying market remains over the breakeven point represented by the exercise price E less the original put premium P, or $E - P$, then the put writer will profit on a net basis and the holder will realize a loss. This profit and loss, respectively, will equal the difference between the breakeven point and the underlying market price at expiration (assuming that the put is in-the-money). Again, the concept of return "zones" may be useful to describe these circumstances.

GROSS AND NET RETURN "ZONES"

Zone		Gross Return	Net Return
I:	In-the-money, U less than $E - P$	Negative	Negative
II:	In-the-money, U greater than $E - P$	Negative	Positive
III:	Out-of-the-money	Zero	Positive

To illustrate the concept of these three return zones, note the following example (also see Figure 6.7):

EXAMPLE.   A trader believes that the price of gold is likely to move upwards somewhat or at least remain relatively static. In order to take advantage of this market scenario, the trader sells a put struck at-the-money at $420 per ounce for a premium of $20 per ounce. What would this trader's returns be should the market move in either direction?

Gold Price at Expiration	Gross Return	Plus $20 Premium Equals	Net Return
$360	($60)		($40)
380	(40)		(20)
400	(20)		0
410	(10)		10
420	0		20
440	0		20
460	0		20

In the foregoing example, zone I extends from the breakeven point of $400 on downwards. In this zone, the option is exercised and the writer's gross losses equal the in-the-money valuation or the exercise price E of $420 less the underlying market price U. The net return is $20 higher by virtue of the receipt of the $20 premium. Zone II extends from the $400 strike price to the $420 exercise price. In this zone, the put sale remains profitable on a net basis. But, of

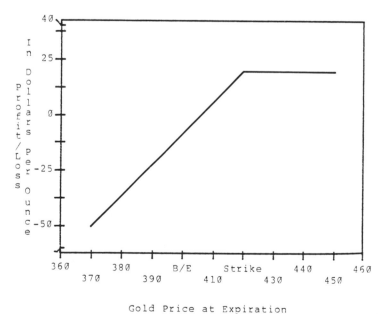

Figure 6.7   Return zones for an outright put writer

course, the profit represented by the premium is eroded by the in-the-money valuation. Put writers may take some comfort in the fact that the market can actually move downwards into-the-money and still permit them to take a net profit. Finally, zone III extends from the $420 strike price on upwards. In this area, the put is out-of-the-money and can be expected to be abandoned. As a result, the writer will retain the full premium of $20.00; this equals the maximum profit potential for the writer.

Earlier, it was implied that the sale of a put was a rather bullish strategy. It is true that a bull movement will provide the outright put writer with a profit, but it is not necessarily true that an enthusiastically bullish trader will prefer to execute a put sale in order to take advantage of this expectation. If the trader were really quite bullish, he may prefer to buy the underlying commodity as an alternative.

EXAMPLE.   A bullish gold bug is faced with the alternatives of selling a put option exercisable for gold futures or buying the underlying gold futures contract outright. The option is struck at-the-money at the prevailing gold futures price of $460 for a $20 premium. What would our trader's returns be under either of the two alternatives (assuming that both positions are held until option expiration)?

Gold Price at Expiration	(1) Returns on Short Put	(2) Returns on Long Futures	Difference (1) − (2)
$400	($40)	($60)	$20
420	(20)	(40)	20
440	0	20	(20)
450	10	(10)	20
460	20	0	20
470	20	10	10
480	20	20	0
490	20	30	(10)
500	20	40	(20)
520	20	60	(40)

As one can see, if an investor were truly quite bullish, the alternative of buying the underlying commodity outright would represent a much more attractive possibility than selling a put. At all points over $480 or the exercise price E plus the premium P, $E + P$, the long futures position is more profitable than the short put. In the area bounded by the exercise price of $460 and $E + P$ or $480, the short put is the more profitable alternative, although by diminishing degrees as the underlying price moves higher. Finally, at all points less than the exercise price of $460, the short put represents the more viable alternative by a consistent $20. In fact in our zone II, bounded by the breakeven point of $E − P$ or $440 and the exercise price E of $460, the short put yields a positive net return while the long futures position renders a net loss. In any event, it is apparent that the short put position is the most attractive when the market is expected to be rather static.

At this point, it may be observed that a long call represents another means of taking advantage of a bullish forecast. If one were truly quite confident in an impending bull movement, the long call may represent a more attractive means of taking advantage of the situation than either a short put or a long position in the underlying commodity.

EXAMPLE.   Let's expand upon the situation illustrated in the prior example by considering the returns that would accrue as a result of the application of both a short put and a long call strategy. Assume that both put and call are struck at-the-money at $460 and both command an identical $20 premium:

Gold Price at Expiration	(1) Return on Short Put	(2) Return on Long Call	Difference (1) − (2)
$380	($60)	($20)	$(40)
400	(40)	(20)	(20)
420	(20)	(20)	0
440	0	(20)	20
450	10	(20)	30
460	20	(20)	40
470	20	(10)	30
480	20	0	20
500	20	20	0
520	20	40	(20)
540	20	60	(40)

As illustrated, it may be much more profitable to buy a call when a large bull movement is possible and although resulting in a loss, a long call represents the more attractive strategy should a large bear movement be realized. But when the market is anticipated to remain relatively stable, the short put strategy dominates the long call. In fact, when the terminal price in the underlying commodity equals the $460 exercise price, the short put strategy renders a return that is $40 per ounce in excess of the returns on the long call. Whenever the terminal value of the commodity remains within the area bounded by the strike price plus or minus the sum of the two premiums, E plus or minus $C + P$, the short put strategy renders a higher return. Although the put writer indeed profits where the market exhibits bullish tendencies, it is rather misleading to forward the short put as a recommended bullish strategy. Instead, this strategy should be used to take advantage of a *neutral* or *slightly bullish* market.

Thus far we have examined only situations where the put was struck at-the-money. Of course, however, a prospective put writer normally has available several puts from which to choose that may be struck at-, in-, or out-of-the-money. To complete our analysis of short put strategies, consider puts exercisable for stock index futures contracts that are struck at 154, 152, 150, 148, and 146 index points while the underlying stock index futures contract is trading at a level of 150.20 index points. In this case, the 154 and 152 puts are struck in-the-money; the 150 put, although not precisely at-the-money (in fact, it is 0.20 index point out-of-the-money), is nonetheless near-the-money; and the 148 and 146 puts are struck out-of-the-money. Assume that there are 90 days until the expiration of these puts, market volatility is at 20%, and short-term rates are around 8%. Under these circumstances, one may calculate the fair market value of these puts as:

	Strike Price	Premium	
Out-of-the-money	146	3.97	Index points
Out-of-the-money	148	4.82	
Near-the-money	150	5.77	
In-the-money	152	6.83	
In-the-money	154	7.99	

As always, the farther the option is in-the-money, the greater the premium it will command. In the case of a short put, the premium represents the maximum profit possible; where the option is out-of-the-money, the maximum potential profit is low relative to the maximum potential profit for an in-the-money option. Where returns are limited, one would expect a lower degree of risk. Let's examine the breakeven point and the "maximum" potential loss (as defined by a three-standard-deviation bear move in the underlying market):

Breakeven Points and Market Moves
to Realize Maximum Profit, Loss, and Breakeven

Strike price	146	147	150	152	154
Max return	3.97	4.82	5.77	6.83	7.99
Market move for max return	0	0	0	1.80	3.80
Breakeven point	142.03	143.18	144.23	145.17	146.01
Market move to break even	8.17	7.02	5.97	5.03	4.19
Max loss	12.49	13.64	14.69	15.63	16.47
Market move for max loss	(20.66)	(20.66)	(20.66)	(20.66)	(20.66)

In this case, the maximum return is represented by the premium received upon put sale. Where the option is out-of-the-money, no market movement whatsoever is required for the put writer to retain the full premium. But where the option is in-the-money, as is the case for the 152 and 154 puts, the market must move upwards over the strike price in order that the option be abandoned and the writer retain the full premium. The breakeven points are represented by the exercise price E less the premium P. As is apparent, the farther the put is out-of-the-money, the less likely it is that the writer will merely break even insofar as successively larger market movements are required to realize that eventuality. When the market is at 150.20 with a standard deviation of market returns equal to 20% per annum and there are 90 days to expiration, the "maximum" downward movement approximated by taking a three-standard-deviation bear move is on the order of 20.66 index points. In other words, we are 99% confident that the market will not move below 129.54 from its current 150.20 over the 90-day life of the puts. This figure is calculated by taking the current level of 150.20 times $e^{(3)(.20)(90/365)}$, or 129.54. Examining the maximum possible losses, it is obvious that where the potential returns are large, the potential losses are similarly large; where potential returns are relatively small, potential losses are also relatively small. This suggests, as shown in Figure 6.8, that conservative put writers may prefer to sell out-of-the-money puts while aggressive put writers may prefer in-the-money puts.

As with other option strategies, there is some risk that once the position is applied, the market will move adversely. These circumstances should be particularly distressing for a put writer. His losses are not constrained to any particular level and the possibility of large losses may exist where a large bear movement occurs. If bearish conditions should prevail after an option trader has applied an outright short put position, the recommended strategy is simply to execute a closing purchase and cut losses short. In-the-money put writers should be particularly careful with respect to monitoring their positions because in-the-money puts may lose their value faster than out-of-the-money

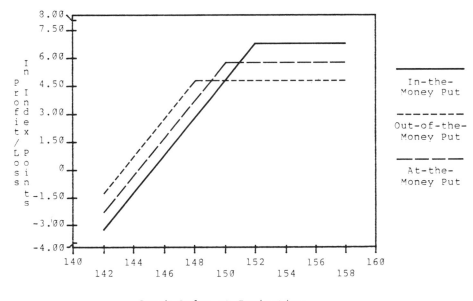

Stock Index at Expiration

Figure 6.8 In-, out-, and at-the-money put sale

puts in response to the same bear movement. Note, however, that the put writer should be interested in extending the time that he holds the short position because no matter whether the put was in- or out-of-the-money initially, its time value will be constantly declining. Obviously, it is in the interest of the put writer that premiums should decline in order that he may buy back the put at a premium less than the premium received upon initial sale.

EXAMPLE. An option trader sells a put exercisable for physical silver bullion struck at $14.00 per ounce; the underlying market price is at $14.15; market volatility is 35%; there are 180 days until option expiration; short-term rates are at 8%; and annual holding costs are about 1%. The put is originally sold at $1.02 per ounce. Although the put sale was motivated by the anticipation of a stable or rising market, in this example we shall assume that the market actually declined to $13.30. It is very important to the put writer to know the period over which this decline could take place. If the decline takes place over the course of 10 days, for example, the fair market premium will appreciate to $1.35. At this point, the put writer may be inclined to execute a closing sale and limit his loss to $0.33 (the difference betwen $1.35 and the original premium of $1.02). If the market moves down $0.85 during the course of only 10 days, this may imply that the market will move down below the breakeven point of $12.98. But if the market moved down $0.85 over the course of 150 days, for example, the put premium would actually decline to $0.89. At this point, the put may be bought back for a *profit* of $0.13 per ounce! This may be attributed to the declining time value associated with the put.

COVERED OPTION TRADING

A "covered" option trading strategy involves the purchase or sale of a particular option in combination with an offsetting or opposite position in the commodity underlying the option. As stated earlier, a call holder and a put writer profit from bullish price movements while call writers and put holders profit in the event of bearish movement. Thus long calls and short puts are offset by a bearish or short position in the underlying commodity market. Short calls and long puts are offset by a bullish or long position in the underlying commodity market. These strategies, although simple compared to some strategies discussed in subsequent pages, are nonetheless complex compared to the outright purchase or sale of an option. Moreover, the application of these strategies can become somewhat confusing when motivated by the intent to capitalize on temporary pricing disparities in the option market relative to the underlying commodity market. These covering strategies are important to understand because they have important implications insofar as commercial or hedging option applications are concerned (discussed in Chapter 7).

"Covering" strategies occur when one, for example, sells a call and is long the commodity. A long position in the underlying commodity market offsets to some degree possible favorable or adverse movements in the value of the option position. Obviously, when the underlying commodity market advances in price, all other things held equal, the call premium may be expected to rise. The former occurrence is favorable to the trader who holds concurrent short call and long commodity positions while the latter occurrence is obviously detrimental to the trader's position. This strategy is covered in the sense that risk is reduced by taking the two positions as opposed to an outright position in either option or commodity. Additionally, the position is covered in that, if the short call is exercised, the trader would be required to sell the underlying commodity, offsetting the long position he had previously held in such commodity.

The strategy that requires the sale of a call in combination with the purchase of the underlying commodity may be referred to as a covered call sale. Similarly, the strategy that requires the sale of a put in combination with the sale of the underlying commodity may be referred to as a covered put sale. For purposes discussed in greater detail below, we do not refer to strategies that involve long puts or calls in combination with offsetting positions in the underlying commodity as "covered put" or "covered call" purchases. Rather, these combinations are referred to as synthetic calls and synthetic puts, respectively, because when we examine the risk and returns potentially associated with these combinations, they closely resemble long calls and long puts.

COVERED OPTION STRATEGIES

		Option Position		Underlying Commodity Position
Covered call sale	=	Short call	+	Long commodity
Covered put sale	=	Short put	+	Short commodity
Synthetic call	=	Long put	+	Long commodity
Synthetic put	=	Long call	+	Short commodity

As we explain in some detail later, the covered call and put sales likewise resemble with respect to risks and returns other strategies that have previously been discussed. Namely, the covered call sale resembles a short put while the covered put sale resembles a short call. Of course, these outright strategies, which the four basic covered strategies resemble, may be motivated by particular pricing forecasts. Similarly, these four covered strategies may be practiced in anticipation of particular future price scenarios. The synthetic call and put strategies, by virtue of the fact that they resemble long calls and long puts, may be practiced where significant bull or bear movements are expected, respectively. Covered call and covered put sales may be practiced where the trader expects the market to remain relatively stable.

PRICING SCENARIOS TO MOTIVATE COVERED STRATEGIES

Covered Strategy	Resembles	Motivated by Price Forecast
Covered call sale	Short put	Neutral to slightly bullish
Covered put sale	Short call	Neutral to slightly bearish
Synthetic put	Long put	Bearish
Synthetic call	Long call	Bullish

Generally, these strategies are employed in situations where the trader already owns a long or short position in the underlying commodity market. This is rather intuitive when one asks why a trader would wish to construct a complex position whose overall risk and return resembles a simple outright option position? Obviously, the transaction costs such as commissions would be lower when executing an outright option transaction because only one trade, rather than two trades, is involved. As discussed in greater detail in Chapter 7, covered option sales are particularly significant for commercial or hedging purposes. More importantly, these strategies have the effect of reducing the risks associated with an outright long or short commodity position. Frequently, options are added to an outright underlying position after this strategy is applied initially to tailor the balance or risk and reward in response to changing market conditions. These strategies may be practiced by holders of outright positions who are caught in a situation where the market is moving in an adverse direction. For one reason or another, it may be easier to reverse one's position by using the option market rather than the underlying commodity market. This may occur when the underlying commodity market is not as liquid as the option market (when, for example, a futures contract underlies the option and the futures trader is fearful of a "lock limit" day). In essence these four covering strategies may be employed as a form of "stop" or "stop loss" order when a position held in the underlying commodity appears to be fluctuating adversely in value.

These simple covering strategies, however, only involve equal units of a commodity in the option and underlying market. There is also the possibility of employing options in combination with the underlying commodity in ratios other than one-for-one. These may be referred to as "delta" or "ratio" strategies. These strategies were considered briefly in Chapter 5 and are motivated by circumstances where the option in question may be under- or overvalued in relation to the underlying commodity. By taking a position in the underlying commodity against the option in proportions indicated by a calculation of the neutral hedge ratio, the option trader hopes to capitalize on these "arbitrage" opportunities. If a call is over- (under-) priced in relation to the underlying commodity, the appropriate strategy is to sell (buy) calls and buy (sell) the underlying commodity. If a put is over- (under-) priced in relation to the underlying commodity, the appropriate strategy is to sell (buy) puts and sell (buy) the underlying commodity. Because these strategies are intended to capitalize on small pricing disparities while carefully managing risk, delta strategies may be regarded essentially as risk-free. If, however, the practitioner does not pay strict attention to the rather subtle methods indicated to carry such an arbitrage off properly, he may be subject to risk and loss.

The following pages illustrate the application of these strategies in greater detail.

Covered Call Sale

A covered call sale involves the purchase of a commodity in combination with the sale or writing of a call option overlying the same commodity. A covered call sale represents a rather conservative strategy insofar as it generally is practiced by those who have already established a long position in some commodity and are intent upon diminishing the risk inherent in the long position. Furthermore, by selling a call against a long commodity position, the trader effectively augments current income by the call premium. Of course, reduced risk and augmented income must come at some price—the price associated with the benefits associated with a covered call sale is that the potential returns associated with the long commodity position in the event of sharp bull movement are limited. However, the losses that would be associated with a major bear movement likewise are reduced, and for many, this may represent an equitable trade-off.

EXAMPLE. A commodity trader believes that silver is fundamentally underpriced and buys physical silver bullion at a price of $12.00 per ounce in anticipation of long-term price appreciation. Although a bull move may be inevitable in the long term, there is some question about short-term movements. In order to limit the risk associated with holding the physical silver over the short term and augment current income, our trader sells a call option on silver bullion struck at $12.00 per ounce for a premium of $1.00 per ounce. What returns would accrue to our trader by the time the option expires in the event of bull or bear price movements in the underlying silver market?

Silver Price at Expiration	(1) Return on Silver	(2) Return on Short Call	Overall Return (1) + (2)
$16.00	$4.00	($3.00)	$1.00
15.00	3.00	(2.00)	1.00
14.00	2.00	(1.00)	1.00
13.00	1.00	0	1.00
12.50	0.50	0.50	1.00
12.00	0	1.00	1.00

Silver Price at Expiration	(1) Return on Silver	(2) Return on Short Call	Overall Return (1) + (2)
11.50	(0.50)	1.00	0.50
11.00	(1.00)	1.00	0
10.00	(2.00)	1.00	(1.00)
9.00	(3.00)	1.00	(2.00)
8.00	(4.00)	1.00	(3.00)

Under these circumstances, our commodity trader locks in a return equal to $1.00 but no more in the case of price appreciation; if the market experiences a bear movement, the covered call writer's losses in the underlying commodity market are cushioned by the receipt of the $1.00 premium. Thus the market must move down below the underlying commodity price to the extent of the premium before the covered call writer experiences a loss. In this case, the option trader is better off having written the call at any terminal commodity price less than $13.00 (or the $12.00 strike price plus the $1.00 premium). At prices in excess of $13.00, the trader simply limits the returns that otherwise would have accrued on the underlying commodity (see Figure 6.9).

The risk/return profile assumed by the covered call writer resembles closely the risk/return profile of a put writer. The profit is limited to the premium received upon option sale and there are large attendant risks in the event of a precipitous price decline. Generally, however, the covered call writer does

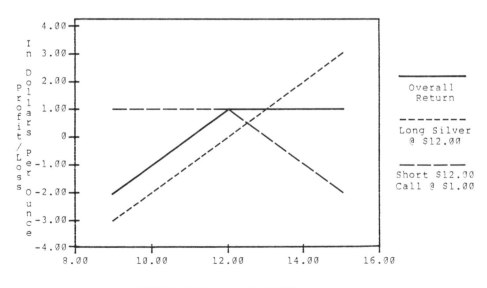

Figure 6.9   At-the-money covered call sale

not see things from the same perspective as an outright put writer. As mentioned above, covered call writing normally is practiced by those who already hold a long position in the underlying commodity market and who see this strategy as a means actually of limiting the risks associated with the long commodity position. As is apparent in the prior example, the range of profit and loss associated with the outright long silver position is reduced through the sale of the call. In effect, the covered call writer is *augmenting his income* through the execution of this strategy insofar as he receives the option premium upon sale. If a sharp upward commodity price movement cannot be expected during the life of the option and the option trader is satisfied to hold the commodity in any event, then he is best advised to sell a call against the option.

Consider the character of the risk and return associated with the covered call sale more closely. In particular, let's employ the concept of return zones once more to examine the risk and returns of a covered call sale. Although the risks and returns associated with this strategy in an overall sense resemble a short put, we will not reiterate our prior section that identified certain return zones for a short put. Instead, let's limit this discussion to a consideration of the difference in returns associated with the outright long commodity versus the aggregate returns associated with the covered call sale. In particular, let's reexamine the results from the previous example where silver was purchased at $12.00 and a call was sold struck at-the-money for a $1.00 premium:

Silver Price at Expiration	(1) Return on Long Silver	(2) Covered Call Sale	Difference (2) − (1)
$16.00	$4.00	$1.00	($3.00)
15.00	3.00	1.00	(2.00)
14.00	2.00	1.00	(1.00)
13.00	1.00	1.00	0
12.50	0.50	1.00	0.50
12.00	0	1.00	1.00
11.50	(0.50)	0.50	1.00
11.00	(1.00)	.0	1.00
10.00	(2.00)	(1.00)	1.00
9.00	(3.00)	(2.00)	1.00
8.00	(4.00)	(3.00)	1.00

In order to compare the extent to which a covered call writer is ahead relative to the simple strategy of holding the underlying commodity outright, please reference the last column. The covered call writer is ahead by virtue of executing the call sale at all prices less than the exercise or underlying commodity price plus the original call premium, or $13.00 ($12.00 plus $1.00). Between this price of $13.00 and the strike and original underlying commodity price of $12.00, the covered call writer is ahead of the outright silver holder but not to the full extent of the premium. Only at prices less than the strike price will the covered call writer's returns better those of the outright long by a full $1.00—or the original call premium.

We have assumed that the covered call writer would have held the long commodity position in any case, whether or not the price increased or decreased. In the event of downward price movement, the outright long is better off having written calls against the underlying commodity position than not— and better off to the extent of the original premium. Where the price appreciates and the call is exercised, the covered call writer still profits, but of course, his profit is not as great as it might have been had he refrained from writing the call. But this loss, as it were, does not represent an out-of-pocket expense, merely a lost opportunity. (Presumably, an opportunity loss is not as painful as an out-of-pocket loss.) Of course, if the call were exercised, the covered call writer would be obliged to sell the underlying commodity at the strike price; if he still wished to maintain a long position in the underlying market, he would have to reestablish it at the higher prevailing price.

So far only at-the-money calls have been considered; what results could be expected if our commodity trader decides to write in- or out-of-the-money calls against the long position? In particular, consider the case where the silver bullion market is trading at $12.00 and there are calls available struck at-the-money at $12.00, out-of-the-money at $13.00, and in-the-money at $11.00 per ounce. There are 90 days until option expiration; market volatility is at 30%; short-term rates equal 8%; and annualized holding costs are 1%:

	Strike Price	Premium
In-the-money	$11.00	$1.48
At-the-money	12.00	0.85
Out-of-the-money	13.00	0.44

As always, the in-the-money option will command a higher premium than the at- or the out-of-the-money options. Because an in-the-money covered call writer receives a greater premium up front than an out-of-the-money covered call writer, he is afforded the greatest degree of downside protection. This protection must be paid for, however, in the form of relatively low profit potential. Consider the breakeven points and maximum returns associated with each of the three aforementioned commodities and as shown in Figure 6.10.

BREAKEVEN POINTS AND MAXIMUM PROFIT POTENTIAL

	Strike Price	Premium	Breakeven Point	Maximum Profit
In-the-money	$11.00	$1.48	$10.52	$0.48
At-the-money	$12.00	$0.85	$11.15	$0.85
Out-of-the-money	$13.00	$0.44	$11.56	$1.44

In the event of a precipitous price decline, of course, the loss potentially associated with the covered call strategy—no matter whether the option is sold

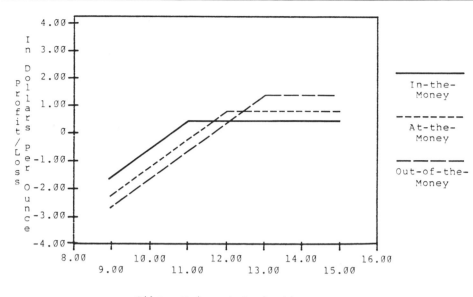

Silver Price at Expiration

Figure 6.10   In-, at-, and out-of-the-money covered call sales

in-, at-, or out-of-the-money—may theoretically be unlimited. In any event, it is possible to identify a pattern emerging out of the foregoing table. Specifically, the breakeven point in all cases equals the price at which the underlying commodity was purchased (U) less the call premium C. The maximum profit in all cases equals the call premium C less the in-the-money amount (where the option is in fact in-the-money), or plus the out-of-the-money amount (where the option is out-of-the-money). Where the option is struck at-the-money, of course, the maximum profit equals the call premium C. This is unadjusted by any reference to the relationship between the exercise and underlying prices.

$$\text{Breakeven Point} = U - C$$
$$\text{Maximum Profit} = C - (U - E)$$

If one were to calculate the breakeven points and maximum profits associated with the three covered call strategies discussed above, one would find that the foregoing formulas would indeed yield the results displayed above. Since the premium associated with the option that is furthest in-the-money will by definition be the greatest, it is obvious that the breakeven point of a covered call strategy employing a deep in-the-money option will necessarily be low relative to other covered call option possibilities. This is obvious when considering the formula for the breakeven point. The underlying market price must be the same for all calls of the same class. Likewise, it is also obvious from the formula for the maximum profit potential that a covered call strategy that utilizes a deep in-the-money option will potentially be least profitable relative to strategies that involve calls that may not be far in-the-money or possibly out-of-the-money. So while there is low risk associated with an in-the-money covered call writing strategy, there is low profit potential (and, of course, this is consistent with many of our previous findings). At the other extreme, covered call strategies that involve out-of-the-money options are associated with relatively high breakeven points and high profit potentials. As such, there are higher risks, which are compensated by higher potential returns.

The fact that there are generally low risks associated with in-the-money covered calls relative to out-of-the-money covered calls may further be explained by reference to the concept of delta. Recall that where an option is deep in-the-money, delta approaches 1.0; and where an option is deep out-of-the-money, the ratio approaches zero. Somewhere in between the two extremes, where the option is at- or near-the-money, delta equals .5. The delta factor provides an indication of the amount by which the premium will fluctuate relative to a particular movement in the underlying commodity market. Where delta equals .5, this suggests that a $1 fluctuation in the underlying commodity market will induce a $0.50 movement in the option premium. Where the option is deep in-the-money and the neutral ratio approaches 1.0, then changes in the value of the subject call option can be expected to mirror changes in the value of the covering or offsetting commodity position. Thus the combined changes in the value of the position may be insignificant. Where the option is extremely out-of-the-money and delta approaches zero, no fluctuation is induced in the option premium in response to a change in the value of the underlying commodity. Under those circumstances, the risks assumed by the out-of-the-money covered call writer resemble closely the risks assumed by the outright buyer of the underlying commodity.

EXAMPLE.   Consider the in- and the out-of-the-money covered call strategies discussed above; calls are available exercisable for physical silver bullion, struck in-the-money at $11.00 and out-of-the-money at $13.00 while the underlying market price equals $12.00. Silver bullion is purchased at $12.00 per ounce, and one strategy calls for the purchase of the $11.00 call for $1.48 while the alternate strategy calls for the sale of the $13.00 call at $0.44. The deltas that may be calculated for the in- and out-of-the-money options equal .79 and .38, respectively. This suggests that the expected fluctuation in the option premiums equal approximately 79% and 38% of any fluctuations realized in the underlying silver market. Of course, delta is dynamic over a range of commodity prices and is effective only for small fluctuations over a short period. These options were written when there were 90 days until option expiration. Assume that over the next business day the price of silver rises to $12.20. Holding all other factors constant, the $11.00 call would rise in value $0.16 from $1.48 to $1.64 (this represents 80% of the change in the value of the underlying commodity) while the $13.00 call would rise in value $0.03 from $0.44 to $0.52 (an increase equal to 40% of the increase in the underlying silver market). Thus the in-the-money covered call writer saw the value of his silver rise 20 cents and the value of the short call position fall 16 cents for a 4-cent profit (should the covered call position be liquidated). The out-of-the-money covered call writer saw the same 20-cent rise in the value of his silver position with only an 8-cent loss on the call for a 12-cent profit (assuming liquidation).

In our previous example, we illustrated a case where the underlying commodity price rises, a favorable circumstance for any covered call writer. Of course, should the underlying commodity price decline, the out-of-the-money covered call writer would be subject to larger losses than the in-the-money covered call writer. Therefore the prudent option trader interested in writing calls against a position in the underlying commodity should assess whether the risks associated with a particular strategy are manageable. Furthermore, these facts suggest certain modifications to the basic covered call theme that may be followed in response to changing market conditions. The writer of a covered at- or near-the-money call assumes a relatively moderate stance with respect to both risk and return. Should the market move substantially upwards, however, such an option trader may prefer to liquidate the original short call in favor of a call with a higher strike price. By assuming a position in the higher-struck option, the covered call writer avoids unduly limiting returns on the profitable position in the underlying commodity. Conversely, should the price of the underlying commodity begin to decline, the option trader may wish to liquidate the original short call in favor of an option with a lower strike price. By assuming a position in the lower-struck call, the covered call writer provides an augmented degree of protection from the adverse price movement. Or he may buy an out-of-the-money put in order to enjoy greater downside protection. The combination of a covered call sale (resembling a short put) and a relatively low-struck out-of-the-money put very much resembles a vertical bullish put spread (discussed below).

Covered Put Sale

The covered put sale strategy is conceptually similar to the covered call sale—with the exception, of course, that a put rather than a call is written and the "covering" or offsetting position in the underlying commodity market is short rather than long. From the perspective of a noncommercial option trader, the covered put sale represents a strategy, the viability of which has been increased tremendously by the availability of options on futures contract. Futures markets permit noncommercial traders to take a short position as well as a long position with equal facility. Contrast this to other markets that may underlie an option—it may be quite difficult for a noncommercial trader to short sell a physical commodity such as gold. While short stock sales represent a rather common transaction, covered put sales nonetheless have not been practiced with frequency in the context of the stock option markets. In this respect, then, the availability of options on futures provides investors with another weapon in their investment arsenals.

Just as a covered call sale represents a rather conservative strategy relative to carrying an outright position in the underlying market, a covered put sale may be considered a risk-reducing and income-augmenting strategy for holders of short commodity positions. Naturally, reduced risk and augmented current income must be bought at some price—in this case, the price paid by the covered put writer is the forfeiture of possible large returns in the event of a sharp price decline. Of course, the risk associated with a major bull move is likewise reduced, and it is the reduction of this risk which motivates covered put writers.

EXAMPLE.   A commodity trader sold a Treasury bond futures contract at 76-00/32nds% of par in anticipation of rising interest rates and declining bond prices. Although our trader is confident of a bear move in the long term, he is nonetheless apprehensive about the possibility of an interim bull movement. That may require the payment of variation margins, diminishing the trader's staying power in the market. In order to augment his staying power, our trader elects to sell a put exercisable for T-bond futures against the short bond position. Specifically, a put struck at 76-00 is sold for 1-32/64ths, or $1,500 for a $100,000 face value bond contract. What returns would accrue to the covered put writer in the event of bull or bear movements in the underlying bond futures market by the time the option expires? (Also see Figure 6.11.)

Bond Price at Expiration	(1) Return on Short Bond	(2) Return on Short Put	Overall Return (1) + (2)
70-00	$6,000	($4,500)	$1,500
72-00	4,000	(2,500)	1,500
74-00	2,000	(500)	1,500
74-16	1,500	0	1,500
75-00	1,000	500	1,500
76-00	0	1,500	1,500
76-16	(500)	1,500	1,000
77-00	(1,000)	1,500	500
77-16	(1,500)	1,500	0
78-00	(2,000)	1,500	(500)
79-00	(3,000)	1,500	(1,500)
80-00	(4,000)	1,500	(2,500)
82-00	(6,000)	1,500	(4,500)

In the event of price depreciation, our covered put writer locks in a return equal to $1,500; this represents the maximum return associated with this particular covered short put position. Of course, our trader is nonetheless subject to the risk of loss in the event of price appreciation, but his losses are cushioned to the extent of the $1,500 premium. If this trader had intended to hold the short position regardless, this $1,500 represents augmented income in the event of price appreciation or relative stability.

An examination of the risk/return profile assumed by the covered put writer is strongly reminiscent of the risk/return profile assumed by an outright call writer: profits are fixed in the event of price decline while losses may be large in the event of a major bull movement. But while the covered put sale may have some appeal in its own right, it is probably more widely practiced by traders who, for one reason or another, already hold a short put or a short commodity position and assume the second component of a covered short put position as a means of limiting or changing the nature of the risk associated with the original position. By selling puts against a short underlying position, the trader retains the original bearish position but with diminished chances of realizing a large loss insofar as the two components of the overall position tend to offset each other. Normally, this strategy is practiced by those who already hold a short position in the underlying commodity and feel that the long-term prospects for a bear move are good but are fearful of an interim bull movement. Because a short put position cannot completely offset movements in the underlying commodity (except, of course, where the subject put is deep in-the-money and delta approaches 1.0), the covered put writer still holds a bearish position but realizes some immediate income through the sale of the put. By selling the commodity against an outright bullish short put position, the trader transforms the overall position into a bearish strategy.

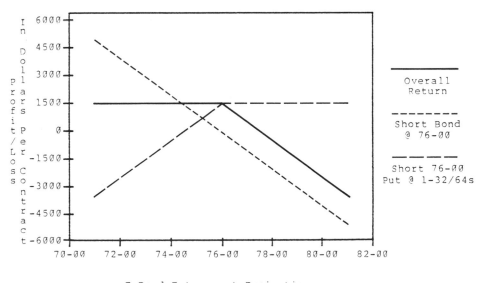

T-Bond Futures at Expiration

Figure 6.11 At-the-money covered put sale

As mentioned above, the risks and returns associated with the covered put sale resemble those associated with an outright short call. By now, a short call should be a very familiar strategy—a short call represents one of the two most simple ways in which to assume a bearish outright option position. Likewise, a commodity trader could simply take an outright short position in the underlying commodity. In order to assess the advantages and disadvantages with selling a put once an outright short position is assumed in the underlying commodity, consider the situation illustrated in our previous example and the difference between the outright short position and the covered put sale:

T-Bond Price at Expiration	(1) Return on Short T-Bond	(2) Covered Put Sale	Difference (2) − (1)
70-00	$6,000	$1,500	($4,500)
72-00	4,000	1,500	(2,500)
74-00	2,000	1,500	(500)
74-16	1,500	1,500	0
75-00	1,000	1,500	500
76-00	0	1,500	1,500
76-16	(500)	1,000	1,500
77-00	(1,000)	500	1,500
77-16	(1,500)	0	1,500
78-00	(2,000)	(500)	1,500
79-00	(3,000)	(1,500)	1,500
80-00	(4,000)	(2,500)	1,500
82-00	(6,000)	(4,500)	1,500

The last column depicts the extent to which the covered put sale strategy compares to the returns on the outright short T-bond. As is apparent, the outright short T-bond strategy dominates the covered put sale strategy in the event of price decline. In fact, where the market experiences a tremendously bearish movement, the trader who is outright short the underlying commodity experiences profits that are considerably in excess of the covered put writer's profits (which are, of course, fixed to $1,500 or the original premium in this example where an at-the-money put is sold). The losses in the event of a bull move are reduced to the extent of the put premium received upon option sale where our commodity trader elected to pursue the covered put sale strategy. So at any point under the strike price at 76-00/32nds less the original put premium of 1-32/64ths or $1,500 for a $100,000 face value bond option, or 76-16/32nds, the trader is best off having sold the T-bond futures contract outright. At underlying market prices equal to or in excess of the strike price 76-00, our trader is best off having sold the put against the short T-bond by a uniform $1,500—the original put premium. Between 76-00 and 74-16, our trader is better off having sold the put but by a decreasing margin as the underlying market price declines. One may note, of course, that a loss is implied even in the case of the covered short put where the underlying market price advances above the breakeven point of 77-16/32nds.

If one assumes that the commodity trader intends to hold the short position in the underlying commodity market regardless (under the belief, perhaps, that a major bear movement is inevitable albeit difficult to anticipate precisely), it is obvious that such a trader may be well advised to sell the put if some interim bull movement occurs. The advantage accruing to the covered put writer in that case may be measured in terms of the put premium. Of course, even if the market does exhibit a major bear movement, the covered put writer still participates in such movement. However, he may realize the full profit implied by the movement by virtue of having sold the put. Obviously, the put will be exercised in the event of price decline and the covered put writer will be compelled to buy the underlying commodity at the strike price, thereby liquidating the original short commodity position. But, just like the covered call writer, a covered put writer may simply chalk this off as an opportunity cost insofar as it does not represent an out-of-pocket expense. Subsequently, our commodity trader could reestablish a short commodity position if he felt that the bear movement would continue.

While it's quite convenient to illustrate an option strategy using an at-the-money option, only rarely will an option trader be able to buy or sell an option when it is precisely at-the-money. In any event, one's risk/return profile may be modified signiicantly through the use of in- or out-of-the-money options as an alternative. In order to illustrate the use of these options, consider the case where the T-bond futures market is trading at 76-00/32nds and puts are available struck at-the-money at 76-00, in-the-money at 78-00, and out-of-the-money at 74-00. There are 120 days until expiration; market volatility equals 18%; and short-term rates equal 8%. Under such circumstances, these options may be trading at the following levels:

	Strike Price	Premium
In-the-money	78-00	$4,061
At-the-money	76-00	2,946
Out-of-the-money	74-00	2,038

As is apparent, an in-the-money option will always command a higher premium than an at- or out-of-the-money option. As a result, the in-the-money covered put writer is afforded a higher level of protection than an at- or out-of-the-money covered put writer insofar as protection generally corresponds to the premium level. Naturally, such protection must be bought at the cost of compromising the profit potential associated with the position. To illustrate this concept, examine the breakeven points and the maximum profits potentially associated with each of the following three strategies:

BREAKEVEN POINTS AND MAXIMUM PROFIT POTENTIAL

	Strike Price	Premium	Breakeven Point	Maximum Profit
In-the-money	78-00	$4,061	82-02	$2,061
At-the-money	76-00	2,946	78-30	2,946
Out-of-the-money	74-00	2,038	76-01	4,038

The careful reader will have observed a pattern developing in the foregoing cases, just as in the case of a covered call sale. The in-the-money covered put writer is afforded a high degree of protection by virtue of a relatively high breakeven point but enjoys relatively low profit potential; the out-of-the-money covered put writer is afforded relatively low protection with a low breakeven point but high profit potential. The breakeven point for a covered put strategy equals the strike or exercise price E plus the put premium P, or $E + P$. The maximum profit potentially associated with a significant price decline equals the put premium P received upon sale less the in-the-money amount or the exercise price E less the underlying market price U (these formulas may be confirmed by working through the situations depicted above):

$$\text{Breakeven Point} = U + P$$
$$\text{Maximum Profit} = P - (E - U)$$

Generally, low risks are associated with in-the-money covered put sales and high risks with out-of-the-money covered put sales. Likewise, high potential returns are associated with out-of-the-money covered put sales and low potential returns with in-the-money covered put sales. These facts may be explained by reference to the concept of delta. Recall that where the subject option is deep in-the-money, delta, of the amount by which the option premium will change in response to a particular change in the underlying commodity price, will approach 1.0. In other words, a 1% change in the underlying market price will result in a near 1% change in the value of the put premium. On the contrary, where the option is exceedingly out-of-the-money, a relatively modest change will be induced in the put premium in response to a movement in the underlying commodity market (in fact, at some point, the option becomes worthless and no change may be induced in the premium). Of course, where the option is at- or near-the-money, delta will approximate .50; this implies that the change in the premium will be about 50% of the change in the underlying market. Thus the farther the amount by which an option is in-the-money, the closer delta will be to 1.0 and the more precisely offsetting the option and underlying commodity positions will be. The farther the option is out-of-the-money, the closer delta will be to zero, implying that the option does not reduce the risks associated with holding a short position in the underlying commodity.

EXAMPLE.   In order to illustrate how the in-the-money covered put sale represents a safer strategy than the out-of-the-money covered put sale,

consider the T-bond strategies illustrated above. T-bond futures
are trading at 76-00/32nds while puts are available struck in-the-
money at 78-00 and out-of-the-money at 74-00. The in-the-money
put may be sold for a total of $4,061 while the out-of-the-money
put may be sold for only $2,038. The deltas associated with the in-
and out-of-the-money puts equal .58 and .38, respectively. This
suggests that the change in the premiums will approximate 58%
and 38% of any (small) change in the underlying T-bond market
(over a relatively short period). There are 120 days until option
expiration; assume that over the next business day, the underlying
T-bond market declines from 76-00/32nds to 75-24/32nds. At the
same time, the in-the-money put appreciates from the original
$4,061 to $4,200 (this is a change on the order of $139 or about 56%
of the $250 fluctuation implied by a movement in the underlying
T-bond market from 76-00 to 75-24). The out-of-the-money put appreciates from $2,038 to $2,140 (this is a $102 change or about 41%
of the change in the underlying commodity). Thus the in-the-
money covered put writer realizes a $139 loss on the put offset with
a $250 profit in the underlying market for a net of $111. On the
other hand, the out-of-the-money covered put writer realizes a
$102 loss on the put and a $250 profit in the underlying commodity
for $148 profit in the aggregate. (This example assumes that the
two components of the covered put sale are liquidated at this
point.)

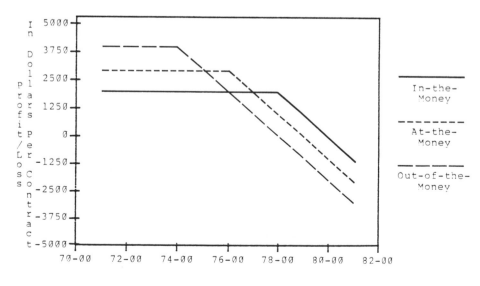

T-Bond Futures at Expiration

Figure 6.12 In-, at-, and out-of-the-money covered put sales

These examples assume that the underlying market price moves downward, in a generally favorable direction for any covered put writer (also see Figure 6.12). If the market moved upwards, in an unfavorable direction, any losses to which the in-the-money covered put writer may be subject would generally be less than any losses realized by the out-of-the-money covered put writer. In such bull movements, the prudent out-of-the-money covered put writer may prefer to liquidate the current put in favor of a put with a higher strike price, that is, an option that is farther towards or in-the-money. In this way, our trader is afforded a higher degree of protection from bull movements. But this assumes that the option trader holds some residual faith in an ultimate bear movement (or at least a certain degree of stability in the market). If the market shows certain signs of rising, the option trader may prefer to liquidate the short commodity position and hold on to the short put position (which by nature favors a bull fluctuation). Another possibility is to buy a high-struck out-of-the-money call. Because the covered put resembles a short call, the combination of a covered put and long high-struck put resembles a bearish vertical call spread.

Synthetic Put

An option contract is quite versatile. Option traders can create an almost endless variety of risk/return scenarios, corresponding closely to the needs of the moment. The use of complex option strategies can permit the trader to construct complex risk/return scenarios; likewise, complex strategies may sometimes be analogous to rather simple strategies when viewed from an aggregate perspective. A synthetic put strategy, as its name implies, is a rather complex strategy that, when reduced to its lowest common denominator, resembles an outright long put strategy.

A synthetic put strategy calls for the purchase of a call in combination with the sale of the underlying commodity. Note that a long call is essentially bullish while the short commodity position is bearish. These are offsetting positions. However, it is interesting to note that, when combined, the synthetic put holder's position becomes essentially bearish (just as a long put position is bearish). In the simplest terms, the short commodity position may be considered "more bearish" than the long call is bullish and the bearish characteristics of the short commodity dominate the bullish characteristics of the long call. Of course, the synthetic put created by the purchase of the call and sale of the underlying commodity does not permit the holder to participate fully in a possible bear movement. But the synthetic put holder is insulated from the risk of a large bull movement. His risk is limited to an amount determined when the synthetic put initially is established.

EXAMPLE.   Options exercisable for stock index futures contracts are the subject of this example: assume that the futures contract is trading at 150.00 and a call struck at-the-money at 150 may be purchased for

4 index points. Likewise, a put is struck at-the-money at 150 and may also be purchased for 4 index points. Compare the risks and returns associated with the creation of the synthetic put relative to buying the put outright:

Index Value at Expiration	(1) Return on Long Call	(2) Return on Short Futures	Synthetic Put (1) + (2)	Return on Long Put
162	8 Points	(12) Points	(4) Points	(4) Points
158	4	(8)	(4)	(4)
154	0	(4)	(4)	(4)
150	(4)	0	(4)	(4)
146	(4)	4	0	0
142	(4)	8	4	4
138	(4)	12	8	8

As is apparent, the risks and returns associated with the synthetic put are the same as the risks and returns associated with the long put (see Figure 6.13). In the event of sharp bear movement, the synthetic put holder and outright put holder enjoy potentially unlimited returns. In the event of a bull movement, both synthetic and outright put holders stand to lose. However, the loss is defined initially, in the foregoing case, by the premium forfeit up front to purchase the call or the put. (Since this example used at-the-money options on futures, both put and call premiums were equal; if they were not equal, an opportunity to earn arbitrage profits may be available.) The question may be

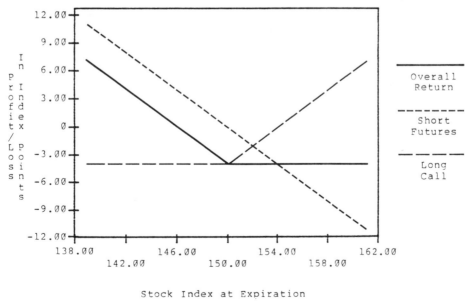

Figure 6.13   Synthetic put

asked: why would any option trader want to create a synthetic put position when an equivalent position may be created through the simple purchase of a put? Before answering this question consider that the outright sale of a put would involve a single commission while the synthetic put holder would normally incur two commissions—one for each leg of the transaction.

To answer this question, consider a commodity trader who has shorted the underlying commodity in anticipation of a decline in price. In particular, assume that our trader has shorted a stock index futures contract. While our trader may firmly subscribe to the inevitability of a price decline, it would nonetheless be unwise to hold the short position in the face of a strong upward move in stock index prices. (Traders are often advised to "cut short your losses and let your profits run.") Under such circumstances, our trader would normally want to liquidate the losing short position by buying back the futures contract. But what if our trader does not have the time to follow the market closely in order to place an order to liquidate the losing position in a timely manner? Normally, the solution to this problem would be to place a "stop loss" order with the broker to buy back the short position in the face of an upward move. But what if the bull move is so unexpected and sharp that it is impossible to execute the closing purchase in a timely fashion? When the market is volatile, a trader may wish to use the long call as a "stop loss" order to liquidate the short position.

If the market moves sharply upwards, the long call leg of the synthetic put becomes profitable to exercise. By exercising the long call, the trader buys the underlying commodity. Since the synthetic put holder is already long the underlying commodity, the exercise of the call simply results in an offsetting position. Thus the short commodity position is liquidated efficiently. If the market moves downwards as expected, the synthetic put holder profits as he maintains the short commodity position and as the long call expires worthless. The "price" of this stop loss order equals the premium paid to acquire the call.

By purchasing an out-of-the-money call, the price of such protection is decreased—but, of course, this diminished cost comes at the expense of forfeiting some degree of protection. To illustrate, consider the purchase of in-, out-, and at-the-money calls to offset a short position in the underlying commodity. In particular, consider a trader who shorts a stock index futures contract at 150.00 and has available an in-, at-, and out-of-the-money call to purchase as a form of stop loss order, selling at the following prices:

	Strike Price	Premium
In-the-money	148 Points	5.69 Points
At-the-money	150	4.69
Out-of-the-money	152	3.80

Assuming that the synthetic put positions are held until the expiration of the long call leg, the following results are associated with the purchase of the in-, at-, or out-of-the-money calls against the short futures contract:

Stock Index at Expiration	In-the-Money Returns	At-the-Money Returns	Out-of-the-Money Returns
158	(3.69)	(4.69)	(5.80)
154	(3.69)	(4.69)	(5.80)
152	(3.69)	(4.69)	(5.80)
150	(3.69)	(4.69)	(3.80)
148	(3.69)	(2.69)	(1.80)
146	(1.69)	(0.69)	0.20
142	2.31	3.31	4.20
138	6.31	7.31	8.20

As is apparent from the foregoing chart (also see Figure 6.14), the safety associated with the sale of an in-the-money call to complete the synthetic put dominates the at- and out-of-the-money options. However, the synthetic put holder who purchases an in-the-money call as opposed to an at- or out-of-the-money call, places a stricter constraint upon possible profits. At points in excess of the long call leg's strike price, the synthetic put holder is subject to a maximum loss. The magnitude of this maximum loss associated with the synthetic put strategy may be calculated as the premium paid up front to secure the call (C) less the difference between the underlying commodity price U and the strike price E, ($U - E$), or:

$$\text{Max Loss} = C - (U - E)$$

The profits potentially associated with this stragey are, at least on a theoretical basis, unlimited. The breakeven point may be calculated as the initial underlying market price U less the call premium C, or:

$$\text{Breakeven Point} = U - C$$

As we can see from the profit/loss chart shown above for the three synthetic put strategies, the maximum losses associated with the in-, at-, and out-of-the-money calls equal 3.69, 4.69, and 5.80 index points, respectively. Although the breakeven points are not overtly shown on the chart, they may be calculated for the in-, at-, and out-of-the-money strategies as 144.31, 145.31, and 146.20, respectively. These results are typical insofar as the safest strategy (the in-the-money strategy) is associated with the breakeven point further from the current underlying market price.

If one examines the risk/return characteristics of the synthetic put, it appears to be rather attractive as risks are limited to a known quantity up front while returns are potentially unlimited. Again, however, we emphasize that the synthetic put strategy would not normally be implemented from scratch to take advantage of an expected bear movement in the underlying commodity. Instead, the outright put purchase produces equivalent results and does not entail the payment of two commissions or the risk that one of the two legs of the position cannot be placed favorably. The synthetic put should be thought

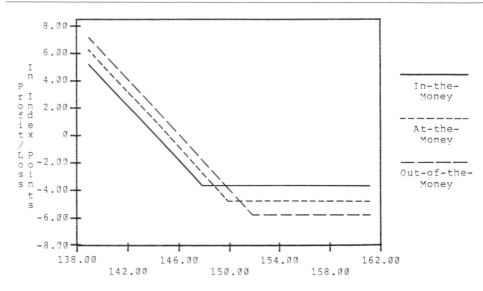

Stock Index at Expiration

Figure 6.14   In-, at-, and out-of-the-money synthetic puts

of as a means of reducing the risk of holding a short outright commodity position in a rising market—as a sophisticated "stop loss" order of sorts.

Parenthetically, one may observe that commodity options originally became popular on domestic commodity exchanges directly as an advanced form of the stop loss order. For example, options on grain futures contracts were available on the Chicago Board of Trade in the early part of this century. They were referred to simply as "bids" and "offers"—bids were today's equivalent of a put, and offers were equivalent to calls. Bids and offers could be purchased at a fixed "commission"—analogous to current-day premiums with the exception that these commissions were fixed and not negotiated. This enabled the bid or offer holder to sell or buy, respectively, at a negotiated discount or premium to the current grain futures price. Thus, originally when an offer was purchased, the holder of an offer had the right to buy at a price just higher than the price at which the futures were sold. As such, bids and offers were uniformly struck out-of-the-money. Although the practices and terminology were different from what is in use today, the concepts were analogous to commodity options as we know them.

Synthetic Call

The synthetic put strategy permits one to assume a risk/return posture similar to an outright long put without taking a position in put options. The synthetic call permits one to assume a position that is similar with respect to both risk and return to an outright long call without taking a position in call options. Specifically, the synthetic call position consists of a long put combined with a long position in the underlying commodity. These positions are offsetting insofar as the long put is essentially bearish while the long commodity is essentially bullish. When combined, however, the holder of the synthetic call has a basically bullish position. In this respect, the bullish long commodity position dominates the bearish put. In effect, the long commodity is "more bullish" than the long put is bearish. The synthetic call holder, just like the outright holder of a call, assumes limited a downside risk at the price of limiting the upside profit potential.

EXAMPLE.   In this example, we examine options exercisable for T-bond futures contracts. Assume that the subject T-bond futures contract is trading at 78-00/32nds% of par and that a put option is struck at-the-money at 78 trading at 2-00/64ths or $2,000 per $100,000 face value contract. Let's compare the synthetic call holder's position to the position of an outright call holder, assuming that a call is likewise available struck at 78 and trading at $2,000:

T-Bond Price at Expiration	(1) Return on Long Put	(2) Return on Long Futures	Synthetic Call (1) + (2)	Return on Long Call
72-00	$4,000	($6,000)	($2,000)	($2,000)
74-00	2,000	(4,000)	(2,000)	(2,000)
76-00	0	(2,000)	(2,000)	(2,000)
78-00	(2,000)	0	(2,000)	(2,000)
80-00	(2,000)	2,000	0	0
82-00	(2,000)	4,000	2,000	2,000
84-00	(2,000)	6,000	4,000	4,000

As illustrated above (also see Figure 6.15), the risk/return posture assumed by the synthetic call holder mirrors precisely the risk/return posture assumed by the outright call holder. Where T-bond rates drop and prices advance, the synthetic and outright call holders profit—potentially to an unlimited extent should the market move up sharply. On the downward side, of course, the risk assumed by the synthetic and outright call holders is limited to the put and call premiums, respectively. As was the case with the synthetic put, one may ask why would an option trader prefer to enter into the synthetic call position as opposed to the outright long call position? Superficially, one may forward the possibility that the put may be purchased at a cheaper price than the call. In our example above, however, we examined the case where both puts and calls were struck at-the-money. We know from Chapter 5 that where there are puts and calls struck at-the-money and exercisable for futures contracts, they should (at least theoretically) trade at the same level. If they do not, arbitrage opportunities may be available, the exploitation of which will tend to drive the put and call prices to equal levels. Although the put and call may not trade at exactly the same levels, the disparity may not be enough to warrant the addi-

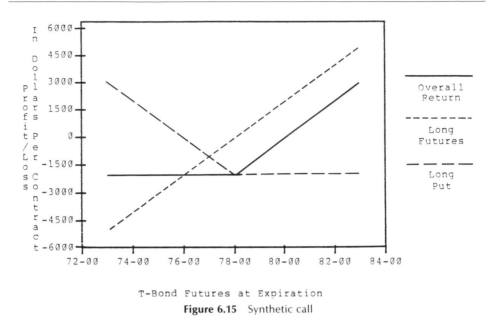

T-Bond Futures at Expiration

Figure 6.15 Synthetic call

tional transaction costs associated with the execution of the synthetic, as opposed to the outright, call strategy.

Where we considered the synthetic put position, we assumed that this
strategy would be most attractive to traders who already held one leg or the
other of the position and applied the opposite leg to reduce risks. In particular,
the trader who holds a position in the underlying commodity may apply the
synthetic put or call position in order to limit possible losses associated with
the outright commodity position. In the case of a synthetic call, one may envi-
sion the holder of a long commodity position who, while confident that the
market will move upwards in the long or intermediate term, is fearful of an interim price decline. This consideration may be especially relevant where long
futures positions are considered because futures are traded on low margin and
may require the trader to meet variation margin calls on short notice. By buying the put against the long commodity, the futures trader effectively limits the
damage potentially associated with a large price decline. In effect, he is placing
a "stop loss" order on the long commodity position.

To understand how the two legs of the synthetic call are offsetting, consider
that if the underlying commodity market should move sharply downwards, the
long put will become profitable to exercise. When the long put is exercised, the
synthetic call holder sells the underlying commodity, offsetting the outstanding
long commodity position. Thus, when the long put is exercised, the put is offset
and the long commodity position is offset. This series of transactions equates in
effect to a stop loss order. If the market moves down against the long outright
commodity position, the synthetic call holder can limit loss to the call premium. The call premium becomes the price one pays for this downside protec-

tion. Should the underlying market experience a bull move, the synthetic call holder will profit. Although a loss will be incurred on the long put position, that loss is limited to the premium forfeit initially while the profit on the long commodity position may be significantly greater.

But what if our option trader decides to use in- or out-of-the-money options as opposed to at-the-money options? As discussed above, in-the-money options will price in excess of out-of-the-money options. By using in-the-money options, one obtains more downside protection but this protection comes at a higher premium. Similarly, out-of-the-money options provide less protection but at a lower price. To illustrate this concept, consider the execution of a synthetic call purchase using in-, at-, and out-of-the-money options. In particular, assume that a T-bond futures trader had bought T-bond futures at a price of 76-00/32nds in anticipation of a major bull move. Unfortunately, market conditions are volatile and our trader fears a price decline. In order to limit possible losses as a result of a decline, our trader is considering the purchase of in-, at-, or out-of-the-money puts struck at 78, 76, or 74, respectively, selling at the following premiums:

	Strike Price	Premium
In-the-money	78-00/32nds	2-46/64ths or $2,719
At-the-money	76-00/32nds	1-51/64ths or $1,797
Out-of-the-money	74-00/32nds	0-45/64ths or $703

Under the assumption that the synthetic call is held until the expiration of the long put leg, the following results are associated with the purchase of the in-, at-, and out-of-the-money puts to offset the long commodity position:

T-Bond Futures at Expiration	In-the-Money Returns	At-the-Money Returns	Out-of-the-Money Returns
82-00	$3,281	$4,203	$5,297
80-00	1,281	2,203	3,297
78-00	(719)	203	1,297
76-00	(719)	(1,797)	(703)
74-00	(719)	(1,797)	(2,703)
72-00	(719)	(1,797)	(2,703)
70-00	(719)	(1,797)	(2,703)

The foregoing table shows that holders of in-the-money synthetic calls have greater downside protection than holders of out-of-the-money synthetic calls. Of course, this protection comes at the price of foregoing possible returns in the event of a large bull movement. The maximum loss associated with the synthetic call is realized at or below the call leg's strike price. This may be defined as the premium paid up front to secure the put (P) less the difference between the strike or exercise price E less the underlying commodity price U ($E - U$) or:

$$\text{Max Loss} = P - (E - U)$$

The profits potentially associated with the synthetic call may be quite large contingent upon a large bull movement. The breakeven point is calculated as the initial underlying market price U plus the put premium P or:

$$\text{Breakeven Point} = U + P$$

These formulas may be used to calculate the maximum losses and breakeven points associated with the in-, at-, and out-of-the-money synthetic call strategies. In particular, the maximum potential losses equal $719, $1,797, and $2,703, respectively. The breakeven points, although not explicitly depicted in the table above, equal 78-46/64ths, 77-51/64ths, and 76-45/64ths, respectively. Note that the in-the-money synthetic call strategy, which provides the maximum degree of protection, is associated with the breakeven point furthest from the current underlying market price of 76 (see Figure 6.16).

Although the results of the synthetic call strategy resemble the results associated with an outright call purchase, this strategy is seldom practiced in order to take advantage of a possible bull movement. If one were intent upon participating in a possible bull movement at a predefined risk, one could elect simply to purchase a call. This would entail a single commission instead of two commissions. Moreover, the purchase of an outright call would reduce the pos-

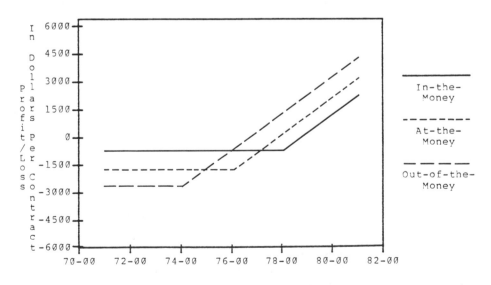

Figure 6.16 In-, at-, and out-of-the-money synthetic calls

sibility of execution errors. In fact, a synthetic call is more often thought of as a means to limit possible losses on a long commodity position.

Ratio Covered Strategies

A "ratio" or "delta" covered strategy involves a long or short position in a commodity underlying an option market that is "covered" by an offsetting position in the overlying put or call option. Fundamentally, these strategies entail the assumption of positions that are identical to the four covered strategies discussed immediately above. The distinction is that, rather than taking equal positions in the option and underlying commodity markets, the trader takes positions in such a ratio as to equalize possible fluctuations in the option versus underlying markets. Ratio trading strategies are motivated by the opportunity to capitalize on temporary pricing aberrations or disparities between the option and underlying commodity prices. By buying the underpriced market and selling the overpriced market in such a ratio as to insure that possible market fluctuations are equalized, a trader may "lock in" an arbitrage profit. The "trick," if there is one, is to identify situations where one market is under- or overpriced relative to the other market.

This discussion takes us back to Chapter 5 in which we examined a method of calculating the "fair market value" of a put or a call option. Once the fair market value of a put or a call option is identified, an option trader may wish to compare that price to the price at which the option is actually trading in the market. If a particular call (put) is overpriced relative to the underlying commodity, the preferred strategy may be to sell the option, simultaneously buying (selling) the underlying commodity. If the call (put) is underpriced relative to the underlying commodity, the preferred strategy is to buy the option, simultaneously selling (buying) the underlying commodity. Of course, these positions must be established in such a ratio as to equalize possible market fluctuations.

A word of caution is in order when considering this practice of referencing the fair market value of an option and comparing that theoretical premium to actual premiums. The models that may be employed to derive these theoretical premiums simply represent the premium at which an option should sell given the theoretical framework that underpins the model and in light of all the assumptions upon which the model may be based. Oftimes, the actual option premium may wander quite far from the theoretical premium and remain at variance from theoretical premiums for extended periods. Option pricing models cannot incorporate all possible factors that impact upon option pricing. The most basic of these factors is simply the demand for option investment. This demand for option investment may be motivated by psychological as well as the more empirical considerations that may be referenced in an option pricing model.

This caveat aside, these ratio strategies may still be quite effective when carefully considered. Perhaps the most important bit of information necessary to implement these strategies is the "neutral hedge ratio" or the reciprocal of delta discussed in Chapter 5. Professional commodity option traders who are interested in pursuing these ratio strategies generally acquire a summary table of theoretical premiums and associated deltas every trading day to help guide their strategies. Even though some professionals may not rely heavily upon calculated theoretical premium valuations, they nevertheless are heavily dependent upon calculated deltas.

Delta is often regarded as a more important number than the theoretical premium because delta provides an indication of the appropriate risk-eliminating ratio of options to underlying commodity units. If delta equals .5, this implies that the option premium may be expected to move on the order of 50% of any fluctuation in the underlying commodity market. By taking the reciprocal of delta, for example, the reciprocal of .5 is 1/.5 or 2, we know how many option

TABLE 6.1 THEORETICAL T-BOND OPTION PREMIUMS AND DELTAS[a]

Underlying/		Strike Prices							
		68	70	72	74	76	78	80	82
75.00	Call	7.00	5.12	3.40	2.22	1.24	0.48	0.23	0.10
	delta	1.00	.86	.74	.59	.42	.27	.15	.08
	Put	0.07	0.19	0.44	1.23	2.23	3.44	5.17	7.01
	delta	.05	.12	.24	.39	.56	.71	.83	.90
75.16	Call	7.32	5.40	4.00	2.41	1.39	0.57	0.29	0.13
	delta	1.00	.88	.77	.63	.46	.30	.18	.09
	Put	0.05	0.15	0.37	1.11	2.06	3.21	4.55	6.36
	delta	.04	.10	.21	.35	.52	.67	.80	.88
76.00	Call	8.00	6.04	4.25	2.62	1.54	1.03	0.35	0.16
	delta	1.00	.89	.80	.66	.50	.34	.21	.11
	Put	0.04	0.12	0.30	1.00	1.54	3.00	4.29	6.08
	delta	.03	.09	.18	.32	.48	.64	.77	.87
76.16	Call	8.32	6.33	4.51	3.19	2.07	1.15	0.42	0.20
	delta	1.00	.91	.83	.70	.54	.38	.24	.14
	Put	0.03	0.10	0.25	0.55	1.39	2.45	4.05	5.45
	delta	.03	.07	.15	.28	.44	.60	.74	.84
77.00	Call	9.00	7.00	5.14	3.42	2.25	1.28	0.50	0.25
	delta	1.00	1.00	.85	.73	.58	.42	.27	.16
	Put	0.02	0.08	0.21	0.46	1.26	2.26	3.46	5.18
	delta	.02	.06	.13	.25	.40	.56	.71	.82
77.16	Call	9.32	7.32	5.41	4.02	2.44	1.42	0.59	0.31
	delta	1.00	1.00	.87	.76	.62	.46	.31	.19
	Put	0.02	0.06	0.17	0.39	1.14	2.09	3.24	4.57
	delta	.02	.05	.11	.21	.36	.52	.67	.79
78.00	Call	10.00	8.00	6.06	4.27	3.00	1.57	1.06	0.37
	delta	1.00	1.00	.89	.79	.66	.50	.35	.21
	Put	0.01	0.05	0.14	0.33	1.03	1.57	3.03	4.32
	delta	.01	.04	.09	.19	.32	.48	.63	.76

[a] Term is 90 days; volatility is 12.5%; and the short-term interest rate is 8.5%.

units must be taken on to balance one unit in the underlying commodity. In this case, the prudent ratio option strategist will take on two option units for every unit in the underlying commodity.

Table 6.1 provides a sample of theoretical T-bond premiums and associated deltas. Note that T-bond options such as those traded on the Chicago Board of Trade are quoted in terms of percent of par in minimum increments of one sixty-fourth (1/64th) of one percentage point while the underlying T-bond futures market is quoted in minimum increments of one thirty-second (1/32nd) of one percentage point. Table 6.1 quotes T-bond futures and T-bond option premiums in terms of thirty-seconds and sixty-fourths, respectively, although for purposes of calculation, we must work in terms of decimals. Tables similar to this are available from many different professional commodity option services.

Once an over- or underpriced option is identified, by whatever method, the appropriate strategy is to sell the overpriced option, hedging the short exposure in the underlying commodity market, or to buy the underpriced option, similarly hedging the long exposure in the underlying commodity market.

EXAMPLE. A call option exercisable for $100,000 face value Chicago Board of Trade T-bond futures contracts is identifed as overpriced relative to the underlying T-bond futures contract in light of prevailing economic conditions. In particular, the call option is trading at a premium of 2-32/64ths or $2,500 per option contract. The call is struck at 76% of par and the underlying T-bond futures contract is trading at 77-00/32nds. Referencing Table 6.1, we find that the theoretical value of this call equals 2-25/64ths, or about $2,391 per contract. Thus the option is overpriced by seven sixty-fourths (7/64ths), or about $109. If our option investor were confident that this theoretical valuation represented a reliable market indicator, he would then sell calls at 2-32/64ths, buying T-bond futures to counterbalance the exposed position in the option market. Table 6.1 indicates that delta equals .6; this implies the neutral hedge ratio equals 1.67 = 1/.6. In other words, 1.67 option units should be sold against every unit in T-bond futures contract. Of course, option contracts are indivisible and so our option trader sells multiples of five calls to three T-bond futures contracts. As long as this ratio of five to three is maintained, our option trader is hedged:

$$1{:}.6 = 5{:}3 \quad 10{:}6 \quad 15{:}9 \quad 20{:}12 \quad 25{:}15 \quad \text{etc.}$$

Assume that our option trader sells five options to three T-bond futures contracts:

Sell 5 calls   @2-32/64ths or $12,500
Buy 3 T-bonds @77-00/32nds

Now let's evaluate our option trader's returns, given that by the end of the same day, the option premium assumes its theoretical value where the option and futures positions are "unwound." Our trader buys back the five calls and sells the three T-bonds. Three different scenarios are evaluated, one in which the T-bond futures price remains at 77-00 for the duration of the day, one in which the T-bond price advances to 77-16, and another in which the T-bond price declines to 76-16:

If T-bonds remain at 77-00:

Sell 5 calls	@2-32 or	$ 12,500
Buy 5 calls	@2-25 or	($ 11,955)
	Profit of	$545
Buy 3 T-bonds @77-00 or		($231,000)
Sell 3 T-bonds @77-00 or		$231,000
	Profit of	0
	RETURN	$545

If T-bonds advance to 77-16:

Sell 5 calls	@2-32 or	$12,500
Buy 5 calls	@2-44 or	($13,437)
	Loss of	$937
Buy 3 T-bonds @77-00 or		($231,000)
Sell 3 T-bonds @77-16 or		$232,500
	Profit of	$1,500
	RETURN	$563

If T-bonds decline to 76-16:

Sell 5 calls	@2-32 or	$12,500
Buy 5 calls	@2-07 or	($10,547)
	Profit of	$1,953
Buy 3 T-bonds @77-00 or		($231,000)
Sell 3 T-bonds @76-16 or		$229,500
	Loss of	$1,500
	RETURN	$453

Under our three scenarios, our option trader was able to realize profits of $545, $563, and $453, respectively. These figures equate roughly to $109 by which the option was overpriced times five options or $545. Where the market fluctuated during the life of the option, our trader's returns did not equate precisely to $545. This is attributable to the fact that the neutral hedge ratio, or delta, is dynamic—as the underlying commodity price moves, delta likewise fluctuates. So by the time the T-bond futures contract moved up to 77-16, delta had moved up to .64, implying that the ratio of option to commodity units should be decreased. Where T-bonds decline to 76-16, delta declines to .55, which implies that the ratio of option to commodity units should be increased. For the purposes of this illustration, we have ignored factors such as commissions, margins, and taxes.

Our previous example illustrated a very short-term ratio strategy where the option premium assumed its theoretical value within a single day. Sometimes, however, one may identify an over- or underpriced option that takes some days or even weeks to return to what one may regard as an "equilibrium" price. And, of course, sometimes the option premium may never fall "into line" so that this ratio strategy may become profitable. Under a somewhat longer term scenario, it will become necessary to constantly reevaluate the neutral hedge ratio and adjust the coverage.

EXAMPLE.   A gold option trader has identified a situation where a call is underpriced relative to the underlying 100-ounce gold futures contract. A call struck at $460 per ounce is trading at a premium of $26.00 per ounce while our trader believes that its fair value is nearer to $29.50. The underlying gold futures contract is trading at $455.00; there are 90 days to expiration; volatility equals 36%; and short-term rates are at 8.5%. At this point, the neutral hedge ratio equals 0.51 or about 0.5, which implies that two calls should be purchased against every gold futures contract. As long as our trader maintains the 2:1 options to futures ratio, he will be appropriately hedged. Assume that he decides to buy 10 calls against 5 futures contracts:

Buy 10 calls @ $26.00/oz. or $26,000
Sell 5 gold contracts @ $455

Because the calls are considered about $3.50 per ounce underpriced, our option trader expects to realize a profit of $3.50 per ounce for each 100-ounce option contract; for ten contracts this amounts to $3,500. Five days later, assume that the price of the underlying futures contract had declined to $435. Unfortunately, the options are still underpriced by about $2.5 per ounce; they are trading at a premium of $17.20 per ounce when our trader calculates their theoretical value at $19.70 per ounce. The value of the ten short calls has declined from $26,000 to $17,200—a $8,800 loss.

At the same time, however, the short futures position has appreciated as the price of gold dropped $20 per ounce. Our trader had sold five 100-ounce contracts for a profit of $10,000 on the futures contracts. Nevertheless, the net return of $1,200 ($10,000 profit on futures less $8,800 loss on calls) is less than the $3,500 profit originally anticipated. Therefore, our trader decides that he will wait the situation out until the option premiums return to their theoretical values. At this point, all other things remaining equal, the neutral hedge ratio equals .41, or about .4. This implies that the appropriate ratio is 2.5 option units to each commodity unit (1/.4 = 2.5). This equates to a ratio of 5:2 or 10:4. Thus our trader buys back one of the five futures contracts at $435 for a profit of $20 per once or $2,000:

Buy 1 gold contract @ $435

In another five days, gold futures have advanced to $440 per ounce. Fortunately, the call premiums have assumed their theoretical value at approximately $20.85 per ounce. At this point, our trader unwinds his positions through the following transactions:

Sell 10 calls @ $20.85 or $20,850
Buy 4 gold contracts @ $440

Thus the value of the 10 long calls appreciated over the last five days from $17,200 to $20,850 for a profit of $3,650. At the same time, the 4 short futures contracts advanced from $435 to $440 for a loss of $5 per ounce or $2,000. Over the second five-day period, our option trader realized a profit of $1,650. Added to the profit of $1,200 over the first five days, this amounts to a net return of $2,850. At this point, let's summarize the net results of all these transactions:

Sell 5 gold contracts @$455 or	$227,500
Buy 1 gold contract @$435 or	($43,500)
Buy 4 gold contracts @$440 or	($176,000)
Profit of	$8,000
Buy 10 calls @$26.00/oz. or	($26,000)
Sell 10 calls @$20.85/oz. or	$20,850
Loss of	$5,150
RETURN	$2,850

Although our trader wasn't quite able to lock in the $3,500 profit originally anticipated he was able to realize a $2,850 profit. Of course, these transactions are somewhat oversimplified because they don't account for transaction costs such as financing, commissions, margins, and taxes. (Don't let the large numbers representing the value of the futures contracts scare you; the margins required to control these futures contracts represent a small fraction of the contract value and typically may be put up in the form of Treasury bills, providing a return on the margin.) For more details on margins see Appendix B.

A final note on ratio covered strategies—it is apparent that option professionals, particularly those who are trading actively on the floor of the exchange, generally will be in a favorable position to apply these ratio strategies. Floor traders are in the midst of the action and can react quickly when a profit opportunity is recognized. As an off-floor trader, it is somewhat more difficult to capitalize on these pricing disparities as they arise. Still it is possible, through careful study, to identify and take advantage of these situations from time to time. Additionally, these ratio strategies may be quite useful in order to hedge the risk of adverse price fluctuation associated with a position in the underlying commodity. These ratio or delta hedging strategies are discussed in more depth in Chapter 7.

OPTION SPREADS

An option spread is a strategy that involves opposite positions in two options of the same type, that is, put or call. For example, one may buy a call and sell a call, or buy a put and sell a put, in order to create an option spread position. However, we know that there are many different option series of the same type. Therefore, option spreads are often categorized on the basis of the relationship between the two option contracts—the two "legs" of the spread—that constitute the spread. Furthermore, option positions are often categorized on the basis of the motivation of the option spread trader—bullish, bearish, or somewhere in between.

Option contracts may vary as to whether they are puts or calls, their expiration date, and their strike price. (These variables define the option type, class, and series.) An option spread involves two options of the same type; beyond that the two legs of the spread may vary with respect to expiration, strike price, or both. An option spread wherein the two legs vary in strike prices but share a common expiration date are often identified as "vertical" spreads. An option spread where the two legs vary in expiration dates but share a common strike price are often identified as "horizontal" spreads and sometimes as "time" or "calendar" spreads. Spreads in which the two legs vary in both expiration date and strike price are often referred to as "diagonal" or "cross" spreads. The terms vertical, horizontal, and cross spread evolved from the common practice of laying out a table of stock option prices in newspapers, other financial publications, and on electronic quotation devices with strike prices quoted vertically and expirations horizontally. Thus one could scan a column to identify "vertical" spread opportunities, scan a row to identify "horizontal" spread opportunities, and scan diagonally to identify "diagonal" spread opportunities. Of course, option quotations may be, and often are, laid out in alternate formats. Nevertheless, the terminology has endured despite the preferences of some publications and quotation vendors to develop alternate layouts.

Different strikes, Same expirations	vertical spread
Same strikes, Different expirations	horizontal spread
Different strikes, Different expirations	diagonal spread

An astute option trader may readily identify an option spread position that may be suitable to take advantage of almost any type of pricing scenario. Note, however, that a spread position entails the assumption of opposite option positions—to buy a call and sell a call, or to buy a put and sell a put. Because the two legs of an option spread are opposites with respect to risk and potential rewards, they tend to offset each other partially. As such, a trader with an option spread generally is not exposed to the same degree of risk as a trader who takes an outright position in a particular option. By moderating the degree of risk associated with the option position, the option spreader further moderates the potential returns associated with the option spread position. Option spreads may generally be thought of as positions that entail a moderate degree of risk and moderate potential rewards.

In any event, one may identify bullish and bearish option spreads as well as option spreads where the motivating pricing scenario is much less straightforward. For example, one may identify option spreads that may be used to take advantage of a stable pricing scenario and one may identify spreads intended to exploit temporary pricing disparities between two options. A catalog of option spread strategies describing some of the most popular spreads is presented below—on the basis of the motivating pricing scenario.

BULLISH OPTION SPREADS

Bullish Vertical Call Spread

A bullish vertical call spread entails the purchase of a call and the sale of a call that share a common expiration date but which vary in strike prices. In order to create a bullish spread, rather than a bearish spread, one buys a call with a low strike price and sells a call with a relatively higher strike price.

When the underlying commodity is valued at a price somewhere in between the two strike prices, this means that the option spreader buys an in-the-money call and sells an out-of-the-money call.

The attractive feature of this bullish vertical call spread is that it permits the spreader to define the risks and potential rewards associated with the position in advance. Although the potential rewards associated with this strategy are rather moderate, the risks are likewise relatively moderate. As such, this strategy may be preferred by option traders who are moderately bullish, as opposed to strongly bullish. If one were strongly bullish, as an alternative to entering a bullish option spread, one might buy a call outright or even purchase the underlying commodity outright.

One disadvantage of this type of spread is that it requires the option spreader to make a cash investment in the spread. We know that an in-the-money or a low-struck call will always command a higher premium than an out-of-the-money or high-struck call. Thus the premium that is paid to secure the long leg of the spread must exceed the premium that is received as a result of the sale of the relatively higher struck call. The spreader's account is debited by the difference between the low-struck call premium and the high-struck call premium for a "net debit."

$$\text{Net Debit} = \text{Low-Struck Premium} - \text{High-Struck Premium}$$

EXAMPLE.   An option trader buys a T-bond call struck at 74 for 1-59/64ths or $1,922 and sells a T-bond call struck at 76 for 61/64ths or $953. The net debit equals the difference between the $1,922 paid to secure the low-struck call and the $953 received from the sale of the high-struck call—or $969.

The net debit associated with the placement of a bullish vertical call spread equals the maximum loss that is associated with the position. In this respect, then, the bullish call spread is similar to an outright call purchase; the maximum possible loss is paid out up front:

$$\text{Maximum Loss} = \text{Net Debit}$$

The maximum loss will occur when the options expire when the underlying commodity price is less than or equal to the lower of the two strike prices. When the underlying commodity price is less than or equal to the lower of the two strikes, both options expire out-of-the-money and are abandoned. Or, at best, the lower struck call is at-the-money, in which case it would likely be abandoned (in any case, it could not profitably be exercised). Should both options be abandoned, the holder of the bullish vertical call spread forfeits the premium received on the high-struck call and retains the premium accepted for the sale of the low-struck call. The loss equals the amount by which his account initially was debited.

Like an outright option purchase, there is limited risk associated with the assumption of a vertical spread. Unlike an outright option purchase, however, the profits potentially associated with the spread may also be defined upon the placement of the spread. If the spread is held until the expiration of the two options, the maximum profit potentially associated with the position may be defined as the difference between the two strike prices less the net debit:

$$\text{Maximum Profit} = \text{High Strike} - \text{Low Strike} - \text{Net Debit}$$

EXAMPLE. The previous example illustrated how to calculate the net debit associated with a bull call spread where the two legs were struck at 74% and 76% of par, respectively. The low-struck T-bond call was purchased for $1,922 and the high-struck call was sold for $953 for a net debit of $969. The maximum loss potentially associated with this position equals the difference between the two strike prices: 76 less 74 or $2,000 for a $100,000 face value contract less the net debit of $969, or $1,031.

The maximum profit occurs when the underlying commodity price equals or exceeds the higher of the two strike prices upon expiration. When the underlying commodity price exceeds the high strike, both options are in-the-money and one may expect that both options will be exercised. The spread holder will, of course, exercise the low-struck call and realize a return equal to the difference between the underlying commodity price and the strike price. The high-struck call will also be exercised (except perhaps where it is right at-the-money at expiration). The spreader will then realize a loss equal to the difference between the underlying commodity price and the strike price. Therefore, the difference between the two strike prices becomes an important factor in determining the maximum potential profit.

A third point of interest is the breakeven point, or the point at which no profit and no loss will accrue. The breakeven point may be defined as the low strike price plus the net debit:

$$\text{Breakeven Point} = \text{Low Strike} + \text{Net Debit}$$

EXAMPLE. To illustrate how to calculate the breakeven point, consider our prior example where the option trader buys the 74 call for $1-59/64ths or $1,922 and sells a 76 call for 61/64ths or $953. The net debit may be calculated as $969, or as 62/64ths. Thus the breakeven point is calculated as the low strike price of 74 plus the net debit of 62/64ths, or 74-62/64ths. Of course, T-bonds prices are normally expressed in terms of 32nds rather than 64ths; therefore the breakeven point may be expressed as 74-31/32nd.

The breakeven point at option expiration always falls somewhere in between the two strike prices. At any point between the low and high strike prices, the low-struck call is in-the-money and profitable to exercise while the

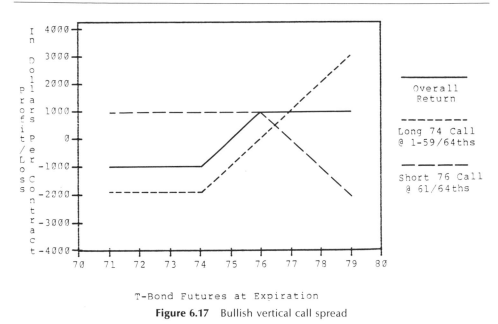

Figure 6.17   Bullish vertical call spread

high-struck call is out-of-the-money and unprofitable to exercise. It is only where the gross profit on exercise of the low-struck long call equals the net debit that the spreader breaks even (see Figure 6.17).

EXAMPLE.   Consider an option investor interested in trading options on gold futures contracts. He purchases a call struck at $400 per ounce for a $25 premium and sells a call struck at $420 for a $15 premium— for a net debit of $10 per ounce. Gold futures are currently trading at $410; thus the $400 call is $10 in-the-money and the $420 call is $10 out-of-the-money. The maximum loss equals the net debit of $10; the maximum profit equals the difference between the two strikes less the net debit or $10; the breakeven point equals the low strike price plus the net debit of $410 per ounce. Let's illustrate the results when the underlying commodity assumes different values at expiration:

Gold Price at Expiration	(1) Return on Long Leg	(2) Return on Short Leg	Overall Return (1) + (2)
$380	($25)	$15	($10)
390	(25)	15	(10)
400	(25)	15	(10)
410	(15)	15	0
420	(5)	15	10
430	5	5	10
440	15	(5)	10

In the prior example, we assumed that the long leg was placed in-the-money and the short leg was placed out-of-the-money. But what if both legs were placed in-the-money or out-of-the-money? In the case of a vertical bull call spread where both legs are placed in-the-money, the investor would effectively increase the probability of realizing a profit. However, this comes at the expense of diminishing the maximum potential profit and increasing the potential risks. A more aggressive investor may prefer to enter this spread when both legs are out-of-the-money. In that case, the investor increases the maximum potential return and decreases the maximum potential loss. However, this comes at the expense of decreasing the probability of realizing a profit altogether.

EXAMPLE.   A vertical bull call spread is placed by buying a $400 call exercisable for gold futures and selling a $420 call. In one case, the spread is placed when both options are in-the-money and when gold futures are trading at $430. In the second case, the spread is placed when gold futures are at $390 and both legs are out-of-the-money. As a rule, the net debit will increase the farther the legs are in-the-money and decrease when the legs are out-of-the-money. When the spread is in-the-money, the $400 leg is purchased at $40 per ounce and the $420 leg is sold at $27 per ounce for a net debit of $13. When the spread is out-of-money, the $400 call is purchased for $18 and the $420 call is sold for $10 for a net debit of $8. Let's compare the maximum profits, losses, and breakeven points of these two strategies (also see Figure 6.18):

	Long Leg Premium	Short Leg Premium	Max Profit	Max Loss	B/E
In-the-money	$40	$27	$7	$13	$413
Out-of-the-money	$18	$10	$12	$8	$408

So far we have confined our discussion to situations where the option spread is held until expiration. A vertical spread may be placed and held for only a short period and then liquidated through a series of two closing transactions. In other words, one may buy back the short high-struck option and sell the long low-struck option. But how will these spreads behave over time?

Let's start simply by examining the value of the spread at expiration and working backwards in time. If the underlying commodity price falls at or below the low strike price immediately prior to expiration, the spread is worthless. It is worthless because at or below the low strike, the spreader realizes the maximum loss (equal to the net debit). If the underlying commodity falls at or above the high strike price, the spread is valued at the difference in strike prices. This difference reflects the maximum profit potentially associated with the position without considering the original net debit. Moreover, this strike price interval equals the profit one would realize by exercising the low-struck call, while the

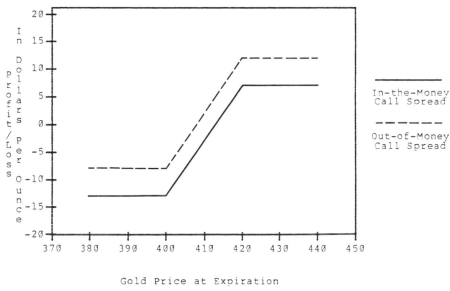

Gold Price at Expiration

Figure 6.18a Vertical bullish call spreads

short high-struck call expires unexercised. Between these two points, the value of the spread falls between zero and the difference in strikes.

Figure 6.18b illustrates the value of a vertical bull call spread at three discrete points: at expiration and with 30 days and with 60 days to expiration, respectively, and over a range of underlying commodity prices. In this particular case, we are examining a bull call spread using options exercisable for T-bond futures contracts. The low-struck and high-struck legs are at 74 and 76, respectively.

EXAMPLE. Assume that there are 30 days to expiration. T-bond futures are trading at 76% of par and a trader enters into a 74/76 spread by buying the 74 call for 2-20/64ths or $2,313 while the 76 call is sold for 1-02/64ths or $1,031. The spreader incurs a net debit of $1,281. If futures remain stable at 76 by expiration, the value of the spread increases to $2,000—or the difference in strike prices. This means that the bull call spreader can realize a profit of $719 by expiration.

The value or net debit associated with placing a vertical spread can vary widely over time. In particular, we can identify a "pivotal price" of about 75 or about midway between the two strikes in the prior example. When futures are over that pivotal point, the net debit associated with applying the position increases over time. Under the pivot, the value of the position decreases over time. Moreover, the value of the position changes most dramatically over the last 30 days of the spread's life. Between the period of 60 to 30 days to expiration, the value of the spread is relatively stable. This suggests that the vertical spreader might be able to retain a spread even when futures fall below the pivotal point when the spread has a long time until expiration. But when there are

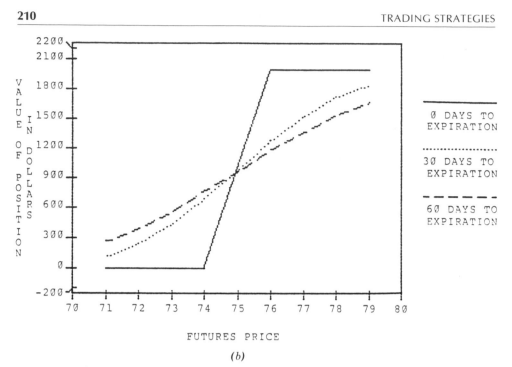

Figure 6.18b   Value of 74/76 bull call spread at different points in time

only about 30 days to expiration, the trader may consider liquidating his position if futures fall under the pivotal point, or holding on to the position if futures fall above the pivotal point.

Many option traders use spreads cautiously, attempting to put time on their side, and thus exploiting the accelerating time value associated with an option. In the prior example, our spreader placed a 74/76 bullish vertical call spread when the underlying futures market was at 76, thus increasing the probability of realizing the maximum return. Figure 6.18c illustrates the value of a 74/76 bullish vertical call spread and a 76/78 bullish vertical call spread over time, holding futures constant at 76% of par. The declining time value of a 76 call is also illustrated. As you can see, the value of the "in-the-money" 74/76 spread *increases* over time while the value of the 76/78 spread *decreases* over time. Note that the value of the spreads change most dramatically over the last 30 days of the spread life.

As is the case with other option strategies, option spreads may be tailored to conform closely to the risk/return preferences of the investor. Bull call spreads are one of the most popular types of option spreads one may undertake. And, as discussed immediately below, they are often preferred over a vertical bull put spread.

Bullish Vertical Put Spread

The risks and returns associated with bullish vertical put spreads are very similar to those associated with call spreads. Both risks and returns are con-

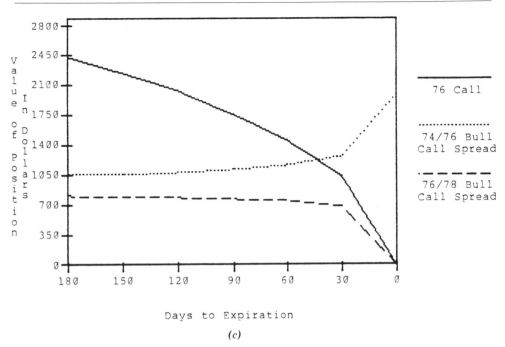

Days to Expiration

(c)

Figure 6.18c   Bull call spread values during option life cycle

fined to rather moderate, predefined levels. Both bull put and call spreads require the purchase of a low-struck option and the sale of a relatively high-struck option that share a common expiration date. The major distinction is that, although the call spread requires the spreader to incur a net debit and on balance pay premium, the put spread may be placed at a "net credit"; in other words, the spreader receives premium on balance.

If we assume that the underlying commodity price falls between the two strike prices, this means that the long leg of the spread is struck out-of-the-money and that the short leg is struck in-the-money. An out-of-the-money option always commands a higher premium than a similar in-the-money option. Therefore, the premium paid to secure the low-struck long put is always less than the premium received from the sale of the high-struck put. The difference between the premium received and the premium paid is credited to the account of the spreader for a net credit.

Net Credit = High-Struck Premium − Low-Struck Premium

EXAMPLE.   An option trader buys a put exercisable for a stock index futures contract struck at 168 and sells a put struck at 170. The low-struck put is purchased for 4.50 index points and the high-struck put is sold for 5.55 index points. This is a net credit of 1.05 index points, or the 5.55 points received from the sale of the high-struck put less the 4.50 points paid to secure the low struck put.

The net credit has further significance insofar as it defines the maximum profit that is associated with the bull put spread. In this respect, the bull put spread is similar to the sale of a put to capitalize on a bullish pricing scenario; the maximum profit potentially associated with the strategy is received up front:

$$\text{Maximum Profit} = \text{Net Credit}$$

The maximum profit will be realized when the underlying commodity price is greater than or equal to the higher of the two strike prices by the time the options expire. When the underlying commodity price is greater than or equal to the higher of the two strikes, both options are out-of-the-money (except that the high-struck put may be at-the-money if the underlying commodity price should equal the higher of the two strikes). In either case, it is likely that both the high- and low-struck options will expire unexercised. Thus the put spreader will forfeit the premium paid to secure the low-struck put and retain the full premium received on the sale of the high-struck put. When this occurs, the spreader's profits are simply calculated as the difference between the two premiums, or the amount by which the spreader's account initially was credited.

Earlier, a comparison had been made between a bull put spread and the outright sale of a put. Specifically, in both cases, the maximum profit is limited to the amount received upon the placement of the position. Unlike an outright put sale, however, the bullish vertical put spread entails limited risk as well as limited potential reward. When the spread is held until the expiration of the two options, the maximum loss potentially associated with the spread equals the difference between the two strike prices less the net credit:

$$\text{Maximum Loss} = \text{High Strike} - \text{Low Strike} - \text{Net Credit}$$

EXAMPLE.   In our previous example, we showed how to calculate the net credit associated with a bull put spread. In that case, a stock index futures put struck at 168 was purchased at 4.50 index points and a put struck at 170 was sold at 5.55 for a 1.05 index point credit. The maximum loss potentially associated with the position equals the difference between the two strike prices, or 2.00 index points less the 1.05 index point credit or 0.95 index point.

The maximum loss is incurred when the underlying commodity price is less than or equal to the lower of the two strike prices at expiration, or at 168 in the case illustrated above. At this point, both puts are in-the-money (except in the special case where the underlying commodity equals the low strike price, in which case the long put is at-the-money). Under these circumstances, the put spreader will be inclined to exercise the low-struck put (except where it is just at-the-money); at the same time, the high-struck put will also be exercised. The difference between the gross loss on exercise of the high-struck put and the gross profit on exercise of the low-struck put will be the difference in the strike prices. The net credit received up front serves to lessen the impact of this loss.

Finally, we are interested in determining the breakeven point at which the put spreader can expect to neither profit nor incur a loss. The breakeven point falls in between the two strike prices, specifically, the breakeven point equals the higher of the two strike prices less the net credit:

$$\text{Breakeven Point} = \text{High Strike} - \text{Net Credit}$$

EXAMPLE.   Our prior example had the put spreader buy a 168 put at 4.50 and sell a 170 put at 5.55 for a net credit of 1.05 index point. The breakeven point is calculated as the high strike of 170.00 less the net credit of 1.05, or 168.95.

Some believe that it is advisable to enter into a bull put spread rather than a bull call spread as it may be preferable to receive a net credit rather than incur a debit. Other option spreaders prefer to incur the net debit and enter into the bull call spread. The reason for this preference is that when the short leg of the option is in-the-money (whenever the underlying commodity price is less than or equal to the strike price), it is a candidate for exercise. The holder of an American option has the right to exercise an option at any point prior to the expiration date. If the short option in the put spread is exercised early, this event may disturb the put spreader's plans. Many spreaders consider the bull call spread as a more certain strategy in this respect.

Nevertheless, the risks and returns associated with this strategy resemble strongly the risks and returns associated with the bull call spread (see Figure 6.19).

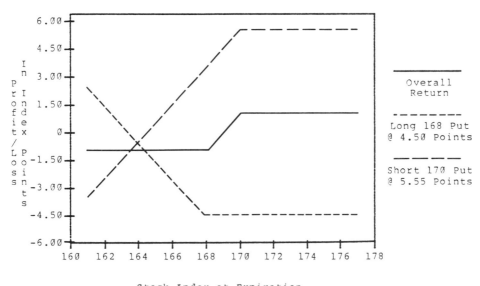

Figure 6.19 Vertical bullish put spread

EXAMPLE.   An option investor purchases a put exercisable for T-bond futures
           struck at 74 for a 1-00/64ths premium or $1,000 for a $100,000 face
           value contract. At the same time, the investor sells a put struck at
           76 for 2-00/64ths or $2,000. The net credit on the opening transac-
           tions equals $1,000; the underlying T-bond futures contract is
           priced at 75-00/32nds. If this position is held until expiration and
           the short put is not exercised early, the spreader's returns under a
           variety of scenarios may be illustrated as follows:

T-Bond Price at Expiration	(1) Return on Long Leg	(2) Return on Short Leg	Overall Return (1) + (2)
72-00	$1,000	($2,000)	($1,000)
73-00	0	(1,000)	(1,000)
74-00	(1,000)	0	(1,000)
75-00	(1,000)	1,000	0
76-00	(1,000)	2,000	1,000
77-00	(1,000)	2,000	1,000
78-00	(1,000)	2,000	1,000

The foregoing example applied the assumption that the spread was placed
when the low-struck put was out-of-the-money and the high-struck put was in-
the-money. But, much like a bull call spread, the bull put spread may be tailored to the preferred degree of risk and return. By placing the spread when
both legs are in-the-money or out-of-the-money, the put spreader can pursue
an aggressive or more conservative strategy, respectively.

EXAMPLE.   A T-bond put spread is placed when both legs are in-the-money: a
           74 put is purchased for 1-40/64ths or $1,625 and a 76 put is sold for
           2-60/64ths or $2,937. The net credit associated with this transac-
           tion equals $1,312 and the underlying T-bond futures contract is
           trading at 73-16/32nds. Another T-bond put spread is placed when
           both legs are out-of-the-money: a 74 put is purchased for 30/64ths
           or $469 and a 76 call is sold for 1-08/64ths or $1,125. The net credit
           is $656 and T-bond futures are trading at 76-16/32nds. (As a rule,
           the net credit will increase as the puts are placed farther in-the-
           money.) The risks and rewards potentially associated with these
           spreads are:

	Long Premium	Short Premium	Max Profit	Max Loss	Breakeven
In-the-money	$1,625	$2,937	$1,312	$688	74-22/32nds
Out-of-the-money	469	1,125	656	1,344	75-11/32nds

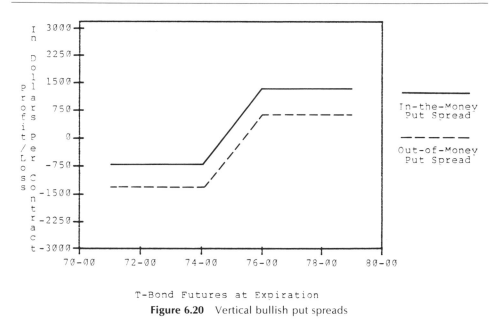

T-Bond Futures at Expiration
Figure 6.20 Vertical bullish put spreads

The in-the-money put spreader pursues a large maximum profit and limits risks to a relatively low level (see Figure 6.20). By definition, however, the underlying commodity price must advance a great deal before the spreader can profit. In the foregoing case, the in-the-money put spread was placed when the underlying commodity price equaled 73-16. But the spreader will not break even until T-bond futures prices advance upward to 74-22. Moreover, he runs the risk that the short put will be exercised unexpectedly. The out-of-the-money put spreader accepts a relatively large risk for the potential to realize a relatively small profit. Note, however, that the spread was placed when T-bond futures prices equaled 76-16—a comfortable measure over the 75-11 breakeven point.

BEARISH OPTION SPREADS

Bearish Vertical Put Spread

Bearish vertical put spreads permit the spreader to benefit from a decline in the price of the commodity underlying the option. Just like its counterpart strategies of a bullish nature, the bear put spread further permits the spreader to define the maximum potential risk and reward in advance, and therefore confine these risks and rewards to relatively moderate levels.

Vertical bull spreads—whether they employ puts or calls—entail the purchase of an option with a low strike price and the sale of a relatively higher-struck option. Vertical bear spreads are just the opposite; they entail the sale of an option with a low strike price and the purchase of an option with a relatively higher strike price. Both legs of the option spread share a common expiration date.

A bearish vertical put spread is more akin to the bullish vertical call than the bullish vertical put spread. Bear put spreads more closely resemble bull call than put spreads because both bear put and bull call spreads entail a net debit to the spreader's account. Assume that the price of the commodity underlying the options falls in between the strike prices of the two option legs. Thus the short low-struck put is out-of-the-money and the long high-struck put is in-the-money. Because an in-the-money option will always command a higher premium than an out-of-the-money option, the bear vertical put spreader will have to pay a higher premium for the long leg of the spread than the premium he receives as a result of the sale of the short leg. The amount by which the high-struck put premium exceeds the low-struck put premium equals the net debit:

$$\text{Net Debit} = \text{High-Struck Premium} - \text{Low-Struck Premium}$$

EXAMPLE.   An investor sells a put struck at 166 and exercisable for a stock index futures contract for 3.30 index points. To complete the spread, he buys a put struck at 168 for 4.35 index points. The net debit equals 1.05 index points or 4.35 less 3.30.

In some respects, bear vertical put spreads resemble the outright purchase of a put to take advantage of a bearish pricing scenario (see Figure 6.21). In particular, the maximum possible loss associated with the bear put spread is confined to the amount that is required initially to secure the spread—in other words, the net debit:

Maximum Loss = Net Debit

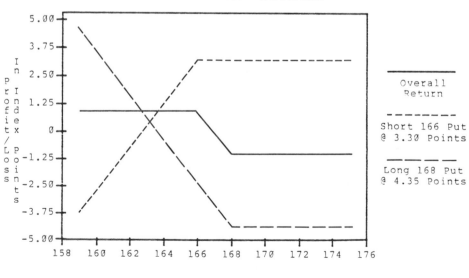

Stock Index at Expiration
Figure 6.21 Vertical bearish put spread

This maximum loss occurs when the underlying commodity price equals or exceeds the higher of the two strike prices on expiration. When this occurs, both puts are out-of-the-money (except where the underlying commodity price equals the upper strike, in which case the long put is just at-the-money). When both options are out- or at-the-money, it is likely that they will be abandoned and expire unexercised. Thus the bear put spreader's losses equal the net debit forfeit up front to establish the position.

But, unlike an outright put purchase, the bear put spreader confines his potential profit to a moderate, predefined level. Should the spread be held until the expiration of the two options, the maximum profit potentially associated with the spread equals the difference between the two strike prices less the maximum risk, or net debit:

$$\text{Maximum Profit} = \text{High Strike} - \text{Low Strike} - \text{Net Debit}$$

EXAMPLE. The previous example illustrated how to calculate the net debit associated with the bear put spread. In that example, the two legs of the option were struck at 166 and 168, respectively. The spreader paid 4.35 index points to secure the long leg struck at 168 and received 3.30 index points for the sale of the 166 put for a net debit of 1.05 index point. The maximum profit potentially associated with this strategy equals the difference between the two strike prices, or 2 index points (168 − 166), less the net debit of 1.05 index point, or 0.95 index point.

This maximum profit is realized when the underlying commodity price is less than or equal to the lower of the two strike prices at expiration. At that point, both options are in- or, at a minimum, at-the-money. Thus they could both be exercised profitably (if the lower-struck put is at least marginally in-the-money). The difference between the gross profit on exercise of the high-struck put and the gross loss on exercise of the low-struck put would equal the difference between the two strikes. This profit is decreased by the net debit initially paid to secure the spread.

Finally, we are interested in the breakeven point at which the spreader can expect to neither profit nor incur a loss. This point may be defined as the high strike price less the net debit:

$$\text{Breakeven Point} = \text{High Strike} - \text{Net Debit}$$

EXAMPLE. Building upon the previous example, the breakeven point may be calculated as the higher of the two strike prices, 168 less the net debit of 1.05; the breakeven point may be calculated as 166.95.

The breakeven point will always fall between the two strike prices. When the underlying commodity price falls between the two strikes, the long high-struck put is in-the-money and the short low-struck put is out-of-the-money. Only where the gross profit on exercise of the long high-struck put equals the net debit will the spreader break even.

EXAMPLE.   T-bond futures are trading at 75-00/32nds. A vertical bear put spread is placed by selling a 74 put exercisable for a T-bond futures contract for a 1-00/64ths or $1,000 premium and by buying a 76 put for a 2-00/64ths or $2,000 premium. This spread is placed for a net debit of $1,000, which equals the maximum risk borne by the spreader. The maximum profit that could accrue to the spreader equals $1,000, or the $2,000 difference between the two strike prices less the net debit. Finally, the breakeven point eqals the high strike price of 76 less the net debit of $1,000 (1-00/64ths) or 75-00/32nds. The returns that accrue to the spreader under a variety of market scenarios are expressed below:

T-Bond Price at Expiration	(1) Return on Long Leg	(2) Return on Short Leg	Overall Return (1) + (2)
72-00	$2,000	($1,000)	$1,000
73-00	1,000	0	1,000
74-00	0	1,000	1,000
75-00	(1,000)	1,000	0
76-00	(2,000)	1,000	(1,000)
77-00	(2,000)	1,000	(1,000)
78-00	(2,000)	1,000	(1,000)

In the prior example, the long leg was struck in-the-money while the short leg was struck out-of-the-money. But by entering the spread when both legs are in- or out-of-the-money, the spreader may conform the level of risk and reward to the desired levels (see Figure 6.22). If both legs are placed in-the-money,

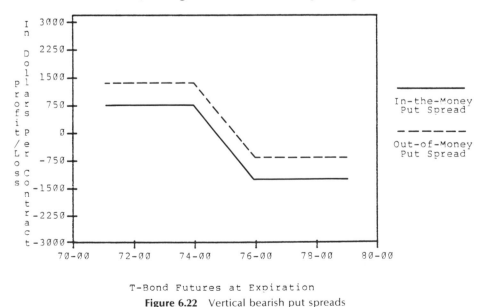

T-Bond Futures at Expiration

Figure 6.22   Vertical bearish put spreads

then the spreader increases the probability of realizing the maximum profit. However, the spreader increases this probability at the cost of diminishing the maximum possible profit and increasing the maximum possible loss. Similarly, the spreader who places both legs of the spread out-of-the-money decreases the probability of achieving a profit. However, this strategy has the merit of increasing the maximum possible profit and diminishing the maximum possible loss; this is an aggressive strategy.

EXAMPLE.   An in-the-money spread is placed by buying a 76 put for 2-60/64ths or $2,937, and selling a 74 put for 1-44/64ths or $1,687. The T-bond futures price equals 73-16/32nds at this point. An out-of-the-money spread is placed by buying a 76 put at 1-08/64ths or $1,125 and selling a 74 put at 30/64ths or $469. The T-bond futures price equals 76-16/32nds at this point. The risks and rewards associated with these strategies may be summarized as:

	Long Leg Premium	Short Leg Premium	Max Profit	Max Loss	Breakeven
In-the-money	$2,937	$1,687	$750	$1,250	74-24/32nds
Out-of-the-money	1,125	469	1,344	656	75-11/32nds

Although the potential profit associated with the in-the-money spread is much less than the profit potentially associated with the out-of-the-money spread, the futures price must advance from 73-16/32nds to the breakeven point of 74-24/32nds before the in-the-money spreader realizes a loss. The futures price must decline froom 76-16/32nds to the breakeven point of 75-11/32nds before the out-of-the-money spreader can realize any profit at all.

Bearish Vertical Call Spread

A bearish vertical call spread entails the sale of a call and the purchase of a call with the same expiration dates but with different strike prices. The long call is placed in an option series with a strike price that is high relative to the short option in the spread. Once more, the attractive feature of a vertical spread is that it permits an investor to participate in an anticipated price fluctuation (a bearish fluctuation in this case) while restricting risks and possible rewards to a rather moderate, predefinable level. As such, the bearish vertical spread may be pursued by a trader who is moderately bearish, rather than strongly bearish.

Another advantage—or at least a superficial advantage—associated with the bearish vertical call spread is that a trader may place the spread and receive a net inflow of premium. The bear call spread requires one to sell a low-struck call and buy a high-struck call. Assume that the underlying commodity price falls between the two strikes. In that case, the short low-struck call will be in-the-money and the high-struck call will be out-of-the-money. All other things being equal, an in-the-money option will invariably command a higher premium than an out-of-the-money option. Thus the premium received from the sale of the low-struck call must exceed the premium paid to secure the high-struck call. The spreader's account is credited for the difference between the low-struck call and the high-struck call for a net credit:

$$\text{Net Credit} = \text{Low-Struck Premium} - \text{High-Struck Premium}$$

EXAMPLE.   A call exercisable for gold futures and struck at $400 is sold for a $25.00 per ounce premium while a call struck at $420 is purchased for a $16.00 per ounce premium. The net credit equals $9.00 per ounce ($25 − $16.00).

The placement of a bearish vertical spread is similar to the sale of a call insofar as both strategies permit the investor to receive premium up front. Another similarity exists in that the maximum profit potentially associated with a short call and a bearish vertical call spread equals the net credit received up front:

$$\text{Maximum Profit} = \text{Net Credit}$$

This maximum profit is achieved when the underlying commodity price is less than or equal to the lower of the two strike prices by the time the options expire. Should the underlying commodity price fall below the lower of the two strikes, both options will be out-of-the-money and expire unexercised. Under these circuumstances, the spreader will retain the premium received from the sale of the low-struck call and forfeit the entire premium paid to secure the high-struck put. In other words, the spreader retains the net credit and counts it as profit.

The bearish vertical call spread is similar to a short outright call in the sense that the maximum profit potentially associated with the position is received initially. The two strategies are different in that the bearish vertical call spreader is subject to a limited loss under adverse circumstances, a loss that may be defined up front. In particular, this loss may be identified as the difference between the high strike price and the low strike price less the net credit:

$$\text{Maximum Loss} = \text{High Strike} - \text{Low Strike} - \text{Net Credit}$$

EXAMPLE.   Building upon the prior example, let's illustrate how the maximum loss associated with the position may be calculated. The low-struck call was sold for $25 per ounce while the high-struck call was purchased for $16, for a net credit of $9. The maximum profit potentially associated with the position equals the difference between the two strike prices: $420 less $400 or $20 less the net credit of $9, or $11.

The trader is subject to the maximum loss when the underlying commodity price is equal to or greater than the higher of the two strike prices at expiration. Assuming that the commodity price exceeds this level, both calls are in-the-money and may be expected to be exercised. The gross profit on exercise accrued by the spreader from the long high-struck call will be less than the gross loss on the exercise of the short low-struck call. The difference will be the difference between the two strike prices. Of course, this loss is reduced by the receipt of the net credit up front.

A third point in which we are interested is the breakeven point at which the bearish vertical call spreader will incur neither a profit nor a loss. The breakeven point falls in between the two strike prices. Specifically, the breakeven point will equal the low strike plus the net credit:

$$\text{Breakeven Point} = \text{Low Strike} + \text{Net Credit}$$

EXAMPLE. Our prior example had the call spreader buy a call struck at $420 for a $16 premium and sell a call struck at $400 for a $25 premium for a net credit of $9 per ounce. The breakeven point is calculated as the low strike price of $400 per ounce plus the net credit of $9, or $409 per ounce.

An obvious advantage associated with the bearish vertical call spread, as opposed to a bearish vertical put spread, is that the put spreader's account is credited, rather than debited, by the difference between the two premiums. It is relatively unobvious, however, that the bearish vertical call spreader is exposed to the risk that the short call will be exercised prior to expiration before the call spreader is prepared for this possibility. As long as the underlying commodity price exceeds the lower of the two strike prices, the short low-struck call is in-the-money and may be exercised. This possibility may be particularly troublesome when the underlying commodity price falls between the two strike prices. At those levels, only the short low-struck call is in-the-money. The long high-struck call is out-of-the-money and the spreader could not be advised to unwind the position by exercising the long call. Because of the increased certainty associated with the bearish vertical put spread as opposed to the bearish vertical call spread, many traders prefer to engage in the former strategy despite the fact that it entails a net debit rather than a net credit.

Of course, in many other respects, the risks and rewards potentially associated with the bearish vertical call spread resemble strongly the risks and rewards associated with the bearish vertical put spread.

EXAMPLE. An option investor purchases a call on a stock index futures contract struck at 168 for a 6.00 index point premium; simultaneously, the investor sells a call struck at 166 for a 7.00 point premium. The net credit equals 1.00 index point. Should this position be held until expiration (assuming that the short call is not exercised

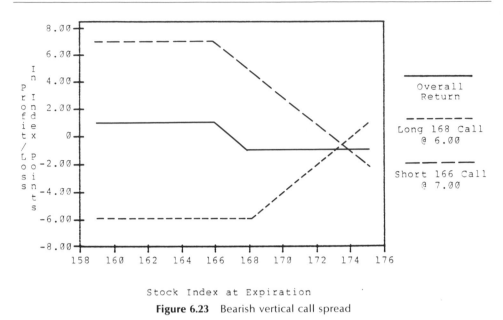

Figure 6.23   Bearish vertical call spread

early), the returns that accrue to the spreader under various scenarios are (also see Figure 6.23):

Index Price at Expiration	(1) Return on Long Leg	(2) Return on Short Leg	Overall Return (1) + (2)
164	(6.00)	7.00	1.00
165	(6.00)	7.00	1.00
166	(6.00)	7.00	1.00
167	(6.00)	6.00	0
168	(6.00)	5.00	(1.00)
169	(5.00)	4.00	(1.00)
170	(4.00)	3.00	(1.00)

The foregoing example applied the assumption that the spread was placed
when the high-struck call was out-of-the-money and the low-struck call was in-
the-money. But, much like the bear put spread, the bear call spread may be
tailored to the preferred balance of risk and reward. By placing the spread
when both legs are in-the-money, or when both legs are out-of-the-money, the
call spreader may pursue a more aggressive or conservative strategy, respectively.

EXAMPLE.   A bearish vertical call spread is placed in the stock index futures
option market when both legs are in-the-money: stock index futures are trading at 168.50 and a 166 call is sold for 7.75 while a 168
call is purchased for 6.75. Another call spread is placed when the
stock index futures market is at 165.50; the 166 call is sold for 6.25

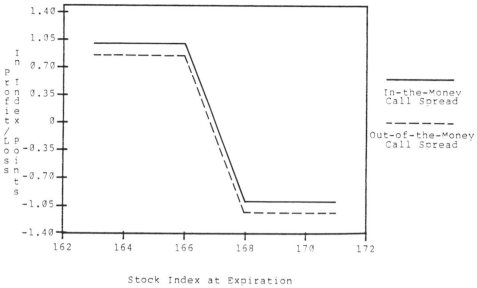

Stock Index at Expiration

Figure 6.24 Vertical bearish call spreads

while the 168 call was purchased for 5.40. The risks and rewards potentially associated with these strategies may be summarized as (also see Figure 6.24):

	Long Leg Premium	Short Leg Premium	Max Profit	Max Loss	Breakeven
In-the-money	7.75	6.75	1.00	1.00	167.00
Out-of-the-money	6.25	5.40	0.85	1.15	166.85

The in-the-money spreader assumes a higher risk of loss because the underlying commodity price must move downwards to 167.00 before he can hope to break even. However, the maximum profit associated with the position is relatively high and the maximum loss relatively low. The out-of-the-money spreader assumes a relatively moderate risk as he could retain the full net credit as long as the underlying commodity price remains out-of-the-money. However, the maximum return potentially associated with the position is low and the maximum risk is relatively high. Moreover, the market need advance only to 166.85 (in the prior example) for the spreader to break even, rather than realizing a positive profit.

NEUTRAL SPREADS

Horizontal or Time Spread

A horizontal spread is placed when the trader sells an option with a relatively short term to expiration and buys an option of the same type and strike price with a longer term to expiration. The idea that underpins this strategy is

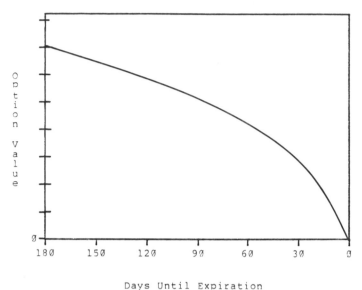

Days Until Expiration

Figure 6.25   Accelerating decline in time value of an at-the-money option

to capitalize on the declining time value associated with the near-term option (see Figure 6.25). As a rule, the time value associated with an option with a short term to maturity will decline quicker than the time value of an option with a relatively longer term to expiration. Therefore, as long as the market remains stable and does not move significantly against the time spreader, he can "ride down" the time value of the short near-term option, realizing a profit thereon. At the same time, a loss may be expected on the long long-term option; however, this loss should be more than offset by the profit on the near-term option *should the market remain stable.*

EXAMPLE.   An option spreader believes that the T-bond futures market is likely to remain quite stable over the next few months. Therefore, he decides to sell a call with 90 days to expiration and struck at 74 for a 1-42/64ths or $1,656 premium and purchase a call with 180 days to expiration and struck at 74 for a 2-18/64ths or $2,281 premium. At the time of these transactions, the T-bond futures contracts underlying both the near- or short-term (S-T) leg and the long-term (L-T) leg are assumed to be equal and at-the-money at 74 (a simplifying assumption). The premiums that may be associated with calls with various terms until expiration and struck at-the-money at 74 are as follows:

Term Until Expiration	Call Premium
180 days	$2,281
90	1,656
0	0

If the market remains stable at 74, both S-T and L-T calls will remain at-the-money. The near-term call can be expected to be abandoned by the opposite long. Simultaneously, our time spreader can sell the long L-T call for its current market value. Since it was originally a 180-day option and 90 days have passed, its value has declined to $1,656. The time spreader's profit equals the $1,656 retained from the sale of the S-T call less the $625 loss on the sale of the L-T call ($2,281 less $1,656) for a net profit of $1,031.

In the prior example, our time spreader was fortunate that the market remained stable and did not fluctuate substantially in either direction. If the market had either advanced or declined, our time spreader's profits would have been diminished. Given a large enough market movement, of course, the spreader would have realized a loss.

EXAMPLE.   Building upon the prior example, a 74 call exercisable for T-bond futures contracts with 180 days until expiration is purchased for 2-18/64ths or $2,281. Simultaneously, a 74 call with only 90 days until maturity is sold for a 1-42/64ths or $1,656 premium. At the time that these transactions were concluded, both options were struck at-the-money at the common strike price of 74 (making the simplifying assumption that the price of the T-bond futures contract underlying the near-term option and the long-term option are, and remain, equal). We are interested in the results where the near-term call is held until expiration. At that point, we assume that the near- or short-term (S-T) call is either exercised or abandoned, depending on whether T-bond futures prices advance in-the-money over 74 or fall out-of-the-money under 74. At the same time, the long long-term (L-T) option is sold for whatever premium it may bring on the market:

T-Bond at Expiration	S-T Leg Premium	S-T Leg Return	L-T Leg Premium	L-T Leg Return	Overall Return
70	$0	$1,656	$359	($1,922)	($266)
71	0	1,656	547	(1,734)	(78)
72	0	1,656	828	(1,453)	203
73	0	1,656	1,187	(1,094)	562
74	0	1,656	1,656	(625)	1,031
75	1,000	656	2,187	(94)	562
76	2,000	(344)	2,828	547	203
77	3,000	(1,344)	3,547	1,266	(78)
78	4,000	(2,344)	4,328	2,047	(297)

In the prior example (also see Figure 6.26a), our time spreader realized the maximum profit when the market remained stable at the common strike price of 74. And, as long as T-bond futures prices remained within the range bounded approximately by 71 on the down side and 77 on the up side, the time

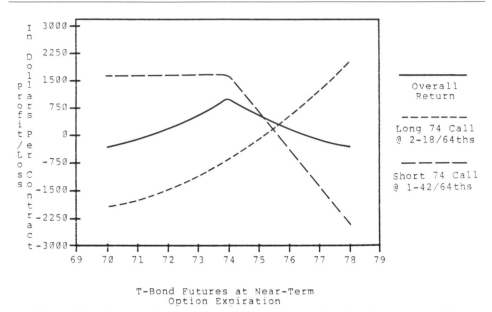

Figure 6.26a   Horizontal option spread (sell near-term option, buy long-term option)

spreader realized a profit (holding all other things equal). Of course, if T-bond futures prices were to fluctuate dramatically in either direction, the spreader could be subject to a large loss.

A horizontal or time spread may be executed just as readily with put options as with call options. Using either puts or calls, a time spreader sells a near-term option and buys a relatively long-term option to capitalize on the accelerating decline in time value as an option approaches expiration.

EXAMPLE.   A one-month 76 option exercisable for March T-bond futures is sold for 1-02/64ths or $1,031. A four-month 76 put is purchased for 2-02/64ths or $2,031. The net debit equals the difference between the two premiums or $1,000; this also equals the maximum profit possible provided that futures remain stable at the 76 strike price. As long as futures do not fluctuate considerably either up or down within the next month, the spreader will be assured of a profit (see Figure 6.26b).

Of course, a horizontal option spread need not be held until expiration of the near-term leg in order to reap a profit (or realize a loss). The short option may subsequently be repurchased prior to its expiration while the long leg of the spread is sold off. Figure 6.26c illustrates the value of a March/June horizontal T-bond call spread over a range of futures prices and at different times, specifically, when the spread has 60 days to expiration, 30 days to expiration, and at expiration of the near-term leg. Both of the legs of the spread are struck at 76. When we refer to the "value" of this spread, we are referring to the net debit paid out to secure the spread.

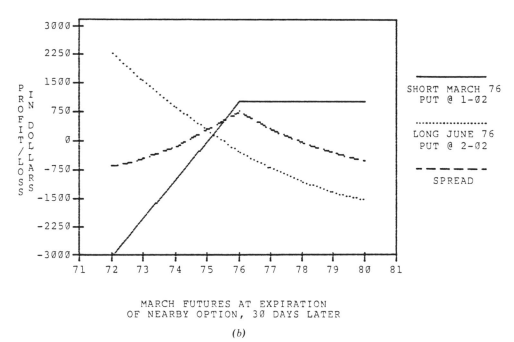

MARCH FUTURES AT EXPIRATION
OF NEARBY OPTION, 30 DAYS LATER

(b)

Figure 6.26b March/June horizontal put spread March and June futures @76

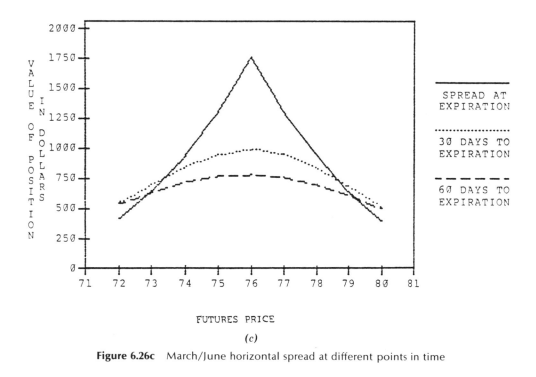

FUTURES PRICE

(c)

Figure 6.26c March/June horizontal spread at different points in time

It is apparent that when futures remain within the range bounded roughly by about 73 and 79, the horizontal spreader's position appreciates in value over time. For example, if futures are around the 76 strike price when there are 30 days to expiration of the near-term option, the spread may be purchased for about $800. Subsequently, the spread will appreciate to about $1,750 if futures remain constant at 76. If, however, futures fall outside of that range, the spreader's position may depreciate in value over time. As one might expect, the value of the horizontal spread changes most dramatically over the last 30 days as opposed to the period between 60 and 30 days to expiration of the near-term leg.

Diagonal Spreads

A diagonal or cross spread involves the purchase and sale of two options of the same type (put or call) but which vary in strike price *and* expiration dates. As a rule of thumb, most diagonal spreads are placed such that the long option has a longer term to expiration than the short option. This is an effort to take advantage of the accelerating decline in an option's time value as it approaches expiration. But, although we have included discussion of this strategy under the subheading "neutral spreads," diagonal spreads may be motivated by a slightly bullish or slightly bearish scenario as well. (If, in fact, one were absolutely neutral, a neutral time spread would be preferred over a diagonal spread strategy.)

A diagonal spread strategy may be employed to take advantage of a mildly bullish or mildly bearish pricing scenario, much like a vertical spread may be used to take advantage of bull and bear scenarios. The difference between a bullish or bearish vertical spread and a bullish or bearish diagonal spread is that the short option position is established in an option with a relatively near-term maturity compared to the long option. As such, a bullish diagonal spread is slightly more bearish and provides more downside protection than a bullish vertical spread. At the same time, a bullish diagonal spread could incur a loss in the event of a strong bull movement. Similarly, a bearish diagonal spread is slightly more bullish than a bearish vertical spread. However, a bearish diagonal spreader could be subject to loss in the event of a strong bear movement.

EXAMPLE. An option trader is only mildly bullish and wants to be careful to protect against the possibility that his market forecasts are incorrect. As a result, he enters into a bullish diagonal call spread. He does this by buying a call, exercisable for a gold futures contract, struck at $400 and with about five months to expiration for a $36.90 per ounce premium. Simultaneously, he sells a call struck at $420 with about one month to expiration for a premium of $10.60. This spread is quite similar to the bullish vertical call spread discussed above, with the exception that the short option position is placed in a relatively near-term expiration month. (Just like the bullish vertical call spreader, the bullish diagonal call spreader's account is debited by $26.30 or the difference between the two premiums: $36.90 less $10.60.) At the time of this transaction, the gold futures contracts underlying both option series are assumed to be equal at about $410. Assume that the spread is held until the short S-T call option expires, at which point it is either exercised or abandoned. At the same time, assume that the long L-T call is liquidated at the current market price. What returns would accrue to the time spreader by the time the S-T call expires under a variety of scenarios?

Gold at Expiration	S-T Leg Premium	S-T Leg Return	L-T Leg Premium	L-T Leg Return	Overall Return
$340	$0	$10.60	$6.70	($30.20)	($19.60)
360	0	10.60	11.90	(25.00)	(14.40)
380	0	10.60	19.00	(17.90)	(7.30)
400	0	10.60	28.40	(8.50)	2.10
410	0	10.60	33.80	(3.10)	7.50
420	0	10.60	39.80	2.90	13.50
440	20	(10.40)	53.10	16.20	5.80
460	40	(30.40)	68.00	31.10	.70
480	60	(50.40)	84.20	47.30	(3.10)

Figure 6.27 shows that even if the market remains neutral or experiences a limited bear move, the bullish diagonal call spreader can still realize a profit.

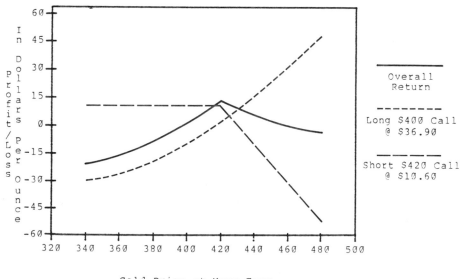

Figure 6.27 shows that even if the market remains neutral or experiences a limited bear move, the bullish diagonal call spreader can still realize a profit.

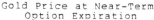

Figure 6.27 Diagonal call spread (sell high-struck, near-term call; buy low-struck, long-term call)

However, he is subject to loss in the event that the market moves strongly upwards or downwards. But if the market advances mildly (to $420, for example), the bullish diagonal call spreader realizes a moderately handsome return.

In the prior example, we illustrated how one can turn a bullish vertical call spread into a position that would permit one to profit even if the market remained relatively stable. Similarly, a bearish vertical put spreader might well consider the execution of a bearish diagonal put spread as an alternative if there is some possibility of a fairly stable market environment.

EXAMPLE. An option trader is mildly bearish and wants to take advantage of that market scenario by entering into a bearish diagonal put spread. He buys a put, exercisable for gold futures, struck at $420 with about five months to expiration for a $37.70 per ounce premium. Simultaneously, he sells a $400 put with only about one month to expiration for a $10.30 premium. This is a net debit of $27.40. For purposes of this example, let's assume that the price of both gold futures contracts were equal at $410 at the time the spread was placed. Assume further that the spread is held until the expiration of the S-T low-struck put. At that point, the S-T put will either be exercised or abandoned by the opposite party. Furthermore, the long L-T put will be sold off by the spreader for whatever premium it will command. Again, we assume that the gold contracts underlying both legs of the spread remain equally priced.

Gold Price at Expiration	S-T Leg Premium	S-T Leg Return	L-T Leg Premium	L-T Leg Return	Overall Return
$340	$60	($49.70)	$81.80	$44.10	($5.60)
360	40	(29.70)	66.00	28.30	(1.40)
380	20	(9.70)	51.90	14.20	4.50
400	0	10.30	39.80	2.10	12.30
410	0	10.30	34.60	(3.10)	7.20
420	0	10.30	29.80	(7.90)	2.40
440	0	10.30	21.80	(15.90)	(5.60)
460	0	10.30	15.60	(22.10)	(11.80)
480	0	10.30	10.90	(26.80)	(16.50)

Even though a bearish diagonal put spread is placed in anticipation of a price decline, the position is still safe in the event of a neutral market or even a mildly bullish market. On the other hand, the bearish diagonal put spreader is subject to loss in the event of strong bearish or bullish movement. In the prior example, the spreader's profits are maximized when the market moves down to about the level of the low strike price by the time the S-T put expires, as shown in Figure 6.28a.

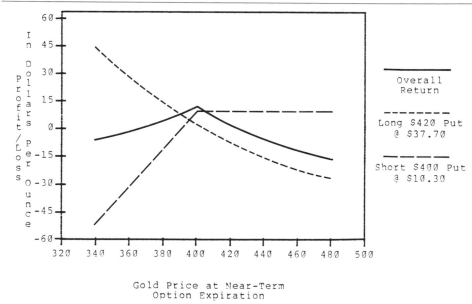

Figure 6.28a   Diagonal put spread (sell low-struck, near-term put; buy high-struck, long-term put)

All of these diagonal spreading examples assumed that the spreader held the position until expiration of the near-term options. Let us reiterate: options may be liquidated through a series of closing transactions at any time after the position initially is placed. In the case of a diagonal call or put spread, the trader simply buys back the short near-term option and sells the long long-term option.

Figure 6.28b illustrates how the value of a diagonal call spread may fluctu-

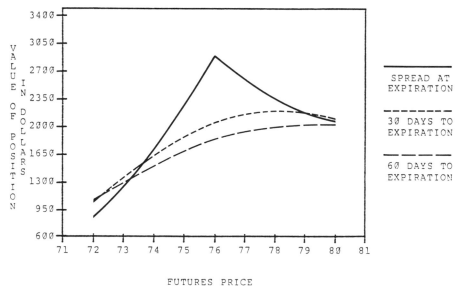

FUTURES PRICE

Figure 6.28b   Diagonal call spread at different points in time

ate over a range of underlying futures prices and at three distinct times: when there are 60 and 30 days to expiration and at expiration of the near-term leg of the spread. The "value" of the position refers to the debit one incurs when initially placing the spread. Obviously, if the value of the position appreciates over the initial debit, the diagonal spreader may realize a profit through a subsequent series of closing transactions.

Note that when futures fall outside of the range bounded in this example by approximately 73 and 79, the value of the spread appreciates over time. But when futures fall outside of that range, the value of the spread declines. Furthermore, the value of the position changes more dramatically during the last 30 days than it does during the period between 60 and 30 days to expiration of the near-term leg. This suggests that diagonal call spreader will neither realize large profits nor incur large losses when the spread involves relatively long-term options. But as the spread approaches expiration of the near-term leg, the spreader may wish to reevaluate his position. If the underlying commodity falls outside of the profitable range and can be expected to remain stable or move adversely, it is probably advisable to consider liquidating the spread. But if the underlying commodity falls within the profitable range and can be expected to stay within range, then it is advisable to hold onto the spread.

Ratio Option Spreading

A "ratio" spread is one in which the spreader takes on unequal numbers of long and short options. The most common form of a ratio option spread has the option spreader selling more options than the number of options purchased. To illustrate, a ratio call spreader may sell two high-struck calls against every single low-struck call he purchases. Similarly, a ratio put spreader may sell two high-struck puts against every single high-struck put he purchases. Generally, these spreads are placed for small credits; the summation of the two short premiums exceed the one long premium by a slight margin. The idea is to take advantage of the declining time value associated with the short options while providing protection against a large bull move (in the case of a ratio call spread) or a large bear move (in the case of a ratio put spread).

EXAMPLE.   T-bond futures are trading at 74-00/32nds. A ratio call spread is established by selling two 74 calls for 1-25/64ths or $1,390 a piece or $2,781 for the two, and by buying one 72 call for 2-37/64ths or $2,578. This is a net credit of $203. The two option series share a common expiration date. The results of this spread if it is held until expiration are as follows:

T-Bond Price at Expiration	Returns on Long Call	Returns on Two Short Calls	Overall Returns
70	($2,578)	$2,781	$203
71	(2,578)	2,781	203

T-Bond Price at Expiration	Returns on Long Call	Returns on Two Short Calls	Overall Returns
72	(2,578)	2,781	203
73	(1,578)	2,781	1,203
74	(578)	2,781	2,203
75	422	781	1,203
76	1,422	(1,219)	203
77	2,422	(3,219)	(797)
78	3,422	(5,219)	(1,797)
79	4,422	(7,219)	(2,797)
80	5,422	(9,219)	(3,797)

As illustrated above, and in Figure 6.29, if the market declines to the lower of the two strike prices at expiration, the spreader's profits are limited to the net credit received up front. Over the lower of the two strikes, the spreader's returns peak, reaching a maximum at the higher of the two strikes and declining at a constant rate thereafter. As long as the market declines, remains neutral, or is only slightly bullish, the spreader may realize a profit. If, however, the market advances dramatically, the spreader may be subject to loss. The reverse is true in the case of a 2:1 ratio put spread: if the market advances, remains neutral, or is only slightly bearish, the spreader can realize a moderate profit. If the market is strongly bearish, the ratio put spreader may be subject to loss:

EXAMPLE.   A 2:1 ratio put spread is placed by selling two puts exercisable for T-bond futures and struck at 72 for 1-22/64ths or $1,344 a piece or $2,688 for the two; at the same time, a 74 put is purchased for

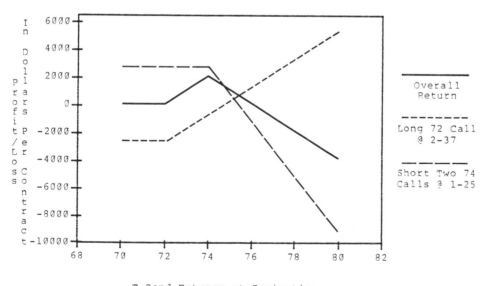

Figure 6.29   Ratio call spread (sell two high-stuck calls; buy one low-struck call)

2-37/64ths or $2,578. T-bond futures are now trading at 72-00/32nds. The spread is placed for a net credit of $110:

T-Bond Price at Expiration	Returns on Long Put	Returns on Two Short Puts	Overall Returns
66	$5,422	($9,312)	($3,890)
67	4,422	(7,312)	(2,890)
68	3,422	(5,312)	(1,890)
69	2,422	(3,312)	(890)
70	1,422	(1,312)	110
71	422	688	1,110
72	(578)	2,688	2,110
73	(1,578)	2,688	1,110
74	(2,578)	2,688	110
75	(2,578)	2,688	110
76	(2,578)	2,688	110

    The spreads illustrated above, and in Figure 6.30, utilize a 2:1 short to long option ratio. But other ratios may be employed as well. For example, if the ratio call spreader above had sold three 72 calls for every single 74 call purchased, he would have succeeded (1) in increasing the net credit and thereby increasing the profit in the event of a bear movement, and (2) decreasing the upside breakeven point and increasing the loss potential should the market exhibit a strong bull movement.

    Another strategy available is to utilize the concept of the neutral hedge

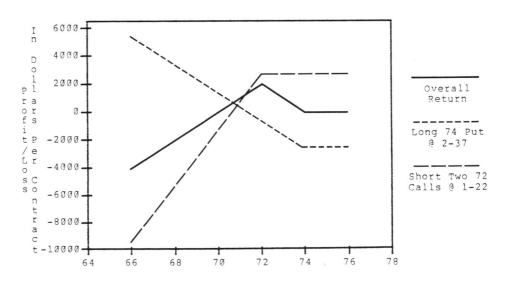

T-Bond Futures at Expiration

Figure 6.30 Ratio put spread (sell two low-struck puts; buy one high-struck put)

ratio to set up an option spread. By spreading options in a ratio such that fluctuations in the value of the long and short components of the spread tend to neutralize each other, the spreader may hope to "ride down" the declining time value of the short options while keeping risk to a minimum.

EXAMPLE.   T-bond futures are trading at 74. Rather than establishing a 2:1 short to long ratio call spread, a "neutral" or "delta" ratio call spread is established. A 72 call is available at 2-37/64ths or $2,578; delta equals .72. A 74 call is available at 1-25/64ths or $1,390 with a delta of .51. The ratio of the low-struck : high-struck deltas equal .73 : .51 or approximately 7:5. This suggests that the ratio call spreader sell seven high struck calls and buy five low struck calls.

Sell seven 74 calls @ 1-25/64ths or $9,730

Buy five 72 calls @ 2-37/64ths or ($12,890)

Net Debit ($3,160)

By establishing a 7:5 short to long position, the spreader can effectively offset loss as a result of price fluctuation. Recall that delta provides a measure of the expected movement in a particular option premium relative to a movement in the underlying commodity. The delta associated with the at-the-money 74 call equals approximately .5, suggesting that these calls will fluctuate on the order of only 50% as quickly as the underlying T-bond futures contract. The delta associated with the in-the-money 72 calls equals approximately .7, suggesting that these calls will fluctuate 70% as quickly as the underlying T-bond futures price. By taking on seven of the slower moving calls against an opposite position in five of the quicker moving options, the spreader effectively enters a neutral position.

If the market remains at 74 in the prior example—the strike price of the short high-struck calls—the ratio spreader will retain the full $9,730 premium received from the sale of the seven calls. But he will realize a loss of $2,890 on the purchase of the five 72 calls for a net option of $6,840. And if the market moves slightly in either direction, the fluctuation in the value of the long and short legs will tend to equalize each other. This, however, still permits the spreader to ride down the time value of the short leg profitably. But if the market moves dramatically in either direction—upwards or downwards—the ratio spreader could be subject to loss. The neutral hedge ratio (the reciprocal of delta) is only effective over a relatively short time period and only for relatively small fluctuations. In order to offset these possible losses, the delta ratio spreader should attempt to adjust the ratio when warranted to maintain a risk-neutral position.

Of course, if it becomes necessary to adjust the ratio frequently, transaction costs will mount up. And if the market moves suddenly before a defensive ratio adjustment can be effected, the ratio spreader may be subject to loss.

Butterfly Spread

The long butterfly spread represents another way in which to take advantage of a neutral market scenario. However, the long butterfly spread is one of the more complicated ways in which to profit in a static market insofar as a butterfly entails four positions in three different option series. The butterfly spread may be applied using either puts or calls with similar results. The long butterfly requires one to buy a low-struck and a high-struck option and sell two options, the strike price of which falls in between the long low-struck and high-struck options. For example, one may buy low-struck and high-struck calls and sell two intermediate-struck calls, or one may buy low-struck and high-struck puts and sell two intermediate-struck puts. A short butterfly may be entered by selling the two extreme-struck options and buying the two intermediate options. Unfortunately, the value of the short butterfly erodes over time and, as such, does not represent a particularly popular trading strategy. Accordingly, this discussion focuses on the long butterfly.

In essence, the long butterfly spread represents two spreads—a vertical bull spread and a vertical bear spread. As such, the butterfly may even be applied using a vertical bull call (put) spread in combination with a vertical bear put (call) spread. The idea, however, is to profit from a neutral or static market rather than a bullish or bearish market movement. This strategy is often considered attractive because the risks incurred by the butterfly spreader are limited to very low levels. These risks are lower than the risks associated with a vertical bull or bear spread. This is because the bull spread component of the butterfly tends to offset the risks associated with the bear spread component of the butterfly. Although the risks inherent in the butterfly spread are limited, the returns are likewise limited to rather modest levels.

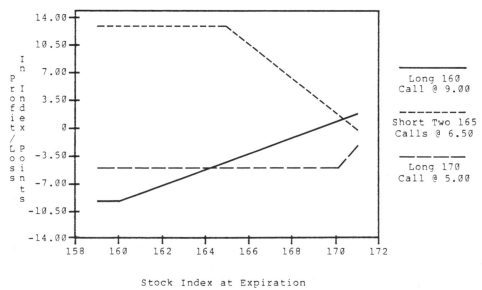

Stock Index at Expiration

Figure 6.31 Butterfly spread legs

EXAMPLE. An option trader enters a butterfly spread using calls exercisable for stock index futures contracts. In particular, our trader buys a call struck at 160 for 9.00 index points, sells two 165 calls for 6.50 index points a piece, and buys a 170 call for 5.00 index points. These various positions are shown in Figure 6.31. This translates into a net debit of 1.00 index point $(9.00 + 5.00 - 2 \times 6.50)$. The holder of the butterfly spread can realize the following returns if the position is held until expiration of the options:

Stock Index at Expiration	(1) Return 160 Call	(2) Return 165 Calls	(3) Return 170 Call	Overall Returns (1) + (2) + (3)
158	(9.00)	13.00	(5.00)	(1.00)
160	(9.00)	13.00	(5.00)	(1.00)
161	(8.00)	13.00	(5.00)	0
163	(6.00)	13.00	(5.00)	2.00
165	(4.00)	13.00	(5.00)	4.00
167	(2.00)	9.00	(5.00)	2.00
169	0	5.00	(5.00)	0
170	1.00	3.00	(5.00)	(1.00)
172	3.00	(1.00)	(3.00)	(1.00)

The maximum loss that can possibly accrue to the holder of the butterfly spread equals the net debit forfeit up front to establish the butterfly spread. In the foregoing case, and as shown in Figure 6.32a, this maximum loss equals 1.00 index point:

$$\text{Maximum Loss} = \text{Net Debit}$$

This maximum loss is realized when the market falls below the lowest of the three strike prices at expiration, or rises above the highest of the three strike prices at expiration. Under the former circumstances, all three options expire worthless and are abandoned. At that point, the holder of the butterfly spread forfeits the entire net debit. Under the latter circumstances, all of the options may be expected to be exercised. But at this point, the loss on the two short calls overwhelms the profits on the two long calls and the butterfly spread holder is again left with a loss equal to the net debit.

On the positive side, the butterfly spread holder realizes the maximum possible profit when the market price equals the intermediate strike price at option expiration. In the foregoing example, this intermediate strike price equals 165 index points. At this point, the long low-struck call will be exercised, while the short intermediate-struck call and the long high-struck call will be abandoned. The gross return on the long low-struck call overcomes the net debit by the difference between the intermediate strike price and the low strike

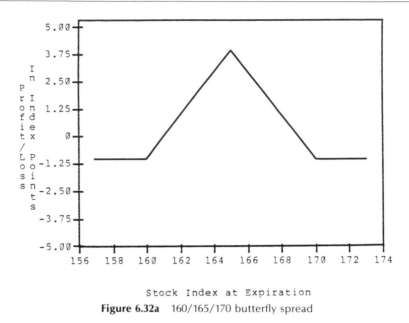

Stock Index at Expiration

Figure 6.32a   160/165/170 butterfly spread

price, or the 165 intermediate strike price less the 160 low strike price less the 1.00 net debit, or 4.00 index points:

$$\text{Maximum Profit} = \text{Strike Price Interval} - \text{Net Debit}$$

Other points of interest include the butterfly spread breakeven points. The butterfly spread has two breakeven points—an upside breakeven and a downside breakeven. The upside breakeven point falls between the intermediate and high strike prices while the downside breakeven falls between the intermediate and low strike prices. Specifically, the upside breakeven equals the high strike price less the net debit; the downside breakeven equals the low strike price plus the net debit. In the foregoing example, the upper breakeven equals the high 170 strike less the 1.00 net debit, or 169. The downside breakeven equals the low 160 strike plus the 1.00 net debit, or 161:

$$\text{Upper Breakeven Point} = \text{High Strike} - \text{Net Debit}$$

$$\text{Lower Breakeven Point} = \text{Low Strike} + \text{Net Debit}$$

The butterfly spread is normally placed when the underlying commodity price is at or near to the intermediate strike price. Thus, if the market should remain quite stable, trading sideways, the holder of a butterfly spread position may hope to realize a profit equal to, or at least reasonably close, to the maximum realizable return.

Like other option strategies considered above, the butterfly represents a *dynamic* strategy. In other words, it need not be held until expiration of the

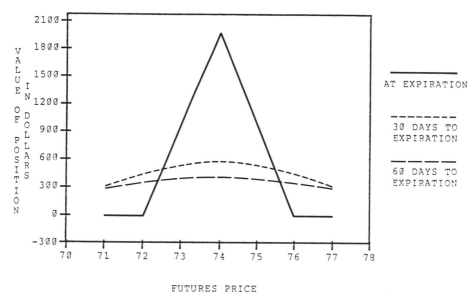

Figure 6.32b   Value of long butterfly at different points in time

four options for the spreader to realize a profit. Instead, the spreader can liquidate the spread by entering into a series of closing sales and purchases. Figure
6.32b illustrates the value of a butterfly spread over a range of underlying commodity prices at different times. Specifically, it depicts 72/74/76 butterfly call
spread in which the options are exercisable for T-bond futures contracts.

A familiar pattern is emerging whenever we consider how an option strategy will fluctuate over time and before the expiration of the nearest term option incorporated within the option strategy. That is, the value of the position
fluctuates most dramatically as it approaches expiration. In the case of the butterfly spread, this effect is most pronounced. Here we see almost negligible
movement between the period when the options have 60 to 30 days until expiration. But over the last 30 days the spread moves considerably. (Of course,
there is nothing particularly magical about 30 days. In fact, the spread will
move a bit more dramatically every day it is available.) In this case, the relevant range runs from approximately 72-16/32nds to about 75-16/32nds. If the
underlying T-bond futures price falls within that range, the net debit associated with putting on this butterfly will increase, leading to profits for the
spreader. But if futures fall out of that range, then the debit melts away over
time, leading to loss.

CALL/PUT COMBINATIONS

All of the strategies examined thus far have employed puts or calls individ-
ually, either in combination with the underlying commodity or in combination
with other options of the same type. But we have not yet examined strategies

that combine puts *and* calls together. By combining puts and calls, an option trader can avail herself of a great deal of added flexibility in pursuing profit opportunities. Two basic put/call combinations are examined herein: straddles and synthetic commodity positions, along with a few variations on these themes.

Straddles are unlike spreads insofar as an option spread entails the purchase and sale of calls, or the purchase and sale of puts. Straddles entail the purchase of a put and a call (a long straddle) or the sale of a put and a call (a short straddle). The most basic option spread strategies (vertical spreads) may be used to take advantage of slightly bullish or slightly bearish pricing scenarios—rather straightforward market forecasts. Straddles, on the other hand, may be used to take advantage of more exotic pricing scenarios. A long straddle position may be used to exploit a very volatile marketplace while a short straddle may be used to exploit a very stable marketplace. If, for example, a trader is confident that the market is likely to move dramatically, but is unsure about which direction this movement may take, he may be advised to go long a straddle. If he is confident that the market is likely to trade sideways or remain quite stable, a market scenario not unlike one that may motivate the execution of a time or horizontal spread, he may be advised to go short a straddle.

Synthetic commodity positions entail the purchase of a call (put) and the sale of a put (call). By pursuing these strategies, respectively, the trader effectively creates a long (short) position in the underlying commodity. In some situations, it may be more convenient or more effective to create a synthetic long or short commodity position to take advantage of a bullish or bearish pricing scenario, respectively.

Long Straddle

A long straddle represents the purchase of a put and the purchase of a call. As a rule, traders who enter a long straddle position do so in anticipation of a very volatile market, but are uncertain as to the likely direction of the market movement. The simplest type of long straddle involves the purchase of a put and a call that share a common expiration date and strike price.

EXAMPLE.   The gold market has been very volatile of late. An option trader is confident that the market will remain volatile but is hesitant to predict the likely direction of future market movement. Therefore, he buys or goes long a straddle by buying a near-to-the-money $440 put and a $440 call exercisable for gold futures contracts. The put and call were purchased for a $20 per ounce premium in piece for a total net debit of $40. Assume that the straddle is held until the common expiration date, at which point the two legs are either abandoned or exercised.

Gold Price at Expiration	(1) Returns on Call	(2) Returns on Put	Overall Returns (1) + (2)
$340	($20)	$80	$60
360	(20)	60	40
380	(20)	40	20
400	(20)	20	0
420	(20)	0	(20)
440	(20)	(20)	(40)
460	0	(20)	(20)
480	20	(20)	0
500	40	(20)	20
520	60	(20)	40
540	80	(20)	60

As is apparent, and shown in Figure 6.33a, large returns may be realized if the market moves dramatically, either upwards or downwards. If the market declines, the long straddle holder will exercise the put and abandon the call. If the market advances, the straddle holder will exercise the call and abandon the put. If, however, the market remains stable, the long straddle holder will forfeit the premiums and be unable to make up this initial setback by exercising one of the two options. It is only when the gross return on exercise from one or the other of the two options is large enough to overwhelm the summation of the two premiums forfeit up front that the long straddle holder can realize a profit.

The long straddle position entails theoretically unlimited rewards but lim-

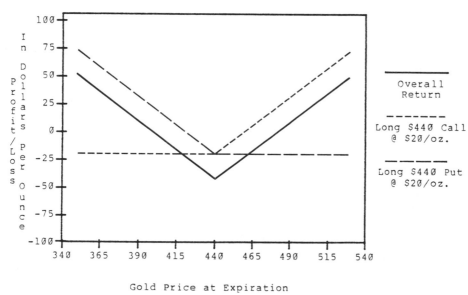

Gold Price at Expiration

Figure 6.33a Long straddle

ited risk. The maximum loss is limited to the sum of the two premiums forfeit up front. In the case of a straddle in which the two legs share a common strike price and expiration date, the maximum loss occurs at the common strike price. In the prior example, the maximum loss equaled the $20 call premium plus the $20 put premium, or $40. This amount is initially debited to the straddler's account. This loss is realized at the $440 strike price:

$$\text{Maximum Loss} = \text{Call Premium} + \text{Put Premium}$$

There are two breakeven points associated with the long straddle—an upside and a downside breakeven point. The long straddler breaks even when the gross return on exercise of the call or the put leg equals the summation of the call and put premiums forfeit up front (the net debit). When the two legs of the straddle share a common strike price, the upside breakeven point may be identified as:

$$\text{Upside Breakeven Point} = \text{Strike Price} + \text{Net Debit}$$

The upside breakeven point is realized when the gross return on exercise of the *call* equals the net debit. In the prior example, the upside breakeven point equals the $440 strike price plus the $40 net debit, or $480. The downside breakeven point is realized when the gross return on exercise of the *put* equals the net debit. In the prior example, this downside breakeven point equals the $440 strike price less the net debit of $40, or $400:

$$\text{Downside Breakeven Point} = \text{Strike Price} - \text{Net Debit}$$

Many of the strategies we have examined so far are attractive in that they put time on the option trader's side. As the term until expiration of the options involved in the strategy draws down, the strategy appreciates in value. Not so with the long straddle. Time works against the holder of a long straddle. Figure 6.33b illustrates this phenomenon. Note that the net debit required to place the spread depreciates from 60 to 30 days to expiration until the expiration date.

Short Straddle

A short straddle is just the opposite of a long straddle. Rather than purchasing a put and a call as in the long straddle, the option trader sells a put and a call. This strategy is practiced frequently in situations in which the market is expected to remain quite stable for the duration of the life of the options sold. The simplest form of this strategy has the option trader sell two options—a put and a call—that share a common strike or exercise price.

EXAMPLE.   A short straddle may be illustrated simply by reversing the parameters in our previous example involving a long straddle. Rather than buying a $440 call and a $440 put exercisable for gold futures

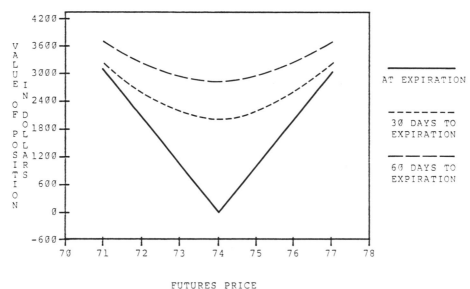

FUTURES PRICE

Figure 6.33b Value of long straddle at different points in time

contract, assume that an option trader sells a near-to-the-money $440 put and a $440 call. The put and call are sold for a $20 premium a piece for a net credit totaling $40. If both legs are held until expiration, the risks and rewards potentially associated with the position under a number of pricing scenarios may be summarized as:

Gold Price at Expiration	(1) Returns on Call	(2) Returns on Put	Overall Returns (1) + (2)
$340	$20	($80)	($60)
360	20	(60)	(40)
380	20	(40)	(20)
400	20	(20)	0
420	20	0	20
440	20	20	40
460	0	20	20
480	(20)	20	0
500	(40)	20	(20)
520	(60)	20	(40)
560	(80)	20	(60)

A short straddle strategy, as shown in Figure 6.34a, is attractive because it permits the option trader to take advantage of the natural decline in an option's time value as it approaches expiration. In the prior example, the short straddler's profits are maximized when the market remains stable and the op-

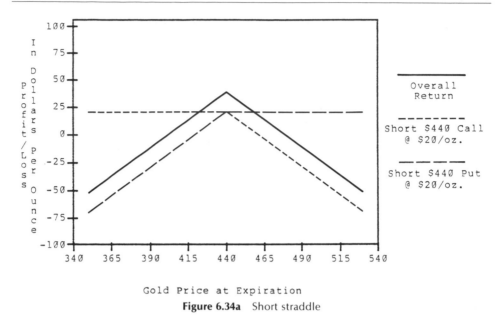

Gold Price at Expiration

Figure 6.34a Short straddle

tions expire at-the-money at the $440 strike price. Under that unique scenario, neither the put nor the call can be expected to be exercised. Meanwhile, the short straddler retains the full premium on both sides, resulting in a profit equal to the net credit. If, however, the market should move dramatically in either direction, either upwards or downwards, the short straddler will be subject to potentially large losses. But it is only when the loss on exercise of the put or the call overwhelms the net credit that the short straddler is subject to loss.

Like an outright short option position, the short straddle entails limited profit potential, but (theoretically) unlimited risks. The maximum profit is restricted to the net credit realized upon sale of the two straddle legs. Of course, this maximum profit is realized at the common strike price (provided that the two legs share a common strike). In the prior example, this maximum profit is realized when the options expire at-the-money at $440. The loss at this point equals the $40 net credit—or the $20 put plus the $20 call premium:

Maximum Profit = Call Premium + Put Premium

Just like the long straddle, there are two breakeven points associated with the short straddle—an upside and a downside breakeven point. The short straddler breaks even on the upward side when the gross loss on exercise of the short call equals the summation of the call and put premiums received up front. Where the two legs share a common strike price, this upside breakeven point is identified as:

Upside Breakeven Point = Strike Price + Net Credit

Thus the upside breakeven point is achieved when the underlying commodity price appreciates over the strike price to the extent of the net credit. In the prior example, this point may be identified as $480—or the $440 strike price plus the $40 net credit. It is at this point that the short straddler suffers a $40 gross loss on exercise of the short call while the put premium is abandoned. Of course, this $40 gross loss is precisely offset by the $40 net credit for no profit and no loss. On the downside, breakeven is realized when the gross loss on exercise of the short put exactly offsets the net credit received up front. In the prior example, the downside breakeven point equals the $440 strike price less the net debit of $40, or at $400:

Downside Breakeven Point = Strike Price − Net Credit

Unlike the long straddle, the short straddle puts time on the option trader's side. Figure 6.34b illustrates that the credit associated with placing the position depreciates as time marches onwards. Note that credit is illustrated as a negative number. Since the short straddle is "sold," the straddle writer profits when the credit associated with placing the position depreciates. When the credit depreciates, this means that the position may be repurchased at a subsequent time at a lower price—this translates into profits.

Of course, not all short straddles are profitable. If the underlying commodity runs significantly over or under the strike price, the short straddler will incur a loss. Nevertheless, the potential to realize a profit by selling a near-to-the-money straddle in a perfectly neutral market is a quite attractive proposition for many option traders.

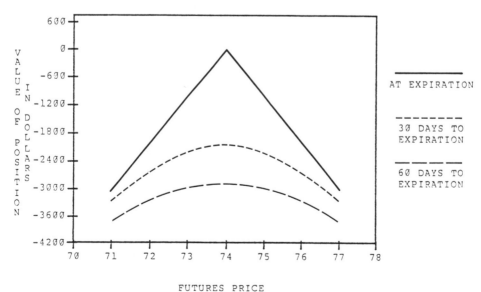

Figure 6.34b Value of short straddle at different points in time

Strangle

The "strangle" represents a special case of the straddle where the two legs do not share a common strike price. In particular, both legs of the straddle are out-of-the-money. Just like the straddle, one may pursue a long or a short strangle strategy in anticipation of a volatile or a stable pricing scenario. Unlike the simple straddles shown above, however, the strangle is characterized by a broad, flat return between the two strike prices. In the case of a short strangle, this flat zone represents profit; in the case of a long strangle, this flat zone represents loss.

Although the strangle may be practiced from the long or short side, it is most frequently employed to take advantage of the declining time value associated with an option in anticipation of a stable market. The short strangle is the more popular of the two strangle strategies. With that in mind, our attention is focused on the short strangle to the exclusion of the long strangle. Bear in mind, however, that whatever holds for the short strangle is equally applicable *in reverse* for the long strangle.

EXAMPLE.   In anticipation of a stable bond market, a trader enters a short strangle by selling an out-of-the-money 74 call and an out-of-the-money 72 put. (At the time, the underlying T-bond futures contract is trading near 75% of par.) Let us apply the simplifying assumption that both legs of the strangle are sold at the same price—1-32/64ths or $1,500 per $100,000 face value contract—for a net credit of $3,000. What results would accrue to the short straddler under a variety of market scenarios, assuming that both legs of the straddle are held until the common expiration date?

T-Bond Price at Expiration	Returns on Call	Returns on Put	Returns (1) + (2)
66	$1,500	($4,500)	($3,000)
68	1,500	(2,500)	(1,000)
69	1,500	(1,500)	0
70	1,500	(500)	1,000
72	1,500	1,500	3,000
73	1,500	1,500	3,000
74	1,500	1,500	3,000
76	(500)	1,500	1,000
77	(1,500)	1,500	0
78	(2,500)	1,500	(1,000)
80	(4,500)	1,500	(3,000)

The most notable feature associated with the short strangle, which is shown in Figure 6.35a, is the zone spanning from strike price to strike price—in the example above, from the 72 put strike price to the 74 call strike price. Be-

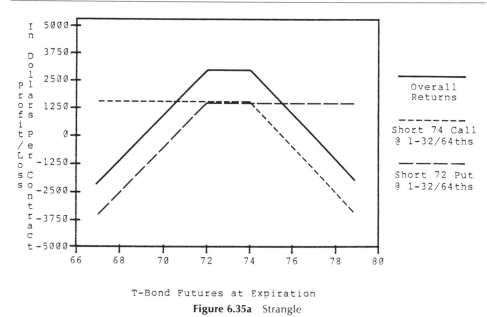

T-Bond Futures at Expiration

Figure 6.35a   Strangle

tween the two strikes, both options are out-of-the-money. And, when both legs of the short straddle expire out-of-the-money, the short straddler retains the full premium, or net credit, received up front upon straddle sale. In the foregoing case, this net credit equals $3,000—or $1,500 on the call and $1,500 on the put. This net credit represents the maximum profit that may be achieved with this strategy. It is realized when the options expire between the strike prices of the two straddle legs:

$$\text{Maximum Profit} = \text{Call Premium} + \text{Put Premium}$$

If, however, one of the two legs of the strangle should expire in-the-money, then the short straddler's profits are diminished. These profits are diminished to the extent of the gross return on exercise of one or the other of the short options. If prices should advance over the call strike price, then it is likely that the short call will be exercised. But it is only when the gross loss on exercise of the call exceeds the net credit realized up front that the short straddler is subject to loss. Since commodity prices may (at least theoretically) climb upwards indefinitely, the losses that may accrue on the short strangle as a result of price appreciation may be dramatic. Therefore, short strangle holders are interested in defining the points at which they can at least break even. On the upwards side, this point may be defined as the call strike price plus the net credit:

$$\text{Upside Breakeven Point} = \text{Call Strike Price} + \text{Net Credit}$$

In the previous example, this upside breakeven point may be identified as the 74 call strike price plus the $3,000 net credit or 3-00/64ths, for a breakeven point of 77% of par.

Likewise, holders of short strangles are likely to be interested in the downside breakeven point. On the downside, short strangle holders have cause for concern that their short puts will be exercised against them, resulting in loss. But it is only when the gross loss on exercise of the short put exceeds the net credit received up front that the short strangle holder is subject to loss. The downside breakeven point may be identified as the put strike price less the net credit. In the previous example, this downside breakeven point may be identified as the 72 put strike less the $3,000 or 3-00/64ths net credit, for a downside breakeven of 69% of par.

$$\text{Downside Breakeven Point} = \text{Put Strike Price} - \text{Net Credit}$$

Interestingly enough, the same risk/reward posture may be assumed through the sale of two *in-the-money* options as well as two *out-of-the-money* options. When the strategy is pursued using in-the-money options, the strategy is often referred to as a "guts" strategy. Of course, the net credit associated with a guts strategy is generally much greater than the net credit associated with the placement of a strangle. This is intuitive in that the guts strategy entails two in-the-money options. The maximum potential profit associated with the guts trade equals the net credit less the difference in strikes.

Like many of the other strategies examined, the strangle may also be studied over time. When a particular commodity is traded outright, this is trading in a "single dimension"—price. But when trading options, there are *at least* two major dimensions to be concerned with—price and time! Figure 6.35b illustrates the dynamic value of a 72/76 T-bond option strangle over a range of

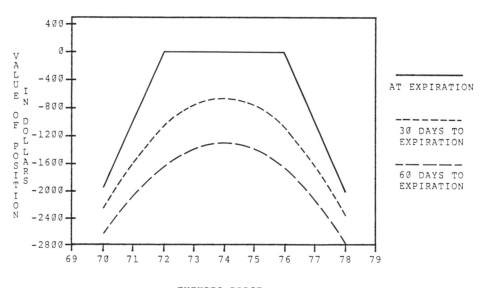

Figure 6.35b Value of short 72/76 strangle at different points in time

underlying futures prices and at three distinct times. Note that the "value" of this position refers to the credit realized by placing the position. Over time, this credit tends to appreciate as long as futures do not fluctuate significantly above the high strike or significantly below the low strike.

Short straddles—strangles or straddles of the simple variety—are considered attractive ways to take advantage of a static pricing scenario and the declining time value of an option. By practicing the short straddle or strangle strategy, the option trader is exposed to limited risk that loss will be incurred. But the rewards that may accrue to the short straddler are limited to the net credit. By entering a short strangle, as opposed to a simple short straddle, the trader further limits the risk of loss. But because both legs of the short strangle are out-of-the-money, the strangle results in a smaller profit potential compared to a simple straddle where both legs may be near-to-the-money. This is obvious since out-of-the-money options always command less premium than comparable at- or near-to-the-money options.

Synthetic Long Commodity

Although this point has been made many times before, it cannot be overemphasized—options represent extremely versatile, flexible investment vehicles. Options can be used, not only to take advantage of the unique attributes of an option contract, but also to simulate or "synthesize" an outright long or short commodity position. In this section, we consider how a combination of puts and calls can be used to create a synthetic long commodity position.

A synthetic long commodity position is created through the purchase of a call option and the sale of a put option where the two legs of the synthetic long position share a common strike price and expiration date. A synthetic long position is, as the name implies, a strongly bullish strategy, intended to take advantage of a rising market.

EXAMPLE. An option trader buys a 160 call and sells a 160 put exercisable for stock index futures for 2 index points a piece. For convenience, assume that both options are struck at-the-money, that is, stock index futures are trading at the 160 level. Since the option trader takes in 2 points on the short put and pays 2 points on the long call, the trader's account is neither debited nor credited. Assume that the synthetic long position is held until the common expiration date. If prices should advance, this trader will be subject to profit. Under those circumstances, the trader will elect to exercise the long call. The short put, being out-of-the-money is an advancing market, will expire worthless. This permits the trader to retain the full premium. If, however, prices should decline, the trader will be subject to loss—at that point, the long call would expire worthless and the short put will be exercised against the trader. At expiration, the synthetic short position strongly resembles, and is shown in Figure 6.36, an outright long futures position at 160:

Stock Index at Expiration	(1) Return on Call	(2) Return on Put	Overall Returns (1) + (2)	Long Futures at 160
152	(2)	(6)	(8)	(8)
154	(2)	(4)	(6)	(6)
156	(2)	(2)	(4)	(4)
158	(2)	0	(2)	(2)
160	(2)	2	0	0
162	0	2	2	2
164	2	2	4	4
166	4	2	6	6
168	6	2	8	8

If the position is established when the call is in-the-money, then the option trader will have to pay more for the long call than is received for the short put. This results in a net debit. However, if the position is established in-the-money, the trader is more likely to be able to exercise the long call profitably and retain the short put premium by expiration. If the position is established out-of-the-money, then the trader will pay less for the long call than the amount received for the short put. This results in a net credit. But, if the position is established

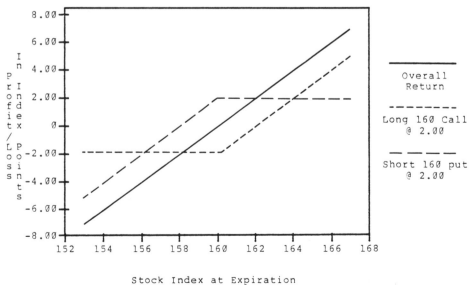

Stock Index at Expiration

Figure 6.36 Synthetic long commodity

out-of-the-money, the trader is less likely to be able to exercise the long call profitably and retain the short put premium by expiration.

The synthetic long position resembles an outright long position but requires the placement of two legs. In many cases, synthetic long positions must be established by "legging" in the long call and the short put separately. This generally entails two commissions and increased uncertainties. Why, then, would anyone want to establish a synthetic long position as opposed to a position in the underlying market? One reason may be identified simply as: leverage. When the option contract entails positive leverage, an option trader can construct a position that is the rough equivalent of a long position in the underlying commodity much more inexpensively. (Note, however, that options on futures entail negative leverage where the option premium must be paid in cash and where futures margins may be made in the form of interest-bearing securities.) Nevertheless, this consideration may be very important where no futures contract exists for a particular commodity but when options *are* available.

Synthetic Short Commodity

A synthetic long commodity position may be constructed by combining a long call with a short put. Conversely, a synthetic short commodity position may be constructed by combining a long put with a short call, in which both legs of the position share a common strike price and expiration date. This strategy may be employed to take advantage of a strongly bearish market, just like an outright short commodity position.

EXAMPLE. Reversing the situation described under our synthetic long example, assume that an option trader buys a 160 put and sells a 160 call exercisable for stock index futures for 2 index points a piece. Again, let's assume that the position is established when both legs are at-the-money, that is, when stock index futures are trading at the common 160 strike price. The option trader is required to pay 2 points to secure the long put but receives 2 points from the sale of the call. Therefore, the account is neither debited nor credited. Assume that the synthetic short position is held until expiration. If prices should decline, this trader will be in a position to profit. Under those conditions, the long put will be exercised for a gross profit implied by the difference between the commodity price prevailing at expiration and the exercise price. At the same time, the short call will be abandoned. But, if prices should advance, the short call will be exercised by the opposite party. This results in a loss equal to the difference between the prevailing commodity price and the strike price. The long put will expire worthless. To underscore the similarity between the synthetic short and the outright short position, consider the returns that may accrue under a variety of circumstances and as shown in figure 6.37:

Stock Index Expiration	(1) Return on Call	(2) Return on Put	Overall Returns (1) + (2)	Short Futures at 160
152	2	6	8	8
154	2	4	6	6
156	2	2	4	4
158	2	0	2	2
160	2	(2)	0	0
162	0	(2)	(2)	(2)
164	(2)	(2)	(4)	(4)
166	(4)	(2)	(6)	(6)
168	(6)	(2)	(8)	(8)

The synthetic short may be established in- or out-of-the-money. If established when the long put is in-the-money, the synthetic short holder will essentially pay for the in-the-money valuation. The long put will be priced at a higher level to reflect the in-the-money value while the short call premium will be discounted to reflect the fact that it is out-of-the-money. If the position is placed when the long put is out-of-the-money, the synthetic short holder will, in effect, be able to establish the position at a discount. Under those circumstances, the long put will be discounted since it is out-of-the-money while the short call will command a higher premium, reflecting its in-the-money valuation.

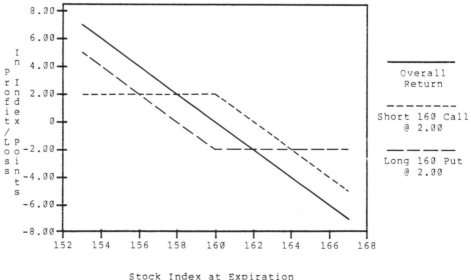

Figure 6.37 Synthetic short commodity

OPTION ARBITRAGE TRANSACTIONS

An "arbitrage" transaction is executed by an "arbitrageur" intent upon capitalizing on a situation in which options are trading at levels apart from their fair market values. If an option is overpriced, an arbitrageur will sell the option; if underpriced, an arbitrageur will buy it. But arbitrage is much more than that—the risk associated with a well-executed arbitrage transaction is practically nil. This near absence of risk is what sets arbitrage transactions apart from other transactions that we have already explored.

How can one buy or sell options and still limit risk to negligible levels? The answer is that is one buys or sells mispriced options in combination with off-setting positions in other option series or in the underlying market. For example, if one buys an underpriced call—an essentially bullish transaction—an arbitrageur offsets the risk that the market will decline by entering into bearish positions that almost completely balance the risks. Since the arbitrageur purchased an *underpriced* option, however, these offsetting positions are tailored to permit the arbitrageur to retain the amount by which the option was mispriced. The idea is to "lock in" the disparity between fair market value and the prevailing market value. Or an arbitrageur may sell an overpriced call—an essentially bearish transaction. In that case, the arbitrageur will offset the risk of an advancing market by entering into offsetting bullish positions. Again, the idea is to "lock in" the disparity between the option's fair market value and its prevailing market price.

Arbitrage transactions tend to "enforce" fair market pricing. If arbitrageurs are constantly following the market in order to buy underpriced and sell over-priced options, this implies that they will bid up underpriced and drive down overpriced options as a result of their activities. And, because arbitrage trans-actions are essentially riskless or at least low in risk, this implies that these transactions will be executed even when the profit potential is quite low. All of this means that arbitrage entails very small returns for each transaction.

In theory, anyone who has access to an option market and the underlying market can engage in arbitrage. In practice, however, arbitrage generally is lim-ited to trading companies whose regular business activities are in the markets underlying the option in question. For example, many of the primary govern-ment security dealers actively arbitrage the Treasury bond option market. Metal bullion dealers and security broker–dealers may be following the metals and stock index option markets for similar arbitrage opportunities. These firms are at an advantage over most private investors because they are regularly in-volved in the markets. This means that their transaction costs may be much lower than the transaction costs to which members of the general public may be subject. Furthermore, these firms may be members of the exchanges on which options are traded—and these firms may trade in very large volumes.

But while arbitrage generally is limited to these professional traders, it is nevertheless recommended that even private investors who may not have the opportunity to "arb" the markets learn about these transactions. As mentioned earlier, arbitrage transactions have the effect of keeping option prices "in line" with their fair market values. And, because professional traders may be subject to lower transaction costs than private investors, this means that professionals will engage in arbitrage even when the profit potential is very low. Remember that one will only enter into any transaction when there is a reasonable likelihood that the reward will provide for a profit *after* considering the costs of entering the transactions, that is, commissions and other possible fees. But since

TABLE 6.2 THEORETICAL OPTION PREMIUMS AND DELTAS[a]

Underlying/		Strike Prices							
		66	68	70	72	74	76	78	80
70.00	Call	4.01	2.16	0.61	0.18	0.04	0.00	0.00	0.00
	delta	.95	.80	.50	.21	.05	.01	.00	.00
	Put	0.03	0.17	0.61	2.17	4.02	6.00	8.00	10.00
	delta	.04	.19	.49	.78	.94	1.00	1.00	1.00
70.16	Call	4.32	2.42	1.14	0.26	0.06	0.01	0.00	0.00
	delta	1.00	.85	.58	.27	.08	.02	.00	.00
	Put	0.02	0.11	0.47	1.57	3.36	5.32	7.32	9.32
	delta	.03	.14	.41	.72	.91	1.00	1.00	1.00
71.00	Call	5.00	3.06	1.34	0.36	0.09	0.01	0.00	0.00
	delta	1.00	.89	.66	.35	.12	.02	.00	.00
	Put	0.01	0.08	0.35	1.35	3.07	5.00	7.00	9.00
	delta	.02	.10	.33	.65	.88	1.00	1.00	1.00
71.16	Call	5.32	3.35	1.57	0.48	0.13	0.02	0.00	0.00
	delta	1.00	.92	.73	.42	.16	.04	.01	.00
	Put	0.01	0.05	0.25	1.16	2.44	4.32	6.32	8.32
	delta	.01	.07	.26	.57	.83	.95	1.00	1.00
72.00	Call	6.00	4.01	2.17	0.63	0.19	0.04	0.01	0.00
	delta	1.00	.95	.79	.50	.22	.06	.01	.00
	Put	0.00	0.03	0.18	0.63	2.18	4.02	6.00	8.00
	delta	.01	.05	.20	.49	.78	.93	1.00	1.00
72.16	Call	6.32	4.32	2.43	1.16	0.27	0.06	0.01	0.00
	delta	1.00	1.00	.84	.58	.28	.09	.02	.00
	Put	0.00	0.02	0.12	0.48	1.59	3.37	5.32	7.32
	delta	.00	.03	.15	.41	.71	.91	1.00	1.00
73.00	Call	7.00	5.00	3.07	1.36	0.37	0.10	0.02	0.00
	delta	1.00	1.00	.89	.66	.35	.12	.03	.00
	Put	0.00	0.01	0.08	0.36	1.37	3.08	5.00	7.00
	delta	.00	.02	.11	.34	.64	.87	1.00	1.00
73.16	Call	7.32	5.32	3.36	1.58	0.50	0.14	0.03	0.00
	delta	1.00	1.00	.92	.73	.43	.17	.04	.01
	Put	0.00	0.01	0.06	0.27	1.17	2.45	4.33	6.32
	delta	.00	.01	.08	.27	.57	.82	.95	1.00
74.00	Call	8.00	6.00	4.02	2.18	1.00	0.21	0.05	0.01
	delta	1.00	1.00	.94	.79	.50	.22	.06	.01
	Put	0.00	0.00	0.04	0.19	1.00	2.20	4.03	6.00
	delta	.00	.01	.05	.21	.49	.77	.93	1.00

[a] Term is 30 days; volatility is 12%; and the short-term rate is 9%.

these professional traders will arbitrage the market for very small profits, they are actually doing a service for others interested in the market—by insuring that competitive pricing prevails.

Three types of arbitrage transactions are examined here: conversions, reverse conversions, and boxes. All of these transactions involve multiple options and, in the case of conversions and reverse conversions (reversals), underlying market positions. All entail minimal risk. And, perhaps most importantly, all are predicated upon one's ability to identify mispriced options.

In order to identify a mispriced option, one may make use of one of the pricing models considered in our discussion of option pricing. That is always the first step in an arbitrage. For the purposes of illustrating these arbitrage strategies, Table 6.2 lists theoretical options on T-bond futures premiums for a range of strike and underlying T-bond futures prices. We reference the prices displayed in Table 6.2 for purposes of constructing arbitrage examples. The second step in arbitrage is execution of the strategy.

Conversions

A conversion entails the sale of a call, purchase of a put, and the purchase of the underlying instrument. Both put and call share a common strike price and expiration date. The motivation behind this series of three transactions is to take advantage of mispriced option relative to the underlying market price.

The important thing to observe is that, no matter which way the market fluctuates subsequent to the initial series of transactions, the conversion will unwind or liquidate itself. If, for example, the underlying market rallies over the strike price that is shared by both put and call, the call falls in-the-money and the put falls out-of-the-money. At expiration, the call will be exercised against the call writer; thus the call writer takes a short position in the underlying market. This exercise has the effect of offsetting the long position in the underlying market. The put expires worthless and unexercised. If the market declines below the common strike price, the long put is exercised. This results in a short position in the underlying market. Of course, this short underlying position offsets the original long position in the underlying market. The call expires worthless and unexercised.

EXAMPLE. June T-bond futures are trading at 72% of par. A 30-day 72 call may be sold for 1-02/64ths or 3/64ths over its fair market value illustrated in Table 6.2. A 30-day 72 put may be bought for its fair value of 63/64ths:

	Debit	Credit
Short 1 June 72 call @1-02/64ths		$1,031
Long 1 June 72 put @63/64ths	($984)	
Long 1 June futures @72-00/32nds		
NET CREDIT		$47

As we can see, this position may be placed at a net credit of $47 or 3/64ths, the amount by which the call was overpriced. Now, no matter which way futures prices move, the arbitrageur has locked in the net credit of $47 by the time the options expire in 30 days:

June futures @70,
30 days later . . .

Abandon   1 Short June 72 call @0-00
Exercise   1 Long June 72 put @2-00   = $2,000
Offset through exercise 1 Long June futures @72-00 = ($2,000)
                                    Net Credit = $47
                              TOTAL RETURN = $47

June futures @72,
30 days later . . .

Abandon 1 Short June 72 call @0-00
Abandon 1 Long June 72 put   @0-00
Sell   1   June futures @70-00 =   0
                   Net Credit = $47

          TOTAL RETURN = $47

June futures @74,
30 days later . . .

Exercised   1 Short June 72 call @2-00   = ($2,000)
Abandon   1 Long June 72 put   @0-00
Offset through exercise 1 Long June futures @74-00 = $2,000
                                  Net Credit = $47

               TOTAL RETURN = $47

In the foregoing example, the arbitrageur locked in a profit equal to the net credit. But this represents a special case in that the two options were struck at-the-money. What would happen if the long put were to be purchased in-the-money, that is, if the underlying futures market price were less than the strike price? In that case, of course, the arbitrageur would be subject to a net debit because he would buy the put at a higher price than he could sell the call. Does this mean that the arbitrageur locks in a loss? If it did, then would that imply that arbitrageurs who entered a conversion when futures were trading over the common strike price would lock in a profit because the call would be in-the-money and would command a higher price than the long put?

Both of these conclusions are wrong. A conversion opportunity may present itself when the put falls in- or out-of-the-money, or where a conversion can be placed at a net credit or debit. The important variable to monitor is the relation between the in- or out-of-the-money amount of the call to the net debit or net credit at which the conversion may be placed.

The amount that an arbitrageur may realize through a conversion can be calculated by comparing the difference between the short call premium and the long put premium with the difference between the underlying market price and the strike price:

$$\text{Conversion Return} = (\text{Call Premium} - \text{Put Premium}) - (\text{Underlying Price} - \text{Strike Price})$$

In the case of the at-the-money conversion executed above, the calculation is quite simple: the conversion profit of $47 may be figured as the call premium ($1,031) less the put premium ($984), or $47 less the difference in underlying and strike prices of zero. The bottom line equals $47. But what if we were to look at a more complicated example?

EXAMPLE.   June bond futures are trading at 71-00. A 30-day June 72 call is sold for 36-64ths ($563) while a 30-day June 72 put is purchased at 1-31/64ths ($1,484), or 4/64ths under its fair value. A net debit of $922 ($563 less $1,484) is realized:

	Debit	Credit
Short 1 June 72 call @36/64ths		$563
Long 1 June 72 put @1-31/64ths	($1,484)	
Long 1 June futures @71-00/32nds		
NET DEBIT	$922	

A profit of $78 is implied in this series of transactions. This profit may be calculated as:

Call premium	$563	
Put premium	($1,484)	($922)
		Minus
Underlying price	71-00	
Strike price	(72-00)	($1,000)
Conversion return		$78

If we follow this conversion until expiration 30 days later, we see that no matter which way prices fluctuate, the arbitrageur locks in the $78:

June futures @68-00
30 days later . . .

Abandon   1 Short June 72 call @0-00
Exercise   1 Long June 72 put   @4-00 = $4,000
Offset through exercise 1 Long June futures @68-00 = ($3,000)
                                             Net Debit = ($922)

                                    TOTAL RETURN = $78

June futures @72-00,
30 days later . . .

Abandon 1 Short June 72 call @0-00
Abandon 1 Long June 72 put   @0-00
Sell   1 June futures   @72-00 = $1,000
                              Net Debit =   ($922)

                         TOTAL RETURN = $78

June futures @76-00
30 days later . . .

Exercise   1 Short June 72 call @4-00   = ($4,000)
Abandon   1 Long June 72 put   @0-00
Offset through exercise 1 Long June futures @76-00 = $5,000
                                             Net Debit =   ($922)

                         TOTAL RETURN = $78

Likewise, if a conversion is placed when the call is in-the-money and the put is out-of-the-money (resulting in a net credit when working with options on futures), we can calculate the returns associated with the transaction. We can also be confident that that return will be achieved.

EXAMPLE. June T-bond futures are trading at 72-16/32nds. An arbitrageur identifies an overpriced June 72 call with 30 days to expiration. The call is sold for 1-20/64ths ($1,313) or 4/64ths above its fair market value illustrated in Table 6.2. A 30-day June 72 put is purchased at 48/64ths ($750) for a net credit of $563. To complete the conversion, June futures are purchased at 72-16/32nds.

	Debit	Credit
Short 1 June 72 call @1-20/64ths		$1,313
Long 1 June 72 put @48/64ths	($750)	
NET CREDIT		$563

The profit that is locked in as a result of this conversion may be calculated as $63:

Call premium	$1,313	
Put premium	($750)	$563

		Minus
Underlying price	72-16	
Strike price	(72-00)	$500

Conversion return	$63

Now, no matter which way prices move, upwards or downwards, the arbitrageur can be confident that he has locked in a return equal to $63:

June futures @70,
30 days later . . .

Abandon	1 Short June 72 call	@0-00	
Exercise	1 Long June 72 put	@2-00	= $2,000
Offset through exercise	1 Long June futures	@70-00	= ($2,500)
		Net Credit =	$563

TOTAL RETURN = $63

June futures @72,
30 days later . . .

Abandon 1 Short June 72 call	@0-00	
Abandon 1 Long June 72 call	@0-00	
Sell 1 June futures	@72-00 = ($500)	
Net Credit	= $563	

TOTAL RETURN = $63

June futures @74,
30 days later . . .

Exercise	1 Short June 72 call	@2-00	= ($2,000)
Abandon	1 Long June 72 put	@0-00	
Offset through exercise	1 Long June futures	@74-00	= $1,500
		Net Credit =	$563

TOTAL RETURN = $63

An important consideration that hasn't been discussed is the cost, or pay-off, associated with holding a conversion. Obviously, if one takes in cash as a result of a net credit, one could invest that cash at interest during the life of the conversion. And, if one were to enter a conversion at a debit, one would have to finance that position as well. Moreover, if one were to enter into conversions that involved an underlying market apart from a futures contract, such as a security or a physical commodity, there may be other costs or payouts involved. For example, an actual bond will generate semiannual interest payments. The holder of a physical commodity may be subject to storage and finance charges. Although we have not explicitly considered these costs or transaction costs such as commissions, they all must enter into a decision to execute a conversion. It is only when options are mispriced to the extent that conversion profits will overcome all these other possible costs that a conversion should be considered.

Another note: since a conversion entails three legs, it is usually impossible to enter a conversion order per se, but rather, it may be necessary to "leg into" the conversion by having a broker or several brokers execute all three transactions separately. Certainly when the underlying instrument is not traded on the same market in which the options are traded, legging in becomes the only way to execute the conversion. This consideration is another reason why these types of transactions are most frequently executed by market professionals, rather than by private, relatively infrequent traders.

Reverse Conversions

Reverse conversions, or simply "reversals," are very similar to straight conversions except that all the legs are reversed. Instead of selling calls, buying puts, and buying the underlying instrument, a reverse conversion means that one buys calls, sells puts, and sells the underlying instrument. Both put and call share a common strike price and expiration date. The motivation behind this set of transactions is the same as that behind a conversion: to capitalize on mispriced options. Of course, when one buys calls and sells puts, this implies that either the calls are underpriced or the puts are overpriced, or both.

Just like the conversion, the reverse conversion unwinds itself. If the market declines below the common strike price by the time the options expire, then the short put may be exercised against the arbitrageur, resulting in a long position in the underlying market. This long exercise cancels the original short position held in the underlying market. The call falls out-of-the-money and is abandoned. If the market advances over the common strike price, then the call falls in-the-money and may be exercised. This exercise results in a long position in the underlying market, canceling the original short position. The out-of-the-money put expires worthless and unexercised.

EXAMPLE.   June T-bond futures are shorted at 72% of par. A 30-day 72 June call is trading at 60/64ths ($938), or three ticks under its fair market value of 63/64ths. An arbitrageur buys this call and sells a 30-day 72 put for 63/64ths ($984). This series of transactions results in a net credit of $47 ($984 less $938 (these numbers are rounded).

	Debit	Credit
Long 1 June 72 call @60/64ths	($938)	
Short 1 June 72 call @63/64ths		$984
Short 1 June futures @72-00/32nds		
NET CREDIT		$47

Now that the reversal is executed, the arbitrageur has locked in a riskless profit of $47 by the time the two options expire in 30 days:

June futures @68,
30 days later . . .

Abandon	1 Long June 72 call @0-00	
Exercised	1 Short June 72 put @4-00 = ($4,000)
Offset through exercise	1 Short June futures @68-00 = $4,000
	Net Credit = $47
	TOTAL RETURN = $47

June futures @72,
30 days later . . .

Abandon 1 Long June 72 call   @0-00
Abandon 1 Short June 72 put @0-00
Buy   1 June futures   @72-00 =   0
                 Net Credit   = $47

                 TOTAL RETURN = $47

June futures @76,
30 days later . . .

Exercise	1 Long June 72 call @4-00 = $4,000
Abandon	1 Short June 72 put @0-00
Offset through exercise	1 Long June futures @76-00 = ($4,000)
	Net Credit = $47
	TOTAL RETURN = $47

It was easy to calculate exactly how much this arbitrageur had locked in, for the profit was equal to the original net credit of $47. But it doesn't always work out so neatly. A reverse conversion may be profitable whether it was intially put on at a net debit or a net credit. It is also relatively easy to calculate the return that may be realized as a result of a reversal. This return may be calculated by comparing the difference between the put and call premiums with the difference between the strike price and the underlying market price:

$$\text{Reversal Return} = (\text{Put Premium} - \text{Call Premium}) - (\text{Strike Price} - \text{Underlying Price})$$

In the prior example, it was quite simple to calculate the reversal return. The put premium less the call premium of $47 ($984 − $938) may be compared to the difference between the strike and original underlying price of zero. But what if one were to place the reversal when the market was trading apart from the common strike price?

EXAMPLE. A single June T-bond futures contract is sold at 70-16/32nds. A 30-day 72 call is purchased for 23/64ths ($359) or 3/64ths less than its fair market value illustrated in Table 6.2. At the same time, a 30-day 72 put is sold for its fair value of 1-57/64ths ($1,891). This results in a net credit of $1,531:

	Debit	Credit
Long 1 June 72 call @23/64ths	($359)	
Short 1 June 72 put @1-57/64ths		$1,891
Short 1 June futures @70-16/32nds		
NET CREDIT		$1,531

Unfortunately for the arbitrageur, he will not retain the net credit of $1,531. He will, however, lock in a profit equal to the net credit less the difference between the strike price and exercise price of $1,500 or $31:

Put premium	$1,891	
Call premium	($359)	$1,531

Minus

Strike price	72-00	
Underlying price	(70-16)	$1,500

REVERSAL RETURN $31

Now, no matter if T-bond futures rally, decline, or remain stable, the arbitrageur locks in a profit equal to $31 by the time the two options expire in 30 days. In addition, since this transaction is placed at a net credit, the arbitrageur has the advantage of being able to apply that credit over the next 30 days to alternate use.

June futures @70,
30 days later . . .

Abandon	1 Long June 72 call	@0-00	
Exercised	1 Short June 72 put	@2-00	= ($2,000)
Offset through exercise	1 June futures	@70-00 =	$500
		Net Credit =	$1,531

TOTAL RETURN = $31

June futures @72,
30 days later . . .

Abandon 1 Long June 72 call   @0-00
Abandon 1 Short June 72 call   @0-00
Buy   1 June futures   @72-00 = ($1,500)
              Net Credit   = ($1,531)
         TOTAL RETURN = $31

June futures @74,
30 days later . . .

Exercise	1 Long June 72 call	@2-00	= $2,000
Abandon	1 Short June 72 put	@0-00	
Offset through exercise	1 Long June futures	@74-00 =	($3,500)
		Net Credit =	$1,531

TOTAL RETURN = $31

EXAMPLE. June T-bond futures are sold at the prevailing price of 72-16/32nds. At the same time a 30-day June 72 call is purchased for 1-16/64ths ($1,250) while a 30-day June 72 put is sold for 52/64ths ($813) or 4/64ths over its fair value. A net debit of $438 is associated with this reverse conversion.

	Debit	Credit
Long 1 June 72 call @1-16/64ths	($1,250)	
Short 1 June 72 put @52/64ths		$813
Short 1 June futures @72-16/32nds		
NET DEBIT	$438	

The return associated with this transaction may be calculated as the difference between the put and call premiums of −$438 less the difference between the strike and underlying price of −$500, or $62:

Put premium	$813	
Call premium	($1,250)	($438)

Minus

Strike price	72-00	
Underlying price	(72-16)	($500)

REVERSAL RETURN $62

Again, the market may move upwards or downwards and the arbitrageur will nevertheless realize a net return equal to $62. Note, however, that the arbitrageur will realize a net debit of $438, which must be financed over the next 30 days until the options expire.

June futures @70,
30 days later . . .

Abandon	1 Long June 72 call	@0-00
Exercised	1 Short June 72 put	@2-00 = ($2,000)
Offset through exercise	1 Short June futures	@70-00 = $2,500
	Net Debit =	($438)

TOTAL RETURN = $62

June futures @72,
30 days later . . .

Abandon 1 Long June 72 call   @0-00
Abandon 1 Short June 72 put   @0-00
Buy   1 June futures   @74-00 = ($500)
                         Net Debit = ($438)

TOTAL RETURN = $62

June futures @74,
30 days later . . .

Exercise	1 Long June 72 call	@2-00 = $2,000
Abandon	1 Short June 72 put	@0-00
Offset through exercise	1 Short June futures	@74-00 = ($1,500)
	Net Debit =	($438)

TOTAL RETURN = $62

Boxes

A box represents another variation on our arbitrage theme. Just like a conversion or a reversal, the arbitrageur should be on the lookout for mispriced options. The arbitrageur will buy underpriced or sell overpriced options. And, to lock in a return implied by the difference between the market price and the fair value of the option, an arbitrageur will enter into a series of offsetting transactions.

In particular, a box entails a series of vertical spreads. A vertical bull call spread may be combined with a vertical bear put spread to form a debit box spread. Or a vertical bear call spread may be combined with a vertical bull put spread to form a credit box spread. All four legs of a box share a common expiration and are spread across two strike prices. It may appear on the surface that a four-leg box may be more difficult to execute than a three-leg conversion or reversal. But sometimes it is easier to execute the box. Note that when one enters a conversion or a reversal, a transaction must be executed in the underlying market. Unless that underlying market is trading on the same purchase on which the options are trading, it may be quite a feat to execute the series of transactions quickly. Conversely, all four legs of the box can be in the same option market. The box is simply the combination of two vertical spreads. When an active market is quoted in vertical spreads, this means that there are effectively only two legs of a box. Thus it can often be easier to execute the box than a conversion or reversal.

A box is self-liquidating at expiration. Consider a debit box—or the combination of a vertical bull call spread and a vertical bear put spread. Let's dissect this series of transactions:

Bull Call Spread	Bear Put Spread
Long low-struck call	Short low-struck put
Short high-struck call	Long high-struck put

Assume that the market falls under the low strike price at expiration. At this point, both calls fall out-of-the-money and expire unexercised. Both puts are in-the-money and are exercised. The short position in the underlying market resulting from the exercise of the long high-struck put is offset by the long underlying market position resulting from the exercise of the short low-struck put. Assume that the market falls in between the two strike prices. At that point, the long low-struck call and the long high-struck put are in-the-money and are exercised. The long position resulting from the exercise of the call is offset by the short position resulting from the exercise of the call. Of course, the out-of-the-money options are abandoned. Finally, if the market should advance over the high strike price, both calls will be in-the-money. The long underlying market position resulting from the exercise of the long call will offset the short underlying market position resulting from the exercise of the short call. Both puts will expire worthless.

Both bull call and bear put spreads represent debit spreads; therefore, this box will also be placed at a debit. The idea is to place the box at a debit that is less than the difference between the two strike prices. The difference between the two strikes and the net debit equal the retuurn that may be realized from the purchase of the debit box spread:

$$\text{Debit Box Return} = \text{Difference in Strikes} - \text{Net Debit}$$

EXAMPLE.   June T-bond futures are trading at 72-16/32nds. Puts and calls are available with 30 days until expiration. In particular, a June 72 call may be purchased for 1-09/64ths ($1,141), or 7/64ths less than its fair value. In order to exploit this situation, our arbitrageur buys the 72 call as part of a 72/74 vertical bull call spread and enters an offsetting 72/74 vertical bear put spread:

	Debit	Credit
Long 1 June 72 call @1-09/64ths	($1,141)	
Short 1 June 74 call @27/64ths		$422
Short 1 June 72 put @48/64ths		$750
Long 1 June 74 put @1-59/64ths	($1,922)	
NET DEBIT	$1,891	

The box spreader has locked in a return equal to the difference in strikes of $2,000 (74 less 72) less the net debit of $1,891, or $109. No matter if the market moves up or down, the spreader has locked in a profit of $109:

June futures @70,
30 days later . . .

Abandon 1 Long June 72 call   @0-00
Abandon 1 Short June 74 call   @0-00
Exercised1 Short June 72 put @2-00   = ($2,000)
Exercise 1 Long June 74 put   @2-00   = $4,000
                        Net Debit = ($1,891)

                  TOTAL RETURN = $109

June futures @73,
30 days later . . .

Exercise 1 Long June 72 call   @1-00   = $1,000
Abandon 1 Short June 74 call   @0-00
Abandon 1 Short June 72 put   @0-00
Exercise 1 Long June 74 put   @1-00   = $1,000
                        Net Debit   = ($1,891)

                  TOTAL RETURN = $109

June futures @76,
30 days later . . .

Exercise 1 LongJune 72 call   @4-00 = $4,000
Exercised1 Short June 74 call @2-00 = ($2,000)
Abandon 1 Short June 72 put @0-00
Abandon 1 Long June 74 put   @0-00

Net Debit = ($1,891)

TOTAL RETURN = $109

A credit box spread is just the opposite of a debit box spread. A credit box entails a vertical bear call spread (the sale of a low-struck call and the purchase of a high-struck call) and a vertical bull put spread (the sale of a high-struck put and the purchase of a low-struck put):

Bear Call Spread	Bull Put Spread
Short low-struck call	Long low-struck put
Long high-struck call	Short high-struck put

Just like the debit box, the credit box is self-liquidating. If prices decline below the low strike price, then both puts are in-the-money. The exercise of the long low-struck put offsets the exercise of the short high-struck put. The long put results in a short underlying market position while the short put results in a long underlying market position. The two calls fall out-of-the-money and expire worthless. If the market should fall between the two strikes by expiration, then the short call and the short put fall in-the-money. The short underlying market position resulting from the short low-struck call will offset the long underlying market position resulting from the short high-struck put. The long call and put will be abandoned. If, however, the market should rise above the high strike price, both of the calls will be in-the-money while the two puts will be abandoned. The long underlying market position resulting from the exercise of the long call offsets the short underlying market position resulting from the exercise of the short call.

Because this box spread is comprised of a credit bull put and a credit bear call spread, the box results in a net credit. The returns that are associated with the credit box spread may be calculated as the net credit less the difference in strike prices:

Credit Box Return = Net Credit − Difference in Strikes

EXAMPLE.   June T-bond futures are trading at 73-16/32nds. Puts and calls are available with 30 days until expiration. In particular, a 72 call is trading at 2-00/64ths ($2,000) or 6/64ths over its fair value of 1-58/64ths. In an effort to exploit this situation, an arbitrageur enters a credit box spread by buying the 72 call, selling the 74 call, buying the 72 put, and selling the 74 put:

	Debit	Credit
Short 1 June 72 call @2-00/64ths		$2,000
Long 1 June 74 call @50/64ths	($781)	
Long 1 June 72 put @27/64ths	($422)	
Short 1 June 74 put @1-17/64ths		($1,266)
NET CREDIT		$2,063

Since the net credit of $2,063 is $63 over the difference in strike prices of $2,000 (74 less 72), we may be assured that, no matter whether T-bond futures move upwards or downwards, the arbitrageur has locked a profit of $63 ($2,063 less $2,000):

June futures @70,
30 days later . . .

Abandon 1 Short June 72 call @0-00
Abandon 1 Long June 74 call @0-00
Exercise 1 Long June 72 put   @2-00 = $2,000
Exercised 1 Short June 74 put @4-00 = ($4,000)
                        Net Credit = $2,063

            TOTAL RETURN = $63

June futures @73,
30 days later . . .

Exercised 1 Short June 72 call @1-00 = ($1,000)
Abandon 1 Long June 74 call @0-00
Abandon 1 Long June 74 put @0-00
Exercised 1 Short June 74 put @1-00 = ($1,000)
                        Net Credit = $2,063
            TOTAL RETURN = $63

June futures @76,
30 days later . . .

Exercised 1 Short June 72 call @4-00 = ($4,000)
Exercise 1 Long June 74 call @2-00 = $2,000
Abandon 1 Long June 72 put @0-00
Abandon 1 Short June 74 put @0-00
                        Net Credit = $2,063

            TOTAL RETURN = $63

Which type of box is most profitable: the debit box or the credit box? Many of the same arguments that may be offered in support of vertical debit and vertical credit spreads are likewise applicable in this case. When one enters the credit box spread, one has use of the credit over the life of the box. By contrast, one is forced to finance the debit associated with the debit box spread. This can be particularly important if the debit associated with the debit box is large. After all, the debit box is comprised of two vertical debit spreads.

A point in favor of the debit spread, however, is that one avoids the uncertainty associated with the potential for an early exercise of one of the spread legs. When one enters the credit spread, one takes on the risk that the short call or short put may be exercised prematurely, that is, before expiration. If that happens and the arbitrageur is unable to exercise the corresponding long option, then the box could be prematurely disrupted. This danger is most serious when the underlying market price falls between the two strike prices, making the short legs in-the-money and the long legs out-of-the-money.

7

Risk Management with Options

Every business or investment enterprise, whether that enterprise is a corporation, a financial institution, a partnership, or even an individual venture, entails some risk. Some risks may be uninsurable, for example, the risk that a business will unwisely decide to introduce an unattractive new product, that unqualified personnel will be retained, or that the competition will prove more resourceful and dominate the field. Many of these so-called management risks are ingrained in the very nature of the business or investment. In many cases it is the challenge and opportunity associated with overcoming those risks that attracts business people. Other risks—the risk of fire, vandalism, theft, or the death of key employees or officers—may be insured in an actuarial sense through an insurance company. These risks are insured through an insurance company because the enterprise decides that it is ill equipped to cope with those risks and that an insurance company can do so more efficiently. In other words, a basic decision is made to pin the prospects of the enterprise in a field apart from those risks.

For some, risk spells trouble, whereas for others, risk implies opportunity. For a manufacturer of electric motors, for example, the risk of fire in the plant means trouble. For an insurance company, however, the risk of fire indicates opportunity. In Chapter 5, we examined the risk associated with the fluctuating market price of "commodities" as diverse as precious metals, interest rates, and stock market trends as well as a number of techniques designed to capitalize on those risks. For many enterprises, these risks are an opportunity. But for many other enterprises, the same risks can mean trouble.

This chapter examines these risks from the perspective of a business or investment enterprise whose activities may entail commodity price risk but which chooses not to accept those risks. Of course, most enterprises can accept a limited degree of these sorts of risks. It may only be when commodity prices appear to be fluctuating adversely or with undue volatility that an enterprise may wish to explore some of the techniques developed in this chapter. The decision to "hedge"—that is, to offset, reduce, or manage—all or part of these risks under some conditions and not under other conditions is another business decision entirely.

This chapter is concerned with some of the techniques that may be employed to manage commodity price risk through the use of options. Note that we refer to "risk-management" techniques rather than "risk-immunization" techniques. We do so for a purpose: although options may effectively be used to offset commodity price risk under many different scenarios, it is never clear that one can *negate* the risks associated with commodity price movement in the sense that one can completely eliminate the possibility of loss. As we discuss later, exchange-traded options are standardized, rather than tailor-made, instruments. As such, these contracts may hold more or less relevance for different enterprises. Therefore, an option may permit one to hedge a great deal of the risk associated with fluctuating commodity prices but may not be used to completely offset that risk. As we shall also see, it may be more appropriate to think of options and futures as tools that may be used to *change* the nature of, rather than negate, the risks to which one may be subject.

Furthermore, we shall see that other techniques may be used to manage price risk. For example, one may be able to avoid such risk through a "natural hedge"; that is, by managing the enterprise's mix of assets and liabilities. Another valid risk-management technique is the use of futures contracts. Today's commodity option markets represent an extension of the futures markets (many commodity option contracts call for the "delivery" of a futures contract upon exercise). We shall spend some time examining the use of futures as a viable alternative to problems that may have prompted exploration of the application of option markets. But before we can examine these risk-management techniques, we must decide how to identify the associated risks and whether or not these risks are amenable to management through the use of options.

IDENTIFYING HEDGEABLE RISKS

The first task that an enterprise faces when considering the risk-management potential of an option market is to assess the nature and magnitude of its commodity price risks. In some cases, an enterprise may determine that it is vulnerable in the event of a price advance. In other cases, an enterprise may be vulnerable in the event of a price decline. Just how vulnerable the enterprise may be to upward or downward price movement is another topic that may be addressed. It may very well be that the enterprise's risk exposure is quite small or even negligible. Under those circumstances, it may be deemed appropriate to accept these small risks. But if these risks become unacceptably large, then the enterprise should answer a second question.

The second question a risk manager must address when considering the use of options is whether or not the enterprise's risk is reflected in the option markets. Only if the question can be answered positively should options be considered. In fact, there may be other risk-management techniques that could be used. This includes the use of futures or of balancing one's risk exposure to avoid risk in the first place. These techniques may more closely conform to the enterprise's risk-management objectives.

If an option market reflects these undesirable cash market risks and buying in this market is deemed the most appropriate risk-management vehicle, a third question must be addressed. It is very easy to decide whether one's cash market risks are reflected in some sense in an option market. But it is quite something else to decide to what extent those risks are reflected. An option market is tied most directly to the instrument that is delivered on exercise of the option. It may be that the option calls for the delivery on exercise of precisely the cash instrument of which the risks are troubling a financial manager. Or it may be that the instrument underlying a particular option contract only indirectly reflects the cash market instrument to be hedged. This latter scenario is more often encountered than the former.

When an option only indirectly reflects the risks associated with a particular cash market risk, one must assess the relation between cash and option. This process may be subjective or mathematical. The product of this assessment is the "hedge ratio" or the number of units of the instrument *underlying* the option. The hedge ratio reflects the risks associated with a given number of units of the cash instrument. (This hedge ratio is different from the hedge ratio or delta that relates movements in the underlying commodity to the option itself.) If the underlying instrument is twice as volatile as the cash instrument, this implies that one should enter two option units for each unit of the cash instrument to be hedged. If the underlying instrument is only half as volatile, this implies that one should enter one-half option units for each unit of the cash instrument to be hedged.

To summarize, the recommended procedure is as follows:

1. Identify the nature and magnitude of the risks to which the enterprise is subject. If these risks are deemed significant, that is, unacceptable financial distress may result if conditions fluctuate adversely, then go on to step (2).

2. Are the cash market risks to which the enterprise may be subject reflected in the option markets? Is there a reasonably high correlation between the cash market instrument(s) to be hedged and the instrument underlying an available option contract? If so, go on to step (3).

3. Define the relation between the cash market instrument(s) to be hedged with the instrument underlying the option market. This relation may be defined mathematically, resulting in a so-called hedge ratio that summarizes the expected price movement in the hedged instrument relative to a given price fluctuation in the instrument underlying the option.

These are only some of the matters that should be considered before an option hedging program is embarked upon. Other steps, such as defining one's risk-management objectives and deciding whether options are the most appropriate instrument to achieve the specified purpose, are discussed later.

Nature of Risk Exposure

There are many types of risks to which an enterprise may be subject. Business risk, "acts of God" risk, liquidity risk, default or asset quality risk, and commodity price risk are all risks to which an enterprise may be exposed. These risks may be defined as follows:

Management Risk.   This is the risk that management will be unable to make or implement the appropriate management decisions to keep up with constantly changing economic risks an enterprise may face. Keeping current with dynamic marketplace conditions and maintaining the foresight and ability to act swiftly to respond to these changing conditions is often one of the most difficult tasks with which a financial manager is charged. Facing and overcoming these obstacles is ultimately what an enterprise is all about.

Acts of God Risk.   Fire, theft, vandalism, death of the enterprise's principals, strikes, civil disorders, and inclement weather are all risks over which an enterprise often has little control. This is not to say that there are not ways to diminish the probability that one will face these unfortunate events. Certainly, there are secuurity measures that may be implemented to diminish the risk of theft or vandalism and fire prevention programs that may be implemented to reduce the risk of fire. And, beyond that, insurance policies may be obtained that provide for compensation in the event any of these unfortunate events should occur. Ultimately, however, there can never be a final guarantee that these events will not occur.

Liquidity Risk.   Wise investment in long-term producing assets does not always insure the viability of an enterprise. Management must always be careful to maintain a sufficient supply of cash or other "near cash" assets that can readily be converted into cash to meet maturing obligations and current accounts payable. The risk that insufficient liquid assets will be available for these purposes has often proven quite difficult to manage.

Asset Quality.   Liquidity risk is the risk that one's short-term cash requirements cannot be matched with incoming cash and that one's assets cannot quickly be liquidated for their fair market value. Liquidity risk is a short-term risk, wherein asset quality risk may be thought of as an ongoing or long-term risk. For example, an enterprise may invest in corporate bonds. The risk that the corporation will go bankrupt or otherwise default on its obligations represents asset quality risk. Asset quality risk may also be thought of in terms of capital plant or equipment. For example, a manufacturing firm may invest in new machinery that, for one reason or another, fails to perform as required or becomes obsolete before its time. (In this respect, asset quality is difficult to distinguish from business risk.) In the final analysis, asset quality risk represents the risk of making poor investment decisions.

Commodity Price Risk.   This is the risk that the market for a particular commodity—whether that "commodity" is defined as a traditional commodity such as grain or metals or a nontraditional commodity such as debt instruments or stock market portfolios—will fluctuate in price adversely.

All of the risks described above share something in common: they can all prove quite dangerous and have all been the downfall of various enterprises at one time or another. Unfortunately, however, options may be used to address only the final type of risk described: commodity price risk.

Asset/Liability Gap

Options are not a panacea in that they cannot be used to manage *any* type of risk to which an enterprise may be subject. Options can, however, prove quite effective in managing commodity price risk. But how does one go about assessing the magnitude of this risk?

The first step is to take an inventory of one's assets and liabilities. In particular, one should pay careful attention to the assets and liabilities of which the value may be sensitive to changing commodity prices. For example, if one were a precious metals dealer concerned about volatility in the gold or silver markets, the first thing one would do is to find out just how much inventory of those metals are at hand. If a bullion dealer accumulates a large store of gold, for example, he may face the possibility of large losses in the event of a price decline.

Commodity inventories are only one type of asset that may be sensitive to commodity price changes. For example, a gold bullion dealer may have ordered large quantities of metal yet to arrive, for which he is bound to pay a previously negotiated contract price. If prices decline, the dealer will find himself carrying additional inventory above the current market price. The dealer's price-sensitive assets may thus be defined as the sum of inventories on hand plus commitments to buy. The sum of these assets may be regarded as the dealer's long cash market position. If prices should advance, the dealer will profit insofar as these assets will appreciate in value. But if prices should decline, these assets will depreciate in value.

On the other side of the coin, we must consider the dealer's liabilities. Just as the dealer may have committed to *buy* metal at a fixed price, he may have committed to *sell* metal at a fixed price. These commitments to sell represent the dealer's short cash market position. If prices decline, the dealer stands to profit. But if prices advance, the dealer stands to lose as a result of these liabilities.

$$\underset{\text{Long Cash}}{\underbrace{\begin{matrix}\text{Inventories}\\+\\\text{Commitments}\\\text{to Buy}\end{matrix}}}\quad\underset{\text{Short Cash}}{\underbrace{\begin{matrix}\text{Commitments}\\\text{to Sell}\end{matrix}}}$$

Inventories
+
Commitments
to Buy
——————
Long Cash
Exposure

Commitments
to Sell
——————
Short Cash
Exposure

Many types of enterprises may have only one of these two types of risk exposures. For example, a gold miner may be quite uncertain as to the ultimate output of a mine shaft. As a result, he cannot contract in advance to deliver particular quantities of metal. Instead, he sells the metal as it is produced. From the time the metal is recovered from the earth until the time he actually sells the metal in the open market, the miner holds an exposed long cash position—exposed to the risk that gold prices will decline. An electronics manufacturer who uses gold in the fabrication of semiconductors may have just the opposite problem. He may anticipate the eventual purchase of gold for fabrication purposes. Although he may also anticipate sales in advance, the price that the electronic components will command may have little to do with the price of gold since gold comprises only a fraction of the cost of the raw materials, labor, and machinery that go into producing the product. As a result, the electronics manufacturer holds an exposed short market position—exposed to the risk that prices will rise.

The problem that our metals dealer faces is a bit more complicated. If the dealer holds metal in inventory or is committed to buy, he is exposed to the risk that prices will decline. This exposure may be managed through an offsetting bearish option position. Similarly, if a metals dealer is liable to deliver metals, that is, has firm commitments to sell at a fixed price, he is exposed to the risk that prices will advance. This exposure may be managed through an offsetting bullish option position. But to get a true measure of the dealer's risk exposure, we must compare the assets with the liabilities to arrive at a net risk exposure. If inventories plus commitments to buy exceed commitments to sell, the dealer retains a *net long exposure*. If these inventories plus commitments to buy fall short of commitments to sell, then the dealer has a *net short exposure*.

EXAMPLE.   A metals dealer holds 5,000 ounces of gold in inventory, is committed to buy another 2,000 ounces at a fixed price, and has accepted orders to sell 3,000 ounces of gold at a fixed price. This gold dealer has a net long exposure of 4,000 ounces of gold (5,000 plus 2,000 less 3,000).

EXAMPLE.   Several months later, our gold dealer has drawn down his inventories to 1,000 ounces and has committed to buy another 1,000 ounces of gold. He has accepted orders to deliver 3,000 ounces of gold at a fixed price. He holds a net short commitment of 1,000 ounces (1,000 plus 1,000 less 3,000).

Not every net long or net short risk exposure may be regarded as significant or worth the trouble of developing and implementing hedge strategies. It may be that only when these net risk exposures run over a certain absolute dollar amount that an enterprise may feel that sufficient risk is entailed in that exposure to warrant the development of a hedging program. Another common method used to determine the significance of these exposures is to calculate the ratio of these net risk exposures as a percentage of earning or producing assets:

Net Risk Exposure/Earning Assets

If that ratio falls above a particular "significance" level as defined by the enterprise, for example, 5% or 10%, then a hedging program will be pursued.

EXAMPLE.   Our metals dealer above has a net long exposure of 4,000 ounces of gold valued at $400 per ounce, or $1.6 million. He holds $10 million in earning assets. His net long risk exposure equals 16% of earning assets—a significant risk.

EXAMPLE.   Our metals dealer has a net short exposure in the gold market of 1,000 ounces valued at $400 per ounce, or $400 thousand. He holds $20 million in earning assets. His net short exposure in gold is only 2% of earning assets—a risk posture that may or may not be regarded as significant. If the dealer had only $5 million in earning assets, his net 8% short exposure would be regarded as much more significant.

Perhaps the best way to manage the cash market risks associated with the dealer's business is to ascertain that long cash exposures always balance with short cash exposures within risk-tolerance levels as defined by management. By executing this so-called natural hedge, there would be no reason for concern about the direction of metals prices *and* there would be no reason to seek protection in options. Unfortunately, it is not always possible to conduct a business in that fashion. Although it may be possible to control inventories and commitments to buy and sell to a certain extent, occasions may arise when the balance between assets and liabilities falls out of tolerance despite the best efforts. For example, the nature of the business may be such that large stocks of inventory on hand become a competitive necessity. Without such stocks ready to deliver upon demand, the metals dealer may be losing sales to the competition.

Asset/Liability Management for Financial Institutions

The situation of many financial institutions is exemplary in that the nature of the business may dictate constant risk exposure. For the most part, financial institutions such as commercial banks and savings and loan or "thrift" institutions face a peculiar kind of interest rate risk due to the nature of their businesses. In particular, these institutions generally borrow from depositors on a short-term basis and loan money to their clients on a relatively long-term basis. The bottom line for a financial institution of this type may be expressed as the "net interest margin" (NIM), or the institution's interest income less its interest expense all divided by earning assets:

NIM = (Interest Income − Interest Expense)/Earning Assets

Presumably, an institution may borrow at a low short-term rate and lend money at a relatively higher long-term rate. Unfortunately, it doesn't always work out quite so neatly as many financial institutions discovered in the early 1980s when the margin between long- and short-term rates was squeezed. For some months, in fact, the yield curve became "inverted" as short-term rates advanced over long-term rates.

The following table represents a typical pattern for many financial institutions. This particular institution—a commercial bank—has $500 million in total assets and $450 million in earning or producing assets. These figures are expressed in millions of dollars. "RSA" represents interest-rate-sensitive assets (including federal funds, investments, commercial, real estate, and installment loans); "RSL" represents interest-rate-sensitive liabilities such as money market certificates, certificates of deposit, and repurchase agreements (repros); and "EA" represents earning or producing assets:

	<6 Months	>6 Months	Total
RSA	$200	$300	$500
RSL and equity	$300	$200	$500
GAP	($100)	$100	-0-
% of EA	22%	22%	-0-

This institution's short-term liabilities, defined as liabilities with less than six months to maturity, exceed its short-term assets by $100 million. Likewise, its long-term assets with maturities greater than six months exceed its long-term liabilities and equity by $100 million. As such, the institution is exposing 22% of its earning assets to interest-rate risk. Assume that short-term rates rise 1% while long-term rates remain stable. This means that the institution is giving up 0.22% of its earning asset base, or $1 million, on a net annualized basis. (Although the institution may earn $2 million more per year on its short-term rate-sensitive assets, it incurs an additional expense of $3 million to service its short-term rate-sensitive liabilities.) Let's assume that the financial manager decides that an asset/liability "gap" of 22% of earning assets is much too high. Therefore, he sets about identifying the gap more precisely as a first step towards reducing its size.

Table 7.1 breaks down the bank's mix of assets and liabilities more precisely. It accounts for the rate-sensitive assets and liabilities by matching their maturities on a monthly basis within the first six months from the date the accounting is drawn and during periods of 5 to 6 years and 10 years and out, thereafter. This type of accounting or "bucket gap analysis" often proves help-

TABLE 7.1 ASSET/LIABILITY WORKSHEET (in millions of dollars)[a]

	1	June	July	Aug.	Sept.	Oct.	Nov.	<6 Months	5–6 Years	10 Years+
RSA										
Federal funds										
Investments										
Commercial loans										
Real estate loans										
Installment loans										
Other										
TOTAL RSA	20	20	42	38	34	27	19	200	40	120
Average % Yield	15.8	12.7	13.1	14.2	15.5	16.1	15.5	14.6	10.4	9.5
RSL										
6-month MMC										
3-month CD										
CDs $100M										
30-month CD										
Repos										
Other										
TOTAL RSL	15	44	45	44	48	60	44	300	4	60
Average % Yield	13.4	11.4	11.9	13.7	13.0	13.9	13.6	13.0	7.0	6.5
$ GAP	5	(24)	(3)	(6)	(14)	(33)	(25)	(100)	36	60
Yield GAP	2.4	1.3	1.2	0.5	2.5	2.2	1.9	1.6	3.4	3.0
GAP/EA	1.1	5.3	0.7	1.3	3.1	7.3	5.5	22.2	8.0	13.3

[a] Figures for *specific* rate-sensitive assets and liabilities are not provided; rather, these categories are aggregated for the purposes of illustrating the identification of maturity gaps.

ful because it allows a financial manager to determine the nature and magnitude of the institution's risk exposures. As we can see, the largest gaps are in June, October, November, in the 5 to 6 year term and the 10 years plus term.

As we can see, Table 7.1 does not break down these rate-sensitive assets and liabilities within particular categories. Although it is necessary to know, for example, the amount of federal funds and six-month money market certificates on the books, we have purposely avoided an explicit accounting. The reason is simple: we are only interested in finding *significant* risks and, at some point, it does not pay to draw up an exact account.

(We should be quick to point out that a bucket gap analysis is *not* the only means of identifying interest-rate exposures. More sophisticated techniques such as "duration analysis" have won an increasingly large following of late. Duration analysis recognizes that a security may generate cash flows currently or at periodic intervals, rather than just at maturation. As such, many financial analysts feel that duration analysis provides a more realistic identification of interest-rate exposure relative to simple bucket gap analysis.)

Ultimately, of course, a policy decision is necessary: how big a "gap" is tolerable? Let's assume that these "period exposures" in June, October, and November in the 5 to 6 year term and 10 years plus term are considered unacceptably large. Let's aggregate the risk exposures during the periods June through September and October through November in order to focus our attention on intolerably sized gaps. From June through September, the bank has a gap of $42 million. This figure includes the $5 million excess of assets over liabilities in the immediate (overnight) maturity range. The bank is likewise exposed to a $58 million gap during the October through November period. These gaps or excesses of liabilities over assets of $42 million and $58 million, respectively, may largely be traced to money market certificates issued and outstanding. The $36 million gap or excess of assets over liabilities in the 5 to 6 year maturity range may largely be attributed to Treasury note and municipal bond holdings. The $60 million excess of assets over liabilities in the 10 years plus range may largely be attributed to mortgage holdings including Government National Mortgage Association (GNMA) certificates (or federally insured FHA and VA mortgages that are "pooled" or bundled for resale in the secondary markets to mortgage investors).

As a result of this analysis, the bank's financial managers have acquired a clear understanding of just where their risk lies. These primary risk centers may be summarized, in millions of dollars as:

	June–Sept.	Oct.–Nov.	5–6 Years	10 Years+
RSA	$154	$46	$40	$120
RSL	196	104	4	60
GAP	($42)	($58)	36	60
Cash instrument	MMCs	MMCs	T-notes Munis	Mortgages GNMAs
Nature of risk	Rate increase	Rate increase	Rate increase	Rate increase

All of these gaps expose the bank to the risk of a rate increase (and corresponding decline in the value of debt instrument holdings or increase in the cost of funding those assets represented by short-term deposits) in the respective maturity ranges.

To the extent that the bank can "plug" these gaps by matching assets and liabilities, that is, executing a natural hedge, the bank will have no need for options or other risk-management vehicles. Often, however, it proves impossible to conduct business in that manner. This is where options *and* futures contracts come in.

CROSS-HEDGING AND THE HEDGE RATIO

As discussed below, options and futures can be used to shorten or to extend the effective maturity of a particular cash market instrument that is the cause of a troublesome risk exposure. In our example above, the cash instruments that exposed the bank to unacceptably large interest rate risks were money market certificates, intermediate-term debt instruments such as T-notes and municipal obligations, and longer-term debt such as mortgage obligations. In order to plug the asset/liability gaps to which the institution is subject, the financial manager may consider lengthening the maturity of the money market certificates synthetically through the use of options or futures; or, conversely, to synthetically shorten the maturity of the longer-term cash instruments. By taking either route and matching up maturities, the financial manager may effectively manage the risk of adverse interest rate movement.

But which route to take? The answer to this question is often found by taking a rather pragmatic, although perhaps a bit mundane, approach. There are many different option and futures markets available to the risk averse financial manager—and the nature and diversity of these markets is constantly growing in scope and depth. Unfortunately, it is not always possible to find option or futures contracts that address the *particular* risks to which the enterprise may be subject. In many cases, there are no markets at all that address the risks to which an enterprise may be subject. In many other cases, markets may be available that call for the delivery upon exercise or maturity of a commodity, the price movements of which closely, but not precisely, resemble those of the cash market instrument to be hedged.

Even when one finds an option or futures market that calls for the delivery of the same kind of cash instrument that is to be hedged, the risk manager may be disappointed. Commodity option and futures contracts often call for the delivery of any of a variety of closely related commodities that vary somewhat in quality or quantity from a standard or "par" grade. Of course, price adjustments may be made to reconcile the quality and quantity of the grade actually delivered to the "par" grade. For example, a bank may hold a portfolio of Treasury bonds and may be fearful that long-term interest rates will rise and as a result the value of the portfolio will decline. There *is* a T-bond option market available. But this option market calls for the delivery upon exercise of a T-bond *futures* contract, not a cash T-bond. In addition, if one examines the contract specifications of the underlying T-bond futures contract, one finds that the contract calls for the delivery of any of a number of actual T-bonds ranging widely in coupon and term to maturity. Unfortunately, the bank may not be holding bonds that are eligible for delivery or bonds that differ from the "par" grade (more will be said about this point below). Or a securities dealer may be considering the use of an option on stock index futures. But the dealer's stock portfolio may differ in composition from the stock issues that are referenced in the underlying stock index. Under these circumstances, there may be concern that these option and futures markets may not "track" the cash market risks to which the enterprise may be subject with sufficient precision to accomplish the financial manager's risk-management objectives.

Rather than express disappointment and give up the hedging program, however, the financial manager should seek means to quantify the relation between the cash instrument to be hedged and option or futures markets that call for the delivery of a commodity that resembles the cash instrument in question. The idea is to find a way to define this relation accurately. Then the financial manager may compare the relative efficiency of using one market or another in terms of the reliability and consistency with which undesirable cash market risks are reflected in the option or futures market.

In the case of the bank described in our prior section, there may be T-bill options that accurately and reliably track the risks associated with money market certificates. Or the manager may find mortgage-based options or futures that more reliably reflect his GNMA and mortgage holdings; or he may find that T-bond options or futures may be used effectively to hedge his T-note and municipal bond holdings.

All of these strategies—using bill options to hedge money market certificates or T-bond options to hedge T-notes—are referred to as "cross hedges." A cross hedge is a strategy wherein the risk associated with a particular cash market instrument is hedged with an option or futures contract that is based on an instrument similar to, but still different from, the cash instrument to be hedged. The distinction between a so-called cross hedge and a "pure hedge," in which the commodity underlying a particular option or futures contract is the same commodity that is the subject of the hedge, is often gray for reasons alluded to above. Rather than bandy about these distinctions, suffice it to say that most hedging situations require one to quantify the relation between the commodity that underlies the option or futures market in question with the cash instrument to be hedged. The fact that this relation may not always be summarized with a one-to-one ratio represents an interesting, but hardly insurmountable, obstacle.

The relation between the commodity underlying an option or a futures contract and a risky cash instrument may be subsumed in the "hedge ratio." This hedge ratio is quite similar to the hedge ratio discussed in prior chapters that is used to balance option premium movements with underlying commodity price movements. But this hedge ratio is somewhat different. We may define this hedge ratio as follows:

> *The expected movement in the instrument underlying an option or futures contract relative to a given movement in the cash instrument to be hedged.*

These movements may be expressed in percentage terms or in absolute unit sizes—dollar units or otherwise. The idea is to quantify the relation between the underlying instrument and the hedged instrument in order to determine how many option or futures contracts should be used to offset as precisely as possible a given quantity of the risky cash instrument. (Commodity options often call for the delivery of a futures contract upon exercise. In that case, the "instrument underlying" the option may be defined as the instrument underlying the *futures contract* itself.)

EXAMPLE. The commodity underlying a particular option contract is expected to fluctuate by 5% coincidentally with a 4% movement in a related cash instrument. One may be advised to hedge five cash commodity units with four option units. To summarize, an expected 5:4 option : cash ratio suggests that one hedge five units of cash with four units of option.

EXAMPLE. A 2% movement is expected in the instrument underlying a futures contract for every 3% movement in a cash commodity, for a 2:3 futures : cash ratio. This suggests that one hedge every two units held in the cash commodity with three units in the futures contract.

Calculating the Hedge Ratio

Unfortunately, there is no single method that may be recommended for the purpose of quantifying the appropriate hedge ratio. We can, however, recommend that one start by studying the contract specifications of the option or futures contract and compare those specifications with the cash instrument one desires to hedge. Sometimes the answer to the problem is even embodied in the contract terms and conditions.

The key question is: how does the instrument underlying the option compare to the cash instrument to be hedged? Often this relation is subsumed in the "basis." The basis is the difference between the price of the cash instrument to be hedged and the instrument underlying the option contract. (Actually, it doesn't make much difference whether the basis is calculated as the price of the cash instrument less the price of the instrument underlying the option or vice versa.) However, we shall express the basis as cash price (C) less the price of the underlying instrument (U) *adjusted* by the number of option or futures contracts (n) used in the hedge:

(7.1) $$\text{Basis} = C - nU$$

EXAMPLE.   The cash price at which a 100-ounce ingot of gold bullion may be bought or sold equals $384.50 per ounce. The price of the 100-ounce gold futures contract for which a gold option may be exercised equals $394. A gold dealer is considering hedging the price of 100 ounces of his inventory with this option with a single put option. The basis equals −$9.50 per ounce, or −$950.00 for 100 ounces.

The gold bullion dealer in the prior example used a 1:1 option to cash hedge ratio. But a one-to-one ratio need not always be employed. Nor is such a ratio always warranted.

EXAMPLE.   A pension fund manager holds $10 million face value of 14% Treasury bonds valued at 120% of par. A $100,000 face value 8% "nominal" coupon T-bond futures contract that is the subject of an option is trading at 73-16/32nds. Superficially, it may appear necessary to hedge with 100 of these $100,000 face value options or $10 million face value in options in the aggregate. But the appropriate hedge ratio may be much greater. A general rule of thumb is that the higher the coupon associated with a fixed-income instrument, the more volatile it will be in response to a given change in prevailing interest rates or yields. Thus a 14% bond will be more volatile than an 8% bond. In this case, a hedger may decide that the 14s are about 162% as volatile as the 8% T-bond futures contract. Applying a hedge ratio of about 1.62, the hedger may use 162 $100,000 face value option contracts. What would the basis be if our pension fund manager decides to use 162 options? In this case, the basis would be 0.93% of par (about 30/32nds), or $93,000 in the aggregate:

$$\text{Basis} = 120\% - 1.62(73.5\%)$$
$$= 0.93\% \text{ or about } 30/32\text{nds}$$
$$OR$$
$$\text{Basis} = \$12 \text{ million} - 162(\$73,500)$$
$$= \$93,000$$

It doesn't matter whether this basis is positive, negative, or zero on average. Under either of these circumstances, a hedge can be quite effective. Superficially, this appears to be an incorrect statement. It is not! What matters when considering the reliability with which the underlying instrument will track the cash instrument is the *variability* of this basis, not its absolute level! The less variable or the less stable the basis is, the more reliable and more predictable the results associated with the hedge will be. So whether the basis that the gold dealer is looking at is negative $9.50 or positive $9.50, a hedge can be very predictable and, hence, may be very effective in achieving the hedger's objectives *if* that positive or negative basis remains *constant*.

The question then becomes: how many option or futures contracts (n) does it take to minimize the variability or volatility of the basis? In many cases, the straightforward approach of implementing a one-for-one cash : option hedge may lead to very good results. Although this "naive" approach is perfectly valid when hedging a cash instrument that is very similar to instrument underlying an option, that approach may prove disastrous in other situations. In order to find the risk-minimizing ratio for whatever commodity we may be interested in, we will explore several techniques that have been used in the context of different markets to find the ratio. These techniques include:

1. "Beta analysis" using statistical regression techniques

2. "Conversion factor" ratios, particularly appropriate for use when hedging long-term debt instruments

3. The "basis point value" method, often appropriate for both short- and long-term debt instruments

Beta Analysis

Beta analysis is a technique that is often used in the stock market to quantify the relation between activity of any individual stock with stock market activity in general. A general market indicator, that is, a stock index such as the Standard & Poor's 500 or the New York Stock Exchange Composite, is often used as a proxy for general stock market movement. This technique may also be used to identify an appropriate hedge ratio, not only to hedge stock with options based directly or indirectly on a stock index (e.g., an option on stock index *futures*), but also to identify an appropriate ratio to hedge other types of "commodities."

The essense of beta analysis is to identify the extent to which price movement of a particular stock issue tracks or parallels price movement in the market in general. Of course, this technique may readily be used to find hedge ratios by identifying the extent to which price movement of a cash instrument to be hedged tracks or parallels price movement in the commodity or instrument underlying an option. This is based on the proposition that all stocks (or all debt instruments, or all grades of a particular commodity for that matter) are affected by a common set of "market factors." For example, all stock issues are affected by a number of broad macroeconomic factors such as inflation, federal fiscal and monetary policy, and the business cycle. These general market factors are referred to as "systematic" influences or "systematic risks."

At the same time, there are a number of economic factors that may impact, more or less, *uniquely* upon a particular stock, a particular type of debt instrument, or a particular grade of a commodity. For example, an individual stock will be affected by the expertise and efficiency of its management, other competitive firms that enter into the same line of business, the availability of raw materials at particular locations where its facilities are located, local strikes, and so forth. These factors may have some minor effect upon other firms and, by implication, the stock market in general. But they may be paramount to an individual firm. These factors are often referred to as firm-specific, "unsystematic" factors or risks.

This analysis suggests that the total risk associated with a particular stock, debt instrument, or commodity is composed of two elements: systematic or general market risk and unsystematic or instrument-specific risk:

$$
\text{Total Risk} = \begin{array}{c} \text{Systematic or} \\ \text{General Market} \\ \text{Risk} \end{array} + \begin{array}{c} \text{Unsystematic or} \\ \text{Instrument-Specific} \\ \text{Risk} \end{array}
$$

Beta analysis can be used to quantify how the cash instrument to be hedged and the instrument underlying the option (or futures contract) share these common systematic risks. Of course, it is somewhat misleading to make a sharp distinction between systematic and unsystematic factors. For example, some factors may affect two instruments but may affect these two instruments in different degrees or in different ways. To illustrate, two U.S. steel manufacturers may both be affected by foreign competition. But perhaps one of the two steel firms is well equipped to be competitive with foreign competition with modern plant and equipment while the other firm is utilizing antiquated facilities and may be much less competitive. Firms in other industries, the textile industry, for example, may be unaffected by the influx of cheap foreign steel. Meanwhile, however, the manufacturer of heavy appliances may enjoy use of this inexpensive steel from overseas.

Beta analysis is often used by stock analysts in order to construct portfolios of stock that yield relatively high returns with minimal risks, or that entail relatively low risk while maximizing returns. They do this by combining stocks into portfolios in such a way as to minimize unsystematic firm-specific risks. By eliminating unsystematic risks, they are left solely with systematic market risks.

Diversification is the key to eliminating unsystematic risks. For example, suppose that an analyst could identify two stocks, both of which could be expected to return 10% over time. But suppose that if the returns on one stock were to decline to 5%, the returns on the other stock could be expected to advance to 15% and vice versa? Under those circumstances, the analyst could recommend a portfolio comprised of both stocks in an equal ratio. In that way, the investor could effectively "lock in" a return of 10% in each period *without* variation, that is, without risk of any kind.

This, of course, is an extreme example, but it does illustrate the benefits of diversification. In that case, both stocks shared all of the same risks. As a result, the investor was able to diversify away systematic and unsystematic risk altogether. Most investors are not so lucky. By investing in a broad sampling of stocks, in many different industries, an investor can eliminate the unsystematic risks that impact uniquely upon a particular firm or industry. This is possible when the unsystematic risks associated with a particular firm or industry are only coincidentally correlated with the unsystematic risks associated with other firms or industries. Presumably, as the portfolio is expanded to include more diverse firms, these unsystematic risks tend to cancel each other out. At some point, as the portfolio is diversified, all of these unsystematic factors are eliminated and the investor's portfolio is affected solely by these undiversifiable systematic market factors.

But this still leaves the investor with systematic risk. Our two stock portfolios also illustrate another point. Note that these two stocks displayed a perfect *negative* correlation with each other. That is, as one stock appreciated, the other declined and vice versa. It is not often possible to find two such perfectly negatively correlated instruments.

But it is possible, in the option and futures markets, to go long *or* short with equal ease. Because of this flexibility, an option or futures contract that shares a good deal of systematic risk with an instrument to be hedged can be used to simulate a perfectly negatively correlated instrument. Thus an investor who uses futures or options to hedge can eliminate *systematic* risk, which is shared by the hedged instrument and the instrument underlying the option or futures contract. The residual unsystematic risk that is left is often referred to as "basis risk." This basis risk may be attributable to risks that impact uniquely upon the cash instrument to be hedged (to the exclusion of the instrument underlying the option or futures) plus certain factors that are unique to an instrument that is slated for *future* delivery (as we shall discuss later in this chapter).

We have discussed the risks that may be measured by beta analysis, but we still have not described how beta analysis may be performed. Beta analysis requires the user to run a statistical regression that relates the prices of the cash (C) and underlying (U) instruments. Specifically, one may regress the cash price on the underlying price:

(7.2) $$C = a + b(U) + e$$

Where *"a"* or alpha equals the regression constant or intercept term, *"b"* equals the beta factor or the slope of the regression line, and *"e"* is the error term. Table 7.2 shows the reader how to perform a regression in order to calclate alpha, beta, and another most important statistic, R^2 or R-squared.

R-squared is particularly important because it summarizes the reliability with which the cash price tracks or parallels the underlying price. It provides a summary measure of the degree to which one can predict the results of a particular hedge. R-squared will vary from zero to 1.0. A result of zero indicates that the two instruments can be expected to exhibit parallel price movements only coincidentally. In other words, they do not track each other at all. This suggests that a hedge using an option or futures contract based on this underlying instrument U to manage the risks associated with the cash instrument C is futile. On the other extreme, if R-squared approaches 1.0, this suggests that the two instruments are very strongly correlated and that a hedge is likely to be predictable and highly effective.

Of course, most R-squared measures fall somewhere between the two extremes of zero and 1.0. For example, if R-squared should equal .75, this suggests that the two instruments tracked each other with about 75% reliability over the

TABLE 7.2   PERFORMING A STATISTICAL REGRESSION

The mathematics behind a statistical regression, although tedious when using a large data sample, are actually rather elementary. Let's set up the form of the regression as:

$$C = a + b(U) + e$$

Beta (b) may be calculated as:

$$b = [\sum UC - n\bar{U}\bar{C}]/[\sum U^2 - n\bar{U}^2]$$

where n equals the number of observations in the data series C and U; $\bar{U}$ and $\bar{C}$ equal the mean average underlying and cash instrument prices or ($\sum U/n$) and ($\sum C/n$), respectively. Alpha (a) is calculated as:

$$a = \bar{C} - b\bar{U}$$

Finally, R-squared (R^2) is calculated as:

$$R^2 = [a\sum C + b\sum CU - n\bar{C}^2]/[\sum C^2 - n\bar{C}^2]$$

period studied. Under those circumstances and lacking a more reliable hedge vehicle, many risk managers may prefer to go ahead and implement the option or futures hedge. If R-squared should be approximately .25, this suggests that the two instruments track each other's movements with only about 25% reliability. Under those circumstances, many risk managers will shy away from using the option or futures contract that overlies the instrument in question as a hedge vehicle. Under those circumstances, the magnitude of basis risk could approach the total risk associated with the cash instrument.

EXAMPLE.   We are interested in finding the relationship between a particular stock with a stock index that is the subject of an option contract. (Whether that option is based directly on the stock index or calls for the delivery of a futures contract based on the same index does not make much difference. In either case, the same techniques for finding the hedge ratio would be recommended.) Let's regress these stock prices on values for the stock index using the formulas provided in Table 7.2 (some of these numbers are rounded):

	Market	Stock	Market^2	Stock^2	(Market) (Stock)
1	158.19	91.25	25,024	8,327	14,435
2	157.06	90.50	24,668	8,190	14,214
3	156.82	90.25	24,593	8,145	14,153
4	159.30	92.00	25,376	8,464	14,656
5	157.51	88.50	24,809	7,832	13,940
6	154.29	86.50	23,805	7,482	13,346
7	154.32	86.75	23,815	7,526	13,387
Totals	1,097.49	625.75	172,090	55,966	98,130

$$\text{Market Average} = 1{,}097.49/7 = 156.78$$
$$\text{Stock Average} \quad = \quad 625.75/7 = \quad 89.39$$

$$
\begin{aligned}
b &= [98{,}130 - 7(156.78)(89.39)]/(172{,}090 - 7(156.78)^2] \\
&= [98{,}130 - 98{,}108]/[172{,}090 - 172{,}069] \\
&= 1.07 \\
a &= 89.39 - 1.07(156.78) \\
&= -77.61 \\
R^2 &= [-77.61(625.75) + 1.07(98{,}130) - 7(89.39)^2]/[55{,}966 - 7(89.39)] \\
&= [-48{,}567 + 104{,}529 - 55{,}937]/[55{,}966 - 55{,}938] \\
&= .85
\end{aligned}
$$

In this example, the regression equation indicates that the relation between the stock and the "market" as represented by a stock index may be modeled as:

$$\text{Stock Price} = -77.61 + 1.07 \text{ (Market Level)}$$

Comparing the graphs of market and stock price movement in Figures 7.1 and 7.2 bear out the regression results. They suggest that the market and individual stock do tend to move upwards and downwards together with a fairly high degree of reliability. The R-squared of .85 indicates that this relation is accurate with 85% reliability over the 7 days observed.

The example above seems to suggest that the hedger utilize 1.07 units of option or futures contract in order to hedge every single unit in the stock. But does it? Note that this example used the absolute levels in the stock price and

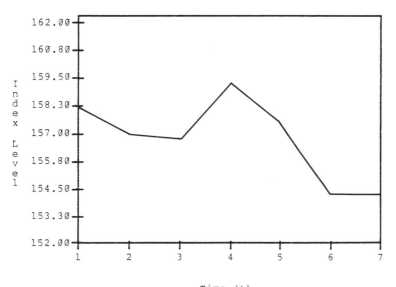

Figure 7.1 Market movements represented by a stock index

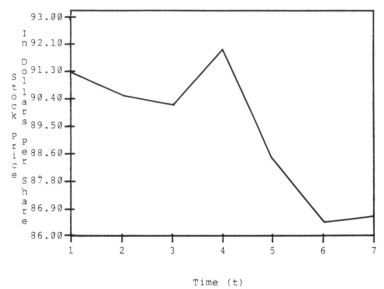

Time (t)

Figure 7.2   Movements of an individual stock

the stock index. But do hedgers attempt to offset the risks associated with the absolute price level of a risky asset or liability? No! Clearly, hedgers must be concerned with offsetting the risks associated with *fluctuating* prices! This suggests that one should use a measure of the *change* in the price of the cash instrument and the underlying instrument. In the prior example, we could have regressed the "first difference" of stock prices against the first difference in index levels. In other words, we could have calculated the price P at time t, or P_t less the price at time $t - 1$, or P_{t-1} $(P_t - P_{t-1})$ for both stock issue and stock index and regressed those price changes one against the other. This is a valid procedure. But most stock analysts prefer to compare the *returns* in individual stock issues against market returns. These returns R at time t, or R_t may be calculated as:

$$R_t = (P_t - P_{t-1})/P_{t-1}$$

Thus, equation 7.2 may be modified to regress stock *returns* (*SR*) on market returns (*MR*):

(7.3) $SR = a + b(MR) + e$

How would our results differ using returns rather than raw price levels?

EXAMPLE.   Let's take the raw prices in our prior example and convert them into returns. (Figure 7.3 provides a comparative illustration of market returns versus stock returns.) Then we shall perform a standard statistical regression. Note that by taking these returns,

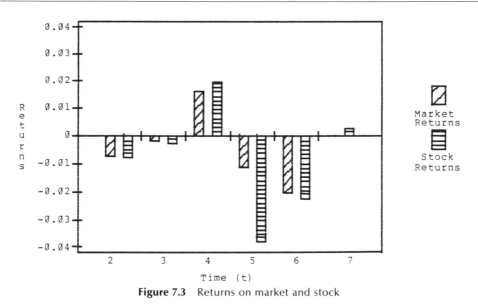

Figure 7.3   Returns on market and stock

we have effectively "lost" one observation, bringing the total down from 7 to 6. Again, note that many of these figures are rounded.

	Market	Stock	Market^2	Stock^2	(Market)(Stock)
2	−.0071	−.0082	.000051	.000068	.000059
3	−.0015	−.0028	000002	000008	000004
4	.0158	.0194	.000250	.000376	.000307
5	−.0112	−.0380	.000126	.001447	.000427
6	−.0204	−.0226	.000418	.000511	.000462
7	.0002	.0029	.000000	.000008	.000001
Totals	−.0243	−.0493	.000848	.002418	.001260

$$\text{Market Average} = -.0243/6 = -.0041$$
$$\text{Stock Average} \;\; = -.0493/6 = -.0082$$
$$b = [.001260 - 6(-.0041)(-.0082)]/[.000848 - 6(-.0041)^2]$$
$$= [.001260 - .000200]/[.000848 - .000099]$$
$$= 1.41$$
$$a = -.0082 - 1.41(-.0041)$$
$$= -.006$$
$$R^2 = [-.006(-.0493) + 1.41(.001260) - 6(-.008224)^2]/[.002418 - 6(-.008224)]$$
$$= [.000123 + .001782 - .0004058]/[.0024175 - .00041]$$
$$= .74$$

In this example, regressing *returns* rather than absolute price levels, our results are a bit different. Here, we see that the beta equaled 1.41, rather than 1.07. This suggests that the stock was about 141% as volatile as the market during the short period studied. Moreover, the R-squared statistic is down from .85 to .74. This is a typical—returns generally display less correlation than raw price levels.

What does this all mean? We can use beta in order to calculate the appropriate hedge ratio. Our first example above suggests that the hedger use 1.07 option or futures units for every single stock unit held. In the case of stock, these "units" simply represent the dollar value of the cash instrument and the option.

EXAMPLE. The option is valued at $100 times the index, that is, $100 times the stock index level. Assume that the hedger holds 10,000 shares—or a hundred "round lots" of 100 shares each of the stock in question. This suggests that the hedger who performs the first of the two regressions shown above may wish to hedge 107% of these shares—10,700 shares or 107 round lots. This translates into 107 option contracts valued at $100 times the index. The hedger who used the latter method would hedge 141% of the shares—14,000 shares or 141 round lots. This translates into 141 option contracts valued at $100 times the index.

Generally, more realistic results will be achieved if the hedger utilizes the beta derived from the regression of stock returns against market returns. In the foregoing example, beta equaled 1.41.

When beta is greater than 1.0, this implies that the stock will fluctuate more dramatically than the market on a percentage basis. This is characteristic of a so-called aggressive investment. (This can be favorable for the investor or unfavorable. When the market is advancing, it is obviously advantageous to hold aggressive investments. But when the market is declining, it is disadvantageous to hold such aggressive investments.) When beta is less than 1.0, this implies that the stock will fluctuate less dramatically than the market on a percentage basis. (Again, this can be favorable or unfavorable.)

What does this imply for our hedger? The "hedge ratio" or the number of option or futures contracts needed to hedge the cash instrument may be calculated as:

$$\text{Number of contracts} = [\text{Beta} \times \text{Cash Value}]/[\text{Contract Value}]$$

EXAMPLE. In order to calculate the hedge ratio using the regression of return on return, we have to adjust for the value of the cash instrument and the option or futures contract, respectively. The option is valued at $100 times the index. Assume that the hedger holds 10,000 shares of the stock in question and will be applying the hedge just subsequent to the last of the seven days from which we took observations. At that point, the stock was valued at $86.75 a share, or $867,500. The stock index was at 154.32, implying an option contract value of $15,432 (= $100 × 154.32). The hedge ratio, or the number of option or futures contracts needed for this hedge, may be calculated as:

Number of
Contracts = [1.41 × $867,500]/[$15,432]
= 79.26 or about 79 Contracts

Regression analysis can be used in even more direct ways to find an appropriate hedge ratio. Rather than performing a regression analysis that relates the returns on the hedged instrument with returns on the underlying instrument, one could regress price *changes* in the hedged market with price *changes* in the underlying market. The resulting beta indicates the expected change in the price of the hedged instrument relative to a given price movement in the underlying market. Since it is our goal to identify hedge ratios that closely match expected *price* movements, rather than percentage returns or yields, this is often regarded as an effective, direct approach to the problem.

EXAMPLE.   An insurance company holds $10 million face value of AT&T 8-3/4% corporate bonds due in the year 2000. The firm wants to hedge these corporates with the use of an option that calls for the delivery of 14% U.S. Treasury bonds maturing in the year 2011. Figure 7.4 illustrates that while these two instruments tend to

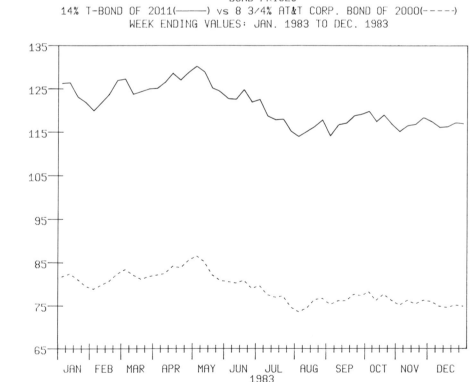

Figure 7.4 Bond prices 14% T-bond of 2011 (----) vs. 8¾% AT&T Corp bond Of 2000 (-----) week ending values: January 1983 to December 1983

move in tandem, the 14% Treasuries far exceed the 8-3/4% corporates in absolute value. In light of these circumstances, it is difficult to reconcile these two price series and determine an
appropriate hedge ratio. Figure 7.5 provides a "scatter graph" of
the weekly price changes of the 14% Treasuries and the 8-3/4%
corporates. As is apparent, a predictable pattern emerges from inspection of this graph. That is, as T-bond prices move upwards or
downwards, the corporates tend to follow with a fairly high degree
of reliability. These patterns may be quantified through the use of
regression analysis, which reveals a beta of .59 and an R-squared of
.78. This suggests that the 8-3/4% corporates are only about 59% as
volatile in absolute price as the 14% Treasuries and that this statement may be made with about 78% reliability. Furthermore, this
suggests that one hedge approximately 59% of the $10 million face
value of the corporate bonds, or $5,900,000. If $100,000 face value
bond option contracts are available, this suggests the use of 59
contracts.

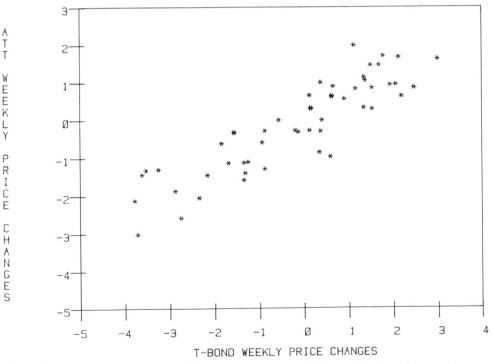

Figure 7.5   14% T-bond of 2011 vs. 8¾% AT&T Corp. Bond of 2000 weekly price changes: January
1983 to December 1983

Regression analysis often proves a very useful tool in defining an appropriate hedge ratio. It is particularly so when one is attempting to define the relation between two instruments that are not readily amenable to mathematical comparisons. For example, how does the price of gold coins compare to the price of gold bullion that may underlie an option or futures contract? How will the price of refined sugar relate to the price of raw sugar that may underlie an option or futures contract? How can the price of an individual stock issue be reconciled to a particular stock index that is the subject of an option or futures contract?

But sometimes the relationship between various cash instruments and the instrument that underlies an option contract is defined in the contract terms. This is true for options that call for the delivery of a "market basket" of closely related commodities. In particular, an option on an interest rate futures contract fits this description.

Conversion Factor Method

The "conversion factor method" is a technique that is uniquely applicable to the interest rate markets. In particular, options on T-bond futures traded on the Chicago Board of Trade (CBOT) call for the delivery on exercise of one $100,000 face value 8% "par" or "nominal" coupon T-bond futures contract. In turn, these T-bond futures call for the delivery of *any* U.S. Treasury bond with at least 15 years to the nearest of the maturity or call date. At any given time, there may be upwards of 20 issues that meet this description. In order to reconcile the value of these bonds, which vary widely with respect to coupon and term to the nominal 8% coupon, a "conversion factor" invoicing system has been developed.

The principal invoice price that is paid by long to short upon tender of T-bonds meeting the description set forth in the contract is calculated as the futures price adjusted by multiplication by a conversion factor. On top of that "principal invoice price" is added the interest accrued since the last semiannual interest payment date of the T-bond actually delivered. Obviously bonds bearing high coupons are worth more than bonds bearing low coupons. As such, the conversion factor system will upwardly adjust principal invoice prices for the delivery of bonds with coupons in excess of the "par" 8% coupon standard. On the other hand, the invoice price for bonds with coupons falling below the standard 8% coupon are downwardly adjusted to reflect the diminished value of such bonds. Conversion factors simply represent the price of the bond actually delivered to yield 8% and may be calculated using a net present valuation method. However, there is no need to attempt to calculate these factors, for these factors are widely available in published sources through the exchange and other financial publishing and quotation services.

EXAMPLE. The conversion factor used to reconcile the par 8% bond for the delivery of the 14% coupon bond that matures in the year 2011 and is callable in 2006 for delivery against the September 1983 contract equals 1.6265. Thus if this contract settles at 72% of par, the principal invoice price may be calculated as:

$$\text{Invoice Price} = \text{Futures Price} \times \$1,000 \times \text{Conversion Factor}$$
$$= 72\text{-}00 \times \$1,000 \times 1.6265$$
$$= \$117,108.00$$

This conversion factor system has some interesting applications. In particular, one can use the conversion factor *directly* as a hedge ratio. In the prior example, the conversion factor for delivery of the 14s of 2006-11 equaled 1.6265. This implies that these 14% bonds are worth roughly 163% of the par 8% coupon bond. Given a parallel yield movement in the cash and futures markets, this implies that these 14% bonds will be roughly 163% as volatile as the T-bond futures contract that underlies an option. Likewise, if the conversion factor for delivery of the 7-5/8% bond equaled 0.9646, this implies that the 7-5/8% bond is worth roughly 96% of the standard 8% coupon bond and, given parallel yield movements, is about 96% as volatile. These results imply that one should hedge 163% of one's 14% T-bonds and 96% of one's 7-5/8% T-bonds. If one held $10 million face value of these cash bonds, that would translate into 163 and 96 $100,000 face value T-bond futures or options on T-bond futures contracts.

Of course, the application of these conversion factors had its limitations. Without going into a full-blown discussion of futures pricing theory, it may be stated that these conversion factors cannot take into account all the peculiarities inherent in the cash bond markets. Conversion factors are simply net present valuation calculations. This introduces certain "biases" in the futures delivery process. Moreover, there are some pecularities in the conversion factor system itself. The bottom line is that, at any one time, a single deliverable cash instrument will stand out as most economic or "cheapest to deliver" against the T-bond futures contract, in light of its cash market price and the principal invoice price it will fetch by delivery against the futures contract. As such, the futures contract and overlying option on T-bond futures contract will most reliably "track" or parallel movements in the cheapest to delivery cash bond. Of course, many hedgers use the conversion factor method regardless when these biases are relatively insignificant.

In other cases, when hedging bonds apart from the cheapest to deliver and particularly when hedging debt instruments that are not deliverable against the T-bond futures underlying the option contract, it may be wholly inappropriate to use these conversion factors. Remember that conversion factors are based on a net present valuation calculation incorporating consideration of term to maturity and bond coupon. Often, however, a financial institution may be interested in hedging a bond that varies from the cheapest to deliver cash bond in terms of coupon and maturity as well as credit risk. Finally, there are other types of debt instruments other than bonds—bills for example—where reference to a conversion factor system is impossible. Under any of these circumstances, other methods may be necessary to identify an appropriate hedge ratio.

Basis Point Value Method

The "basis point value" or "dollar equivalency" method represents an even more sophisticated technique. This method is often used by financial managers to compare the relative volatilities of two debt instruments. The essence of this method is to measure the dollar value fluctuation in the price of a debt instrument in response to a one basis point (0.01%) change in the yield of the debt instrument. By comparing the basis point value of the instrument that is to be hedged with the basis point value of the debt instrument that underlies an option or futures contract, one can identify an appropriate hedge ratio. This technique is quite flexible and powerful—it can be used for both short- and long-term debt instruments. In addition, as we shall see, one can extend the model to adjust for varying degrees of credit risk associated with a particular debt instrument.

Short-term debt instruments may differ considerably from long-term debt instruments on a number of levels. For example, long-term Treasury, corporate, and municipal bonds once issued entitle the holder to the semiannual receipt of interest income. They are normally quoted in percentage of par value in minimum increments of one thirty-second (1/32) of 1% of par. By contrast, short-term debt such as Treasury bills are issued on a discount basis and do not pay a stated rate of interest. Instead, returns are implied by the difference between the original issue price and the face value that is received upon maturity. Often T-bills are quoted in terms of the "discount rate," which, although not strictly comparable to a T-bond yield, may be thought of as the interest rate on the bill.

EXAMPLE. $1 million face value of U.S. Treasury bills maturing in 90 days may be quoted at a discount rate of 10.00%. The actual sale price of these bills equals $975,000.00 while the "bond equivalent yield" equals 10.40%.

EXAMPLE. $1 million face value of U.S. Treasury bills maturing in 180 days may be quoted at a discount rate of 9.00%. The actual sale price of these bills equals $955,000.00 while the "bond equivalent yield" equals 9.55%.

The formula used to calculate the value of the bill given the discount rate and the term until maturity is:

(7.4)
$$\text{Price} = \text{Face Value} - \frac{(\text{Days to Maturity})(\text{Rate})(\text{Face Value})}{360}$$

To illustrate the application of this method, consider the price of the $1 million face value 90-day bills quoted at a rate of 10.00% (0.10):

$$\text{Price} = \$1,000,000 - \frac{90 \times 0.10 \times \$1,000,000}{360}$$
$$= \$1,000,000 - \$25,000$$
$$= \$975,000$$

The "bond equivalent yield" may be calculated using the face amount, the actual dollar price, and the days until maturity using the following equation:

(7.5)
$$\text{Yield} = \frac{(\text{Face Value} - \text{Price})}{\text{Price}} \times \frac{365}{\text{Days to Maturity}}$$

Illustrating the application of equation 7.5:

$$\text{Yield} = \frac{\$1,000,000 - \$975,000}{\$975,000} \times \frac{365}{90}$$
$$= 10.40\%$$

Note that these discount rates always "low ball" the actual yield, or the yield that would be comparable to yields quoted on bonds. The reason why the discount rate underestimates the actual yield is twofold. In particular, the yield implicitly assumes (1) a 360-day, rather than a 365-day, year, and (2) that the face value equals the principal amount invested in the bill, whereas the principal amount or price is really much lower since a bill is sold at a discount.

The basis point value of a bill may be calculated by (1) taking the discount rate at one point and calculating a price, and (2) comparing that price with the price of the bill given a one basis point (0.01%) change in the discount rate.

EXAMPLE.   The price of $1 million face value bills maturing in 90 days given a discount rate of 10.00% equals $975,000. The price of the bills given a 10.01% discount rate equals $974,750. The difference between the two prices equals $25.00 = $975,000 − $974,750.

As a rule, the basis point value of $1 million face value 90-day bills equals $25.00. This applies uniformly no matter how high or low the discount rate varies. By contrast, the basis point value of a 180-day bill equals twice as much, or $50.00.

EXAMPLE.   The price of $1 million face value bills with 180 days to run at a discount rate of 9.00% equals $955,000.00. The price of $1 million face value bills with 180 days to run quoted at 9.01% equals $954,-950. The difference between these two prices, or the basis point value, equals $50 = $955,000 − $954,950.

This relation may readily be extended to 270- or to 360-day bills. The basis point value of $1 million face value 270-day bills equals $75.00 while the basis point value of $1 million face value 360-day bills equals $100.00. As a general rule, one can use a 90-day bill as a reference point—the basis point value of any $1 million face value bill may be calculated by multiplying the ratio of the maturity of the particular bill to 90 days by the $25.00 standard:

$$BPV = \frac{\text{Days to Maturity}}{90\ \text{Days}} \times \$25.00$$

Thus the basis point value of $1 million face value of 45-day bills equals half that of the 90-day bills, or $12.50. Likewise, the value of $1 million face value 135-day bills equals one and one-half times the $25.00 standard, or $37.50. If one were to reference $0.5 million face value 90-day bills, the basis point value could be figured as half the basis point value of $1 million 90-day bills, or $12.50. Similarly, the face value of $0.5 million 360-day bills equals $50.00.

These basis point values may be used to calculate the appropriate hedge ratio. To illustrate, assume that a financial institution holds $10 million face value T-bills with 180 days to maturity. Furthermore, assume that this institution is considering hedging these holdings with an option contract exercisable for $1 million face value 90-day bills. In order to reconcile the hedged securities with the option contract, the institution could use the following formula:

(7.6)
$$\text{Number of Contracts} = \frac{BPV(\text{cash}) \times \text{Cash Face Value}}{BPV(\text{underlying}) \times \text{Contract Face Value}}$$

This means that our institution may consider the use of 10 option contracts:

$$\text{Number of Contracts} = \frac{(\$50)\ (\$5\ \text{million})}{(\$25)\ (\$1\ \text{million})}$$
$$= 10\ \text{Contracts}$$

Because basis point values change over time, this implies that hedgers should be careful to continually monitor the relation between the hedged cash security and the instrument that underlies the option contract. As the maturity of the hedged security winds down, it would be appropriate to liquidate some of the option contracts that make up the hedge. For example, when 18 days have passed and there are only 162 days until bill maturity, the basis point value of $1 million face value bills equals $45. As such, the hedge ratio may be calculated as 9 contracts = ($45)($5 million)/($25)($1 million). This suggests that the hedger liquidate one of the original 10 contracts at this point. After another 18 days pass, the appropriate hedge ratio will drop to 8 contracts, and so on. Thus it is important to think of the hedge ratio as a dynamic, rather than a static, concept.

Thus far, we have discovered how the basis point value method can be applied in the context of short-term debt securities. (In particular, the foregoing discussion centered upon Treasury bills. However, there are other types of short-term debt securities that are not priced like T-bills. Care should be taken to apply the correct analysis under these alternate situations.) Now let's extend the discussion to long- and intermediate-term securities such as Treasury and corporate bonds and notes.

To repeat what was mentioned earlier: bonds and notes, including Treasuries, corporates, agencies, state, and municipals, are often quoted in percentage of par in minimum increments of one thirty-second (1/32) of 1%. These issues entitle the holder to semiannual interest payments.

EXAMPLE.   14% T-bonds maturing on November 15, 2011, and callable in 2006 are quoted on 110-23/32nds to yield 12.53%. The actual sale price of $100,000 face value of this bond equals $110,718.75 plus interest accrued since the last semiannual coupon payment date.

EXAMPLE.   8-3/4% T-bonds maturing on November 15, 2008, and callable in 2003 are quoted at 71-19/32nds to yield 12.44%. The sale price of $100,000 face value of this issue equals $71,593.75 plus interest accrued since the last semiannual coupon payment date.

The formula used to calculate the price of a bond given the term to maturity or call (market analysts usually refer to the yield to call rather than maturity), coupon, and yield:

$$(7.7) \quad P = (1 + Y)^{-A}[C + (C/Y) \times (1 - (1 + Y)^{-N}) + (1 + Y)^{-N}] - [C \times (1 - A)]$$

where P equals the bond price, Y equals semiannual yield, A equals the fraction of the current coupon period until the next interest payment, C equals the semiannual coupon, and N equals the number of semiannual coupon payments remaining until issue maturity.

To illustrate the application of equation 7.7, consider a 14% ($C = 0.07$ semiannual coupon payment) T-bond yielding 10.5% ($Y = 0.0525$ semiannually) with 23 years ($N = 46$ payments over 23 years), 4 months to maturity ($A = 0.667$ of the 6-month coupon period until the next interest payment date).

$$P = 1.0525^{-0.667}[0.07 + (0.07/.0525)(1 - 1.0525^{-46}) + 1.0525^{-46}] - [0.07(1-0.667)]$$
$$= 1.3023278 \text{ or about } 130\text{-}08/32\text{nds}$$

The basis point value (BPV) may be calculated by finding the price of the bond given prevailing yields and comparing that price to the price of the same bond calculated given a one basis point (0.01%) change in the yield.

EXAMPLE.   The price of $100,000 face value 8-3/4% bonds maturing in exactly 20 years given a 10.50% yield may be calculated as $85,485.95. The price of that 8-3/4% bond given a 10.51% yield equals $85,412.79. The difference between these two prices, or the basis point value, equals $73.16 (= $85,485.95 − $85,412.79).

EXAMPLE.   The price of $100,000 face value 14% bonds maturing in 23 years given a 10.5% yield is calculated as $130,166.22. The price of the same bond given a 10.51% yield equals $130,058.28. The difference between these two prices, or the basis point value, equals $107.94 (= $130,166.22 − $130,058.28).

Unfortunately, there are no convenient conventions or reference points that may be used to calculate a basis point value as there was when we considered the basis point value associated with a Treasury bill. The fact is: basis point values for the same bond with the same coupon and term to maturity will vary over a range of yields.

EXAMPLE.   The basis point value of the 8-3/4%, 20-year bonds equaled $73.16 when yields were at 10.50%. But when yields are at 10%, the basis point value equals $78.41; and when yields are at 11%, the basis point value equals $68.35%.

This underscores the idea that hedge ratios are dynamic in character and hedges should be adjusted over time and over changing yield ranges.

To illustrate how these basis point values may be used to calculate a hedge ratio, consider a financial institution that holds $10 million face value of the 8-3/4% bonds yielding 10.5% and which is considering the use of an option contract that calls for the delivery on exercise of $100,000 face value 14% bonds also yielding 10.5%. The appropriate hedge ratio may be calculated using equation 7.6 as follows:

$$\text{Number of Contracts} = \frac{(\$73.16)(\$10\text{ million})}{(\$107.94)(\$100,000)}$$
$$= 67.78 \text{ or } 68 \text{ Contracts}$$

This suggests that the hedger "underweight" the hedge or hedge only 68% of the face value of the cash securities. This underweighted hedge is appropriate insofar as 8-3/4% bonds are not expected to react as dramatically in response to changing yields as the 14% bond issue. But what if we're using an option contract that calls for the delivery, not of an actual 14% bond on exercise, but of a bond futures contract?

The answer is that the calculations are very similar. But this requires an identification of the so-called cheapest to deliver cash bond. Our discussion of conversion factors provided above indicated that, although there may be upwards of 20 different bond issues eligible to be delivered against a bond futures contract, typically a single issue stands out as most economic or cheapest to deliver in light of its current cash market value and the T-bond futures contract's invoicing system. In order to identify a workable hedge ratio, we must take a twofold approach. First, we must reconcile the basis point values of the hedged security with the cheapest to deliver cash bond. Secondly, we must reconcile the value of the cheapest to deliver cash bond with the futures contract price. Fortunately, we already have all the tools to accomplish both tasks.

Equation 7.8 incorporates both of the considerations discussed above:

$$(7.8) \quad \text{Number of Contracts} = \frac{BPV(\text{cash}) \times (\text{Cash Face Value}) \times CF(cd)}{BPV(cd) \times (\text{Contract Face Value})}$$

By comparing the basis point values of the cash instrument to be hedged $BPV(\text{cash})$ with the basis point value of the cheapest to deliver security $BPV(cd)$, we can reconcile cash and cheapest to deliver securities. By adjusting this ratio by the conversion factor of the cheapest to deliver cash security $CF(cd)$, we can reconcile the price of the cheapest to deliver cash security with the price of the futures contract underlying the option.

EXAMPLE.   A financial institution holds $10 million face value of 8-3/4% bonds and is considering the use of an option exercisable for T-bond futures contracts to hedge the risk of rising rates and declining bond prices. The institution identifies the 14% bond as cheapest to deliver. The conversion factor associated with the bonds equals 1.6238. Given a prevailing yield of 10.5%, the appropriate hedge ratio may be determined as:

$$\text{Number of Contracts} = \frac{(\$73.16)(\$10 \ \text{million})(1.6238)}{(\$107.94)(\$100,000)}$$
$$= 110.06 \text{ or } 110 \text{ Contracts}$$

This result suggests that the 8-3/4% cash bonds can be expected to be about 110% as volatile as the 8% futures contract nominal or par coupon. But this result holds with one important caveat. These results assume *parallel yield shifts*. In other words, the basis point value method is based upon the assumption that the yield fluctuations associated with the cash security to be hedged will equal yield fluctuations associated with the security underlying the option.

Risk-Adjusted Basis Point Value Method

In many cases, it may be appropriate to assume parallel yield curve shifts. In other words, to apply the assumption that cash bond yield fluctuations will parallel yield fluctuations in the underlying cash security. When considering the hedge of a Treasury security with an option that is based on other Treasury securities, this assumption may be applied to good effect. Unfortunately, the two methods to calculate hedge ratios considered above—the conversion factor and the basis point value method—only incorporate consideration of the coupon, term to maturity, and yield level of the cash and underlying securities. These methods do *not* incorporate consideration of the *credit risk* associated with particular securities.

For example, one would expect a corporate or municipal bond to behave a bit differently from a Treasury bond insofar as these instruments entail different levels of credit risk. Credit risk refers to the risk that the entity that issued the bond may default, subjecting the bondholder to possible loss of principal and interest. As a rule, Treasuries are regarded as essentially "risk-free." The rationale is that if a default on Treasuries were to occur, destabilizing ripple effects would be felt throughout the economy. These effects would clearly be disastrous in almost every sector of the economy. Therefore, all resources available would be mustered to prevent the default. The bottom line is: if you cannot count on the Treasury, on whom can you count?

So if one takes the risk that the Treasury will default as the base reference point, one concludes that securities issued by other corporate, state, or municipal entities are "risky" in comparison. As a rule, the more credit risk associated with the security, the more the security must yield in order to offset those risks from the perspective of the bondholder. And if the yields associated with these non-Treasury securities are higher, could they also be more volatile? And if they these yields are more volatile, can the hedge ratio be made to incorporate these variations?

The answer to both of these questions is sometimes and yes! In order to determine whether the yields associated with a cash bond to be hedged are more or possibly less volatile than the yields associated with the underlying security, one could readily perform a regression analysis. That is, to regress the changes in yield of the hedged security with the changes in the yield of the security underlying the option contract, or in the case of an option exercisable for a futures contract, the security that is cheapest to deliver against the futures contract. The beta that results from the regression analysis may be used as a "risk adjustment" factor (RAF) to modify the appropriate hedge ratio. Let's apply that adjustment to equation 7.9:

(7.9)
$$\text{No. of Contracts} = \frac{BPV(\text{Cash}) \times (\text{Cash Face Value}) \times CF(cd)}{BPV(cd) \times (\text{Contract Face Value})} \times RAF$$

EXAMPLE. A financial institution holds $5 million face value 10% corporate bonds maturing in 15 years and wants to hedge the bonds using options exercisable for T-bond futures contracts. The cheapest to deliver cash bond is identified as the 14s maturing in 23 years—the conversion factor associated with delivery of these 14s into the underlying bond futures contract equals 1.6238. The basis point values associated with the corporates currently yielding 11% equals $68.62, whereas the basis point value associated with the 14% Treasuries yielding 10.5% equals $107.94. By performing a statistical regression of the changes in these corporate yields against changes in the yields of the 14s, the financial manager determined that the corporate yields are 110% as volatile as the Treasury yields. In other words, the beta from the regression equals 1.10. The hedge ratio is calculated as:

$$\text{Number of Contracts} = \frac{(\$68.62)(\$5 \ \text{million})(1.6238)}{(\$107.94)(\$100,000)} \times 1.10$$
$$= 56.77 \text{ or } 57 \text{ Contracts}$$

Of course, one could avoid a good deal of these tedious calculations by using a hedge ratio based upon a regression of price changes in the hedged security versus price changes in the T-bond futures contract. In many cases, that may be a perfectly valid approach. The real question is: does a stronger linear relation exist between price changes or between yield changes? The answer to this question determines which method one chooses to utilize.

Do the yields associated with bonds apart from Treasuries always display more volatility than Treasury yields? Not necessarily!

EXAMPLE.   Figure 7.6 illustrates the yields associated with the 8-3/4% AT&T corporate bond of the year 2000 with the yields associated with the 14% Treasuries of 2006-11 during 1983. We see that the yields associated with the corporate bonds were generally higher than the yields associated with the Treasuries. Surprisingly, there were some brief periods when the Treasury yields exceeded the corporate yields. This may be attributed to the simple fact that the corporates are on a different rung on the yield curve, that is, they mature in the year 2000 while the Treasuries mature in 2011 and are callable in 2006. By regressing changes in corporate yields

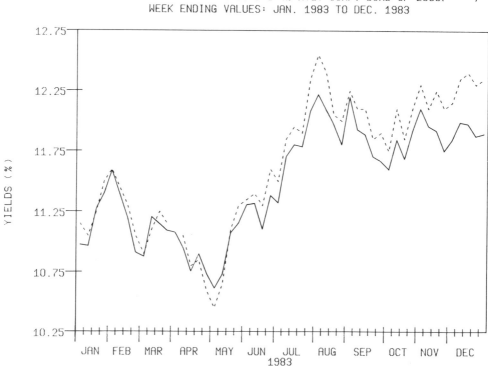

Figure 7.6   Bond yields 14% T-bond (-----) 2011 vs. 8¾% AT&T Corp. Bond of 2000 (-----) week ending values: January 1983 to December 1983

against changes in Treasury yields over this period, a beta of 0.97 is calculated, suggesting that the corporate yields are in fact slightly less volatile than the Treasury yields. Again, bear in mind that these corporate bonds fell into a different maturity range than did the Treasuries.

The foregoing pages reviewed a number of ways of identifying an appropriate hedge ratio. Which method is recommended? The answer can only be that it depends upon the particular situation. No one method dominates. Nor can it be said that any single method can be used to completely eliminate basis risk. Residual basis risk will be present whenever the cash commodity to be hedged varies from the commodity underlying the option or futures contract. The best that can be done is to reduce basis risk to manageable levels. Once a hedge is placed, hedgers are best advised to monitor the basis carefully. By actively managing a hedge, rather than placing the hedge and passively expecting it to perform, a hedger can increase tremendously the probability of achieving the desired results.

HEDGING ASSETS

The availability of options in addition to futures on a particular commodity opens up tremendous new opportunities to tailor the balance between risk and reward associated with asset holdings. This section reviews some of the major strategies that can be used to accomplish these ends. Because futures provide a valid alternative to commodity options and, in fact, represent the "traditional" method to hedge commodity price risk, futures hedging strategies are examined in addition to option hedging strategies.

As a review, consider the risks associated with a price-sensitive asset—a grain farmer who anticipates the harvest of soybeans, a gold dealer holding a sizable inventory of bullion, and a commercial bank invested in long-term Treasuury bonds. All of these situations are analogous because all of these commercial entities are exposed to the risk that the price of these assets or inventories will decline. This is not to say that these commercial entities are faced with an immediate difficulty. The grain farmer anticipates the harvest of soybeans sometime in the future. A great deal can happen between the time the farmer is considering the hedge and the time that he actually brings his produce to market. For example, prices may decline and then rebound. Or the farmer may harvest the grain and store it for subsequent resale. Likewise, the commercial bank may be carrying its investments at book value and may not realize an accounting loss immediately if rates should rise and the value of its holdings decline.

If prices should in fact decline, however, these losses are bound to catch up to all of these commercial entities. And in the interim, they are often faced with many troubling problems. For example, the gold dealer may be collateralizing a loan with bullion inventories. If the value of the bullion should decline, this could adversely affect the loan terms.

Of course, prices are not necessarily bound to decline. In fact, prices may very well rise and all of them will realize profits. But is this what the grain farmer, the gold dealer, and the commercial bank is in business for? Chances are that these entities are not practiced speculators in the cash markets for these commodities. And when an opportunity becomes available to introduce a degree of certainty in an uncertain economic environment, this opportunity should not be ignored.

This section examines four basic hedging strategies using futures and options that may be used to hedge the risk of price decline and the adverse impact that this may have on asset holdings. Remember that the commercial entity that holds exposed, price-sensitive assets essentially is speculating that cash prices will rise. By being so exposed, this implies that the commercial entity holds a basically bullish market outlook. But often, the entity's outlook does not conform to his cash position. When this is the case, the commercial entity needs to assume an offsetting bearish futures or option position.

This section examines four basically bearish futures and option strategies that may be used to offset the risks associated with the bullish cash position: (1) sell futures, (2) buy puts, (3) sell calls, and (4) buy a bearish vertical put spread. All of these strategies have been examined to one degree or another in prior sections. But they have all been examined from the perspective of the risk-taker, that is, an individual or institution that hopes to profit by taking a position in the market. By contrast, this treatment of these strategies are drawn from the perspective of the risk-shifter, that is, the individual or institution that hopes to shift the risk associated with a cash position to risk-takers through the futures or option market mechanism.

Furthermore, all of these strategies accomplish different ends. At the risk of oversimplification, let us summarize the results associated with these strategies in terms of costs and benefits:

	Benefits	Costs
Sell futures	Lock in a specific price	Forfeit opportunity to participate in price advance
Buy puts	Lock in a floor price	Forfeit premium
Sell calls	Augment current income	Lock in a ceiling price
Bear put spread	Lock in a partial floor price	Forfeit debit

The following pages consider each of these four strategies in turn.

Sell Futures

The short futures strategy is the most direct of the four asset hedging strategies considered in this section. The idea is simply that a bullish cash market position is matched with a fundamentally bearish short futures market position. Ideally, cash market losses would be matched with futures market gains; or cash market gains would be matched with futures market profits such that the hedger's assets would be insulated from price risk. Two questions immediately come to mind: (1) why would a hedger want to offset cash market gains, and (2) is it possible to precisely match these gains and losses?

Of course, hedgers are most concerned with their ability to offset cash market losses. In the process of hedging with futures, however, they must as a matter of course forfeit the potential to participate in favorable price movements. Many hedgers attempt to pick and choose the occasions for executing a hedge transaction in order to avoid the possibility of limiting their ability to participate in favorable price movements. Some hedgers are more successful in this type of activity than others. By selectively hedging only when there appears to be a high probability of an adverse cash market movement, hedgers implicitly accept the possibility that their judgment may be wrong. In other words, that the market may in fact move adversely and that their interests will be damaged before they can reverse their judgment and execute a hedge transaction. More conservative hedgers will not attempt to call the market and will hedge whenever their cash market exposure exceeds a certain tolerance with which they are comfortable.

Which approach is recommended? This is a very subjective question that cannot be answered universally. The best that can be offered is that a hedger's past experience in calling possible market movements and their risk tolerance should play into these considerations.

The second question is: can hedgers be assured that their futures transactions will precisely offset their cash market risks? Of course the answer is that there can be no such assurance. Futures market hedgers essentially replace outright cash market risks with basis risk. When the futures contract they select correlates highly with the price movements of the cash market instrument they wish to hedge, then basis risk will be low and the hedge may be quite effective. When the futures contract they select correlates with low precision to the movements of the cash instrument they desire to hedge, the hedge may be quite ineffective. In fact, there may be some cases where basis risk actually exceeds cash market risk.

In instances where the cash instrument to be hedged is deliverable against the futures market in question and particularly when that cash instrument represents the cheapest to deliver item against the futures contract, basis risk is likely to be low. Hedgers can vastly increase their chances of executing a successful hedge by utilizing some of the hedge ratio techniques discussed above. Still, it may not be necessary to use a ratio other than one-for-one when hedging a commodity that is directly deliverable into a futures contract.

EXAMPLE.   A precious metals dealer holds 5,000 ounces of gold bullion and is fearful of a potential price decline. As a result, he sells 50 gold futures contracts covering 100 ounces each, thereby matching up the long cash market risk exposure with an offsetting short futures market exposure. At the time of this transaction, there were three months until the futures contract delivery month, cash gold prices were near $400 per ounce, and the futures contracts were sold at a price of $412 per ounce. Subsequently, the hedger's fears were confirmed as the cash market and futures markets declined to $360. The hedge was unwound as the futures contracts approached expiration. In other words, the short futures were bought back at the prevailing market price. As a result of these transactions, the gold dealer's inventories declined in value by $40 per ounce. At the same time, these losses were more than offset by a profit of $52 in the futures market. The bottom line is a net gain of $12 per ounce.

Cash Market	Futures Market
Holds 5,000 ounces of gold @$400 per ounce	Sells 50 100 ounce gold futures @$412
Holds 5,000 ounces of gold @$360 per ounce	Buys 50 100 ounce gold futures @$360
Loss: $40.00 per ounce	Gain: $52.00 per ounce

Net Gain: $12.00 per ounce

In the foregoing instance, the basis moved to the advantage of the gold dealer. The original basis was −$12 per ounce ($400 cash price less $412 futures price). Subsequently, the basis narrowed to zero as the cash and futures prices converged in the delivery month. Remember that buying or selling futures in the delivery month is tantamount to buying or selling the cheapest deliverable cash commodity as delivery may occur at any time during the delivery month. This basis movement worked to the benefit of the gold dealer.

In order to understand why the basis narrowed in this instance, recall the relationships between a cash commodity and a futures contract outlined in Chapter 5. Equation 5.15 provides a convenient way to reconcile a futures price with the price of a physical commodity underlying the futures contract. This reconciliation is made in light of the short-term interest rate at which the commodity purchase may be financed and any related holding costs including storage, insurance, and so on. In our example, we applied some very simple assumptions: short-term rates equaled 10% per annum and holding costs equaled 2%. In other words, it cost the gold dealer 12% of the cost of the metal to hold inventory for a year. Applying simple interest compounding, that amounts to 3% over 3 months, or $12 when gold is at $400. Thus we assumed that gold futures were trading at a price of $412, or $12 over spot sprices. Subsequently, the basis narrowed as the delivery month approached and these carry considerations became less and less relevant.

Not only did the gold dealer in our example transfer the risk of adverse price movement to others by selling futures, he also essentially offset the costs of carrying the inventory. Of course, in this case the basis behaved very predictably and in accordance with our assumptions about the cost of carry. This is not always the case as cost of carry pricing does not always prevail. Futures will only price in accordance with these carry considerations when there are arbitrageurs who are willing and able to step in and take advantage of situations where futures prices are "out-of-line" with spot prices and in light of prevailing market conditions.

Nor is it always the case that the basis will work to the hedger's advantage in such an obvious manner. Physical commodities are characterized by "negative carry." In other words, there are out-of-pocket expenses associated with the leveraged purchase and carry of a cash commodity in the form of financing and other holding costs. But other commodities are characterized by "positive carry" (at least under some conditions). For example, the leveraged purchase and carry of a long-term Treasury bond generally results in a net inflow of funds. The relationship between a security such as a T-bond and futures prices is quantified in equation 5.16.

A long-term Treasury bond will result in positive carry when long-term interest rates exceed short-term interest rates. If the bond throws off more income than it costs to finance, then a futures contract that may be exercised for the long-term T-bond will tend to price at a discount to the cheapest to deliver cash security. Of course, the long-term U.S. Treasury bond futures contract calls for the delivery of any of a number of different cash securities varying widely in terms of coupon and maturity. Therefore, futures prices must be adjusted by multiplication by the "conversion factor" discussed above. This means that the futures price times the conversion factor for the cheapest to deliver will price at a discount to the cheapest to deliver cash security when long-term rates exceed short-term rates, that is, when the yield curve is upwardly sloping. And each successively deferred bond futures contract will price at a successively deeper discount because the positive carry grows with the holding period.

But sometimes the yield curve is not "normal" in that it is not upwardly sloping such that long-term rates exceed short-term rates. Sometimes short-term rates exceed long-term rates. This describes an "inverted yield curve." Under these conditions, a long-term bond will throw off less income than it costs to finance. As a result, futures prices times the conversion factor will price at a premium to the cheapest to deliver cash security. And each successively deferred futures contract will price at a wider and wider premium as the negative carry grows with the holding period (see Figure 7.7). Although negative carry is unusual in the context of fixed-income security futures, stock index futures typically price at a premium to the spot value of the subject stock index insofar as dividend yields typically fall short of short-term interest rates.

What are the implications for the hedge of a fixed-income security? By shorting futures contracts against a long-term security, the hedger is essentially converting a long-term instrument into a short-term instrument. As a result, the hedger should not expect to lock in a long-term rate as a result of a hedge

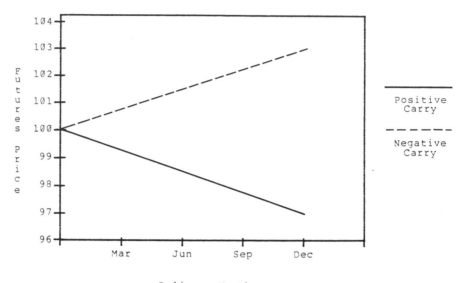

Figure 7.7   Cost of carry futures pricing cheapest to deliver cash security @100

transaction. Instead, the hedger should expect to lock in a short-term rate (subject to some basis risk).

EXAMPLE.   A government securities dealer holds $10 million face value of 14% long-term bonds due in November 2011 and callable in 2006. These bonds are currently priced at 120-00/32nds percent of par to yield on a current basis 11.7%. The bond dealer decides to hedge the 14s by selling 162 March 1983 bond futures. Why sell 162 contracts or the equivalent of $16.2 million face value rather than 100 contracts or the equivalent of $10 million face value? This bond dealer is using the conversion factor method for determining an appropriate hedge ratio. The conversion factor for delivery of these 14s against the March 1983 contract equals 1.6216. There are 80 days until the delivery month and March futures are trading at 73-16. What would happen if the cash bonds declined to 115% of par?

Cash Market	Futures Market
Holds $10 million face value 14s @120	Sells 162 bond futures @73-16
Holds $10 million face value 14s @115	Buys 162 bond futures @70-29
Loss: $500,000	Gain: $420,187

Net Loss: $79,813

As a result of this hedge transaction, the hedger offset a loss that would otherwise have amounted to $500,000. Still, the $420,187 profit in the futures market offset only a part of the cash market loss. A net loss of $79,813 results.

The foregoing example assumed that long-term rates exceeded short-term rates. As a result, the original hedger price times the conversion factor of 119.18% of par (73-16/32nds × 1.6216) fell short of the price of the 14s at 120, which we assume to be cheapest to deliver against the contract. Over the 80-day life of the hedge, the basis converged—the cash bonds fell to 115 while the futures price times the conversion factor fell to 114.98% of par (70-29/32nds × 1.6216), or just short of the cash price. This "convergence loss" amounted to about $80,000.

In this case, a convergence loss resulted as futures prices times the conversion factor, which was initially at a discount to the cheapest cash security, eventually converged to the price of the same. This convergence loss will occur in a normal yield curve environment whether the market rallies or declines. Remember that the hedger is long cash and short futures. Holding cash prices constant, futures will rise to converge to cash. Holding futures prices constant, cash will decline to converge with futures. Under either scenario, the hedger who is long cash and short futures will suffer this convergence loss. Of course, in an inverted yield curve environment, the hedger may enjoy a convergence gain as futures prices times the conversion factor, which is initially at a premium to the price of the cheapest cash security, converges to the same. Under that scenario, holding cash constant, futures will decline to converge with cash; holding futures constant, cash must advance to converge with futures. Under either scenario, this convergence loss or gain means that the hedger locks in a short-term, rather than a long-term, rate. This short-term rate is often referred to as the "implied repo rate." (A "repo rate" is a short-term interest rate at which repurchase agreements are executed. A repurchase agreement is a short-term transaction wherein an institution sells securities on a short-term basis, often just overnight, and agrees subsequently buy them back. The difference in the sale and purchase price of the collateral implies a short-term interest rate.)

Thus far we have looked only at the dollar returns potentially associated with a hedge transaction. To a financial institution, however, percentage figures may be more useful than dollar figures. The percentage returns associated with the hedge transaction, or the implied repo rate, may be calculated by referencing the dollar inflows and outflows compared to the value of the bond being hedged:

$$\frac{\text{Implied}}{\text{Repo Rate}} = \frac{\text{Interest} + \text{Bond Return} + \text{Futures Return}}{\text{Bond Value}} \times \frac{365}{\text{Days}}$$

If we were to apply this formula to our prior example, we would find that the implied repo rate that the hedger locked in was equal to 8.6%:

$$\frac{\text{Implied}}{\text{Repo Rate}} = \frac{\$306{,}849 - \$500{,}000 + \$420{,}187}{\$12 \text{ Million}} \times \frac{365}{80}$$
$$= 8.6\%$$

This compares favorably to an unhedged return of −7.3%. (Actually, the formula that we have applied is not exactly precise but it is precise enough to get a good idea as to the relative effectiveness of the hedge.) This means that, as long as the basis behaves as predictably as we have assumed, the hedger can expect to lock in a return of about 8.6% by shorting futures. By contrast, the returns associated with the long cash bonds provided they were unhedged varies widely. In particular, let's illustrate what would happen if the cash price should remain stable or advance, rather than decline.

Cash price	@115	@120	@125
Futures price	70-29	74-00	77-03
Unhedged return	−7.3%	11.7%	30.7%
Hedged return	8.6%	8.6%	8.6%

Although the hedged returns fall short of the unhedged return when cash prices remain stable or advance, the bond dealer enjoys the advantage of certainty. He gives up the opportunity to participate in windfall capital gains but also insulates himself against the possibility of large capital losses. Figure 7.8 illustrates the essence of hedging long bonds with short futures in a normal yield curve environment. Although the hedger who shorts futures cannot be absolutely sure of locking in a particular return (due to basis risk), the probability is nonetheless high that a particular return will in fact be realized.

Buy Puts

The long put strategy may be thought of as an attractive alternative to the short futures strategy. Essentially, a commercial entity who buys puts against a risk-sensitive asset is buying price insurance. That price insurance policy guar-

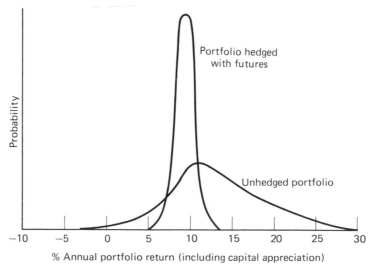

Figure 7.8   Return distribution for a bond portfolio hedged by selling futures

antees a fixed sale price for the asset over the life of the policy no matter how far the price of that asset may decline. If prices should decline below the put strike price, the hedger can be expected to exercise the option to at least partically offset cash market losses. At the same time, the commercial entity that buys a put against a long asset retains the ability to participate in an upward price advance. If prices should advance, the put will simply be abandoned and the put premium paid initially to secure the option will be chalked off as the price of insurance.

Of course, basis considerations can still play an important part when considering the possible results of a long put hedge if the instrument underlying the option is different from the cash instrument to be hedged. An example is when the commodity option is exercisable for a futures contract rather than directly exercisable for the cash commodity.

EXAMPLE. Our gold dealer holds 5,000 ounces at a cash price of $400 and is fearful of a price decline. Rather than selling gold futures contracts, the hedger decides to buy put options in order to retain the ability to participate in an upward price advance. The dealer buys 50 puts struck at $400 per ounce and exercisable for 100-ounce gold futures contracts at a price of $14.30 per ounce. At the time of this sale, there were 90 days to expiration and the underlying gold futures contract was trading at $412.00 per ounce. In other words, the gold dealer bought puts that were $12.00 per ounce out-of-the-money. As a result of this transaction, the gold dealer locks in a floor price equal to the $400 strike price less the $14.30 premium, or $385.70. This assumes that futures will fully converge to cash by the time the option expires. Actually, options on futures typically expire a few weeks prior to the delivery month of the underlying futures contract. As a result, one cannot expect full convergence by that time. But for the purposes of illustration, we will apply the simplifying assumption of full convergence. What would happen if the cash market were to decline to $360 by expiration?

Cash Market	Option Market
Holds 5,000 ounces of gold @$400 per ounce	Buys 50 100-ounce $400 puts @$14.30 when futures @$412
Holds 5,000 ounces of gold @ $360 per ounce	Exercises 50 100-ounce $400 puts for profit of $40 per ounce when gold futures @$360
Loss: $40.00 per ounce	Gain: $25.70 per ounce
	Net Loss: $14.30 per ounce

Figure 7.9 provides a graphic illustration of the results of the foregoing example. In this case, convergence worked to the advantage of the hedger. For example, if futures failed to converge to the cash price by expiration and the basis remained stable at −$12.00 per ounce, the net return would have been re-

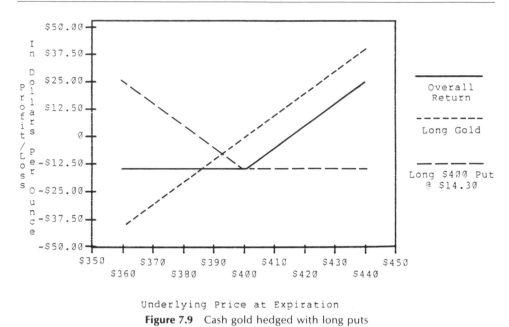

Underlying Price at Expiration
Figure 7.9   Cash gold hedged with long puts

duced by $12.00, for a loss of $26.30. But as convergence did occur in our example, the cost of the price insurance represented by the put hedge equaled the
price of the puts, or $14.30 per ounce. Essentially, the hedger offset both the
risk of a price decline as well as transferring the carrying costs associated with
the metal inventories to put sellers.

As we already know, basis movements do not always work to the advantage
of the hedger. In the case of a hedger of long-term Treasury bonds in a normal
yield curve environment, the basis actually works against the hedger. As a result, a long put hedge must be thought of as a play aimed at protecting the
hedger's ability to lock in a short-term, rather than a long-term, rate.

EXAMPLE.   A financial institution holds $10 million face value of 14% T-bonds
due 2006-11 and is fearful that rates will rise and the value of the
bonds, currently trading at 120-00/32nds, will decline. At a price of
120, the bonds are yielding 11.7% on a current basis. This is an important reference point against which the effectiveness of the
hedge may be measured. A put option exercisable for a T-bond futures contract and struck at 74 is available for a premium of
1-27/64ths. There are 40 days until expiration of this option and
the T-bond futures contract underlying the option is trading at a
price of 73-16/32nds. Using a conversion factor weighted hedge
(the conversion factor equals 1.6216), the institution buys 162 puts
for an aggregate price of $230,344. Subsequently, the value of the
14s declines $500,000 to 115 while the underlying bond futures
contract declines to 70-29. At that point, the institution exercises
the puts for a gain on exercise of $3,094 per option, or $501,187 for

the 162 puts. The net result of these transactions is that the institution has realized a net loss of $229,157.

Cash Market	Option Market
Holds $10 million face value 14s @120	Buys 162 74 puts @1-27/64ths, or $230,344
Holds $10 million face value 14s @115	Exercise puts when futures @70-29 for gain of $501,187
Loss: $500,000	Gain: $270,843

Net Loss: $229,157

It is not immediately obvious in the example above how convergence worked against the hedger. But, in fact, convergence did work to the detriment of this hedge. Originally, futures were assumed to be trading at 73-16, or 16/32nds *under* the cash price divided by the conversion factor of 74-00 (120/1.6216). Furthermore, we assumed that futures would converge completely to the cash price divided by the conversion factor by the time the options were about to expire. This can be confirmed by noting that 70-29 approximates 115/1.6216. This means that the hedger had to pay 16/32nds, or $81,000 of intrinsic value initially, to secure the puts. When convergence occurs, this suggests that the hedger essentially gives up this intrinsic value. This "convergence loss" is roughly equivalent to the convergence loss calculated in the context of the short futures hedge. Thus this hedge may be thought of as a way to protect a short-term, rather than a long-term, rate. (Note that the full convergence assumption is conservative since options on T-bond futures expire shortly before the delivery month of the underlying T-bond futures contract.)

So far we have examined the results of this hedge strategy by looking at the dollar returns associated with the hedge. But fixed-income portfolio managers generally measure their performance, not in absolute dollar terms, but in relative terms, that is, on earnings in proportion to available resources. Just as one may calculate the implied repo rate associated with the combination of a cash bond and a short futures contract, one may calculate the percentage returns associated with the long put hedge. These returns may be found by referencing dollar gains and losses in relation to the value of the asset being hedged.

$$\text{Return} = \frac{\text{Interest} + \text{Bond Return} + \text{Option Return}}{\text{Bond Value}} \times \frac{365}{\text{Days}}$$

Although this formula is not precise, it does provide a reasonable measure of the results of an option hedge. In the foregoing example, the results of the hedge may be measured as follows:

$$\text{Return} = \frac{\$153,425 - \$500,000 + \$270,843}{\$12 \text{ million}} \times \frac{365}{40}$$

$$= -5.8\%$$

This return of −5.8% does not appear particularly attractive until one considers that the unhedged return would have equaled −26.4%. This −5.8% return also equals the maximum loss that is associated with this hedge, assuming that the basis behaves predictably in accord with our assumptions. By buying puts, the hedger essentially locks in a minimum return, guarding against the possibility of large capital losses. At the same time, however, the long put hedger gives up the option premium, a cost that may be regarded as a price insurance premium. Still, the long put hedger retains the ability to participate in possible favorable rate declines and corresponding price advances.

Cash price	@115	@120	@125
Futures price	70-29	74-00	77-03
Unhedged return	−26.4%	11.7%	49.7%
Hedged return	−5.8%	−5.8%	32.2%

In this example, the worst possibility to which the hedger is exposed is the possibility of realizing a return of −5.8%. Some hedgers may balk at the prospect of locking in a negative floor return and look to the possible purchase of other put options. Our prior example examined the sale of an option that was relatively near-to-the-money (actually, the option was just in-the-money). For convenience sake, let's refer to that put as an at-the-money option. What if the hedger were to buy an in- or an out-of-the-money put instead?

EXAMPLE. At the same time that a 74 put option was trading at a price of 1-27/64ths, an in-the-money 76 put was available at 2-51/64ths while an out-of-the-money 72 put was available at 35/64ths. What results would be realized if the purchase of 162 of these puts were matched up with the $10 million face value of 14% bonds?

Cash price	@115	@120	@125
Futures price	70-29	74-00	77-03
Unhedged return	−26.4%	11.7%	49.7%
Hedged returns:			
In-the-money hedge	1.9%	1.9%	15.2%
At-the-money hedge	−5.8%	−5.8%	32.2%
Out-of-money hedge	−19.6%	4.9%	42.9%

Here we see that the in-the-money long put hedge is the most conservative of the three strategies while the out-of-the-money hedge is the most aggressive. The in-the-money strategy allows the hedger to lock in a relatively high minimum floor return but at the same time limits the hedger's participation in a possible price advance to relatively modest levels. Because the in-the-money hedger pays a relatively high premium, he receives a relatively high degree of protection from downward price movements. By contrast, an out-of-the-money put is relatively cheap but provides relatively little protection from adverse price movements. The out-of-the-money long put hedge entails a relatively low

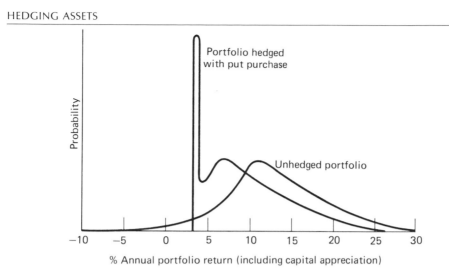

Figure 7.10 Return distribution for a bond portfolio hedged by purchasing put options

floor return but permits the hedger to retain much of his ability to participate in a possible price advance. Of course, the at-the-money strategy falls somewhere in between the in- and the out-of-the-money strategies in terms of risk and possible rewards.

Figure 7.10 illustrates the essence of hedging with long puts. As is apparent, the long put hedger locks in a minimum floor return. But at the same time, the return distribution is shifted to the left by virtue of the forfeiture of the put premium up front.

Bear Put Spread

The long put strategy can be very effective in locking in a floor price or return for a particular asset. But many hedgers point to the forfeiture of the option premium, sometimes indicating a reluctance to pay such premiums in return for price protection. Fortunately, there *are* ways to reduce the cost of hedging. Of course, these methods may not provide the same degree of protection as the purchase of a put option.

One alternative to the purchase of a put option against a long asset is to enter into a vertical bear put spread. While the long put strategy permits the hedger to lock in a particular floor return, the bear put spread permits the hedger to lock in a *partial* floor return. The advantage of this strategy is that it entails a lower initial commitment to capital relative to the long put hedge.

As discussed in Chapter 6, a vertical bear put spread is the purchase of a high struck put coupled with the sale of a low struck put where both legs of the spread share a common expiration date. In and of itself, this strategy results in a limited potential loss as prices bull up at or over the high strike price and a limited potential profit should prices fall at or below the low strike price. As a rule, this strategy entails a net debit in the option market insofar as the long high struck put must command a premium in excess of the premium brought in through the sale of the low struck put. The maximum potential loss equals that net debit while the maximum potential gain equals the difference in strike prices less that net debit.

When coupled with a long position in the underlying commodity market, the bear put spread hedge stabilizes the returns on the cash instrument given that prices fall between the two strike prices.

EXAMPLE.   Gold is trading at $400 in the cash market and our gold dealer, holding 5,000 ounces of the metal, is fearful that prices may decline. To partially hedge that risk, the dealer buys $420 puts for $24.23 per ounce and sells $400 puts for $14.30 per ounce for a net debit of $9.93 per ounce. These puts are exercisable for gold futures that are trading at $412. The maximum loss on the option spread equals the net debit of $9.93 per ounce if gold futures should be at or above $420 at expiration while the maximum gain equals $10.07 per ounce if futures should fall at or below $400. Assume that cash and futures fully converge by option expiration at $385. This means that the hedger suffers a $15 per ounce decline in the value of his cash gold holdings. But at the same time, the hedger can exercise the long puts struck at $420 for a $35 per ounce gain on exercise; the short $400 put will be exercised against the hedger for a loss on exercise of $15 per ounce. These two transactions translate into a $20 gain in the option market reduced by the $9.93 initial debit for a $10.07 per ounce gain. All of this means that the hedger's net loss is reduced from $15 to $4.93 per ounce.

Cash Market	Option Market
Holds 5,000 ounces of gold @$400 per ounce	Buys 50 $420/$400 bear spreads @$9.93 debit, futures @$412
Holds 5,000 ounces of gold @305 per ounce	Liquidate spread for $20 gain on exercise, futures @$385
Loss: $15.00 per ounce	Gain: $10.07 per ounce

Net Loss: $4.93 per ounce

Figures 7.11 and 7.12 illustrate the construction and results of this bear put spread. As is apparent in Figure 7.12, the gold dealer locks in a particular return only within a limited range bounded by the strike prices of the two spread legs. In this example, convergence worked to the advantage of the hedger. If cash gold remained stable at $400, futures would have declined, applying our full convergence assumption, to $400. At $400, the hedger would have reaped the maximum gain of $10.07 per ounce from the option positions.

This begs the question: which strikes to use in connection with a bear put hedge? An "in-the-money bear put spread" where both legs of the spread are in-the-money will entail a relatively high debit and low profit potential. An "out-of-the-money bear put spread" where both legs are out-of-the-money will entail a relatively low initial debit and high profit potential. Balancing these

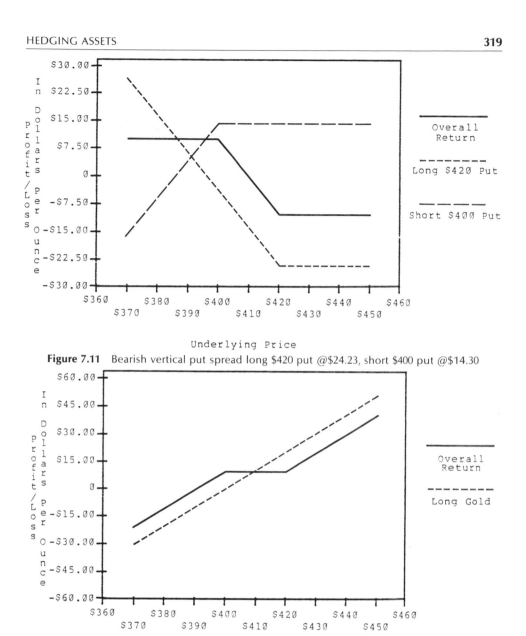

Figure 7.11   Bearish vertical put spread long $420 put @$24.23, short $400 put @$14.30

Figure 7.12   Cash gold hedged with bear put spread long $420 put @$24.23, short $400 put @$14.30, long cash gold @$400

considerations is the fact that the hedger has a greater probability of realizing the maximum return on an in-the-money spread and a relatively low probability of the same with the out-of-the-money spread.

EXAMPLE.   An institution holds $10 million 14% 2006-11 bonds at 120. T-bond futures are at 73-16 and the institution is considering the purchase of an in-the-money 76/74 bear put spread for 1-24/64ths or an out-of-the-money 74/72 bear put spread for 56/64ths. Because the conversion factor for the underlying bond futures is 1.6216, the institution will buy 162 spreads. Assuming full convergence over the 40-day life of the options with the cash price divided by the conversion factor by expiration, the following results would accrue from the two alternative spread strategies.

Cash price	@116	@118	@120	@122	@124
Futures price	71-17	72-24	74-00	75-08	76-15
Unhedged return	−18.8%	−3.6%	11.7%	26.8%	42.1%
Hedged Returns:					
In-the-money spread	−11.1%	4.1%	19.2%	19.2%	25.1%
Out-of-the-money spread	−4.9%	1.0%	1.0%	16.0%	31.3%

As is apparent, the in-the-money spread may be used to augment income in the event of relatively stable prices while the out-of-the-money spread results in diminished returns in a neutral market. This is because, holding prices constant, the in-the-money spread will actually appreciate in value over time while the out-of-the-money spread depreciates. On the other hand, the in-the-money spread results in more dispersed returns in the event of extreme price movements—either bullish or bearish. These returns were constructed using the same method used to calculate returns in the context of the long put hedge.

This strategy is said to allow the hedger to lock in a "partial" floor return insofar as returns are stabilized between the two strike prices. Note once again that this example assumed full convergence by the time the options expired. This means that, holding cash prices constant at 120% of par, futures bulled up from 73-16 to 74—to the apparent disadvantage of the bond hedger.

Sell Calls

The long put strategy allows a hedger to set a floor price for the sale of a particular commodity at the cost of forfeiting the option premium. In effect, the put purchaser buys price insurance. A short call strategy is quite the opposite: a short call hedge, often referred to as a "covered call sale" or as a "buy/write" strategy, allows the hedger to take in the option premium at the cost of setting a ceiling price for the sale of the particular commodity. In so doing, the call writer essentially is granting price insurance to the call buyer. But, of course, when an essentially bearish short call is combined with an essentially bullish long commodity position, the hedger can succeed in reducing risk while at the same time augmenting income.

To many, the idea that one may be able to augment income *and* reduce risk is hard to swallow. Still, many option professionals will attest that the covered call sale has been perhaps *the* most effective option trading strategy practiced since the advent of exchange-traded equity options in 1973. This strategy has produced similar results in the relatively short time that commodity options have been available as well. This has occurred despite the fact that the covered call sale is one of the most straightforward of the myriad option strategies available.

EXAMPLE.   Let's return to our example of the gold dealer holding 5,000 ounces when cash prices are prevailing at $400. Gold futures are at $412 and a $400 call is sold for a $26.01 per ounce premium. Assume that cash and futures prices rally to $440 by the time the option is about to expire. At that time, the hedger's inventories have appreciated $40 per ounce. Unfortunately, the $400 call can be exercised against the gold dealer for a loss on exercise of $40, cushioned by the initial receipt of the $26.01 premium for a $13.99 per ounce loss in the cash market. This reduces the $40 cash market gain to a net gain of only $26.01 per ounce.

Cash Market	Option Market
Holds 5,000 ounces of gold @$400 per ounce	Sells 50 $400 calls @$26.01 when gold futures @$412
Holds 5,000 ounces of gold @$440 per ounce	Calls exercised for $40 loss when gold futures @$440
Gain: $40.00 per ounce	Loss: $13.99 per ounce

Net Gain: $26.01 per ounce

In this case, the cash market fluctuated in the hedger's favor (although it could have gone either way). As a result, the hedger realized a return equal to $26.01 per ounce. This $26.01 represents the maximum return potentially associated with the hedge. This means that the hedger effectively has locked in a ceiling price of $426.01 on his gold holdings. Although the hedger may have made more by remaining unhedged, this "loss" is an opportunity loss only and *not* an out-of-pocket expense.

At all prices *under* the $400 strike price, the gold dealer augments his income by the amount of the option premium—$26.01. This represents a cushion against loss in a "southbound" market. Of course, at a price of $373.99, the hedger's net returns become negative as cash losses mount up beyond the $26.01 cushion.

But perhaps the most interesting area is that between cash prices of $373.99 and $426.01. If prices remain within that range by the time expiration rolls around, the hedger will have successfully realized a positive return by shorting the call. *And* this return will exceed the returns associated with the uncovered cash market position. In other words, as long as prices remain neutral—and there is a rather wide margin for error—the gold dealer will be successful in augmenting income and reducing the risks associated with the cash position. Figure 7.13 shows the above return alternatives.

What if the hedger were to use calls with higher or lower strike prices? The outright sale of an in-the-money call is a more aggressive strategy than the sale of an out-of-the-money call. Remember that in-the-money options will always

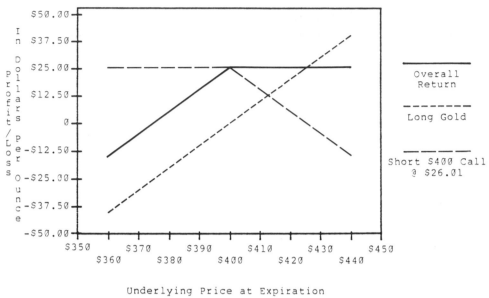

Underlying Price at Expiration
Figure 7.13   Cash gold hedged with short calls

command higher premiums than comparable out-of-the-money options. But while there is higher profit potential associated with the outright sale of an in-the-money call, this is balanced by a relatively low breakeven point. But when combined with a long commodity position, the in-the-money covered call sale can be shown to be more conservative than an at- or out-of-the-money covered call sale.

EXAMPLE.   Our financial institution once again holds $10 million face value 14s of 2006-11 at 120-00/32nds. Bond futures are trading at 73-16/32nds and there are calls available struck in-the-money at 72, out-of-the-money at 76, and near-the-money at 74 (we will refer to this 74 call option as an at-the-money call for convenience). These calls are trading at 2-02/64ths, 21/64ths, and 59/64ths, respectively. What results would be realized if our hedger combined 162 short calls with the $10 million face value 14% cash bonds?

	@115	@120	@125
Cash price	@115	@120	@125
Futures price	70-29	74-00	77-03
Unhedged returns	−26.4%	11.7%	49.7%
Hedged returns:			
In-the-money hedge	−1.4%	12.0%	12.0%
At-the-money hedge	−15.0%	22.9%	22.8%
Out-of-money hedge	−22.4%	15.7%	40.2%

As is apparent, the in-the-money covered call sale is the most conservative of the three strategies. It provides quite a bit of downside protection by virtue of the receipt of a relatively high premium. At the same time, the in-the-money covered call sale locks in a relatively low ceiling return of about 12% in this case. By contrast, the at- and out-of-the-money covered call sales provide less downside protection but permit the hedger to participate more fully in possible price appreciation.

This has some important implications for hedgers. Assume that the hedger initially enters into an at-the-money covered call sale but that the market starts declining quickly. One alternative is to liquidate the original at-the-money short call—most likely at a profit insofar as the premium should decline as prices back off—and at the same time enter into a lower-struck short call. By "rolling down" the hedge into an in-the-money covered call sale, the hedger can effectively extend his protection downward.

Another alternative is to buy a cheap, out-of-the-money put option. This effectively creates a bullish vertical put spread. To understand this "hedge wrapper" strategy, consider that the at-the-money short call combined with the long commodity behaves much like a short put option. By combining the short put with a low-struck long put, the hedger synthetically creates a bullish vertical put spread. In addition, it is likely that the proceeds from the short call will fund the purchase of the low-struck put. This means that the hedger enjoys limited downside risk *and* limited upside potential. In other words, the net position displays characteristics similar to the covered call sale and the long put hedge.

Figure 7.14 illustrates the essence of hedging with short calls. This graph illustrates percentage returns on the horizontal axis and the probability of achieving that return on the vertical axis. Although the hedger effectively is precluded from participating in windfall capital gains, again, it should be stressed that these losses are opportunity losses only and not out-of-pocket expenses. Even though this strategy entails the forfeiture of the opportunity to participate in windfall capital gains, it effectively shifts average returns upwards to the right.

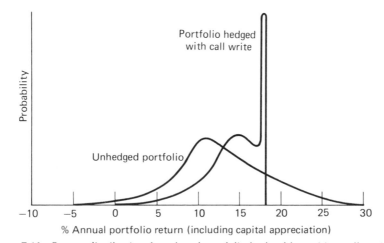

Figure 7.14 Return distribution for a bond portfolio hedged by writing call options

HEDGING LIABILITIES AND ANTICIPATED ACQUISITIONS

When an enterprise holds a price-sensitive liability or anticipates the acquisition of a commodity, it is exposed to the risk of advancing costs. But that risk may be offset and modified with the use of futures and options. The strategies illustrated in this section are the exact opposite of the strategies illustrated in the prior section, which dealt with hedging assets exposed to the risk of price decline. So rather than take on essentially bearish futures and option market positions to hedge an asset, liabilities and anticipated acquisitions may be hedged with essentially bullish futures and option market positions.

In some cases, however, it is somewhat misleading to suggest that liabilities are sensitive to advancing prices. Consider the case of a financial institution that is funding itself with short-term deposits and is lending on a relatively long-term basis. The risk to which that institution's liabilities (short-term deposits) are exposed is the risk of advancing costs in the form of interest rates. Of course, when rates advance, the value of debt instruments declines. This means that a financial institution's liabilities may be hedged using the strategies described in the prior section: short futures, buy puts, buy bear spreads, or sell calls.

Notwithstanding a special case, we shall consider the risks associated with liabilities as essentially similar to the risks associated with the anticipated acquisition of an asset. For example, a metals dealer may have accepted orders for the purchase of gold or silver that exceed his inventories on hand. These unfilled orders represent liabilities that will be satisfied by the purchase and delivery of metal. By the same token, a financial institution may anticipate the purchase of debt instruments with funds from operations or maturing investments. The four hedging strategies considered in this section include: (1) buy futures, (2) buy calls, (3) buy a bullish vertical call spread, and (4) sell puts. How these strategies alter the risks associated with a liability or an anticipated acquisition is summarized as follows:

	Benefits	Costs
Buy futures	Lock in a specific price	Forfeit opportunity to benefit from price declines
Buy calls	Lock in a ceiling price	Forfeit premium
Bull call spread	Lock in a partial ceiling price	Forfeit debit
Sell puts	Augment current income	Lock in a floor price

Buy Futures

The long futures strategy is the most straightforward of the four strategies considered in this section. The risks associated with an essentially bearish cash market position is offset to some degree by an opposite long position in the futures market. Although the ideal is to offset precisely possible losses in the cash market with gains in the futures market, the ideal is seldom realized in practice. Rather than precisely offsetting cash market risk, it is more appropriate to think of a long futures hedge as the replacement of cash market risk with basis risk.

EXAMPLE. A soybean crusher anticipates the purchase of 50,000 bushels of beans for further processing but is fearful of the prospect of an advancing price. In order to hedge that risk, the crusher decides to buy 10 5,000-bushel soybean futures contracts. Cash bean prices are at $7.00 per bushel while a soybean futures contract that calls for the delivery of beans two months later is trading at $7.14 per bushel. The −14 cent basis or the difference between the $7.00 cash and $7.14 futures price may be accounted for by short-term financing rates and storage costs, which we assuume to equal aboout 12% per annum, or 14 cents for two months. Let us make the simplifying assumption that the futures contract will precisely track the cash market. In other words, the crusher is interested in beans of a grade and in a location that represent the "cheapest to deliver" cash beans in light of the soybean futures contract's system of premiums and discounts. With that assumption, we may also assume that cash and futures prices will converge by the time the futures contract reaches maturity. What if beans were to rally to $7.40 in two months? That means that the crusher is forced to pay 40 cents per bushel more for the cash beans than originally anticipated. But at the same time he realizes a profit of 26 cents in the cash market as futures prices likewise rally to $7.40.

Cash Market	Futures Market
Anticipates purchase of beans @$7.00	Buys bean futures @$7.14
Buys beans @$7.40	Sells bean futures @$7.40
Loss: $0.40 per bushel	Gain: $0.26 per bushel

Net Loss: $0.14 per bushel

By buying bean futures in anticipation of the purchase of cash beans, the soybean crusher was able to offset a good deal of the risk of rising prices. Of course, the bean processor was unable to offset all of the risk as the futures market gain fell short of the loss in the cash market due to convergence. To some, this net loss may be regarded as an opportunity loss in the sense that the bean processor missed the opportunity to buy beans at a relatively low price of $7.00. But consider the implications if the bean processor had purchased cash beans at $7.00 for use two months hence. Under those circumstances, the costs of carrying the beans for the two months—financing costs and storage costs— would have been incurred by the bean processor. Essentially, buying futures represents a substitute for the initial purchase of cash beans. If futures are

fairly priced in accordance with carry considerations, the hedger should be indifferent between buying cash initially or buying futures as a temporary substitute for the anticipated acquisition. Of course, other factors may dictate the use
of futures. For example, futures are traded on low margins relative to the value
of the cash commodity and initial margins may be put up in securities. Moreover, the crusher may not have sufficient facilities available to store beans in
the quantities that may be needed in the future. Or the crusher may simply
find it more attractive to go long futures because of a favorable basis relationship.

Because soybean futures prices are affected by negative carry, that is, a net
outflow of funds is required to carry or hold physical soybeans, the long hedge
suffered a convergence loss. A convergence gain would be realized in the event
of a positive carry structure. Long-term debt securities typically are characterized by a positive carry structure insofar as long-term yields typically exceed
short-term financing costs. In that situation, a long hedge could result in a net
gain rather than a net loss.

EXAMPLE.   A financial institution anticipates the inflow of funds from matur-
            ing investments and wants to invest in T-bonds, specifically, the
            12% issue of 2008-13. These 12s are currently trading at 94% of par
            to yield 12.7% on a current basis. Short-term rates are around 10%.
            June 1984 T-bond futures are trading at 65-26/32nds and there are
            40 days until the delivery month. The conversion factor associated
            with the delivery of these 12s into the June contract equals 1.4239.
            As the institution anticipates the acquisition of $10 million face
            value of these bonds, it buys 142 June bond futures contracts.
            Subsequently, cash prices rally to 98 while futures rise to 68-26.
            (Full convergence is factored into this example.) At that time, the
            institution acquires the 12s for $400,000 more than expected and
            sells the futures contracts for a $426,000 gain. A net gain of $26,000
            results.

Cash Market	Futures Market
Anticipates purchase of	Buys 142 bond futures
$10 million 12s @94-00	@65-26
Buys $10 million 12s	Sells 142 bond futures
@98-00	@68-26
Loss: $400,000	Gain: $426,000

Net Gain: $26,000

The bottom line is that the hedger has effectively assumed the positive
carry associated with the 12% T-bonds. The long futures contracts essentially
act as a temporary substitute for the purchase of the cash bonds. Assume that
the institution previously had the funds that were applied to the purchase of
the 12% bonds invested in short-term debt instruments at a 10% rate. Then it is

clear that, by buying bond futures, the hedger effectively achieves a long-term, instead of a short-term, rate over the 40-day life of the hedge. This may be confirmed by examining the percentage returns achieved over the 40-day holding period under three different scenarios: stable, advancing, and declining cash prices.

Cash price	@90	@94	@98
Futures price	63-07	66-00	68-26
Unhedged return	48.8%	10.0%	−28.8%
Hedged return	12.5%	12.5%	12.5%

These returns are calculated using $9,400,000 as the base value, or the amount that the hedger originally expected to pay for the bonds. The variance from the amount that is actually required to secure the bonds is accounted for as a gain or loss in the calculation. Finally, a 10% return on the base investment is incorporated into the calculation.

As is apparent, the long hedge stabilizes the hedger's returns over the 40-day life of the hedge. Moreover, the returns achieved resemble those that would be expected from a long-term investment in a normal, upward sloping yield curve environment, relative to the prevailing 10% short-term rate.

Buy Calls

The long call strategy may be thought of as a "low-maintenance" alternative to the long hedge with futures. By buying calls, the hedger guarantees that he will be able to purchase the subject commodity at a fixed price at any time prior to expiration despite possible price advances. In return for this option, the hedger forfeits the option premium, which may be thought of as the cost of the price insurance. This is a low-maintenance strategy because, once paid, the option premium represents the maximum cost potentially associated with the strategy, outside of basis risk. This is shown for the following example in Figure 7.15.

EXAMPLE.   Our soybean crusher is interested in acquiring 50,000 bushels of beans in the near future and wants to insulate himself from possible price advances. Cash beans are trading at $7.00 per bushel; a $7.00 call option exercisable for soybean futures is trading at $0.30 per bushel while the underlying bean futures contract is trading at $7.14. The crusher buys 10 of these 5,000-bushel call options to cover the risk of a rally. Let's make the simplifying assumption of full convergence. Two months later, as the calls are about to expire, cash beans and bean futures have rallied to $7.50. At this point, the crusher can exercise the calls by buying bean futures at the $7.00 strike price when they are actually valued at $7.50, which implies a $0.50 per bushel profit. On the other hand, the crusher

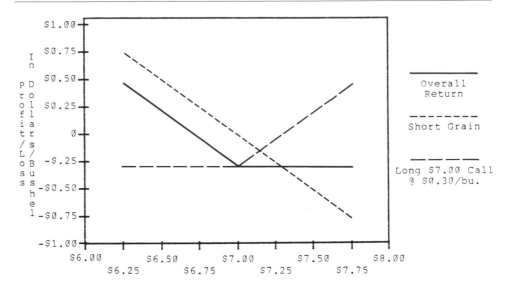

Underlying Price at Expiration

Figure 7.15 Anticipated soybean purchase hedged with long calls

has to buy cash beans at $7.50, or $0.50 above the original target price of $7.00. The gain on exercise of the calls offsets the additional costs in the cash market. But this must be reduced by the initial call premium for a net loss of 30 cents per bushel.

Cash Market	Option Market
Anticipates purchase of beans @$7.00	Buys $7.00 calls for $0.30 per bushel when futures @$7.14
Buys beans @$7.50	Exercises $7.00 calls when bean futures @$7.50 for $0.50 per bushel gain
Loss: $0.50 per bushel	Gain: $0.20 per bushel
	Net Loss: $0.30 per bushel

In this case, the soybean crusher was able to offset less than half of the loss in the cash market through the purchase of calls. Part of this result is because convergence worked against the hedger. When considering the use of options, the effects of basis convergence are sometimes less obvious than when considering the use of futures. But remember that the calls were bought when they were 14 cents in-the-money. Subsequently, the futures price rose only 36 cents relative to a 50-cent advance in the cash market.

In the foregoing example, the long call hedge did not seem to work very well. Why would the crusher want to implement the long call hedge and give up the 30-cent premium? One of the most attractive features of this strategy is that it permits the crusher to enjoy the benefits associated with a possible decline in price. At the same time, the hedger is assured that he has *locked in a ceiling price* for the purchase of grain. In this case, the effective purchase price of the grain was the original $7.00 target price plus the $0.03 call premium, or $7.30 per bushel. So if the crusher feels comfortable knowing that he can realize a profit buying beans at $7.30 but wants to retain the ability to participate in a possible price decline, the long call strategy may be quite attractive. And because there will be a number of options available at different strike prices and premiums, a hedger can assume a risk/reward structure that most closely suits his needs.

EXAMPLE.   Let's reconsider the financial institution that anticipates the purchase of $10 million face value 12% bonds of 2008-13. This bond is trading at 94-00 to yield 12.7%. T-bond futures are trading at 65-26/32nds and the conversion factor for the delivery of the 12s equals 1.4239. Calls exercisable for T-bond futures and struck at 64 are trading at 2-08/64ths, or $2,125; 66 calls are trading at 60/64ths, or $937; and 68 calls are at 20/64ths, or $312. There are 40 days to expiration and we shall assume full convergence. What would happen if the institution were to buy 142 of the nearest-to-the-money 66 calls? Assume that 40 days later as the options are about to expire, the 12s have rallied to 98-00. This implies a 4-point, or $400,-000, opportunity loss in the cash market. At the same time, assume that futures have rallied to 68-26 and the calls are exercised for their in-the-money value of 2-26/32nds a piece, or $399,375 for the 142 calls. This gain more than offsets the original $133,125 cost of the options. The bottom line is that the hedger realized a $266,250 gain in the option market against a $400,000 loss in cash. In this case, convergence worked to the advantage of the hedger as futures rallied to equal the cash price divided by the conversion factor. If it is not clear how this benefitted the hedger, consider that the options were purchased out-of-the-money when futures were trading at a level *less* than the prevailing cash price of 94 divided by the 1.4234 conversion factor, or 66-00.

Cash Market	Option Market
Anticipates purchase of $10 million 12s @94-00	Buys 142 66 calls @60/64ths or $133,125
Buys $10 million 12s @98-00	Exercises calls when futures @68-26 for a gain of $399,375
Loss: $400,000	Gain: $266,250
Net Loss: $133,750	

Of course, there were other options struck in- and out-of-the-money at 64 and 68, respectively, available as well as the near-to-the-money 66 call. We are interested in finding the percentage returns that would have accrued under a range of scenarios had the hedger used any of these three call options. We shall assume that the target $9.4 million price is currently invested in short-term securities at a 10% rate.

Cash price	@90	@94	@98
Futures price	63-07	66-00	68-26
Unhedged return	48.8%	10.0%	−28.8%
Hedged returns:			
In-the-money hedge	19.5%	8.3%	8.3%
At-the-money hedge	35.9%	−2.9%	−2.9%
Out-of-money hedge	44.6%	5.7%	−21.9%

The in-the-money call purchase is the most conservative of the three strategies shown above while the out-of-the-money call purchase represents the most aggressive. The in-the-money call purchase permits the hedger to lock in a relatively low ceiling price and, consequently, a high floor return (8.3%). This comes at the cost of restricting potential participation in price declines. However, the out-of-the-money call purchase entails a relatively high ceiling price and, consequently, a low floor return (−21.9%). But this strategy permits the hedger to participate richly in possible price declines.

Bull Call Spread

The long call strategy described above provides a good deal of assurance for the hedger insofar as the strategy may be used to lock in a ceiling price for the acquisition of a commodity. Still, many hedgers may be reluctant to part with the option premium in order to obtain price protection. Additionally, some may point to the fact that option holders become victims of time value decay.

An alternative to the purchase of a call option is represented in the bull call spread. Generally, this strategy will require a smaller investment up front and insulate the strategy practitioner from time value decay. Unfortunately, this strategy cannot provide a similar measure of protection. Rather than locking in a ceiling price, the bull call spread may be thought of as a strategy aimed at establishing a partial ceiling price or stabilizing acquisition prices over a limited price range.

A vertical bullish call spread represents one of, if not *the,* most popular option spread. The bull call spread represents the purchase of a low-struck call coupled with the sale of a relatively high-struck call where both legs of the spread share a common expiration date. This results in limited risk in the event that the price of the instrument underlying the option falls at or below the low strike price by expiration, and limited profit potential in the event prices advance at or over the upper strike by expiration. A bull call spread invariably results in a net debit, which represents the maximum risk. The difference in strike prices less the net debit represents the maximum profit potential.

When combined with a short position in the underlying commodity market, the bull call spread tends to stabilize returns between the two strike prices.

EXAMPLE. The soybean crusher intending to buy 50,000 bushels of beans enters a bull call spread by buying a call struck at $7.00 per bushel for 30 cents and selling a $7.25 call for 17 cents. This results in an initial net debit of 13 cents per bushel. At the time of this transaction, cash beans are at $7.00 while bean futures are trading at $7.14. Subsequently, bean prices—both cash and futures—rally to $7.30 per bushel. At that point, the long $7.00 call is exercised for a 30-cent per bushel gain while the $7.25 short call is exercised against the hedger for a 5-cent loss; a net gain of 25 cents per bushel is realized at expiration. Deducting the 13-cent debit, the hedger is left with a 12-cent gain in the option market to be matched with a 30-cent loss in the cash market for a net 18-cent loss.

Cash Market	Option Market
Anticipates purchase of beans @$7.00	Buys $7.00/$7.25 bull call spread for $0.13 debit, futures @$7.14
Buys beans @$7.30	Liquidate spread for $0.25 gain on exercise, futures @$7.30
Loss: $0.30 per bushel	Gain: $0.12 per bushel

Net Loss: $0.18 per bushel

In this case, the hedger realized the maximum possible profit associated with the bull call spread—12 cents, or the difference in strikes (25 cents) less the net debit (13 cents). No matter how far bean prices advance, the hedger's income from the bull spread will not exceed that 12-cent level. As prices fall, however, the hedger's loss as a result of the bull call spread cannot exceed the net debit. Only between the two strikes will the losses and gains in the cash market be roughly matched with gains and losses in the option market. Figures 7.16 and 7.17 illustrate how the bull call spread is constructed and, once constructed, how the spread stabilizes prices between the two strike prices.

A question that often arises when considering the use of an option spread as a hedge vehicle is: which strikes to use? "In-the-money spreads" where both legs of the spread are in-the-money entail relatively large net debits and correspondingly low profit potential. Yet these spreads may be used to achieve the maximum possible returns with relatively high probability. "Out-of-the-money spreads" entail relatively high profit potential and lower risk. Yet these spreads have a lower probability of paying off.

EXAMPLE. Our financial institution holds $10 million 12% bonds trading at 94-00 to yield 12.7%. T-bond futures are at 65-26/32nds. The institution is considering the purchase of either an "in-the-money" 64/66

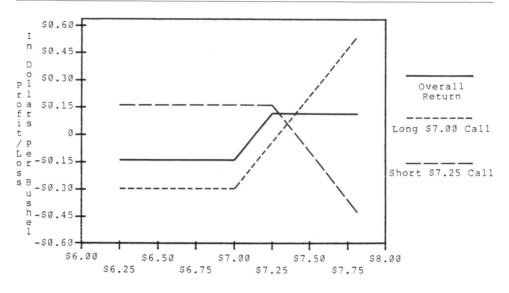

Figure 7.16   Bullish vertical call spread long $7.00 call @$0.30, short $7.25 call @$0.17

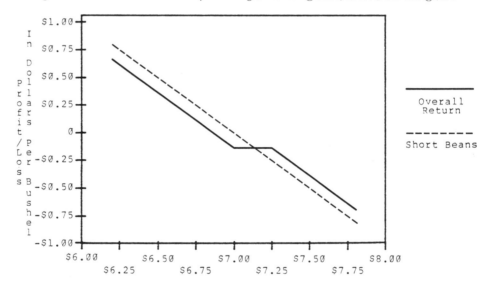

Figure 7.17   Anticipated soybean purchase @$7.00 hedged with bull call spread long $7.00 call
@$0.30, short $7.25 call @$0.17

bull call spread or an "out-of-the-money 66/68 bull call spread.
The 64 call is trading at 2-08/64ths, the 66 call at 60/64ths, and the
68 call at 20/64ths. Thus the 64/66 spread may be entered at a
debit of 1-12/64ths, or $1,187, while the 66/68 spread is going at a
debit of 40/64ths, or $625. What returns might be realized over the
40-day life of the options under a variety of price scenarios, assum-

ing that futures will fully converge to the cash price divided by the
1.4234 conversion factor within that time?

	@90	@92	@94	@96	@98
Cash price	@90	@92	@94	@96	@98
Futures price	63-07	64-20	66-00	67-14	68-26
Unhedged return	48.8%	29.4%	10.0%	−9.4%	−28.8%
Hedged returns:					
In-the-money spread	32.5%	21.4%	21.4%	1.8%	−17.6%
Out-of-the-money spread	40.2%	20.8%	1.5%	1.5%	−9.8%

As shown above, the in-the-money 64/66 spread permits the hedger to
augment income in the event of a neutral market where futures drift to the 66-
00 level by the time the options expire. At 66 and above, the in-the-money
spread yields its maximum return. On the other hand, the out-of-the-money
66/68 spread yields its maximum loss at 66. As a result, the out-of-the-money
hedger's returns are diminished if cash prices remain stable. As discussed in
Chapter 6, the in-the-money spread will appreciate over time, holding prices
constant, while the out-of-the-money spread will depreciate. Because the in-
the-money spreader's position will actually appreciate over time, he is insulated from time value decay—an importgant disadvantage associated with the
long call strategy. The out-of-the-money spread will dominate the in-the-
money spread only if prices appreciate significantly.

Note that, between the two strike prices of the spread legs, the hedger can
stabilize returns. As such, the bull call spread allows the hedger to establish a
"partial" ceiling price for the anticipated acquisition.

Short Puts

The short put strategy is analogous to the covered call strategy. By selling
puts against an anticipated acquisition, the hedger can augment income that
will provide a cushion against the possibility that prices will advance. If, however, prices decline, the hedger will be unable to fully benefit from that eventuality. In effect, and as shown in Figure 7.18, the hedger locks in a floor price for
the purchase of the commodity in question.

EXAMPLE. The soybean crusher interested in buying 50,000 bushels of soybeans decides to sell puts to hedge the risk of a price advance. Cash
beans are at $7.00 while a $7.00 call option exercisable for bean futures is trading at a premium of 16 cents per bushel. Bean futures
are at $7.14. Two months later, as the option is about to expire,
soybeans—cash and futures—are trading at $6.50. At this point,
the short puts are exercised against the hedger: the crusher must
buy bean futures at $7.00 when they are actually valued at $6.50.
This implies a 50-cent loss on exercise cushioned by the 16-cent
premium for a net loss of 34 cents per bushel in the option market.

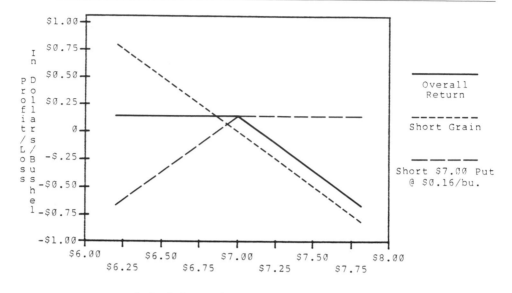

Figure 7.18 Anticipated soybean purchase hedged with short puts

Of course, the crusher is able to buy beans at $6.50, or 50 cents under the original price of $7.00, for 50-cent gain. On balance, the hedger acquires beans at 16 cents under the $7.00 target price, or $6.84. This $6.84 per bushel represents the floor purchase price for the beans.

Cash Market	Option Market
Anticipates purchase of beans @$7.00	Sells $7.00 puts for $0.16 per bushel when futures @$7.14
Buys beans @$6.50	$7.00 puts exercised when bean futures @$6.50 for a $0.50 per bushel loss
Gain: $0.50 per bushel	Loss: $0.34 per bushel
	Net Gain: $0.16 per bushel

In the foregoing example, the market declined and the hedger locked in the floor price. But if the market were to advance, the hedger's effective purchase price would increase over the target price. The only compensation is that the hedger earns the premium from the original put sale. Let's look at what might happen if the market were to decline, advance, or remain neutral using at-, in-, or out-of-the-money options.

EXAMPLE.   Our financial institution wants to buy $10 million face value 12% bonds of 2008-13 trading at 94. Bond futures are trading at 65-26/32nds and the hedger is considering the sale of puts struck in-the-money at 68, near to or essentially at-the-money at 66 and out-of-the-money at 64. These puts are trading at prices of

2-62/64ths ($2,969), 1-30/64ths ($1,469), and 32/64ths ($500), respectively. There are 40 days until option expiration over which time a full convergence assumption is applied. The hedger is considering the purchase of 142 options execute a conversion factor weighted hedge. Currently, the hedger has $9.4 million (the target price of the bonds) invested in short-term securities at 10%. What kind of returns might be expected if the market were to decline, advance, or remain stable?

	@90	@94	@98
Cash price			
Futures price	63-07	66-00	68-26
Unhedged return	48.8%	10.0%	−28.8%
Hedged returns:			
With 64 puts	44.9%	16.9%	−21.9%
With 66 puts	30.4%	30.4%	−8.6%
With 68 puts	23.5%	23.5%	12.1%

As is apparent, the sale of the in-the-money 68 puts represents the most conservative strategy of the three. By selling in-the-money puts, the hedger locks in a relatively low maximum return (23.5%). (Looking at it from another angle, the hedger locks in a relatively high floor purchase price.) On the other hand, the in-the-money put sale provides much better insulation from advancing prices as the hedger brings in a relatively large premium up front. By contrast, the out-of-the-money put sale represents the most aggressive of the three strategies. The out-of-the-money put sale permits the hedger to take greater advantage of possible price declines. As is apparent, the ceiling return in this case equals 44.9%. But this comes at the cost of relatively large losses in the event that prices advance.

DELTA HEDGING TECHNIQUES

When one attempts to hedge price risk by using futures contracts, the idea essentially is to match cash market losses and gains with futures market gains and losses. "Delta hedging" with the use of options begins with essentially the same objective. The hedger wishes to offset cash gains and losses with losses and gains in the option premium. Although the basic motivation is similar when comparing futures and delta hedging techniques, the actual execution of the hedge becomes much more involved when using the delta technique. In addition, because of the special properties of delta, these two techniques are most appropriate under very different circumstances.

A delta hedge is predicated upon one's ability to identify the expected change in the price of an option—the option premium—relative to a given change in the price of the commodity for which the option may be exercised. This figure is, of course, "delta." To briefly review material found elsewhere in this book, a delta of .50 implies that the option premium may be expected to fluctuate by 50 cents for every dollar fluctuation in the price of the underlying commodity. If the price of the underlying commodity appreciates by one dollar, a call option with a delta of .50 may be expected to appreciate in price by 50 cents; similarly a put option with a .50 delta may be expected to decline in price by 50 cents. As a result, long put deltas and short call deltas are sometimes denoted with a negative sign in front of the value. A delta of about .50 and −.50 is characteristic of at- or near-to-the-money call and put options, respectively. But as an option trends into-the-money, its delta will approach 1.0 in the case of calls and −1.0 in the case of puts. As an option trends out-of-the-money, its delta will approach zero.

In order to hedge a particular commodity with an option that has a delta of about .50, one must "double up" on the options. By taking two option units for every single unit held in the underlying commodity, the hedger can effectively match premium with underlying price fluctuations. In other words, the hedge ratio is found by taking the reciprocal of delta. The reciprocal of a .50 delta (1/.5) is 2.0. Of course, the appropriate hedge ratio will change when using different options. The hedge ratio may also be adjusted to reflect the relationship between the hedged commodity and the commodity that is actually deliverable upon the exercise of an option.

It cannot be stressed enough that delta is dynamic. Deltas will fluctuate over price and over time. This suggests that it becomes necessary to continually adjust the ratio of options to the hedged commodity, not only as prices fluctuate but also as time marches on. Transaction costs may mount up quickly in a volatile market where the hedge ratio must continually be adjusted. In addition, as we shall see in a subsequent section, it may not be possible to adjust fully for the effects of time. Thus a delta hedge strategy is most effectively practiced over a short period of time and over a limited price range. By contrast, a futures contract hedge generally requires much less effort in managing the hedge once placed.

Why effect a delta hedge under these circumstances? Why not simply use futures when the idea is to match cash market losses and gains with gains and losses in an offsetting market? For some, delta hedging may represent the only available means of achieving this match where an option market is available and there is no corresponding futures market. Still others may find the prospect of paying cash variation margins on futures market losses unmanageable. These hedgers may be more comfortable with the idea of using long options in the delta hedge and thereby limiting the maximum possible outlays to the premium. Still others may find that the dynamic nature of the delta hedge position conforms to their risk/reward preferences. This final point is discussed in more detail below.

Applying the Delta Hedge

We have discussed how the delta hedge represents a dynamic strategy requiring continual management. This fact is underscored when one examines Figure 7.19. As shown in Figure 7.19, the delta associated with an option

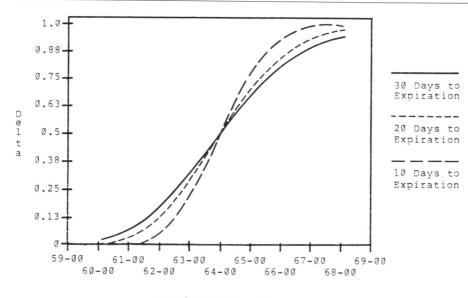

Figure 7.19   Delta at 30, 20, and 10 days to expiration for 64-00 T-bond call option

changes as the price of the underlying commodity changes and changes
through the simple passage of time. Only when an option is just at-the-money
does its delta remain constant—at the pivotal .50 level. As the call option
trends into-the-money, its delta approaches 1.0; and as it trends out-of-the-
money, its delta approaches zero.

Although delta is constant when the option remains just at-the-money,
Figure 7.19 suggests that delta is in fact most unstable when the option is near-
to-the-money. In other words, a slight change in the underlying commodity
price may give rise to a relatively large change in the delta when the option is
near-to-the-money. Delta is most stable over small fluctuations in the underlying price when it falls deep in- or out-of-the-money. Moreover, this effect is exacerbated as the option approaches expiration. In other words, the deltas
associated with near-term options are less stable than the deltas associated
with deferred options.

The stability of delta itself is often measured by a companion statistic
known as "gamma." While delta provides an indication of the expected change
in the option premium relative to a change in the underlying commodity price,
gamma is sometimes used to provide an indication of the rate of change in delta
relative to a fluctuation in the underlying commodity price. Gamma may be
thought of as the slope of the line depicting delta. As we can see, that slope becomes steeper and steeper as the option approaches expiration. Still, delta and
gamma in and of themselves provide no indication of the effect of time on the
option premium. This fact implies that a delta hedge has vastly different implications over an extended period than it does over a short period of time.

Enough has been said about delta and the need to continually monitor the
dynamic nature of the resulting hedge ratio. The real question is: just how
might this strategy be applied?

EXAMPLE.   A financial institution holds $1 million face value Treasury bonds and is concerned about the possibility of rising rates and declining prices in the near term. As a result, this institution has decided to employ a delta hedging strategy to match changes in the value of the cash instrument with changes in the premiums of the options employed in the hedge. To make our example quite straightforward, we will employ a number of simplifying assumptions. Assume that the hedger has decided to use options exercisable for U.S. Treasury bond futures contracts. These cash T-bonds bear an 8% coupon and represent the cheapest to deliver cash security. We shall also assume that the yield curve is perfectly flat, that is, short-term rates equal long-term rates. As a result, the price of these cash bonds should approximate quite closely the price of the T-bond futures that may be delivered against the option contract in the event of an exercise. In fact, we shall assume that these prices are equal. T-bonds—cash and futures—are trading at 64% of par, and the hedger decides to use at-the-money long puts struck at 64 to delta hedge the risk associated with the $1 million face value of cash bonds. Since the options are at-the-money, their delta approximates negative .50. This implies that 20 $100,000 face value puts must be used to match the risks associated with the $1 million face value cash bonds.

30 Days to Expiration

Long $1 million face value 8% cash bonds @64-00/32nds	
Buy 20 64 puts @56/64ths, or $875 a piece	$17,500 debit

On the next day, cash bond price decline to 63-16/32nds% of par. At that point, the put premium has advanced to 1-08/64ths, or $1,125 a piece. As a result, the value of the cash holdings has dropped $5,000. The value of the 20 puts, however, has advanced $250 a piece, or $5,000 in the aggregate. As a result, the hedger has managed to preserve the value of his cash holdings.

29 Days to Expiration

Long $1 million face value 8% bonds @63-16/32nds	$5,000 paper loss
Long 20 64 puts @1-08/64ths, or $1,125 a piece	$5,000 paper gain
Net result	No gain or loss

At this point, the delta associated with the long puts has gone from −.50 to −.58. This suggests that the hedger take steps to adjust the hedge ratio. In particular, the new hedge ratio becomes −1.72 (1/-.58). In other words, the hedger should liquidate 3 of the 20 puts, bringing the total down to 17 long puts.

Sell 3 64 puts @ 1-08/64ths,
or $1,125 a piece $3,375 credit

Now, let's assume that prices advance to 64-16/32nds on the third day. At that point, the hedger has a $10,000 paper gain in the value of the cash bonds. The 17 long puts decline in value to 40/64ths, or $625 a piece, for a $8,500 paper loss in the option market. This puts our hedger ahead by $1,500 on paper.

28 Days to Expiration

Long $1 million face value 8% bonds @64-16/32nds	$10,000 paper gain
Long 17 64 puts @40/64ths, or $625 a piece	$8,500 paper loss
Net result	$1,500 paper gain

Although few hedgers may quarrel with the idea of a $1,500 gain, this result nonetheless illustrates the importance of staying on top of the situation and continually adjusting the ratio of options to cash commitments. Remember that the idea is to offset cash losses *and* gains with gains and losses in the option market. Perhaps the best way to illustrate this point is with the use of short call options in a delta hedge.

EXAMPLE.   Our financial institution decides to sell 20 calls struck at 64% of par against the $1 million face value 8% bonds as a delta hedge. There are 30 days to expiration and cash and futures bonds are trading at the 64 strike price. At this point, the calls have a delta equal to .50. Since the hedger is going short the calls, this effectively changes the sign of the delta from positive (.50) to negative (−.50).

30 Days to Expiration

Long $1 million face value 8% bonds @64-00/32nds	
Sell 20 64 calls @56/64ths, or $875 a piece	$17,500 credit

Over the next day, cash and futures prices decline to 63-16/32nds. This implies a paper loss in the cash market of $5,000. At the same time, the calls decline to 40/64ths, or $625 a piece. This represents a paper gain of $250 per option, or $5,000 for the 20 short calls.

29 Days to Expiration

Long $1 million face value 8% bonds @63-16/32nds	$5,000 paper loss
Short 20 64 calls @40/64ths, or $625 a piece	$5,000 paper gain
Net result	No gain or loss

Since the calls have fallen out-of-the-money, the delta has fallen to .41. This implies that the appropriate hedge ratio has risen to 2.43.

In other words, the hedger should sell 4 more calls to bring the total up to 24.

Sell 4 64 calls @40/64ths, or $625 a piece	$2,500 credit

If prices now advance to 64-16/32nds on the third day, the hedger has a $10,000 paper gain in the value of the cash bonds. But the 24 short calls have now appreciated from 40/64ths to 1-07/64ths. This implies a $484 paper loss per option, or $11,625 in the aggregate. This puts our hedger in the red by $1,625 (at least on paper).

28 Days to Expiration

Long $1 million face value 8% bonds @64-16/32nds	$10,000 paper gain
Short 24 64 calls @1-07/64ths, or $1,109 a piece	$11,625 paper loss
Net result	$1,625 paper loss

Obviously, the long put and short call delta hedges produced very different results. But the real point here is that the hedger must continually be aware of market movements—even movements within a day—in order to maintain a proper delta hedge. In the case of the long put hedge, the hedger should have been applying additional contracts during the daily trading session as the market moved significantly upwards. Likewise, the short call hedger should have been liquidating calls as the market moved upwards. In our example, of course, the hedger neglected to maintain the appropriate hedge ratio. As a result, neither delta hedge met the original objective of a net flat return.

Inattention to the Hedge

The prior two examples underscore a very important point: the delta hedge ratio is dynamic and must continually be adjusted as prices fluctuate. In the case of the long puts, the hedger benefitted from the effects of volatility. In fact, the long put hedger would have enjoyed positive returns in the event of upward *or* downward price movement. The opposite holds true in the case of the short call hedger. Price variability, upwards or downwards, can result in a loss to the delta hedger using short calls. But this is just one aspect of the delta hedge.

Remember that a delta hedge is only effective over a limited price range without readjustment. And since delta does not measure the effects of time, a delta hedge can only be effective over a limited time period.

We have already shown how volatility works for the delta hedger long puts and works against the delta hedger short calls. (A more precise rule of thumb is that volatility works for a delta hedger long options whether they are puts or calls; likewise, volatility works against a delta hedger short options, either calls or puts.) The effects of time, however, will work to the advantage of the delta hedger short calls and to the detriment of the delta hedger long puts. This is easy to understand when one considers that, over time, the time value asso-ciated with an option will decay. Longs suffer from and shorts benefit from time value decay.

Figure 7.20 illustrates the effects of volatility and time on the delta hedge using long puts. The hedger's unadjusted delta hedge position is insulated over a rather limited price range above and below the original price of 64 on the first day that the hedge is applied. But if the market should bull upwards or take a tumble, the long put hedge will show a gain. Over time, however, the long put hedge begins to deteriorate. Specifically, the time value associated with the long puts will decay and show a larger and larger loss as the options approach expiration. Figure 7.21 illustrates how this position ultimately comes to resem-ble a long straddle position. This is because the long bonds in combination with 10 of the long puts resemble a long call position. This synthetic long call com-bined with the remaining 10 long puts will resemble a long straddle over time.

Figure 7.22 illustrates the effect of volatility and time on the short call delta hedge. As we can see, the unadjusted call hedge provides protection on the first day only over a limited price range. If prices advance or decline, the hedger's position will suffer a loss. As time marches on, however, the hedger's position benefits from time value decay. Figure 7.23 illustrates how this position comes to resemble a short straddle. The long bonds coupled with 10 of the short calls will resemble a short put position. This synthetic short put coupled with the remaining short calls may be identified as a short straddle.

A delta hedger may take steps to adjust the hedge ratio and maintain a so-called delta neutral position by adding or liquidating options. This continual readjustment may not prove feasible in a volatile market to the extent that transaction costs may mount up quickly. Be that as it may, a delta hedger can-not neutralize time value decay using all short or all long options. (Of course, a delta hedger short options may not wish to neutralize the effects of this time value decay.)

If, however, the delta hedger were to use a combination of long puts and short calls, transaction costs as a result of readjustments will practically be re-duced to nil. In addition, the effects of time will be all but eliminated. Delta hedgers liquidate short calls and add to long put positions as the market ad-vances; they add to short call and liquidate long put positions as the market advances. Thus a combination of long puts and short calls can be expected to remain delta neutral as the market moves up or down. Similarly, the ill effects of time value decay associated with the long options are negated by the bene-fits of time value decay that accrue from the short options.

Perhaps it is easiest to understand this hedge position as being essentially similar to a conversion. By selling calls and buying puts in combination with a long position in the underlying market, the hedger can effectively lock in a price with the assurance that the hedge requires very low maintenance. Or this position may be understood in that the combination of long puts and short calls represents a synthetic short position in the underlying commodity market. This short combined with a long will tend to lock in a particular price, similar to the results of a futures hedge.

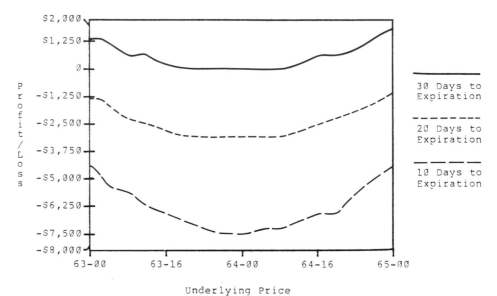

Figure 7.20 Unadjusted delta hedge over time—20 long 64 puts @56/64ths vs. $1 million face value 8% bonds @64 hedge placed with 30 days to expiration

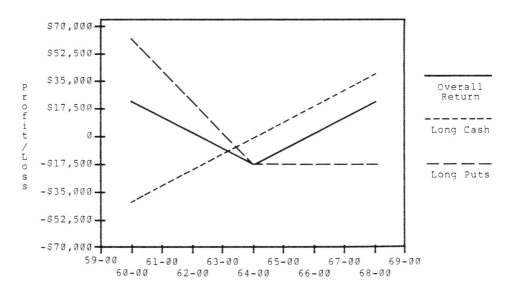

Figure 7.21 Unadjusted delta hedge at expiration—20 long 64 puts @56/64th vs. $1 million face value 8% @64

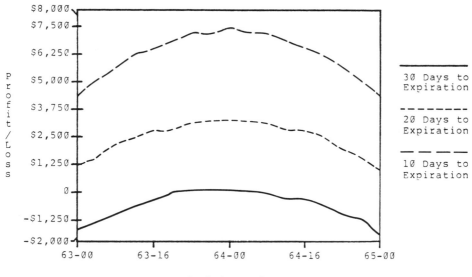

Figure 7.22 Unadjusted delta hedge over time—20 short 64 calls @56/64ths vs. $1 million face value 8% bonds @64 hedged placed with 30 days to expiration

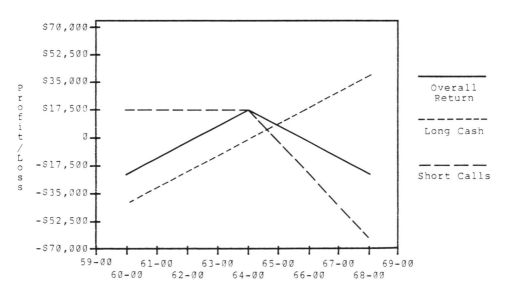

Figure 7.23 Unadjusted delta hedge at expiration—20 short 64 calls @56/64ths vs. $1 million face value 8% bonds @64

Appendix A

Cumulative Normal Distribution

CUMULATIVE NORMAL PROBABILITY DISTRIBUTION
WHERE $d(1)$ OR $d(2)$ IS POSITIVE

	.00	.01	.02	.03	.04	.05	.06	.07	.08	.09
0.00/	.5000	.5040	.5080	.5120	.5159	.5199	.5239	.5279	.5319	.5358
0.10/	.5398	.5438	.5478	.5517	.5557	.5596	.5636	.5675	.5714	.5753
0.20/	.5793	.5832	.5871	.5909	.5948	.5987	.6026	.6064	.6103	.6141
0.30/	.6179	.6217	.6255	.6293	.6331	.6368	.6406	.6443	.6480	.6517
0.40/	.6554	.6591	.6628	.6664	.6700	.6736	.6772	.6808	.6844	.6879
0.50/	.6915	.6950	.6985	.7019	.7054	.7088	.7123	.7157	.7190	.7224
0.60/	.7257	.7291	.7324	.7356	.7389	.7421	.7454	.7486	.7517	.7549
0.70/	.7580	.7611	.7642	.7673	.7703	.7734	.7764	.7793	.7823	.7852
0.80/	.7881	.7910	.7939	.7967	.7995	.8023	.8051	.8078	.8106	.8133
0.90/	.8159	.8186	.8212	.8238	.8264	.8289	.8315	.8340	.8365	.8389
1.00/	.8413	.8437	.8461	.8485	.8508	.8531	.8554	.8577	.8599	.8621
1.10/	.8643	.8665	.8686	.8708	.8729	.8749	.8770	.8790	.8810	.8830
1.20/	.8849	.8869	.8888	.8906	.8925	.8943	.8962	.8980	.8997	.9015
1.30/	.9032	.9049	.9066	.9082	.9099	.9115	.9131	.9147	.9162	.9177
1.40/	.9192	.9207	.9222	.9236	.9251	.9265	.9279	.9292	.9306	.9319
1.50/	.9332	.9345	.9357	.9370	.9382	.9394	.9406	.9418	.9429	.9441
1.60/	.9452	.9463	.9474	.9484	.9495	.9505	.9515	.9525	.9535	.9545
1.70/	.9554	.9564	.9573	.9582	.9591	.9599	.9608	.9616	.9625	.9633
1.80/	.9641	.9649	.9656	.9664	.9671	.9678	.9686	.9693	.9699	.9706
1.90/	.9713	.9719	.9726	.9732	.9738	.9744	.9750	.9756	.9761	.9767
2.00/	.9772	.9778	.9783	.9788	.9793	.9798	.9803	.9808	.9812	.9817
2.10/	.9821	.9826	.9830	.9834	.9838	.9842	.9846	.9850	.9854	.9857
2.20/	.9861	.9864	.9868	.9871	.9875	.9878	.9881	.9884	.9887	.9890
2.30/	.9893	.9896	.9898	.9901	.9904	.9906	.9909	.9911	.9913	.9916
2.40/	.9918	.9920	.9922	.9925	.9927	.9929	.9931	.9932	.9934	.9936
2.50/	.9938	.9940	.9941	.9943	.9945	.9946	.9948	.9949	.9951	.9952
2.60/	.9953	.9955	.9956	.9957	.9959	.9960	.9961	.9962	.9963	.9964
2.70/	.9965	.9966	.9967	.9968	.9969	.9970	.9971	.9972	.9973	.9974
2.80/	.9974	.9975	.9976	.9977	.9977	.9978	.9979	.9979	.9980	.9981
2.90/	.9981	.9982	.9982	.9983	.9984	.9984	.9985	.9985	.9986	.9986
3.00/	.9986	.9987	.9987	.9988	.9988	.9989	.9989	.9989	.9990	.9990

CUMULATIVE NORMAL PROBABILITY DISTRIBUTION
WHERE $d(1)$ OR $d(2)$ IS NEGATIVE

	.00	.01	.02	.03	.04	.05	.06	.07	.08	.09
−3.00/	.0014	.0013	.0013	.0012	.0012	.0011	.0011	.0011	.0010	.0010
−2.90/	.0019	.0018	.0018	.0017	.0016	.0016	.0015	.0015	.0014	.0014
−2.80/	.0026	.0025	.0024	.0023	.0023	.0022	.0021	.0021	.0020	.0019
−2.70/	.0035	.0034	.0033	.0032	.0031	.0030	.0029	.0028	.0027	.0026
−2.60/	.0047	.0045	.0044	.0043	.0041	.0040	.0039	.0038	.0037	.0036
−2.50/	.0062	.0060	.0059	.0057	.0055	.0054	.0052	.0051	.0049	.0048
−2.40/	.0082	.0080	.0078	.0075	.0073	.0071	.0069	.0068	.0066	.0064
−2.30/	.0107	.0104	.0102	.0099	.0096	.0094	.0091	.0089	.0087	.0084
−2.20/	.0139	.0136	.0132	.0129	.0125	.0122	.0119	.0116	.0113	.0110
−2.10/	.0179	.0174	.0170	.0166	.0162	.0158	.0154	.0150	.0146	.0143
−2.00/	.0228	.0222	.0217	.0212	.0207	.0202	.0197	.0192	.0188	.0183
−1.90/	.0287	.0281	.0274	.0268	.0262	.0256	.0250	.0244	.0239	.0233
−1.80/	.0359	.0351	.0344	.0336	.0329	.0322	.0314	.0307	.0301	.0294
−1.70/	.0446	.0436	.0427	.0418	.0409	.0401	.0392	.0384	.0375	.0367
−1.60/	.0548	.0537	.0526	.0516	.0505	.0495	.0485	.0475	.0465	.0455
−1.50/	.0668	.0655	.0643	.0630	.0618	.0606	.0594	.0582	.0571	.0559
−1.40/	.0808	.0793	.0778	.0764	.0749	.0735	.0721	.0708	.0694	.0681
−1.30/	.0968	.0951	.0934	.0918	.0901	.0885	.0869	.0853	.0838	.0823
−1.20/	.1151	.1131	.1112	.1094	.1075	.1057	.1038	.1020	.1003	.0985
−1.10/	.1357	.1335	.1314	.1292	.1271	.1251	.1230	.1210	.1190	.1170
−1.00/	.1587	.1563	.1539	.1515	.1492	.1469	.1446	.1423	.1401	.1379
−0.90/	.1841	.1814	.1788	.1762	.1736	.1711	.1685	.1660	.1635	.1611
−0.80/	.2119	.2090	.2061	.2033	.2005	.1977	.1949	.1922	.1894	.1867
−0.70/	.2420	.2389	.2358	.2327	.2297	.2266	.2236	.2207	.2177	.2148
−0.60/	.2743	.2709	.2676	.2644	.2611	.2579	.2546	.2514	.2483	.2451
−0.50/	.3085	.3050	.3015	.2981	.2946	.2912	.2877	.2843	.2810	.2776
−0.40/	.3446	.3409	.3372	.3336	.3300	.3264	.3228	.3192	.3156	.3121
−0.30/	.3821	.3783	.3745	.3707	.3669	.3632	.3594	.3557	.3520	.3483
−0.20/	.4207	.4168	.4129	.4091	.4052	.4013	.3974	.3936	.3897	.3859
−0.10/	.4602	.4562	.4522	.4483	.4443	.4404	.4364	.4325	.4286	.4247
−0.00/	.5000	.4960	.4920	.4880	.4841	.4801	.4761	.4721	.4681	.4642

Appendix B

Option Margin Comparisons

OPTION MARGIN COMPARISONS[a]

CBOE (OPTIONS ON STOCKS AND T-BOND ACTUALS); CSCE, COMEX, CBT, CME (OPTIONS ON FUTURES)[b]
COMPILED BY JAMES MEISNER, HENRY OTTO, AND JEANNE SINQUEFIELD

Strategy	Maximum Potential Loss	CBOE Stock Option Margin	CBOE T-Bond Option Margin	CSCE and COMEX[b] Option Margin	CBT and CME[b] Option Margin
1. Long put or long call	Entire premium	Option premium paid in full; no margin required	Same as CBOE stock option	Same as CBOE	Same as CBOE
2. Short call or short put	Futures loss minus premium received	30 percent of security value plus in-the-money amount or minus out-of-the-money amount; minimum of $250	Option premium (marked-to-market) plus $3500; margin reduced by out-of-the-money amount; minimum of $500	Option premium (marked-to-market) plus futures margin; for CSCE, futures margin reduced by the out-of-the-money amount to a minimum of $250	Option premium (marked-to-market) plus the greater of (a) the futures margin minus one-half the out-of-the-money amount or (b) initial $1000 ($1500), maintenance or hedging $750 ($1250); long-term T-bonds (80% of market value) acceptable by CBT Clearing Corporation as margins

3a. Long security and short call (covered call) or long futures and short call, same months for futures and call (synthetic short put)	Futures loss minus premium received	Half of security value; no margin calls	No margin required if one owns the T-bond	Option premium (marked-to-market) plus futures margin minus in-the-money amount; minimum of option premium plus the futures spread margin (50% of futures margin for CSCE and 10% for COMEX)	Option premium (marked-to-market) plus the greater of (a) the futures margin minus one-half the in-the-money amount or (b) initial $1000 ($1500), maintenance or hedging $750 ($1250)
3b. Short security and short put or short futures and short put, same months for futures and put (synthetic short call)	Same as 3a	Same as 3a	No special margin treatment; short option treated as naked short position	Same as 3a	Same as 3a
4. Short call and short put, same months for call and put (short straddle)	Futures loss (on either side) minus total premiums received	Greater of the margin requirements for a naked position in the call or put plus in-the-money amount of the other option	Same as CBOE stock option (but note that naked short margins differ)	Sum of both option premiums (marked-to-market) plus futures margin	Same as CSCE and COMEX

OPTION MARGIN COMPARISON

Strategy	Maximum Potential Loss	CBOE Stock Option Margin	CBOE T-Bond Option Margin	CSCE and COMEX Option Margin	CBT and CME Option Margin
5. Vertical spreads	A vertical spread (also called a money spread) consists of a long and short call option or a long and short put option, both options having the same expiration dates but different strike prices				
5a. Long call (put) strike price less (greater) than short call (put) strike price (bull call or bear put spread)	Long option premium minus short option premium; debit transaction	Long option premium paid in full; no margin required for the short option	Same as CBOE stock option	Same as CBOE	Same as CBOE
5b. Long call (put) strike price greater (less) than short call (put) strike price (bear call or bull put spread)	Difference between strike prices plus long option premium minus short option premium; credit transaction	Long option premium paid in full; margin equals difference in strike prices	Long option premium paid in full; margin equals minimum of difference in strike prices and margin for naked short option	Long option premium paid in full; margin equals the difference in strike prices not to exceed futures margin for CSCE, not to exceed margin for naked short option for COMEX	Long option premium paid in full; margin equals the difference in strike price not to exceed margin for naked short option (same as CBOE)
6. Horizontal spreads	A horizontal spread (also called a time or calendar spread) consists of a long and short call option or a long and short put option, with the two options having different expiration dates; the strike prices may be the same or different (if different the position is also called a diagonal spread)				

6a. Long call (put) strike price less (greater) than or equal to short call (put) strike price	Long option premium minus short option premium plus underlying futures spread risks plus time value of long option if long option expires before short option	(1) *Short option expires before long option:* long option premium paid in full; no margin required for the short option (2) *Long option expires before short option:* no special margin treatment; short option treated as naked short position	Same as CBOE stock option	Long option premium paid in full; margin equals short option premium minus long option premium (marked-to-market) if short premium exceeds long premium plus futures spread margin (50% of futures margin for CSCE, 10% for COMEX)	Long option premium paid in full; margin equals short option premium minus long option premium (marked-to-market) if short premium exceeds long premium, plus futures spread margin ($200 if underlying months are 1 year or more apart, zero otherwise for CBT, $400 for CME) plus for the CBT if the long option expires before the short option, initial $750, maintenance or hedging $500

OPTION MARGIN COMPARISONS

Strategy	Maximum Potential Loss	CBOE Stock Option Margin	CBOE T-Bond Option Margin	CSCE and COMEX Option Margin	CBT and CME Option Margin
6b. Long call (put) strike price greater (less) than short call (put) strike price	Difference between strike prices plus long option premium minus short option premium plus underlying futures spread risk, plus time value of long option if long option expires before short option	(1) *Short option expires before long option:* long option premium paid in full; margin equals difference in strike prices (2) *Long option expires before short option:* no special margin treatment; short option treated as naked short position	Same as CBOE stock option	Long option premium paid in full; margin equals short option premium minus long option premium (marked-to-market) if short premium exceeds long premium plus the difference in strike prices not to exceed futures margin	Same as CSCE and COMEX
7a. Long call and short futures (synthetic long put)	Entire premium plus out-of-the-money	None	None	(1) *In- or at-the-money:* option premium paid in	Option premium paid in full, margin equals futures

7b. Long put and long futures (synthetic long call)	amount or minus in-the-money amount at time position is assumed		full; margin equals futures spread margin (50% of futures margin for CSCE, 10% for COMEX); if underlying months are the same, margin reduced by in-the-money amount to a minimum of zero (2) *Out-of-the-money:* option premium paid in full; margin equals futures margin	margin minus any amount by which the market value of the option premium exceeds futures spread margin ($200 if underlying months are 1 year or more apart, zero otherwise for the CBT, $400 FOR CME);[c] FCM may loan in-the-money amount of the long option to meet variation margin payments on the futures contract	Same as CSCE and COMEX
8a. Short call, long put, long futures, same months and strike prices (conversion)	Risk-free arbitrage; gains or losses fixed at time the position is assumed	None	Long premium paid in full; no margin required for the short option	Long option premium paid in full; margin equals amount by which short	
8b. Long call, short put, short futures, same months and strike prices (reverse condition)	Same as 8a	None	Same as 8a	option premium exceeds long option premium; FCM may loan in-the-money amount of the long option to meet variation margin payments on the futures contract	Same as 8a

OPTION MARGIN COMPARISONS

Strategy	Maximum Potential Loss	CBOE Stock Option Margin	CBOE T-Bond Option Margin	CSCE and COMEX Option Margin	CBT and CME Option Margin
9. Box spread	A box spread consists of a long call and a short put with the same exercise price, coupled with a short call and a long put with the same exercise price (all options have the same expiration month); a box represents risk-free arbitrage; gains or losses fixed at time the position is assumed				
9a. Credit box—total short option premiums exceed total long option premiums	A liability at expiration equal to the difference in strike prices fixed when the position is assumed	No special margin treatment	No special margin treatment	Long options paid in full; margin equals the difference in strike prices (plus for COMEX the futures spread margin if the options expire in different months)	Long option premiums paid in full; margin equals the difference in strike prices
9b. Debit box—total long option premiums exceed total short option premiums	A value at expiration equal to the difference in strike prices fixed when the position is assumed	No special margin treatment	No special margin treatment	Long option premiums paid in full; no further margin required (for Comex if options expire in different months margin equals the futures spread margin)	Long option premiums paid in full; no further margin required

A butterfly spread consists of four options: one vertical bull spread (put or call) combined with one vertical bear spread (put or call); the vertical spreads share one common strike price, which lies between the two other strike prices (all options have the same expiration month)

10. Butterfly spread		No special margin treatment	No special margin treatment
10a. Debit spread—total long premiums exceed total short premiums when position is assumed	(1) *Middle strike price exactly halfway between outer strike prices;* long option premiums less short option premiums (2) *Middle strike price not exactly halfway between outer strike prices;* long option premiums less short option premiums; for some positions, an additional amount equal to the smallest difference between any two strikes	Long option premiums paid in full; margin equals amount short option premiums exceed short option premiums plus the greater of (a) the amount that the short in-the-money amount exceeds the long in-the-money amount or (b) the futures margin	(1) *Middle strike price exactly halfway between outer strike prices;* long option premiums paid in full; no further margin required (2) *Middle strike price not exactly halfway between outer strike prices;* long option premiums paid in full; the butterfly margined as two vertical spreads

OPTION MARGIN COMPARISONS

Strategy	Maximum Potential Loss	CBOE Stock Option Margin	CBOE T-Bond Option Margin	CSCE and COMEX Option Margin	CBT and CME Option Margin
10b. Credit spread—total long premiums exceed total short premiums when position is assumed	*(1) Middle strike price exactly halfway between outer strike prices;* the difference between adjacent strike prices less the net premiums required *(2) Middle strike price not exactly halfway between outer strike prices;* the largest difference between adjacent strike prices less the next premiums received	No special margin treatment	No special margin treatment	Same as 10a	*(1) Middle strike price exactly halfway between outer strike prices;* long option premiums paid in full; the butterfly margined as two vertical spreads *(2) Middle strike price not exactly halfway between outer strike prices;* long premiums paid in full; margin equals between two adjacent strikes, not to exceed the futures margin plus the amount by

which the short
option premi-
ums exceed long
option premi-
ums

---

[a] Option margins can be changed by the exchanges with little or no notice. These margins are also minimum exchange requirements. Brokerage and Commodity Firms can set higher margins.

[b] CSCE—Options on Sugar Futures, COMEX—Options on Gold Futures, CBT—Options on T-Bond Futures, CME—Options on S&P 500 Stock Indices.

[c] The futures position may also be a CBT GNMA or 10-year T-note contract. In this case the spread margin is larger. See CBT regulations for intermarket spread margin requirements.

Bibliography

Many of these references are geared toward stock options insofar as commodity options are only now reemerging as significant trading and hedging vehicles. Literature is expected to be available shortly from the exchanges that will trade the options described in this book.

Black, F. "The Pricing of Commodity Contracts." *Journal of Financial Economics* (January/March 1976).

Black, F. and Scholes, M. "The Pricing of Options and Corporate Liabilities." *Journal of Political Economy* (May/June 1973).

Blume, M. and J. Friedman, eds. *Encyclopedia of Investments.* Boston: Warren, Gorham and Lamont, 1982.

Bokron, N. *How to Use Put and Call Options.* Springfield, MA: John Magee, 1975.

Bookstaber, R. M., *Option Pricing and Strategies in Investing.* Reading, MA: Addison-Wesley Publishing Company, 1981.

———. *Option Strategies for Institutional Investment Management: A Guide for Improving Portfolio Performance.* Reading, MA: Addison Wesley Publishing Company, 1983.

Clasing, H. *The Dow Jones Irwin Guide to Put and Call Options.* Homewood, IL: Dow Jones Irwin, Incorporated 1978.

Cox, J. C., S. Ross, and M. Rubinstein. "Option Pricing: A Simplified Approach." *Journal of Financial Economics,* Vol. 7, 229–263.

Davis, G. and Jacobson, M. *Stock Option Strategies.* Cross Plains, WI: Badger Press, 1976.

Gastineau, G. *The Stock Options Manual.* New York: McGraw-Hill, 1979.

Kaufman, P., ed. *Handbook of Futures Markets.* New York: John Wiley and Son's, 1984.

Malkiel, B. and Quandt, R. *Strategies and Rational Decisions in the Securities Options Market.* Cambridge, MA: MIT Press, 1969.

McMillian, L. *Options as a Strategic Investment.* New York: New York Institute of Finance, 1980.

Mehl, P. "Trading Privileges on the Chicago Board of Trade." U.S. Department of Agriculture Circular No. 323, 1934.

Noddings, T. *How the Experts Beat the Market.* Homewood, IL: Dow Jones Irwin, Incorporated, 1976.

Rebell, A. and G. Gordon. *Financial Futures and Investment Strategy.* Homewood, IL: Dow Jones-Irwin, Incorporated, 1984.

Glossary

AMERICAN OPTION: An option contract that may be exercised at any time prior to expiration. This contrasts with a "European option," which may only be exercised on the expiration date.

AT-THE-MONEY: An option is at-the-money when the underlying market price equals the strike price. When an option is at-the-money, there is no obvious incentive for the option holder to exercise the option.

CALENDAR SPREAD: See "horizontal spread."

CALL OPTION: A call option gives the option buyer or holder the right, but not the obligation, to buy, and obliges the option seller or writer to sell the underlying commodity at a specific strike price upon the holder's demand.

CLASS OF OPTION: All options of the same type (see "type of options") with the same expiration date are considered to be of the same class. For example, all Treasury-bond put options that are exercisable for March Treasury-bond futures are considered to be of the same class.

CLOSING PURCHASE: A closing purchase cancels an outstanding short option position. For example, an option trader may have sold an option yesterday. By buying an option of the same series today, the trader may cancel or offset the outstanding obligation. A closing transaction results in diminished open interest.

CLOSING SALE: A closing sale cancels an outstanding long option position. For example, an option trader may have bought an option yesterday. By selling an option of the same series today, the trader may cancel or offset the outstanding option. A closing transaction results in diminished open interest.

COVERED WRITER: An option writer is "covered" when the writer holds an offsetting position in the underlying commodity market. For example, a short put option is covered by a short position in the underlying commodity. Conversely, a short call option is covered by a long position in the underlying commodity.

DELTA: The amount by which an option premium will fluctuate as a percentage of the fluctuation in the underlying commodity market.

DIAGONAL SPREAD: A diagonal option spread involves the purchase and sale of two options of the same type that have different strike prices and different expiration dates.

DOUBLES: See "straddles."

EUROPEAN OPTION: A European option may be exercised only on its expiration date. This contrasts with "American options," which may be exercised at any time prior to the expiration date.

EXERCISE: When a call option holder exercises an option, the holder buys the underlying commodity from the option seller. Conversely, a put option holder who exercises an option sells the underlying commodity to the option seller.

EXERCISE PRICE: See "strike price."

EXPIRATION DATE: Every option contract becomes null and void subsequent to its expiration date. An option that is not offset by a closing transaction or exercised by the expiration date expires or lapses.

EXTRINSIC VALUE: The price of an option over and above the intrinsic value. This value is sometimes referred to as the option's "time value."

FAIR VALUE: An option's fair value is the premium that the buyer might pay to the seller wherein both parties to the contract might expect to break even, without considering transaction costs. The actual purchase price of an option may vary from the fair value insofar as fair value is a theoretical concept.

FUTURES CONTRACT: A futures contract is a contract to make or take delivery of a commodity at some future date. Some option contracts are exercisable for futures contracts rather than the actual or physical commodity.

HOLDER: An option holder has bought an option and therefore owns the right to exercise it. The terms "option buyer" and "holder" are synonomous.

HORIZONTAL SPREAD: A horizontal or calendar spread involves the purchase and sale of two option contracts of the same type that have the same strike prices but different expiration dates.

INSURANCE VALUE: An option has insurance value insofar as an option buyer has unlimited profit potential and limited downside risk.

IN-THE-MONEY: An option is in-the-money when it may be exercised for a gross profit by the holder. A call option is in-the-money when the underlying market price exceeds the strike price. Conversely, a put option is in-the-money when the underlying market price is less than the strike price.

INTRINSIC VALUE: An option's intrinsic value is equal to its in-the-money valuation. An option premium will never be less than the option's intrinsic value. If the fair value of the option is less than its intrinsic value, the option is likely to be exercised.

LEVERAGE: Leverage refers to one's ability to participate in profits that result from favorable price fluctuations of a particular commodity without putting up the full purchase price of the commodity.

MARGIN: The monetary deposits required to secure an investment position.

MARK-TO-MARKET: This refers to the practice of assessing the requirement for more or less margin to secure a position that has lost in value or gained in value, respectively.

NAKED OPTION: An option is naked when it is bought or sold while the buyer or seller does not hold an offsetting position in the underlying commodity market.

NEUTRAL HEDGE RATIO: Option premiums normally do not fluctuate in a one-to-one ratio with fluctuations in the underlying commodity market. For example, a 10% change in the underlying market price may give rise to a 5% change in the option premium. In this case, the neutral hedge ratio equals 2. For example, one could buy two call options to offset the risk of a short position in the underlying commodity.

OPENING PURCHASE: An opening purchase establishes an open or outstanding long position in the option market.

OPENING SALE: An opening sale establishes an open or outstanding short position in the option market.

PREMIUM: The option buyer pays the option seller a premium in order to secure the rights associated with holding the option. This is the option price and is usually quoted in units of the underlying commodity rather than in the aggregate. For example, a premium for a $100,000 Treasury-bond option may equal 2% of par, or $2,000 in the aggregate.

PUT OPTION: A put option gives the option buyer or holder the right, but not the obligation, to sell, and obliges the option seller or writer to buy the underlying commodity at a specific strike price upon the holder's demand.

SERIES OF OPTIONS: All options of the same type and of the same class that are exercisable at the same price are considered to be of the same series.

SPREAD: An option spread involves the purchase and sale of two options of the same type that vary in terms of their strike prices or their expiration dates, or both.

STRADDLE: An option straddle or double involves the purchase of two different types of options, that is, a put and a call, or the sale of two different types of options.

STRIKE PRICE: The price at which the option may be exercised. Normally, options are available at a number of different striking prices for the same underlying commodity with the same expiration date.

TIME VALUE: See "extrinsic value."

TYPE OF OPTION: Options are of two types—puts and calls.

UNDERLYING COMMODITY: The commodity for which the option may be exercised. There are generally three types of commodities underlying a commodity option contract: interest-bearing commodities, such as debt instruments, non-interest-bearing commodities, such as physical gold, and futures contracts. The former two types of commodities are also referred to as "actual" or "physical" commodities.

VERTICAL SPREAD: A purchase and sale of two options of the same type with the same expiration date and different strike prices.

Index